# DOZER'S QUINTESS
# GUIDE TO
# COMPUTER LITERACY

## 14th Edition

Written by
Steve Pannell

Edited by
Diane S. Pannell

Inspired by
Dozer Pannell

# Dozer's Quintessential Guide To Computer Literacy
## 14th Edition

**Published by**

**Majestic D & Associates, LLC**
**Las Vegas, Nevada**
**email: D@MajesticD.com**

Dozer's Quintessential Guide To Computer Literacy was written with the express purpose of assisting folks with no prior computing experience to become computer literate. The software used in this publication include Microsoft® Windows, Microsoft® Word, Microsoft® Excel, Microsoft® PowerPoint®, and Microsoft® Access. This book is compatible with versions 2002 (XP) and 2003 of Word, Excel, PowerPoint, and Access.
All brand names and product names mentioned in Dozer's Quintessential Guide To Computer Literacy are trade names, service marks, trademarks, and/or registered trademarks of their respective owners. Usage in this publication is merely for identification purposes.

Screen shots reprinted by permission from Microsoft Corporation.
Microsoft is a trademark of Microsoft Corporation in the United States and other countries.
This book is not sponsored or endorsed by or affiliated with Microsoft Corporation.

The Pet's Bill of Rights is copyrighted by Rodale Press, Inc. and is reprinted by permission.

**ISBN 0-9744008-6-6**
**Printed in the United States of America**

My old man, Steve, wrote this manual to assist folks
with no prior computer training to become computer literate.
The book was inspired by me, and is, therefore, named after me
(my picture is on the cover).  By the way, I'm "Dozer" because
I take lots of naps, which I highly recommend for humans as well.
Anyway, this book covers Computer Concepts, Microsoft Windows,
The Internet, and Microsoft Word, Excel, PowerPoint, and Access.
Each topic is presented in a series of projects.  Each project provides
two pages of step-by step instructions followed by two pages of exercises.
After reading and doing the four pages in a project, you will be ready
for the next project.  I've heard humans say that "A journey of a thousand
miles begins with a single step."  I suppose this applies to the journey
towards computer literacy as well as to any other journey.
So, turn the page and let's get going!

**Your Pal, Dozer**

# DOZER'S QUINTESSENTIAL GUIDE TO COMPUTER LITERACY

## TABLE OF CONTENTS

HARDWARE    PIRACY    MONITORS

GB   BITS   SOFTWARE    UPGRADE

PROCESSOR    MOUSE    PRINTERS

BYTES   geeks   CLICK   MB   ZIP

CLONES   DISKETTES   KB   VERSION   KB

CD-ROM    USB    SCANNERS

# Dozer's Quintessential Guide To Computer Concepts
## T A B L E   O F   C O N T E N T S

When most folks talk about a computer, they are really talking about a computer system, which consists of a computer and all the components connected to it. This stuff is often referred to as **hardware**. If you were to disassemble a computer system into its components, you could place the parts in four piles based upon each part's function (what each part does). That is, hardware components can be classified as either **input**, **processing**, **storage**, or **output** devices. This project explains the function of these various components.

## INPUT COMPONENTS

In order for a computer to work, it needs a program and data. Thus, we need some sort of device to allow us to input the programs and the data in a form that a computer can deal with. These devices are classified as input components. Common input components include a mouse, keyboard, scanner, digital camera, microphone, and bar code reader.

The **mouse** is an input device that typically has two buttons on the top and a ball on its underside. Basically, a mouse can do six things. The mouse can be **clicked** (rapidly press the left button), **double-clicked** (rapidly press the left mouse button twice), or **right-clicked** (rapidly press the right mouse button). In addition, it can point to on-screen objects, it can be moved across a surface to move the mouse pointer on the screen, and if you hold down the left mouse button and **drag** the mouse, you can use a mouse to move objects on the screen.

Some data is inputted via a **keyboard**, which has a variety of enhancements over a typewriter keyboard. **Function keys** (F1, F2, F3, etc.) each execute a program-specific command. The **Delete** and **Backspace** keys delete characters on the screen. The **Ctrl** (**control**) and **Alt** keys are used with other keys to execute commands. The **arrow** keys move the insertion point and the **Esc** (**escape**) key cancels an action. In addition, the numeric keypad provides for rapid entry of numeric values.

In addition to the mouse and the keyboard, you can input data with digital cameras, scanners, microphones, bar-code readers, and a variety of other devices. A **digital camera** works much like a camera in that a picture is taken. However, instead of developing the film, the image is saved in a digital format. A **scanner** works much like a copy machine in that a hard copy of the data is scanned. However, unlike a copier, instead of producing a paper copy, the data is digitized. A **microphone** can be used with voice-recognition software to input data. A **bar-code reader** (like at the grocery store) reads codes. By the way, while we most often think of a monitor as being an output device (more on that topic on the next page), some monitors are in fact input devices. That is, some monitors have a "touch" screen that permits commands to be executed by merely touching the screen with your finger.

## PROCESSING COMPONENTS

While a computer system may consist of many devices, the actual **computer** in a computer system is the **CPU** (**central processing unit**), also called a **processor**, which uses a **program** (set of instructions), also referred to as **software**, to process **data** (raw, unorganized details) in such a way that the data is converted into **information**. CPU chips are produced for either Apple machines or for **IBM-compatible** machines (also called **Clones**), which are machines produced by organizations other than IBM, but utilize the same type of CPU. Over the years, these chips have become more powerful. Most of the chips used in IBM and IBM-compatibles are produced by either Intel or Advanced Micro Devices (AMD). Intel makes **Pentium** and **Celeron** chips; AMD makes **Athlon** and **Sempron** chips.

In addition to a processor, a computer system uses **expansion cards** (circuit boards that can be installed to expand a system's capabilities), **ports** (sockets to plug in other devices), and **buses** (the circuitry that connects the devices). All of these can be found in the **system unit** (the box the monitor typically sits on, or in the case of a tower, the box that typically sits on the floor). The processor chip is plugged into the **system board** (also called the **motherboard**) which is the main circuit board located inside the system unit.

Processing speed is a function of the **bus width**, which determines how many bits can be worked on simultaneously and the system's **clock speed**, which is the rate at which the system clock beats per second. A **megahertz** (MHz) is one million beats (cycles); a **gigahertz** (GHz) in one billion beats. Thus, a 2-GHz machine produces two billion cycles per second, each of which executes one or more instructions.

## STORAGE COMPONENTS
### BITS AND BYTES

Since a computer can only understand machine language, programs and data must be stored in binary form. A **bit** (**b**inary dig**it**) represents one of two possible states. A circuit is either open or closed, a magnetic particle on a diskette is either negatively or positively charged, a pit on a CD either exists or does not exist. In an open/closed, positive/negative, pit/no pit world, bits (0 or 1) are used to represent programs and data. Each keyboard character is represented by a unique combination of eight bits (referred to as a **byte**). In other words, a byte is composed of eight bits in a unique sequence. The storage capacity is measured in bytes. A **kilobyte** (**KB**) is roughly a thousand bytes, a **megabyte** (**MB**) is about a million bytes, and a **gigabyte** (**GB**) is approximately a billion bytes.

### SECONDARY STORAGE

As previously mentioned, in order for a computer to work, it needs a program and it needs data. The program and the data are stored in two places--primary and/or secondary storage. Programs and data not currently being used are stored in **secondary storage**. Secondary storage is **non-volatile**, which is a fancy word for **permanent** (programs and data stored here are not lost when the power is turned off). Secondary storage is provided primarily with diskettes, hard drives, CD-ROMs, CD-RWs, CD-Rs, zip drives, USB drives, and magnetic tape drives. The next few paragraphs provide details about each of these.

DISKETTES. Most **diskettes** (**floppy disks**) are 3-½ inch, **high-density** diskettes, upon which data is stored via positively or negatively charged magnetic particles. A diskette has a storage **capacity** of **1.44 MB** (capacity is how much can be stored: density is how tightly bits of data are packed on a diskette). The surface of the diskette is protected with a **shutter mechanism** (designed to automatically close to cover the recording window when the disk is extracted from the drive).

The disk surface is accessed by the read/write heads (found in the floppy drive) through a **recording window** (found on the diskette). At two of the corners of a diskette, there is a square hole. The hole with the movable button is the **write-protection square**. If it is open (you can see through it), you will not be able to save a file to the disk. To save a file to the disk (write to the disk), you should close the window so you can't see through the hole. Before a diskette is usable, it must be formatted. Most diskettes are formatted when you buy them; some are not. **Formatting** a diskette removes all files from the diskette, divides the diskette into addressable locations, and creates a file directory. To use a diskette, insert it (shutter-end first and label up) into the floppy drive (often referred to as the **A-drive**). When the drive is **reading** from the diskette (retrieving data) or **writing** to the diskette (saving/storing data), the **A-drive indicator light** is on and you can hear the drive running. By the way, many new computers are now sold without floppy drives. This technology is being replaced by other storage options.

HARD DRIVES. Another secondary storage device is a **hard drive**. It gets its name from the fact that, unlike a floppy disk, the hard drive utilizes hard platters. Data is stored on a platter via positively or negative charged magnetic spots. The hard drive (often referred to as the **C-drive**) is sealed in an air-tight box in the system unit. This prevents contaminants like dust particles from entering the drive and causing damage.

CD-ROM. Another type of secondary storage is **CD-ROM** (**Compact Disk-Read Only Memory**). Data is stored on a CD as tiny pits burned in with a laser beam. Bits are distinguished by the presence or absence of a pit. Once the pits are burned into the surface, a CD-ROM cannot be written to; it can only be read from (this is why it is called "Read-Only" Memory). Therefore, data produced by the user cannot be stored on this type of secondary storage. The only data stored on it would be the data placed there by the CD manufacturer.

CD-RW and CD-R. As noted above, data produced by the user cannot be saved to a CD-ROM. However, with the proper hardware, data can be saved with a **CD-RW** (**Compact Disk-ReWritable**) or a **CD-R (Compact Disk-Recordable)**.

ZIP DRIVES. A **zip drive** is similar to a floppy drive in that the data is stored on a removable medium. However the speed of a zip drive is much faster than a floppy and with a storage capacity of 100 MB (or 250 MB, depending on the type), you can store as much data as 70 (or 175 ) diskettes would hold.

USB DRIVES. A **USB drive** (sometimes called a flash drive, keychain drive, or a mini drive) is a storage device about the size of your thumb. When plugged into a computer's USB port, it acts like a floppy disk, except its storage capacity greatly exceeds that of a floppy disk (16MB to 256MB are common).

MAGNETIC TAPE. **Magnetic tape** systems use a tape drive unit in which a cartridge is inserted much like a cassette tape is inserted into a cassette player. Data is stored sequentially (like a cassette). Magnetic tape storage is much cheaper than disk storage. But, since the data is stored on a linear tape, retrieving specific data requires that the data be retrieved in the order in which it was recorded (similar to a cassette tape that must be heard in the order in which it was recorded). Thus, magnetic tapes are used in circumstances where speed is not important (e.g., backing up data).

ROM. **Read-Only Memory** (**ROM**) is used to store programs that need to be accessed more quickly by the CPU than would be possible if the programs were stored in any of the previously mentioned secondary storage devices. The permanent nature of ROM permits it to be used when a machine is **booted up** (the process of turning on a computer). Therefore, the set of instructions that are used to activate the machine are found in a ROM chip which is located on the system board.

**PRIMARY STORAGE**
The programs and data currently being used by the computer are stored in **primary storage** (more commonly referred to as either **RAM, random access memory**, or simply **memory**). Since a computer can process data only if the program and the data are in memory, when a program or data is needed by the computer, a copy of the program or data is taken from secondary storage and is placed into memory. RAM is provided via chips installed on the system board. RAM is **volatile**, which is a fancy word for **temporary** (since RAM requires a constant source of electricity, programs and data stored in RAM are lost when the power is turned off). **Cache** (pronounced "cash") is a small block of very fast memory where frequently-used data and instructions are stored. **Virtual memory** extends RAM by placing parts of the program on the hard drive and reciprocating between the hard drive and RAM as needed.

**OUTPUT COMPONENTS**
In addition to input, processing, and storage devices, we will need to have some way to obtain the computer's output. For this, we will primarily rely on **monitors** (for **soft copy**) and **printers** (for **hard copy**).

MONITORS. A monitor is either a **CRT** (Cathode Ray Tube) which operates like a TV or a **flat-panel** which is a thin, light-weight monitor commonly used on **laptop** computers. An important consideration is the **resolution** (clarity) of the picture produced by the monitor. The determining factor in resolution is the **density** of the **pixels** (the thousands of small dots that create the image on the screen). The more pixels per square inch of screen space, the higher the density, and subsequently, the higher the resolution. Other factors to consider are the **dot pitch** (the distance between pixels) and the **refresh rate** (the number of times per second that the image is reconstructed). The dot-pitch is measured in millimeters (mm), the current standard being .28 mm. The refresh rate is measured in Hertz (Hz). Since each Hertz is one cycle per second, if the refresh rate is 80 Hz, then the image on the screen is recreated 80 times per second. A small dot pitch and a rapid refresh rate will provide a sharper picture.

PRINTERS. There are many times when you will want to have a hard copy of your output to send to someone who does not have a computer or because a hard copy is just easier to carry from place to place than a computer would be. In such a case, a printer will be your best friend. Most printers are either dot-matrix, ink-jet, or laser. A **dot-matrix** printer constructs characters on the paper by striking the ribbon with pins that form the characters. Like a typewriter, it produces characters by physically striking the ribbon (dot-matrix printers and typewriters are impact devices). An **ink-jet** printer sprays a mist of ink to form the characters. A **laser printer** utilizes a laser beam to form the characters. By the way, a printer (or any other device) that is in communication with a computer is said to be **online**. And, if it ain't online, it's **offline**.

## EXERCISE 1: CROSSWORD

Use the clues below to complete the crossword puzzle (Note: the answers for this and many other exercises can be found in the Answer Key, beginning on page A-25).

### ACROSS

1. A diskette has a ___ mechanism, which is designed to automatically close to cover the recording window when the disk is extracted from the drive.
4. If I hold down the left mouse button and ___ the mouse, I can use a mouse to move objects on the screen.
5. Another name for memory is ___ storage.
7. A ___ drive is similar to a floppy drive. However, this device is faster and has a higher storage capacity.
10. The "M" in RAM stands for ___.
11. A ___ printer utilizes a laser beam to form the characters.
14. The dots that create the image on the screen.
15. The circuitry connecting devices in a computer system.
16. How tightly bits of data are packed on a diskette.
17. Programs and data not currently being used by the computer system are stored in secondary ___.
19. Instructions used by a computer to process data.
22. The device that provides soft copy to the user.
23. A billion bytes is abbreviated as ___.
26. Monitors produce this type of copy.
27. The distance between pixels on a monitor is the dot ___.
31. A million bytes is abbreviated as ___.
32. Another word for turning on a computer.
33. Memory is ___, which means programs and data in memory require electricity at all times or they are lost.
35. Another name for memory.
36. A socket into which another device can be plugged.
37. A ___ panel monitor is commonly used on laptops.
38. The ___ width determines how many bits can be worked on simultaneously by the computer.
39. An acronym for Central Processing Unit.
40. Another name for the A-drive is the ___ drive.

### DOWN

2. One cycle per second.
3. The physical devices that make up a computer system.
6. A CD- ___ is a disk the allows you to retrieve data from it, but you can't save data to it.
8. Another name for the computer in a computer system.
9. Approximately a million bytes is a ___ byte.
12. The main circuit board in a computer system is the ___ board.
13. The clarity of the picture produced by a monitor.
15. Eight bits.
17. The box that contains the circuit boards, hard drive, ports, buses, chips, etc.
18. An ___ device is not in communication with a computer.
20. To store data on a disk, I ___ to the disk.
21. The number of times per second that the image is reconstructed on the screen is its ___ rate.
24. A binary digit is a ___.
25. A ___ camera saves the image in a digital format so that a computer can recognize it.
28. A machine produced by an organization other than IBM, but utilizes the same type of processor as an IBM is sometimes referred to as IBM-___.
29. Another name for 28 Down.

30. The hole in the corner of a disk with a movable button is the write ___ square.
33. This type of memory extends RAM by placing parts of the program on the hard drive and reciprocating between the hard drive and RAM as needed.
34. A small, portable computer.

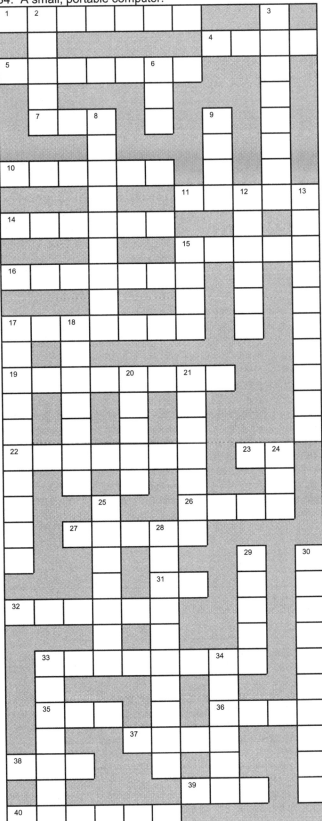

## EXERCISE 2: MATCHING

The physical components that make up a computer system are referred to as hardware, which can be categorized in four ways: Input, Processing, Storage, and Output. Below is a list of the four categories. Below the list is another list of specific devices. For each device, identify the type of device by writing the letter on the line preceding each device.

A. Input
B. Processing
C. Storage
D. Output

1. ___ Bar Code Reader
2. ___ CD-ROM
3. ___ CD-RW
4. ___ Celeron Chip
5. ___ CRT Monitor
6. ___ Digital Camera
7. ___ Diskette
8. ___ Dot-Matrix Printer
9. ___ Flat Panel Monitor
10. ___ Hard Drive
11. ___ Ink-jet Printer
12. ___ Keyboard
13. ___ Laser Printer
14. ___ Magnetic Tape
15. ___ Microphone
16. ___ Sempron Chip
17. ___ Mouse
18. ___ Pentium chip
19. ___ Scanner
20. ___ Zip disk

## EXERCISE 3: MATCHING

Storage capacity is measured in units called bytes. Draw a line to match the following terms to the number each represents.

| | |
|---|---|
| Gigabyte | 1 |
| Megabyte | 1,000 |
| Kilobyte | 1,000,000 |
| Byte | 1,000,000,000 |

## EXERCISE 4: IDENTIFY ACRONYMS

In the computer world, there are lots of acronyms. An acronym is a word created by taking the first letter of each word in a series of words and forming a new word. Using acronyms to refer to stuff saves time. For instance, we often refer to a list of Frequently Asked Questions as a FAQ (pronounced "facts") and we refer to a Dual In-Line Memory Module as a DIMM. In this project, you have already encountered several computer-related acronyms. In the space next to each of the acronyms below, write out its full name.

| ACRONYM | FULL NAME |
|---|---|
| 1. BIT | |
| 2. CD-ROM | |
| 3. CD-RW | |
| 4. CD-R | |
| 5. CPU | |
| 6. GB | |
| 7. KB | |
| 8. MB | |
| 9. RAM | |
| 10. ROM | |

## EXERCISE 5: FIND A WORD

The answers to the following statements can be found in the matrix below. Some are backwards, some are diagonal, some are vertical, and some are horizontal. Circle each word.

1. The type of monitor that looks and operates like a TV.
2. This input device works like a copy machine, but instead of producing a paper copy, the data is digitized.
3. This input device is used to click, right-click, double-click, point, and drag.
4. Approximately a billion bytes is a ___.
5. A small block of very fast memory.
6. Printers and monitors are ___ devices.
7. Another name for the system board is the ___ board.
8. Another name for the processor or CPU.
9. A diskette's surface is read through its recording ___ which can be seen if you open the shutter mechanism.
10. ___ cards are added to expand a system's capabilities.
11. A ___ printer sprays ink to form the characters on paper.
12. Raw, unorganized details.
13. I enter text by pressing keys on a ___.
14. The rate at which the system clock beats is its clock ___.
15. To remove all files from a disk, divide it into addressable locations, and create a file directory, I would ___ the disk.
16. RAM stands for ___ Access Memory.
17. A ___ matrix printer constructs characters on the paper by striking the ribbon with pins.
18. Intel makes this very popular processor.
19. A magnetic ___ drive works much like a cassette player in that data is stored on tape.
20. How much can be stored on a device is called its ___.
21. Eight bits is a ___.
22. The hard drive is also called the ___ .
23. A mouse and a keyboard are examples of ___ devices.
24. A thousand bytes is abbreviated as ___.
25. An acronym for Read Only Memory.
26. You cannot save data to a CD-ROM, but you can save data to a CD-___ drive.

| K | E | Y | B | O | A | R | D | R | A | H |
|---|---|---|---|---|---|---|---|---|---|---|
| B | M | O | T | H | E | R | O | M | A | M |
| E | X | P | A | N | S | I | O | N | D | A |
| P | W | I | N | D | O | W | U | W | R | R |
| A | C | A | P | A | C | I | T | Y | I | G |
| T | C | D | R | I | V | E | P | X | V | O |
| S | O | D | C | O | M | P | U | T | E | R |
| T | C | D | R | O | M | X | T | X | I | P |
| X | R | X | D | W | O | N | L | I | N | E |
| P | E | N | T | I | U | M | X | N | P | T |
| C | A | C | H | E | S | P | D | K | U | Y |
| R | D | S | P | E | E | D | A | J | T | B |
| T | G | I | G | A | B | Y | T | E | M | K |
| X | B | X | F | O | R | M | A | T | I | C |

While the physical components that make up a computer system are referred to as hardware, the sets of instructions are referred to as **software** (also called **programs**), which can be broadly classified as either systems or applications software. A computer program tells the processor what to do and how to do it (e.g., where to find the data and how to process it).

## SYSTEMS SOFTWARE

**Systems software** includes several types of programs that manage the computer resources and communicate with the mouse, keyboard, printer, etc. One type of systems software is the **operating system** (sometimes called the "O.S."). The most widely-used operating system on the planet is Microsoft Windows, which can be found in several versions (Windows 95, Windows 98, Windows Me, Windows NT, Windows 2000, and Windows XP). Other operating systems include Netware, DOS, Macintosh System Software, UNIX, and Linux.

A **user** is a person who uses the hardware and software associated with a computer system. The way a program interacts with a user is referred to as the **user interface**. Most of our interaction with a computer will be via a **graphical user interface** (abbreviated as **GUI** and pronounced as "goo-eey"). In a GUI environment, we work with **windows** (boxes that display information) which appear on a **desktop** (the entire area on the screen where documents, folders, and programs are displayed). In addition, a GUI includes **icons** (on-screen graphical images that are used to execute commands).

## APPLICATIONS SOFTWARE

**Applications** software (also called **productivity** software) includes the specific programs used to create documents. There are hundreds of different programs that fall under the category of applications, each of which is task-specific, which means its purpose is to perform a specific task. In fact, within the world of applications software, the various types are categorized based on the specific task performed. Thus, if the software was primarily designed to process words, it is called a word processing program; if it was designed to permit you to access the Internet, it is called a web browser. A brief description of various types of productivity software follows.

## WORD PROCESSING

**Word processing** programs not only allow you to enter text like a typewriter, but you can later modify the document by inserting, moving, copying, or deleting text. In addition, you can insert graphics and format the document in a variety of ways to give it a professional appearance. Therefore, if you wanted to write a letter, a memo, or a novel, you would use a word processing program. The most popular ones currently on the market are Microsoft Word, Corel WordPerfect, and WordPad. WordPad is part of the Windows operating system. It is a very simplistic word processor. On the other hand, Microsoft Word (Dozer's favorite word processor) and Corel WordPerfect are very sophisticated programs.

## SPREADSHEETS

If you want to create a budget, amortization schedule, or some other document that utilizes formulas to calculate values, you will want to use a **spreadsheet** (worksheet) program. A spreadsheet permits you to ask "what if?" questions to test various scenarios. That is, once the data and the formulas are in place, you can change a key figure and any formula tied to that figure will be recalculated with the new result appearing instantaneously. For example, you can create an amortization schedule covering a 30-year time span representing your mortgage payments. This schedule may contain thousands of calculations, many of which are based on the interest rate of the loan. Once completed, you can simply change the interest rate and all the values will be recalculated to reflect the new rate. You can then ask "What if the interest rate was 6% instead of 7%?" You can even convert your data into a chart. Commonly used spreadsheet programs include Lotus 1-2-3, Corel Quatro Pro, and the most widely used spreadsheet program, Microsoft Excel (which is Dozer's favorite). All three work very similarly, such that, once you know how to use one of them, you will have the knowledge and skills to readily master either of the others, if needed.

## WEB BROWSERS

To find, load, view, print, or create web pages, you will use a **web browser**, such as Internet Explorer (IE) or Netscape Navigator. Since they work similarly, once you know how to use one of them, you will have the knowledge and skills to readily master any other browser. By the way, Dozer's favorite web browser is Internet Explorer.

## SLIDE SHOW PRESENTATIONS

If you need to give a speech or present an idea to a group of folks, you might want to jazz up the event with a computerized slide show in which you could incorporate graphics, sound, and animations. To create such a slide show, you would use some type of **presentation** software, such as Corel Presentations or Microsoft PowerPoint (Dozer's favorite).

## DATABASE

A **database** program (e.g., Microsoft Access) permits you to store, organize, and retrieve data. All types of organizations use database programs. For instance, colleges use database programs to keep track of students. The database contains information about each student, such as name, address, phone number, etc. Likewise, retailers use database programs to keep track of customer accounts. The power behind a database program is its ability to retrieve data in various customized ways based upon any field in the database. For example, if a national retailer has a sale on snow shovels and winter coats, the retailer can use its database of customers to extract all the records for customers who have zip codes that indicate they live in northern regions of the country. The retailer could then send each of these customers information about the sale. After all, it would be fruitless to try to sell a snow shovel to someone living in South Florida (unless those folks need snow shovels to remove coconuts from their sidewalks)

## DESKTOP PUBLISHING

Due to the growing sophistication of word processing programs, the distinction between word processing and desktop publishing has become blurred. However, with desktop publishing, you can produce a professional-quality magazine, announcement, newsletter, advertisement, or brochure. Desktop publishing software includes Corel Ventura, Microsoft Publisher, Adobe PageMaker, and QuarkXpress.

## PERSONAL FINANCE

To create budgets, manage bank accounts, or operate a small business, you might want to use a personal finance program such as Microsoft Money or Quicken. These inexpensive, yet powerful programs are readily available at any software store. And, they are relatively easy to learn how to operate. You can perform financial forecasts, write checks, and basically keep the books for your home or small business. In addition to managing finances with Money and Quicken, you can obtain programs to calculate your tax liability and print the proper tax forms for submission to the IRS.

## GRAPHICS AND PHOTO EDITING

Graphics and photo-editing programs, such as CorelDraw, MGI PhotoSuite, and Paint allow you to create drawings and edit photos. By the way, Paint is a simple-to-use art program that comes as a part of the Windows operating system.

## EDUCATIONAL PROGRAMS

Young folks can learn math by drawing pictures or by interacting with cartoon characters. High school students can prepare for college entrance exams with programs that provide instruction on how to increase scores on nationally standardized tests (e.g., the ACT or SAT). College students can prepare for graduate school with programs designed to enhance scores on the GRE, GMAT, or MAT tests. Anyone can learn to type using a typing tutor, such as Mavis Beacon's typing tutor. By the way, if you can't type, you should learn how, NOW!

## GAMES

Computer games have come a long way since Pong was played on a black and white monitor. In addition to games that utilize video and sound in fast-paced action incorporating virtual reality and 3-D graphics (**multimedia**), you can play a relaxing game of checkers, solitaire, or poker. Or, you can play computerized versions of popular games such as Scrabble or Monopoly. The opportunities to waste time playing games on a computer are endless. In Dozer's Quintessential Guide To Computer Literacy, we'll waste no time on such frivolous activities.

## SUITES AND INTEGRATED PACKAGES

Many software marketers bundle their most popular software in a **suite** (a collection of full-fledged programs packaged as a single unit). For example, the Corel Corporation sells WordPerfect, Quatro Pro, and Presentations in a single package called WordPerfect Office. Microsoft does the same with Word, Excel, and PowerPoint, selling these popular programs in a suite called Microsoft Office. Therefore, you can economically purchase the most commonly-used programs in one bundle instead of buying each separately.

Some software makers create less-powerful programs and bundle them together. An **integrated program** is a single program that does a variety of things, such as process words, crunch numbers, and create a database. For instance, Microsoft Works includes a word processor, spreadsheet, and a database program in a single package. Sometimes, this package comes with a computer when it is purchased. When compared to the full-fledged software available, these programs may be less-sophisticated. However, for what many folks want to do with a computer, they are more than adequate.

## SOFTWARE PIRACY AND COPYRIGHTS

Some software developers want to make their products available at no charge to users; others wish to be compensated for their efforts and creativity. How the product is distributed and under what conditions others are granted the right to use the software is determined by the developers of the software. Generally, software can be classified as either public domain, freeware, shareware, or proprietary (buy-it-to-use it).

## PUBLIC DOMAIN

Software that is not under copyright protection is said to be **public domain** software. It can be copied, used, and/or redistributed without cost to the user. That is, it is provided free of charge without restrictions on its usage.

## FREEWARE

Similar to public domain software, **freeware** is given away free of charge. However, the similarities end there, because the developer of freeware retains a copyright to the program and can, therefore restrict the way it can be used.

## SHAREWARE

**Shareware** is provided free for a limited period of time or a limited version, sometimes referred to as **liteware**, is provided. If the borrower likes it, she should pay the owner who will then permit her to use it for an unlimited time (or, in the case of liteware, the full-scale version of the software will be provided). By permitting limited use of the software, developers can give potential users the opportunity to try the software, much like a car dealer will let you test drive a car to see if you want to own it. Since this type of software is copyright protected, any unauthorized duplication or use is illegal.

## PROPRIETARY (BUY-IT-TO-USE-IT)

Since most software developers wish to be compensated for their efforts, it is illegal to copy or use some software without paying for the right to do so. Generally, you purchase the right to use the software in a prescribed manner. If you wish to install the program on multiple machines, you can purchase a **site license** specifying how the software is to be used in your organization. Any violation of the terms of use is **software piracy**. The Software & Information Industry Association (www.siia.net) is an organization committed to education about (and enforcement of) laws that protect computer software.

## BUYING SOFTWARE

All newly-purchased computers come with many programs pre-installed. Additional programs can be purchased at a variety of places, such as computer stores, discount stores, office supply stores, bookstores, and from Internet vendors.

Students can save big bucks by buying "academic" versions of many of the most popular programs. College bookstores, as well as many other stores, offer this type of software. In addition to "academic" versions, many folks save major bucks by buying the "upgrade" version of the software they want. Upgrade versions only work if you already have an older version of the same (or similar) product. Be sure to read the package carefully to ensure you are buying the right version of the program, because many retailers will not allow you to return software that has been removed from its sealed container.

## EXERCISE 1: CROSSWORD

Use the clues below to complete the crossword puzzle.

### ACROSS

1. Copying or using software illegally is ___.
5. An on-screen graphical image that executes a command.
6. If you wish to install a program on multiple machines, you can purchase a ___ license which specifies how the software is to be used in your organization.
7. When I use a program that makes use of sight (video) and sound (audio), I am using ___.
8. A ___base program stores, organizes, and retrieves data.
10. A person who uses a computer system.
12. Are freeware and shareware the same thing?
13. An abbreviation for a billion of 14 Across.
14. Eight bits.
16. When Microsoft bundles various programs, such as Word, Excel, and PowerPoint in a single package to be sold as a single unit, this package is called a ___.
17. Another name for a processor.
18. An abbreviation for a thousand of 14 Across.

### DOWN

1. Programs used to create documents such as letters, spreadsheets, and newsletters are called ___ software.
2. Another word for 1 Down.
3. On page A-3, we learned that a binary digit is called a ___.
4. The boxes that display information on the desktop.
9. Software that is copyrighted, but is given away without charge, is called ___ ware.
11. ___ domain software is not under copyright protection, and can be copied, used, and/or redistributed without cost.
13. "Graphical User Interface" is abbreviated as ___.
15. The ___top is the entire area on the screen upon which documents, folders, files, and programs are displayed.

## EXERCISE 2: MATCHING

The sets of instructions used by a processor are referred to as software (programs). Various categories of software exist. Below is a list of six of the most widely used types of software. Below that list, specific programs are listed. For each program, identify which type it is by placing the letter of the type on the line next to the program.

A. Database
B. Operating System
C. Slide Show Presentation
D. Spreadsheet
E. Web Browser
F. Word Processing

| | |
|---|---|
| 1. ___ Access | 9. ___ NetWare |
| 2. ___ Corel Presentations | 10. ___ PowerPoint |
| 3. ___ WordPad | 11. ___ Quatro Pro |
| 4. ___ Excel | 12. ___ UNIX |
| 5. ___ Internet Explorer | 13. ___ Lotus 1-2-3 |
| 6. ___ Linux | 14. ___ Word |
| 7. ___ Windows | 15. ___ DOS |
| 8. ___ Netscape Navigator | 16. ___ WordPerfect |

## EXERCISE 3: COMPLETION

As mentioned previously, some software developers want to make their products available at no charge; others wish to be compensated for their efforts and creativity. How the product is distributed and under what conditions others are granted the right to use the software is determined by the developers. Generally, software can be classified as either freeware, shareware, proprietary (buy-it-to-use it), or public domain. Use the four terms below to complete the statements.

Freeware
Shareware
Proprietary
Public Domain

1. _____ software is provided free for a limited period of time or a limited version (liteware) is provided. If, after using the software, the borrower wants to continue to use it or if she wants the full version of the program, she will pay the owner who will then permit her to use it for an unlimited time (or, in the case of liteware, the full-scale version of the software will be provided). Lots of this type of software can be downloaded from the Internet.

2. _____ software is not under copyright protection. It is provided free of charge without restrictions on its usage. It can, therefore, be copied, used, and/or redistributed without cost to the user. Lots of this type of software can be downloaded from the Internet.

3. _____ software is given away free of charge. However, the developer of this type of software retains a copyright to the program and can, therefore restrict the way it can be used. Lots of this type of software can be downloaded from the Internet.

4. _____ software requires payment for its usage. This type of software has tremendous market value and is sold in retail stores and over the Internet. It is illegal for the user to copy or redistribute this type of software.

## EXERCISE 4: FIND A WORD

The answers to the following statements can be found in the matrix below. Some are backwards, some are diagonal, some are vertical, and some are horizontal. Circle each word.

1. To find, load, view, print, or create web pages, you will need to use a web ___, such as Internet Explorer or Netscape Navigator.
2. A collection of full-fledge programs packaged as a single unit, such as Microsoft Office or WordPerfect Office. By buying software this way, you can save lots of money.
3. A person who uses the hardware and software associated with a computer system.
4. Boxes on the screen that display information (hint: it's also the name of the world's most widely used operating system).
5. The type of software that is given away free, but the developer retains a copyright to the program and can, therefore restrict the way it is used. So, while you can use it without paying anything, there are some restrictions concerning its use.
6. Another name for programs.
7. If you make illegal copies of software or use it in other illegal ways, you are involved in software ___.
8. The entire area of the screen where documents, folders, and programs are displayed.
9. On-screen graphical images that are used to execute commands.
10. Microsoft Windows is an ___ system.
11. An abbreviation for Graphical User Interface.
12. The way a program interacts with a user is its user ___.
13. Software that is not under copyright protection is said to be ___ domain software.
14. If you wish to install a program on multiple machines, you can purchase a site ___.
15. A program (e.g., Microsoft Access) that permits you to store, organize, and retrieve data.
16. A program (e.g., Microsoft Excel) that permits you to create a budget or some other document that utilizes formulas to calculate values is called a spreadsheet or a ___.

| B | G | O | P | E | R | A | T | I | N | G |
|---|---|---|---|---|---|---|---|---|---|---|
| R | A | U | D | F | S | U | I | T | E | O |
| O | T | W | I | S | T | N | S | E | U | P |
| W | I | N | D | O | W | S | O | E | B | C |
| S | M | C | E | R | A | W | E | E | R | F |
| E | C | S | O | F | T | W | A | R | E | I |
| R | Q | P | X | N | Y | C | A | R | I | P |
| Y | L | W | D | E | S | K | T | O | P | U |
| V | I | N | T | E | R | F | A | C | E | B |
| J | G | H | D | E | S | N | E | C | I | L |
| D | A | T | A | B | A | S | E | A | E | I |
| L | W | O | R | K | S | H | E | E | T | C |

## EXERCISE 5: EXPLAIN CONCEPTS

Dozer has been to a few computer stores recently. While looking at software, he's noticed that some packages have an "Upgrade" label and others do not. Furthermore, he's noticed that the ones marked as "Upgrade" are much cheaper in price. Explain the difference between those programs so he will know under what circumstances he can save some money by buying the "Upgrade" version?

_____
_____
_____
_____
_____
_____
_____
_____
_____
_____
_____
_____
_____
_____
_____
_____
_____

## EXERCISE 6: TRUE-FALSE

For each of the following eight statements, place a T or an F on the line to indicate if the statement is True or False.

1. ___A printer and a scanner are sometimes called software.
2. ___GUI stands for "Geographic Utility Integrator"
3. ___Microsoft Office is a suite (a collection of software).
4. ___Application and productivity software are the same thing.
5. ___Windows XP is an operating system.
6. ___A "user" is a person who uses a computer system
7. ___A database stores, organizes, and retrieves data.
8. ___ Public domain software is not under copyright protection.

## EXERCISE 7: SYNONYMS

Synonyms are words with similar meanings (e.g., big and large). For each word below, provide a synonym.

| WORD | SYNONYM |
|---|---|
| Programs | |
| Worksheet | |
| Productivity | |

## EXERCISE 8: TRUE-FALSE

For each of the following eight statements, place a T or an F on the line to indicate if the statement is True or False.

1. ___Copying or using software illegally is piracy.
2. ___Windows XP is a database program.
3. ___A computer program is also called software.
4. ___Freeware and shareware are the same thing.
5. ___Shareware software is not under copyright protection.
6. ___An icon is a graphical image that executes a command.
7. ___O.S. stands for "Office Software".
8. ___A web browser lets me find stuff on the Internet.

☞ Dozer's Quintessential Guide To Computer Concepts ☜

Nowadays, colleges have computer labs with the equipment (hardware) and the programs (software) that you will need. You and other taxpayers paid for the labs, the equipment, the software, the paper, the electricity, and the salaries of the lab technicians and lab instructors. You should take advantage of these facilities. After all, since you have already paid for them, using them is free. Think of it as though you were spending the day at Disneyland. Once you pay for your ticket, the rides are free. Likewise, since you have already paid for the labs, using them is free. At Disneyland, your goal is to ride each ride as many times as possible to get your money's worth. In the computer labs, your goal should be to invest as much time as possible to get your money's worth.

In using Dozer's Quintessential Guide To Computer Literacy, there's no need for you to buy a computer and software. Many students don't own a computer. Even if they do, they may not have the versions of the software used in Dozer's Guide. Therefore, use the lab to learn. Besides, when working in the lab, they get free use of the equipment, paper, toner, and electricity. And, they get to ask the lab assistants questions.

You will soon discover that a computer can be educational as well as entertaining and given the low cost of today's computers, you may decide to buy one--if not now, certainly sometime. This project helps you understand how to buy a computer system.

Many people think that they need to own a computer system. Some of these people are right; some of them are wrong. To determine if you need to own a computer system, and, if so, what kind of system, you should answer the following seven questions. Doing so will ensure that you obtain the right system for your needs and you'll save time, money, and grief later.

### WHO WILL BE USING THE COMPUTER SYSTEM?
Consider the other folks who will use the computer (e.g., your kids or grandkids; your parents or grandparents). Make a list of the folks who might use your computer.

### WHAT DO THEY WANT TO DO WITH A COMPUTER?
How will each of these people use a computer? You might want it to write letters, memos, or novels. Someone else might be interested in creating graphic-intensive presentations. And, yet another person might want to play interactive games. These are distinctly different needs and each should be considered when researching what computer system to purchase. In addition to assessing the current needs of these people, you should consider how their needs might change in the near future. For instance, you might have a youngster who currently would use a computer to draw pictures; in a couple of years, that child may be sophisticated enough to navigate the Internet. Or, you may be considering starting your own business in the near future, in which case, you may need to use a computer to perform accounting functions such as the creation of budgets and financial statements. Your decision to purchase one system over another should be made with some thought to the future, as well as to current users and uses for the system.

### WHERE WILL THE COMPUTER BE USED?
While this might seem like an odd question, it is important. For instance, will all your computing be done in your home? Or, will you want to take your computer on vacation with you, or to the office? If you plan to use your computer in more than one location, portability is an issue. While not impossible, it is tough to move a desktop computer. If this is your desire, consider buying a laptop. Otherwise, get a desktop machine.

### WHAT SOFTWARE WILL BE NEEDED?
If your needs include word processing, accounting, and access to the Internet, you will need to locate software to perform each function. With word processing, decide if you prefer Microsoft Word or WordPerfect. For accounting, you will need some sort of accounting software, such as Quicken or Peachtree. By the way, you will find that these software packages come in two versions. One for Macintosh machines and one for IBM-compatibles. When selecting software, you will need to make this decision. For most folks the choice is easy--go with the IBM-compatible version of software and be sure to buy an IBM-compatible machine (discussed further in a moment).

Most computers are sold with an lots of great software already installed. Before you buy any software, choose the computer system (hardware). The system you choose may very well have the software you need already installed on it. Buying software before buying a computer system may, therefore, be a waste of your financial resources. So, for now, you are just locating the software. You aren't buying it. When you get ready to buy it, you'll want to compare prices. For now, don't buy anything.

### WHAT HARDWARE WILL BE NEEDED?
**Processor**: Processor speed, measured in GHz (gigahertz) is a major consideration. But, not much to worry about since most computers sold today have very fast processing speeds.

**Memory**: Look on the software boxes to see how much memory is required. Consider the possibility that you will want to work with multiple programs simultaneously (**multitasking**). If so, you will need sufficient memory to run two or more programs at once. More memory will cost, but you should consider spending the extra bucks to get plenty of memory. The memory needs of future versions of software will, no doubt, be greater than the current needs. Be ready for the future: invest in memory.

**Hard Drive**: The primary consideration is storage capacity, measured in GBs (gigabytes). The amount you need depends on how many programs you will install and how byte-intensive are the files stored on the hard drive. For instance, if you work with lots of graphics, you will need more hard drive storage capacity than if you only work with text-based documents.

**Floppy Drive**: Until recently, all computers came with a floppy drive. Many still do: some don't. As time goes by, fewer will. If you need to store and retrieve data from floppy disks, be sure to buy a machine with a floppy drive.

**Modem**: Since most computers come with a 56Kbps modem, you don't need to decide if you want one (you do) or how fast it should be (it will be 56Kbps). By the way, Kbps stands for KiloBits Per Second, which means that it is capable of transmitting 56 thousand bits per second, which is sometimes referred to simply as a 56K modem. Remember, a modem is the device that connects a computer to a phone line.

**CD-ROM**: The primary consideration here is the speed. A 40x CD-ROM is 40 times faster than the first available CD-ROM drive. If you will be running interactive games from a CD, speed is important. Otherwise, don't be overly concerned.

**CD-RW**: Many computer systems are sold with a CD-RW, which will permit you to save lots of stuff on a CD instead of having to save lots of stuff on lots of diskettes. Of course, most of your files will be saved to the hard drive of your machine. But, you will always want to backup your files to protect yourself in the event that your valuable data is lost, deleted, or corrupted in some way. A great way to backup your work is to save a copy of it to a CD-RW, which will hold up to 680 MB of data.

**DVD**: Many computers have a DVD drive which lets you watch movies on your computer or store lots of music. Since a DVD holds much more data, they will eventually replace CD-ROMs. By the way, DVD stands for either Digital Versatile Disc or Digital Video Disc, depending on whom you ask.

**Monitor**: The important features are the size of the monitor (measured diagonally like TV screens are measured) and the resolution (clarity), which is mostly determined by the number of pixels (dots that create the image) and the dot pitch (the space between the pixels). Most any monitor will perform satisfactory. However, if you will be using graphics, you might want to consider paying a few extra bucks for a monitor with higher resolution. As with a TV, the bigger the screen, the happier you will be. Buy the best and the biggest monitor you can afford.

**Speakers**: To hear CDs (regular music CDs) or to hear audio on web sites, you will want speakers. Since most computers come with speakers, the only decision for you to make is whether you want to upgrade the standard speakers for better ones. For most folks, the standard stuff is sufficient.

**Printer**: To choose the proper printer, you will need to answer three questions: Do you want a color printer, how sharp an image is desired, and how fast do you want it to produce printouts? For text-based documents, get a B&W printer; for photos and graphics, get a color printer. If resolution is important, get a printer with lots of dpi (dots per inch). If speed is important, pay attention to the ppm (pages per minute) rating. An ink-jet printer uses ink to make the characters and images; a laser printer uses a powdery substance called toner to do so.

**Scanner**: You need one if you will want to scan photos or documents. Otherwise, you don't need one. In any event, it is something you can always buy later and add to your system.

**Ports**: Computers have multiple ports, including USB ports that will permit you to attach a printer, scanner, or digital camera. The more such devices you have, the more ports you will need. But, most computers have lots of them, so don't worry much.

**Tower vs Desktop**: The system unit can be a tower or a desktop. The tower can be placed on the floor so that your monitor sits lower on the desk, but unless you have some special needs, it won't matter either way.

### WHEN SHOULD I BUY A COMPUTER?
Technology is changing rapidly. In the world of computers, this means that what is sold today will be technologically obsolete without much delay. In fact, it will probably be technologically obsolete the moment you buy it, because many computers for sale today are already stale (they utilize features no longer being used in computers coming off the assembly line).

So, the age-old argument is: "If I wait, I can get a faster, more efficient machine which incorporates up-to-date technological advancements." Yes, that is true. However, back when PCs were sold without a hard drive, that argument was used to postpone the purchase in anticipation of the introduction of computers with built-in hard drives. And, when hard drives with capacities measured in kilobytes were included, that argument was used to postpone the purchase in anticipation of the availability of hard drives whose capacities were measured in megabytes, and the argument was again used to postpone the purchase of a computer in anticipation of gigabyte-sized hard drives. Then there was the transition from 5-1/4" to 3-1/2" floppies, the addition of a CD-ROM drive, and the increased processing speed from 33 MHz to 66MHz . . . to 2.8 GHz etc..

Yes, if you wait you can get a faster, more powerful machine with more bells and whistles. Meanwhile you are denying yourself the opportunity to use a computer. Prices are low: features are high. If you need a computer now; buy it now!

### WHERE SHOULD I BUY THE SYSTEM?
There are five sources from which you can buy a computer.

From a friend who will sell you his old system for a few hundred bucks. He may be selling his old computer for the same reason you should not buy it. It will no longer do what he wants it to do. Perhaps it has inadequate memory to run the programs currently on the market. Perhaps, the speed of the processor is too slow. Perhaps it lacks a sound card, a video card, or even a modem. Perhaps the hard drive is too small. He wants to discard it to buy a machine that will be faster or better. You should follow his lead--buy a faster and better machine yourself. Let him keep his old junk. After all, you deserve good stuff too!

From a mail order firm. If you encounter problems putting it together, you can call them on the phone for help. Some mail order firms are reputable; others are not. If you go this route, go with a well-known, proven name in the business.

From a computer/office warehouse such as CompUsa, Office Max, or Office Depot, where you can test drive the computers in the store, ask questions, and find an abundance of software and peripherals. If the machine does not perform as expected, you can go yell at a real, live human being until you get satisfaction. After all, it's more fun to yell at a real live person than it is to yell at some nameless, faceless humanoid on a phone. Besides, the guy on the phone might hang up on you.

From a computer builder. Some firms specialize in custom building computers. Since most folks don't have special needs, having a computer custom built is typically unnecessary.

From a discount store that sells everything from candy to toys. You may find that the prices are as low as the level of service. But, if you know what you want, you might save some bucks. In addition, you can buy a pair of shoes while you are there.

Whatever you do, don't buy a computer from a dude selling stuff from the back of a U-Haul truck. Especially, if you hear the motor running.

## EXERCISE 1: CROSSWORD
Use the clues below to complete the crossword puzzle.

### ACROSS

1. The physical components that make up a computer system (e.g., monitor, scanner, printer, etc.).
3. When a computer ad refers to the processor, it will very likely tell you something about its ___, which will be measured in GHz (gigahertz).
6. A CD is inserted into a CD-___ drive.
7. The device that permits a computer to be connected to a phone line to allow data to be transmitted.
10. Dot pitch, pixels, and size are three important features of ___.
13. If you want to be able to easily take a computer with you, you'd probably want to buy a ___ computer.
14. An abbreviation for Digital Video (or Versatile) Disc.
15. The type of port into which you might plug a scanner, a printer, or a digital camera.
17. When referring to a monitor, you'd probably want to know about the clarity of its image. Another word for clarity is ___.
18. An abbreviation for how many dots a printer will use to create the characters or images per square inch of space on the paper.
20. PPM stands for ___ Per Minute, which indicates the speed at which a printer will create printed pages.
22. When referring to printers, DPI stands for ___ Per Inch.
23. A computer can store data and programs on a ___ drive located within the system unit. When buying a computer, you might want to consider the importance of getting sufficient capacity to hold all of your programs and data.
25. Computer systems come with one of two types of system unit. A ___ usually will be placed on the floor so that it doesn't take up valuable space on your desk.
26. A laser printer creates characters and images on the paper with a powdery substance called toner; an ink-___ printer sprays ink on the paper to create the characters and images.
27. Before you buy a computer system, it's a good idea to find the programs that you will need. On the box you will then see the specification of the computer required to run each program. Another name for program is ___.

### DOWN

2. You can listen to music on a CD or hear sounds from a web site if you have headphones or speakers. Another word for "sound" is ___.
4. One of the important features to consider when selecting a printer is its speed, which is measured in ___, an abbreviation for how many pages a printer will create in one minute.
5. The temporary location where the data and programs currently being used by a processor reside. When you buy a computer, one of the most important things to consider is the capacity of this temporary storage location. You want as much as you can afford.
6. You can't create (burn) your own CDs in a CD-ROM drive, but a computer with a CD-___ drive will let you do so, which means you can create your own music CDs and store lots of other stuff on CDs.
8. The dots that create the image on a monitor are called

pixels; the space between the pixels is the ___ pitch. You want lots of pixels and very little space between them.
9. Should you buy a computer before you go looking for software?
10. Simultaneously working with more than one program is called ___. If you want to do this (and most folks want to do this), your computer system will need lots of memory.
11. Is a CD-ROM and a CD-RW the same thing?
12. A device that works like a copy machine, except instead of producing a paper copy, it creates a digital copy of the document.
14. Computer systems come with one of two types of system unit. A ___ is typically placed under the monitor.
16. PPM stands for Pages Per ___.
19. If you want to listen to music or hear the audio found on some web pages, your computer system will need to either have headphones or ___.
21. The most important feature of a hard drive is its ___ capacity, which is measured in GBs (gigabytes).
24. Dozer is the world's smartest cyber ___.

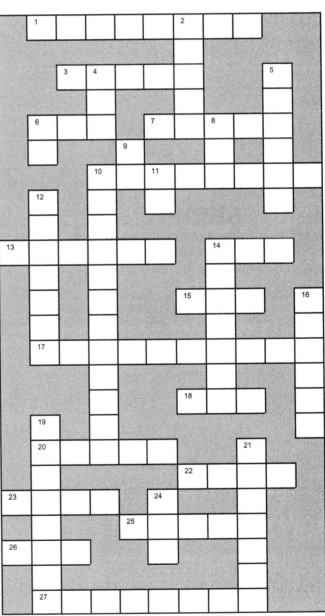

## EXERCISE 2: UNDERSTANDING COMPUTER ADS

Dozer is thinking about buying a new computer. He's been reading ads. Please review the ads below and answer Dozer's questions:

---

**COMPUTER SYSTEM A**

Price: $349
2.2 GHz Intel Celeron Processor
128 MB RAM
40 GB Hard Drive
48X CD-ROM Drive
56 K Modem
Software: Windows XP, Microsoft Works

Monitor Sold Separately

---

**COMPUTER SYSTEM B**

Price: $829
2.08 GHz AMD Athlon Processor
17" .28 Color Monitor
512 MB RAM
120 GB Hard Drive
40X CD-ROM
56 K Modem
Software: Windows XP, WordPerfect Office

---

**COMPUTER SYSTEM C**

Price: $1899
3.2 GHz Pentium 4 Processor
17" .24 Monitor
1 GB RAM
250 GB Hard Drive
48X CD-ROM Drive
CD-RW Drive
56 K Modem
Software: Windows XP, Microsoft Office

---

1: Which computer system has the fastest processor?

2. What does "GHz" stand for and what is one GHz?

3. Why would anyone pay for the faster processor?

4. What does .24 and .28 tell you about each monitor?

5. How is the monitor size measured?

6. Which computer system has the most RAM?

7. When measuring RAM, what do the terms "MB" and "GB" stand for?

8. What is one MB? What is one GB?

9. What does "RAM" stand for and what else is it called?

10. Why is the amount of RAM important?

11. Why would anyone pay for lots of RAM?

12. Which computer has the highest capacity hard drive?

13. Why is the amount of hard drive capacity important?

14. Why would anyone pay for the larger hard drive?

15. What does "CD-ROM" stand for?

16. What does 40X and 48X tell you about each CD-ROM?

17. What is a modem used for?

18. In describing a modem, what does the "K" stand for?

19. What does "CD-RW" stand for?

20. Why would anyone pay for a CD-RW?

21. None of the ads mentions a floppy drive. Should you assume that they all come with a floppy drive?

22. Only the second ad tells you the monitor is a color monitor. Do you think the other monitors are black & white?

23. What is meant in the first ad by "Monitor Sold Separately"?

24. One system comes with Microsoft Works, one comes with WordPerfect Office, and another comes with Microsoft Office. What's the difference? Hint: You might want to reread the information about suites and integrated packages found on page A-8.

Whether you buy a computer now or use someone else's, you will need to know a few things about protecting the equipment, your data, and yourself. There will also come a time when you will need to diagnose some computer-related problems to avoid unnecessary expense and down-time. In addition, eventually, you will own a machine and will realize that your machine is outdated. You will then need to decide whether it is time to buy a new machine or upgrade your existing one by purchasing new hardware components or new software. This project covers these topics with the goal of providing a working understanding of these activities.

## PROTECTING THE EQUIPMENT

Whether you purchased your own computer or you are using someone else's, a substantial investment in finances and time have been made to acquire and maintain the equipment. To protect that investment, consider the following.

### SURGE SUPPRESSOR

A surge or spike is a momentary increase in voltage. This boost in electrical power can harm the circuitry in a computer. The damage may happen immediately or it may slowly wear out the components over time. To absorb power surges and/or spikes, you can buy a **surge suppressor**, which looks like a multi-outlet power strip, but has additional components that absorb the spikes. A surge suppressor costs anywhere from five to five hundred bucks depending on the level of protection desired. It can be installed in about five seconds. All you do is plug it in an electrical outlet and plug your computer components into it. By the way, you should have a surge suppressor for all the valuable electronic devices in your home (e.g., TV, VCR).

### SCREEN SAVER

**Screen savers** (software that creates random patterns when the keyboard and mouse have been idle for a given period of time) were developed to protect monitors from being exposed to the same image for extended periods of time, which would burn the image into the screen. Now, with advancements in monitor design, screen savers provide more entertainment than protection. Microsoft Windows comes with a variety of screen savers. In addition, you can purchase screen savers or you can download lots of free screen savers from the Internet.

### PASSWORDS

One of the most common destructive forces to a computer system is a friend who wants to use your computer. You may consider your friend to be a computer wiz who knows all about computers. You may think that he could not, nor would not, do anything to harm your machine. If you let enough friends use your computer system, eventually one of them will delete some needed files or will tamper with the machine in some way that will prove to be less-than-desirable. Whenever a computer wiz wants to use your computer, try to recall the following: Steve McQueen, in addition to being an actor, was considered to be a highly-skilled driver and he wrecked more cars in his life than you and I will ever own. To prevent your friends from driving your car, you keep the keys away from them. Likewise to keep your friends from using your computer, keep your friends physically away from your computer and use a **password**. Not only will they not be able to harm your machine, but they will not be able to read files containing sensitive information.

## VIRUS PROTECTION

A **computer virus** is a piece of code that was deliberately designed to maliciously cause unexpected and/or undesirable consequences for the victim (e.g., delete files, perform pranks, etc.). Computer viruses enter a computer disguised as normal information, sometimes disguised as Trojan horses (programs designed to attract attention in hopes that folks will be enticed to download the program). The real purpose of the program is to transmit the virus to damage your system. To reduce the likelihood of contracting a virus, be careful when you borrow diskettes or when you download programs via the Internet. Use an **anti-virus program** to detect and eliminate common viruses. These programs can be purchased for less than fifty bucks (many computer systems are now sold with such a program). You should scan your diskettes before you use someone else's machine so that you do not infect their machine with any virus that may be on your diskette. Before leaving their machine, you should scan your diskettes to be sure that any virus you may have acquired from their computer is detected before you take the diskette home and infect your computer with the virus. The best protection from viruses is to maintain several generations of backups (discussed below). If one copy contracts a virus, you still have other copies of your data.

### ANTI-STATIC MATS

When you walk across many carpeted floors, you build up static electricity. When you touch someone else or some objects, you can hear the snap and feel the bite of the static electricity leaving your body. If you were to touch a computer, the static electricity can harm the delicate circuitry. To protect your computer system from such harm, you can buy and install an **anti-static mat**. These basically come in two varieties. You can buy a floor mat that is placed under your chair. It looks like a regular plastic carpet protector mat, but it has an anti-static property. When you sit down in front of your computer, the static electricity is dissipated into the mat before you touch the computer keyboard. The other type is a mat placed under your keyboard. When you touch the keyboard, the static is removed.

### BACKUPS

You should periodically make a **backup** (a duplicate copy) of all of your important data. While secondary storage is said to be permanent, this merely means that its integrity is maintained in the absence of electricity. There are many events that can cause your data to be lost or corrupted in such a way that it will be unaccessible. For instance, you can delete a file that you now need, your files can be damaged by a computer virus, or your hard drive could crash. In addition, you can format a disk containing a needed file, your disk can be lost or stolen, or your disk could be damaged from excessive heat, dirt, magnetic fields, water, or the family pet iguana. Therefore, if your data is of any value to you, backup your work. By the way, there are two groups of computer users. Those who have previously lost important files and had no backups. Having learned their lesson, they now backup their work. The other group of folks have not yet lost their important files, but will one day. Then, they will learn their lesson. Which group are you in?

### DISKETTE CARE

In times past, a diskette had a thin cover that could easily be bent and a recording window that exposed the disk surface.

Nowadays, diskettes have a few enhancements that help to protect the data residing on them. For instance, the diskettes in use today have a hard plastic cover that is difficult to bend and they have a spring-loaded shutter mechanism that protects the disk surface when the diskette is removed from a floppy drive. Even with these built-in protections, you should treat your diskettes with respect by following these rules:

- Keep diskettes away from magnetic objects (remember, the data is stored via positively or negatively charged magnetic particles, which can be altered by the force of a magnet).
- Protect diskettes from extreme heat.
- Don't touch the surface of a diskette.
- Don't bend a diskette or stack heavy stuff on top of it.
- Don't use a diskette with a bent shutter mechanism. If it is bent, remove the mechanism and the small spring. Insert the diskette into a floppy drive and copy its contents to another diskette. Then throw the defective diskette away.

### PROTECTING THE USER

Some folks suffer from sundry physical and/or psychological consequences from computer usage. For instance, some **novices** (beginning computer users) suffer from **cyberphobia** (the fear of computers in general or the fear of using a computer). This fear may make the user so nervous that she can't concentrate on what she is doing, thus inhibiting the user's ability to learn about computers. If you suffer from cyberphobia, relax. One of the goals of Dozer's Quintessential Guide To Computer Literacy is to provide you with the experience needed to eliminate any such fears. There is nothing to fear, except the fear that you are not willing to invest the time and effort required to become computer literate. If you have the time and expend the effort, you will succeed. By the way, the opposite of a novice is a **geek** (also called a **nerd**). Becoming a geek is our goal. After all, Dozer is proud to be a geek. So should you.

Backaches and fatigue experienced from using computers for extended periods of time have little to do with the computer itself, but with the position of the computer user. To reduce the risk of experiencing these problems, use a properly adjusted ergonomic chair and adjust the height of the monitor so that it is at, or slightly below, eye level. Most importantly, you should periodically get up and walk around for a few minutes.

Straining to focus on a screen can lead to **computer vision syndrome** with symptoms that include eyestrain, blurred vision, headaches, and dry burning eyes. While the symptoms normally disappear when you are not using a monitor, there are some things you can do to reduce the risk of developing this condition. For example, you can use an anti-glare filter for the screen, reduce the amount of lighting in the room, wear tinted sunglasses, set the computer to display less-irritating colors, and take regular breaks from computer work.

At the base of the palm of your hand is the carpal tunnel (a small tunnel through which tendons and the median nerve pass). This tunnel is barely large enough for the tendons and one nerve to pass through. Sometimes, the nerve becomes pinched in the small space, resulting in a painful condition called **carpal tunnel syndrome**. The repetitive nature of using a keyboard for extended periods of time can result in this condition, because the size of the carpal tunnel changes depending on the position of the wrist. When the wrist and hand are straight, the carpal tunnel is at its maximum size. The tunnel becomes slightly smaller when the hand is bent up or down at the wrist. Most computer keyboards are based on the design used on typewriters. They fail to take into account the way a human body works, forcing most typists to twist their arms and wrists in unnatural positions which results in pressure being exerted on the median nerve as it passes through the carpal tunnel. To reduce the risk of developing this condition, use a wrist rest and an ergonomic (natural) keyboard and periodically take breaks from extended periods of keyboarding. Treatments for carpal tunnel syndrome range from immobilizing the wrist with a brace to taking medications. In severe cases, surgery is required (Ouch!).

### TROUBLESHOOTING

Everything eventually fails to work as expected. Cars stop running, washing machines quit spinning, and phones cease to ring. Computers are no different. If you own one, it will, without a doubt, one day act weirdly. So, periodically, you will need to do some **troubleshooting** (diagnosing and solving problems). If all else fails, have a technician look at your machine. Before calling her, try doing the following:

- Whatever you were trying to do, try it again.
- Reboot the machine and try again.
- Check the connections from the computer to the electrical receptacle and from peripheral devices to the computer. If the printer is not connected to the computer, the printer will not work. If the power is off, nothing will work.
- Think about what happened just prior to the trouble. What were you doing? What did you see or hear? Does any of that give you a clue as to what might be wrong?
- Test your system by using diagnostic software which is designed to find problems and suggest solutions.
- Take a break. Go for a walk. When you return, try again. You will be amazed how many problems disappear by this approach. Even if the walk does not solve the problem, you probably needed a break to reduce the likelihood of back aches, eyestrain, or wrist pain as described earlier.

### UPGRADING

Just as a car becomes outdated, so does a computer system. A computer system can become outdated in two ways. When a new **version** of software becomes available (e.g., you are operating under Windows Me and Windows XP is released) or when new hardware components are available (e.g., faster processors), your system is **technologically obsolete**, which probably occurs the day after you bought your system. On the other hand, your system is **functionally obsolete** when it will no longer do what you want it to do. This can happen years after it is technologically obsolete. For instance, you might need a new program that requires more memory than your system has or you may want to download sounds from the Internet and your system lacks a sound card and speakers. When you determine that your system will no longer do what you want it to do, you need to **upgrade** your current system by obtaining the new software and/or hardware. Or, you need to buy a new system. The decision to upgrade or to buy a new system is one that many people face every couple of years. The distinction between technological and functional obsolescence is important. While you may <u>want</u> to upgrade when your system becomes technologically obsolete, you only <u>need</u> to upgrade if your system is functionally obsolete. In short, technological obsolescence deals with what can be done; functional obsolescence deals with what you want to do. So, if your computer system is currently doing all you want it to do, don't waste your money on new stuff.

# EXERCISE 1: CROSSWORD

Use the clues below to complete the crossword puzzle.

## ACROSS

1. If you are afraid of computers in general, or fear using a computer, you suffer from ___. You may be a bit anxious, but there is no need for you to fear a computer.
4. When you walk across some carpeted floors, you generate static electricity. If you were to touch a computer, the static electricity can harm the delicate circuitry. To protect your computer system from damage due to static electricity, you can use an anti-___ mat. One type is placed under the keyboard; another type is placed under the chair.
6. In Project 1, we learned that the abbreviation for a thousand bytes is ___.
7. A backup is a duplicate ___ of your data.
9. In Project 1, we learned that a flat-panel monitor is used on a small portable computer called a ___top.
10. A ___ saver is software that creates random patterns when the keyboard and the mouse have been idle for a given period of time.
11. In Project 1, we learned that another way of saying "turn on" a computer is to say "boot __" a computer.
12. In Project 1, we learned that a typical desktop monitor is a CRT (Cathode Ray Tube), that works much like a ___.
15. A beginning computer user.
16. In Project 1, we learned that ___ is used to store programs that need to be accessed quickly. These programs are used when a machine is booted up.
18. To reduce the likelihood of contracting a computer virus, you should be careful from whom you borrow diskettes and from where you download files. In addition, you should use an ___ program to detect and eliminate common viruses.
20. Your system is ___ obsolete when it will no longer do what you want it to do.
25. The abbreviation for a billion bytes is ___.
26. Diagnosing and solving computer-related problems is called ___shooting.
27. Dozer is the smartest cyber ___ on the planet.
29. Eyestrain, blurred vision, and headaches caused by straining to focus on a monitor's screen is called computer ___ syndrome.
30. The most widely used operating system in the world is called ___.

## DOWN

1. The repetitive nature of using a keyboard for extended periods of time can result in a painful wrist condition called ___ syndrome.
2. There are many events that can cause your data to be lost or corrupted. To protect your data, you should periodically make a ___ (a duplicate copy) of your data.
3. To prevent unauthorized people from accessing your data, you can use a ___, which is a secret code used by you to access your data.
5. When a new version of software becomes available (e.g., you are operating under Windows Me and Windows XP is released) or when new hardware components are available (e.g., faster modems or faster processors), your computer system is ___ obsolete.
8. In Project 1, we learned that a socket into which another device can be plugged is called a ___.

13. A ___ is a piece of code that was deliberately designed to maliciously cause undesirable consequences.
14. In Project 2, we learned that in a GUI environment, such as Windows, an ___ is an on-screen graphical image that is used to execute a command.
17. In Project 1, we learned that approximately 1000 bytes is a ___ byte.
19. In Project 1, we learned that a printer, or any device, in communication with a computer is said to be ___ line.
21. When your system will no longer do what you want it to do, you need to ___ your current system by obtaining the new software and/or hardware.
22. In Project 1, we learned that when a floppy drive is reading from or writing to the disk, the drive indicator ___ is on and, if you listen carefully, you can hear the drive running.
23. A spike in electrical power can harm the circuitry in your computer. To absorb these potentially harmful power spikes, you can buy a ___ suppressor, which looks like a multi-outlet power strip, but it has additional components that absorb the spikes.
24. When a software developer improves the software, the new, improved software is a new ___.
28. Is a megabyte a trillion bytes?

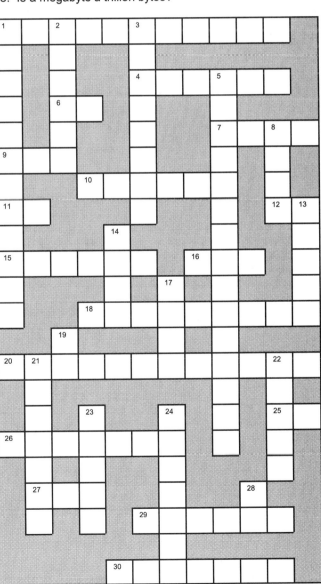

## EXERCISE 2: EXPLAIN CONCEPTS

Dozer thinks that only sissies and crybabies create backups of their work. After all, careful computer users never need backups because they're too smart to ever lose their work. Is he right? If not, explain why he's wrong.

_____
_____
_____
_____
_____
_____
_____
_____
_____

## EXERCISE 3: TRUE-FALSE

For each of the following eight statements, place a T or an F on the line to indicate if the statement is True or False.

1. ___A backup is a duplicate copy of your work.
2. ___Carpal tunnel syndrome is a painful wrist condition.
3. ___Geekophobia is the fear of computers.
4. ___An anti-influenza program can find and eliminate viruses.
5. ___Diagnosing and solving problems is troubleshooting.
6. ___When I buy new software or hardware, I am upgrading.
7. ___Sometimes a nerd is called a geek.
8. ___A screen saver and an anti-static mat are the same thing.

## EXERCISE 4: EXPLAIN CONCEPTS

If your computer is not working properly, you can call a technician to diagnose and fix the problem. What could you do to attempt to fix the problem yourself?

_____
_____
_____
_____
_____
_____
_____
_____
_____

## EXERCISE 5: EXPLAIN CONCEPTS

Dozer knows that the computer systems being sold today are faster, more powerful, and have enhanced capabilities when compared to the computer system he bought just three months ago. Therefore, he has concluded that his computer system is outdated, old, and without value. He thinks he needs to buy a new system. In fact, he thinks he needs a new system every few months to keep up with advances in technology. Is he right? In your answer, explain the difference between technological and functional obsolescence.

_____
_____
_____
_____
_____
_____
_____
_____

## EXERCISE 6: FIND A WORD

The answers to the following statements can be found in the matrix below. Some are backwards, some are diagonal, some are vertical, and some are horizontal. Circle each word.

1.  There are many events that can cause your data to be lost or corrupted. To protect your data, you should periodically make a ___ (a duplicate copy) of your data.
2.  When your system will no longer do what you want it to do, you need to ___ your current system by obtaining the new software and/or hardware.
3.  If you are afraid of computers in general, or fear using a computer, you suffer from ___.
4.  A spike in electrical power can harm the circuitry in your computer. To absorb these potentially harmful power spikes, you can buy a ___ suppressor, which looks like a multi-outlet power strip, but it has additional components that absorb the spikes.
5.  A ___ saver is software that creates random patterns when the keyboard and the mouse have been idle for a given period of time.
6.  A ___ is a piece of code that was deliberately designed to maliciously cause undesirable consequences.
7.  The repetitive nature of using a keyboard for extended periods of time can result in a painful wrist condition called ___ tunnel syndrome.
8.  When a new version of software becomes available (e.g., you are operating under Windows Me and Windows XP is released) or when new hardware components are available (e.g., faster modems or faster processors), your computer system is technologically obsolete. However, your system is ___ obsolete when it will no longer do what you want it to do.
9.  A beginning computer user.
10. To prevent unauthorized people from accessing your data, you can use a ___, which is a secret code used by you to access your data.
11. Another word for nerd.

| F | P | A | S | S | W | O | R | D | T | D |
|---|---|---|---|---|---|---|---|---|---|---|
| U | N | S | C | O | T | Y | V | N | U | A |
| N | S | G | R | L | U | S | N | B | L | G |
| C | Y | B | E | R | P | H | O | B | I | A |
| T | K | A | E | S | G | T | V | P | V | T |
| I | N | R | N | U | R | Y | I | R | K | J |
| O | E | U | T | R | A | C | C | E | U | O |
| N | C | B | V | I | D | O | E | B | P | S |
| A | K | A | W | V | E | G | R | U | S | J |
| L | L | O | R | L | C | R | K | E | V | F |
| L | R | G | W | P | M | C | W | I | A | R |
| Y | T | J | P | M | A | E | F | Q | O | E |
| J | U | A | T | B | T | L | P | N | U | A |

The rapid change in technology coupled with the need for organizations to embrace these new technologies to improve productivity will continue to fuel the need for computing professionals in the coming years. Perhaps, no other industry will see the levels of growth as will the computer industry. While the lines are somewhat blurred as to the specific duties of various specialists, the following should provide some starting point to understand the diversity of careers available. You need only choose a path and acquire the knowledge and skills needed by employers.

### GETTING THE JOB
Once on the job, you'll have the opportunity to demonstrate your proficiency. But, how do you convince a prospective employer that you are qualified so she will hire you in the first place? Basically in three ways. First, through experience. If you can document prior experience performing the duties associated with your specialty, that would, no doubt, suffice. However, if you have inadequate prior experience, you will need to demonstrate your skills via either formal education and/or through obtaining the relevant certification. Most colleges provide dozens of courses that employers will recognize as indicators of your level of expertise. In addition, you can take Industry-wide tests to become certified in your area of interest. The **certification** serves as a standard for documenting your competencies. Why not obtain both the formal education and the certification in your chosen field? Classes will prepare you for the certification tests. Your college transcript coupled with your certifications will demonstrate your proficiency. The two might just be your ticket to a new career!

### THE FIRST STEP
For many students, the first step in acquiring the knowledge for entry into the computer industry is to take an introductory level course in computers, such as the one you are now taking. In such a class, you will lay a foundation for further studies by learning about basic computer concepts, the Windows operating environment, the Internet, word processing, spreadsheets, and presentation software. Many of the topics covered in Dozer's Quintessential Guide To Computer Literacy are assumed to be known by anyone who enters any of the more specific areas of computing discussed below. That is, entering any of the following career paths assumes that the student has mastered the body of material found in an introductory-level computer class.

### NETWORK ENGINEER
In many organizations, individual computers are connected to each other via cables forming what is called a LAN (Local Area Network) or a WAN (Wide Area Network). Thus, various computers can share software, data, and hardware devices (e.g., shared printers). Since specialized software and hardware is needed, specialists are needed to install, maintain, troubleshoot, and repair these systems. The majority of networks use either Novell NetWare and/or Microsoft Windows. Along with either of these, most networks use products and technology developed by Cisco Systems.

### NOVELL NETWARE
The Novell Corporation markets a widely-used network software called **Novell NetWare**. Network administrators and network engineers possess knowledge of this type of software. A network administrator performs day-to-day maintenance of elements (e.g., sets up user workstations, manages resources, installs and configures print servers, and handles routine software maintenance), while a network engineer performs more technical work (e.g., troubleshooting network problems, performing system upgrades, and planning for technological changes, as well as working with network cards, cabling, and routers). In summary, the engineer is hardware oriented while the administrator is software oriented. College classes can prepare you for a career in this area of the computer industry. Once you obtain the required knowledge, you will probably want to obtain Novell certification, which is recognized world wide as an indication that you have a particular level of knowledge. For instance, passing the **CNA (Certified Novell Administrator)** test or the series of **CNE (Certified Novell Engineer)** tests, will demonstrate to any prospective employer that you have acquired a level of expertise about Novell networks. Some folks pass the CNA test and then after learning more, take the CNE tests. If interested, go to www.novell.com to learn more about Novell certification.

### MICROSOFT NETWORK
Microsoft competes with Novell NetWare in the networking market with its own widely-used software. To qualify for jobs in this area of the computer industry, you will need to gain the knowledge and skills that will permit you to plan, set up, maintain, and troubleshoot networks running under the Microsoft Windows and Microsoft Server products. College classes can prepare you for a career in this area of the computer industry. Once you gain the requisite knowledge, you will probably want to become a **MCSA (Microsoft Certified Systems Administrator)**. Then, after you learn even more, you may want to become a **MCSE (Microsoft Certified Systems Engineer)**. For detailed information about these certification programs, you can go to www.microsoft.com.

### CISCO ASSOCIATE
Cisco Systems is a major producer of the hardware, software, and technology used in **LANs** (Local Area Networks) and **WANs** (Wide Area Networks). College classes can prepare you for a career in this area of the computer industry. Once you've gained the requisite knowledge, you may wish to become certified to demonstrate to potential employers that you possess the knowledge and skills they seek. While a **Cisco Certified Network Associate (CCNA)** is a person who is recognized as having an introductory level of expertise in this area, more advanced certifications exist (e.g., **CCNP** and **CCIE**). If you would like to learn more about Cisco certification programs, go to www.cisco.com.

### GIS (GEOGRAPHIC INFORMATION SYSTEMS)
Many organizations need information that can be provided by a person proficient in the use of **GIS** (geographic information system) software. This software permits you to query a database and have the results appear in the form of a map or graph. The information provided can be used for a variety of purposes (e.g., forecasting population trends, planning efficient land use, determining traffic patterns, etc.). College classes can prepare you for a career in this area of the computer industry. To learn more about GIS software, go to www.esri.com.

## PROGRAMMER

A computer program tells the processor what to do and how to do it (e.g., where to find the data and how to process it). A **programmer** uses a programming language such as COBOL, Java, C++, or Visual Basic to code the specific instructions followed by the computer. He then runs the program to test it to ensure that it works as desired. When **bugs** (errors) are found, the program is modified to **debug** it (remove the errors). Thus, programmers must be detail-oriented, logical thinkers. College classes can prepare you for a career in this area of the computer industry. According to the U.S. Department of Labor's Occupational Outlook Handbook, "Job prospects should be best for college graduates with knowledge of a variety of programming languages and tools; those with less formal education or its equivalent in work experience should face strong competition for programming jobs." For information about various certifications, you should go to www.sun.com or www.iccp.org.

## WEBMASTER

**Webmasters** (also called web designers or web developers) design, create, post, and maintain web pages. An in-depth understanding of **HTML** (HyperText Markup Language) is needed since this is the code used to create web pages. This code consists of markups (tags) that determine the format of the web page along with the placement of text and graphics. According to the U.S. Department of Labor's Occupational Outlook Handbook, "The growth of the Internet has generated a variety of occupations relating to design, development, and maintenance of websites." For your first class, you should take an introductory-level class about the Internet. However, if you already possess a basic knowledge of the Internet, you might want to proceed ahead and take a course covering web page construction techniques. You also might want to become a Certified Internet Webmaster (CIW). For information about webmaster certification, take a look at www.ciwcertified.com or www.comptia.com.

## SECRETARY/DATA ENTRY

With the widespread migration from typewriters to computers, the job of a secretary has become increasingly sophisticated. Where typing pools once existed, now a single secretary produces a wide range of documents. He is expected to know how to use a computer and various programs, such as word processing, spreadsheets, database, email, and web browsers. As the typical office continues to evolve toward a more technologically-advanced workplace, a secretary is expected to participate in continuing education to learn about new software or a new version of the old software. According to the U.S. Department of Labor's Occupational Outlook Handbook, "Opportunities should be best for applicants with extensive knowledge of software applications." College classes can prepare you for a secretarial career. Once you are fortified with the knowledge and skills, you may want to obtain an industry-wide certification to further prove your worth to potential employers. For instance, Microsoft has **Microsoft Office Specialist** certifications for Microsoft Office in its entirety or for specific programs within the Microsoft Office suite, such as Excel, Access, PowerPoint, and Word. If you want to learn more about these certifications, you can go to www.microsoft.com. In addition to Microsoft Office Specialist certifications, secretaries can acquire the Certified Professional Secretary (CPS) designation. Information about the CPS designation, can be found at www.iaap-hq.org.

## HELP DESK TECHNICIAN

Help desk technicians (also called technical support specialists or customer service representatives) troubleshoot hardware and software problems and provide technical support for customers and users. While some technicians work for a computer or software vendor assisting customers, others work directly within an organization providing in-house assistance to other employees. According to the U.S. Department of Labor's Occupational Outlook Handbook, "Job prospects should be best for college graduates who are up to date with the latest skills and technologies; certifications and practical experience are essential for persons without degrees." One place where you can find information about help desk certification is www.thinkhdi.com.

## GRAPHIC ARTIST

While some graphic artists still create art by hand, the speed and instant editing capabilities available by using a computer makes it the tool of choice for many graphic artists. These folks work for advertising agencies, publishing firms, retail stores, and commercial art houses designing a variety of documents, such as brochures, reports, web pages, and logos. College classes can prepare you for a career in this area of the computer industry.

## REPAIR AND MAINTENANCE TECHNICIAN

This computer professional installs hardware and software, performs maintenance, and troubleshoots and fixes problems on computers, printers, and other peripherals. When equipment breaks down, field technicians travel to customers' workplaces to make repairs. On the other hand, bench technicians work in repair shops. According to the U.S. Department of Labor's Occupational Outlook Handbook, "Workers qualify for these jobs by receiving training in electronics from associate degree programs, the military, vocational schools, equipment manufacturers, or employers." The Handbook also states that "opportunities for computer repairers should be excellent." A widely-acknowledged certification in this area is called the A+ Certification. You can learn more about this certification by going to www.comptia.com.

## COMPUTER AIDED DRAFTING & DESIGN (CADD)

**CADD** software is used by architects, engineers, and artists to create meticulous drawings and illustrations. CADD software can be used to create two-dimensional (2-D) drawings or three-dimensional (3-D) models. CADD solves architectural and engineering problems in the planning stages, allowing folks to avoid the expense of having to build the building or machine to test it for its usability. For example, an airline manufacturer can use CADD to create a computer version of a newly-designed plane to test its flyability instead of having to manufacture a prototype plane only to discover that it won't fly. (Besides, test flying a virtual plane from the comfort of an office chair is safer than test flying a real plane). Thus, the costs and time of developing new products is reduced. College classes can prepare you for a career in CADD. Typically, you'd take a class in basic drafting principles. Then, you would take a variety of manual and computerized drafting and design classes.

## EXERCISE 1: CROSSWORD
Use the clues below to complete the crossword puzzle.

### ACROSS
1. Some computers are connected to other computers in what is called a network. The software produced by Novell that permits computers to communicate with each other is called Novell ___.
3. A Cisco Certified Network Associate has expertise in the hardware, software, and technology used in LANs (Local Area Networks) and WANs (Wide Area Networks). Instead of saying "Cisco Certified Network Associate," some folks simply say ___.
7. The process of coding the detailed instructions used by a computer is called ___.
8. Geographic information system software, permits you to query a database and have the results appear in the form of a map or graph. Instead of saying "geographic information systems," folks simply refer to this collection of software as ___ software.
10. Computers that are connected together, yet not located near each other, compose a Wide Area Network, which is often referred to as a ___.
11. Computers located near each other and connected together compose a Local Area Network, which is often referred to as a ___.
12. The "M" in MCSE stands for ___soft.
15. The "E" in CNE and the "E" in MCSE stand for ___.
16. To remove an error from a program, a programmer will ___ it.
18. HTML stands for Hypertext Markup ___.

### DOWN
2. A ___ is a professional who designs, creates, posts, and maintains web pages.
4. Once a person selects a specific area of the computer industry in which to specialize, she will want to learn as much as possible about her specialty. To prove to prospective employers that she has achieved a certain level of expertise in her chosen field, she will want to pass tests developed by organizations such as Novell, Microsoft, and Cisco. The goal is to gain ___ in her chosen field which documents her competency.
5. A ___ is a professional who writes the code that contains instructions followed by a computer.
6. A Certified Novell Administrator performs day-to-day maintenance of elements (e.g., sets up user workstations, manages resources, installs and configures print servers, handles software maintenance). Instead of saying "Certified Novell Administrator," some folks would simply refer to this person as a ___.
9. A major producer of the hardware, software, and technology used in LANs (Local Area Networks) and WANs (Wide Area Networks) is a company called ___.
12. A Microsoft Certified Systems Engineer is a professional who plans, sets up, maintains, and troubleshoots networks running under Windows and Microsoft server products. Instead of saying "Microsoft Certified Systems Engineer," most folks simply refer to this person as a ___.
13. A Certified Novell Engineer works with network cards, cabling, and routers. She performs system upgrades, troubleshoots network problems, and plans for changes. Instead of saying "Certified Novell Engineer," some folks would simply refer to this person as a ___.
14. CADD stands for Computer ___ Drafting and Design.
17. An error in a program is called a ___.

## EXERCISE 2: TRUE-FALSE
For each of the following seven statements, place a T or an F on the line to indicate if the statement is True or False.

1. ___An error in a program is called a snail.
2. ___An MCSE designs web pages.
3. ___The "L" in LAN stands for "License".
4. ___Certification is a standard that documents your skills.
5. ___Maps can be created with GIS software.
6. ___A help desk technician helps users solve problems.
7. ___CNE stands for "Certified Novell Engineer".

## EXERCISE 3: TRUE-FALSE
For each of the following seven statements, place a T or an F on the line to indicate if the statement is True or False.

1. ___HTML stands for "HyperText Markup Language".
2. ___A webmaster designs web pages.
3. ___The "M" in MCSA and in MCSE stands for "Microsoft".
4. ___A bug is an error in a program.
5. ___CCNA, CCNP, and CCIE are Cisco certifications.
6. ___A LAN and a WAN are exactly the same thing.
7. ___GIS stands for "Graphical Interpreter Software".

## EXERCISE 4: IDENTIFY ACRONYMS

In the computer world, there are lots of acronyms. An acronym is created by combining the first letter of each word in a series of words. In this project, you have encountered several computer career related acronyms. In the space next to each of the acronyms below, write out its full name.

| ACRONYM | FULL NAME |
|---------|-----------|
| 1. CCNA | |
| 2. LAN | |
| 3. HTML | |
| 4. CADD | |
| 5. MCSE | |
| 6. CNA | |
| 7. WAN | |
| 8. GIS | |
| 9. CNE | |
| 10. MCSA | |

## EXERCISE 5: TRUE-FALSE

For each of the following seven statements, place a T or an F on the line to indicate if the statement is True or False.

1. ___Architects and engineers use CADD software.
2. ___To "debug" is to remove errors found in a program.
3. ___A network is two or more computers connected together.
4. ___GIS stands for "Geographic Information Systems".
5. ___CNE stands for "Computer Nerd Engineer".
6. ___The "W" in WAN stands for "Webmaster".
7. ___CADD stands for "Computer Animated Dozer Dog".

## EXERCISE 6: EXPLAIN CONCEPTS

How does the work of a CNA and a CNE differ? Also, which of these certifications would indicate the most knowledge?

_____
_____
_____
_____
_____
_____
_____
_____
_____
_____
_____
_____
_____
_____
_____
_____

## EXERCISE 7: FIND A WORD

The answers to the following statements can be found in the matrix below. Some are backwards, some are diagonal, some are vertical, and some are horizontal. Circle each word.

1. The smartest cyber dog on the planet. To be sure you get this one right, it's highlighted.
2. Some computers are connected to other computers in what is called a network. The software produced by Novell that permits computers to communicate with each other is called Novell ___.
3. A professional who designs, creates, posts, and maintains web pages.
4. An error in a program.
5. Once a person selects a specific area of the computer industry in which to specialize, she will want to learn as much as possible about her specialty. To prove that she has achieved a certain level of expertise in her chosen field, she will want to pass tests developed by organizations such as Novell, Microsoft, and Cisco. The goal is to gain ___ in her chosen field which documents her competency.
6. A professional who writes the code containing instructions followed by a computer.
7. The first "C" in CCNA, CCNP, and CCIE stands for ___, a major producer of the hardware, software, and technology used in LANs (Local Area Networks) and WANs (Wide Area Networks).
8. CADD stands for Computer Aided ___ and Design.
9. Computers that are connected together, yet not located near each other, compose a Wide Area Network, which is often referred to as a ___.
10. To ___ is to remove errors found in a program.
11. GIS stands for ___ Information Systems.
12. Computers located near each other and connected together compose a Local Area Network, which is often referred to as a ___.
13. An abbreviation for HyperText Markup Language.
14. The "M" in MCSE and the "M" in MCSA stands for ___.

| B | W | R | Y | C | I | S | C | O | X | V |
|---|---|---|---|---|---|---|---|---|---|---|
| U | S | D | B | E | Q | S | F | B | M | J |
| G | E | O | G | R | A | P | H | I | C | P |
| A | G | Z | E | T | R | U | T | D | Q | R |
| L | Y | E | V | I | V | U | M | R | Y | O |
| E | J | R | C | F | M | E | L | A | L | G |
| C | U | Y | P | I | T | A | H | F | F | R |
| B | H | P | W | C | U | N | B | T | N | A |
| N | E | T | W | A | R | E | N | I | I | M |
| B | D | I | V | T | N | C | I | N | S | M |
| L | A | N | E | I | E | I | L | G | V | E |
| T | F | O | S | O | R | C | I | M | J | R |
| O | U | L | H | N | D | E | B | U | G | C |
| A | R | E | T | S | A | M | B | E | W | M |

## COMPUTER CONCEPTS COMPREHENSIVE
# E X E R C I S E S

### EXERCISE 1: MATCHING

Match each of the following terms with the word or phrase that is its best synonym by placing the letter of the term in the left column in the blank next to its counterpart in the right column.

| | | | |
|---|---|---|---|
| A. | Backup | 1. __ | A-Drive |
| B. | Byte | 2. __ | Application Software |
| C. | Clarity | 3. __ | Beginner |
| D. | Clone | 4. __ | Billion Bytes |
| E. | Cyberphobia | 5. __ | C-Drive |
| F. | Diskette | 6. __ | CPU |
| G. | Floppy Drive | 7. __ | Dot |
| H. | Gigabyte | 8. __ | Duplicate Copy |
| I. | Graphical User Interface | 9. __ | Eight Bits |
| J. | Hard Drive | 10. __ | Fear of Computers |
| K. | Hard Copy | 11. __ | Floppy Disk |
| L. | Kilobyte | 12. __ | GUI |
| M. | Megabyte | 13. __ | IBM-Compatible |
| N. | Megahertz | 14. __ | Million Bytes |
| O. | Memory | 15. __ | Million Cycles |
| P. | Novice | 16. __ | Monitor Display |
| Q. | Permanent | 17. __ | Motherboard |
| R. | Pixel | 18. __ | Non-volatile |
| S. | Processor | 19. __ | Paper Copy |
| T. | Productivity Software | 20. __ | Program |
| U. | Reading From Disk | 21. __ | RAM |
| V. | Soft Copy | 22. __ | Resolution |
| W. | Software | 23. __ | Retrieving Data |
| X. | System board | 24. __ | Saving Data |
| Y. | Temporary | 25. __ | Thousand Bytes |
| Z. | Writing To Disk | 26. __ | Volatile |

### EXERCISE 2: IDENTIFY TERMS

Below are eight definitions. Below the definitions are eight lines. In each line, write the word that matches the definition.

1. The physical components that make up a computer system.
2. Eight bits.
3. Circuit boards added to expand a system's capabilities.
4. The box the monitor typically sits on.
5. Working with multiple programs simultaneously.
6. The distance between the dots on the screen.
7. The number of times per second a screen is reconstructed.
8. Diagnosing and solving problems.

1. _____     5. _____
2. _____     6. _____
3. _____     7. _____
4. _____     8. _____

### EXERCISE 3: MATCHING

Match each of the following terms with the word or phrase that is its best description by writing the letter of the term on the line next to its description.

| | | |
|---|---|---|
| A. Click | 1. ___ | rapidly press the right button once. |
| B. Double-click | 2. ___ | rapidly press the left button once. |
| C. Drag | 3. ___ | rapidly press the left button twice. |
| D. Right Click | 4. ___ | hold left button down & move mouse. |

### EXERCISE 4: EXPLAIN CONCEPTS

While Dozer is computer literate, his sister, Skooter, is a novice. She often gets confused and needs some help. Sometimes, she gets help from Dozer. From time to time, perhaps you could help her. For instance, Skooter is confused about the difference between technological obsolescence and functional obsolescence? Can you explain it to her? Please write your response on the lines below.

_____
_____
_____
_____
_____
_____
_____
_____
_____
_____

### EXERCISE 5: TRUE-FALSE

For each of the following eight statements, place a T or an F on the line to indicate if the statement is True or False.

1. ___ The F1, F2, F3, keys are format keys.
2. ___ A computer turns information into data.
3. ___ The circuits that connect devices are called buses.
4. ___ A megahertz is one million beats (or cycles) per second.
5. ___ A high-density disk can hold up to 1.44 MB of data.
6. ___ A binary digit is called a bingit.
7. ___ Places to plug in devices are called plugs.
8. ___ An online printer is in communication with a computer.

### EXERCISE 6: IDENTIFY ACRONYMS

In the computing world, lots of terms are referred to by an acronym. What do each of the following acronyms stand for?

| ACRONYM | FULL NAME |
|---|---|
| 1. CD-ROM | |
| 2. CD-RW | |
| 3. CNA | |
| 4. CNE | |
| 5. CPU | |
| 6. GB | |
| 7. GIS | |
| 8. GUI | |
| 9. KB | |
| 10. LAN | |
| 11. MB | |
| 12. RAM | |
| 13. ROM | |
| 14. WAN | |

## EXERCISE 7: TRUE-FALSE

For each of the following eight statements, place a T or an F on the line to indicate if the statement is True or False.

1. ___ A zip drive is faster than a floppy drive.
2. ___ The A drive and the C drive are both the same thing.
3. ___ A dot-matrix monitor will help prevent eye strain.
4. ___ An offline printer is in communication with a computer.
5. ___ A suite is a set of full-fledged programs sold together.
6. ___ A CRT uses toner to print text on the paper.
7. ___ All data is removed from a diskette when it is formatted.
8. ___ A gigabyte is one trillion bytes.

## EXERCISE 8: IDENTIFY TERMS

Below are eight definitions. Below the definitions are eight lines. In each line, write the word that matches the definition.

1. A beginning computer user.
2. A secret code used to access your data.
3. The small dots that create the image on the screen.
4. The process of turning on a computer.
5. A device that protects your system from static electricity.
6. The way a program interacts with a user.
7. The fear of computers or the fear of using a computer.
8. Using software illegally.

1. _____    5. _____
2. _____    6. _____
3. _____    7. _____
4. _____    8. _____

## EXERCISE 9: EXPLAIN CONCEPTS

Skooter has a couple of questions. She went to ask Dozer, but he is currently taking a nap. She wants to know what's the difference between a scanner and a digital camera? Under what circumstances would she use each of these? Can you help her? Please write your response on the lines below.

_____
_____
_____
_____
_____
_____
_____
_____

## EXERCISE 10: IDENTIFY TERMS

Below are eight definitions. Below the definitions are eight lines. In each line, write the word that matches the definition.

1. The rate at which the system clock beats per second.
2. A device that will absorb potentially harmful power spikes.
3. A program that finds and eliminates some viruses.
4. The small square hole with a movable button on a diskette.
5. A program that incorporates sight (video) and sound (audio).
6. The process of obtaining new software and/or hardware.
7. Boxes that display information on the screen.
8. A small block of very fast memory.

1. _____    5. _____
2. _____    6. _____
3. _____    7. _____
4. _____    8. _____

## EXERCISE 11: MATCHING

The programs and the data needed by a computer are stored in primary or secondary storage. The main difference between these two types of storage is the degree of permanency of the programs and data. Some storage is volatile (temporary); other storage is non-volatile (permanent). For each of the following types of storage, indicate if it is volatile or nonvolatile by placing a T (Temporary) or a P (Permanent) on the line.

| T (Temporary-Volatile) | P (Permanent-Nonvolatile) |
|---|---|
| 1. ___ CD-R | 5. ___ Hard Drive |
| 2. ___ CD-ROM | 6. ___ Magnetic Tape |
| 3. ___ CD-RW | 7. ___ RAM (Memory) |
| 4. ___ Floppy Disk | 8. ___ Zip Drive |

## EXERCISE 12: UNDERSTANDING COMPUTER ADS

Below is the type of information you might typically see in an ad for a computer system. Review the information provided and answer the seven questions.

| COMPUTER SYSTEM |
|---|
| Price: $759 |
| 1.2 GHz Intel Celeron Processor |
| 15" .28 Color Monitor |
| 256 MB RAM |
| 60 GB Hard Drive |
| 40X CD-ROM Drive |
| 56 K Modem |
| Software: Windows XP |

**1.** What does "1.2 GHz Intel Celeron Processor" tell you?
_____

**2.** What does "15" and ".28" tell you about the monitor?
_____

**3.** What does "256 MB RAM" tell you about the system?
_____

**4.** What does "60 GB" tell you about the hard drive?
_____

**5.** What does 40X tell you about the CD-ROM drive?
_____

**6.** What is a modem used for and what does "56K" refer to?
_____

**7.** What kind of software is Windows XP?
_____

## EXERCISE 13: MATCHING

Match each of the following computer chips with the company that produces them by writing the name of the company on the line next to the processor chip it produces.

| AMD | Intel | |
|---|---|---|
| 1. _____ | Athlon |
| 2. _____ | Celeron |
| 3. _____ | Sempron |
| 4. _____ | Pentium |

## PAGE A-5: EXERCISE 1

| Across | Down |
|--------|------|
| 1. Shutter | 2. Hertz |
| 4. Drag | 3. Hardware |
| 5. Primary | 6. ROM |
| 7. Zip | 8. Processor |
| 10. Memory | 9. Mega |
| 11. Laser | 12. System |
| 14. Pixels | 13. Resolution |
| 15. Buses | 15. Byte |
| 16. Density | 17. System Unit |
| 17. Storage | 18. Offline |
| 19. Software | 20. Write |
| 22. Monitor | 21. Refresh |
| 23. GB | 24. Bit |
| 26. Soft | 25. Digital |
| 27. Pitch | 28. Compatible |
| 31. MB | 29. Clone |
| 32. Bootup | 30. Protection |
| 33. Volatile | 33. Virtual |
| 35. RAM | 34. Laptop |
| 36. Port | |
| 37. Flat | |
| 38. Bus | |
| 39. CPU | |
| 40. Floppy | |

## PAGE A-6: EXERCISE 2

1. A   4. B   7. C   10. C   13. D   16. B   19. A
2. C   5. D   8. D   11. D   14. C   17. A   20. C
3. C   6. A   9. D   12. A   15. A   18. B

## PAGE A-6: EXERCISE 3

Gigabyte = 1,000,000,000      Kilobyte = 1,000
Megabyte = 1,000,000      Byte = 1

## PAGE A-6: EXERCISE 4

1. Binary Digit
2. Compact Disk-Read Only Memory
3. Compact Disk-ReWritable
4. Compact Disk-Recordable
5. Central Processing Unit
6. Gigabyte
7. Kilobyte
8. Megabyte
9. Random Access Memory
10. Read Only Memory

## PAGE A-6: EXERCISE 5

| | |
|--|--|
| 1. CRT | 14. Speed |
| 2. Scanner | 15. Format |
| 3. Mouse | 16. Random |
| 4. Gigabyte | 17. Dot |
| 5. Cache | 18. Pentium |
| 6. Output | 19. Tape |
| 7. Mother | 20. Capacity |
| 8. Computer | 21. Byte |
| 9. Window | 22. C-drive |
| 10. Expansion | 23. Input |
| 11. Ink-jet | 24. KB |
| 12. Data | 25. ROM |
| 13. Keyboard | 26. R or RW |

## PAGE A-9: EXERCISE 1

| Across | Down |
|--------|------|
| 1. Piracy | 1. Productivity |
| 5. Icon | 2. Applications |
| 6. Site | 3. Bit |
| 7. Multimedia | 4. Windows |
| 8. Data | 9. Free |
| 10. User | 11. Public |
| 12. No | 13. GUI |
| 13. GB | 15. Desk |
| 14. Byte | |
| 16. Suite | |
| 17. Computer | |
| 18. KB | |

## PAGE A-9: EXERCISE 2

1. A   4. D   7. B   10. C   13. D   16. F
2. C   5. E   8. E   11. D   14. F
3. F   6. B   9. B   12. B   15. B

## PAGE A-9: EXERCISE 3

1. Shareware      3. Freeware
2. Public Domain      4. Proprietary

## PAGE A-10: EXERCISE 4

| | | |
|--|--|--|
| 1. Browser | 7. Piracy | 13. Public |
| 2. Suite | 8. Desktop | 14. License |
| 3. User | 9. Icons | 15. Database |
| 4. Windows | 10. Operating | 16. Worksheet |
| 5. Freeware | 11. GUI | |
| 6. Software | 12. Interface | |

## PAGE A-10: EXERCISE 5

Upgrade versions only work if you already have an older version of the same product. Dozer should read the package carefully to make sure he's buying the right version of the program.

## PAGE A-10: EXERCISE 6

1. F: The physical components are hardware; the instructions that tell the processor how to perform its tasks is software.
2. F: GUI stands for Graphical User Interface.
3, 4, 5, 6, 7, and 8 are all T.

## PAGE A-10: EXERCISE 7

Programs = Software
Worksheet = Spreadsheet
Productivity = Applications

## PAGE A-10: EXERCISE 8

1. T
2. F: Windows XP is an operating system.
3. T
4. F: While freeware can be used without paying a fee, shareware can be used for a specified period of time for free, but then the user is expected to pay to continue to use it.
5. F: Shareware is copyrighted.
6. T
7. F: O.S. stands for Operating System.
8. T

## PAGE A-13: EXERCISE 1

| Across | Down |
|--------|------|
| 1. Hardware | 2. Audio |
| 3. Speed | 4. PPM |
| 6. ROM | 5. Memory |
| 7. Modem | 6. RW |
| 10. Monitors | 8. Dot |
| 13. Laptop | 9. No |
| 14. DVD | 10. Multitasking |
| 15. USB | 11. No |
| | 12. Scanner |
| | 14. Desktop |
| | 16. Minute |
| | 19. Speakers |
| | 21. Storage |
| | 24. Dog |

(continued)
| | |
|--|--|
| 17. Resolution | |
| 18. DPI | |
| 20. Pages | |
| 22. Dots | |
| 23. Hard | |
| 25. Tower | |
| 26. Jet | |
| 27. Software | |

## PAGE A-14: EXERCISE 2

1. System C (3.2 GHz)
2. Gigahertz (one billion cycles per second)
3. To permit faster processing of commands
4. The dot pitch (distance between pixels)
5. Diagonally (from corner to corner)
6. System C (1 Gigabyte)
7. MB (megabyte), GB (gigabyte)
8. One million bytes, one billion bytes
9. Random Access Memory (Memory)
10. Programs and data are stored there
11. They use big programs or want to multitask
12. System C
13. Programs and data are stored there
14. They store lots of stuff (e.g., graphics)
15. Compact Disk-Read Only Memory
16. Speed (40x is 40 times faster than first CD)
17. Connects computer to phone line for Internet
18. Kilobits per second (56 K = 56,000 bits)
19. Compact Disk-ReWritable
20. To create their own CDs
21. No. Some computers do: some do not
22. No. All monitors bought today will be color
23. You need to buy one, or use on old one
24. Works = integrated program; Office = suite

## PAGE A-17: EXERCISE 1

| Across | Down |
|--------|------|
| 1. Cyberphobia | 1. Carpal tunnel |
| 4. Static | 2. Backup |
| 6. KB | 3. Password |
| 7. Copy | 5. Technologically |
| 9. Lap | 8. Port |
| 10. Screen | 13. Virus |
| 11. Up | 14. Icon |
| 12. TV | 17. Kilo |
| 15. Novice | 19. On |
| 16. ROM | 21. Upgrade |
| 18. Anti-virus | 22. Light |
| 20. Functionally | 23. Surge |
| 25. GB | 24. Version |
| 26. Trouble | 28. No |
| 27. Dog | |
| 29. Vision | |
| 30. Windows | |

## PAGE A-18: EXERCISE 2

Dozer is wrong. There are many events that can cause his data to be lost or corrupted. For instance, he could delete a file, his files could be damaged by a virus, his hard drive could crash, he could format a disk containing a needed file, his disk could be lost or stolen, or his disk could be damaged from heat, dirt, magnetic fields, or water. Therefore, he needs to back up his work.

## PAGE A-18: EXERCISE 3

1 and 2 are T.
3. F: Cyberphobia is the fear of computers. I

have no idea what geekophobia is (maybe it's the fear of geeks?).
4. F: An anti-virus program finds and eliminates viruses.
5, 6, and 7 are all T.
8. F: A screen saver is software that creates random patterns on the screen. An anti-static mat protects your computer system from the harmful effects of static electricity.

## PAGE A-18: EXERCISE 4
Before calling a technician, try the following:
☞ Whatever you were trying to do, try it again.
☞ Reboot the machine.
☞ Check the connections to the electrical receptacle and from peripheral devices to the computer to make sure it's all connected.
☞ Think about what you were doing prior to the trouble. Did you see or hear anything that might be a clue to what is wrong?
☞ Test your system with diagnostic software.
☞ Take a break. When you return, try again.

## PAGE A-18: EXERCISE 5
When new software or hardware is available, Dozer's system is technologically obsolete; when it will no longer do what he wants it to do, it's functionally obsolete. Only when his system is functionally obsolete does he need to upgrade. So, if his system is currently doing all he wants it to do, he shouldn't waste his money on new stuff. Instead, he should buy himself some dog biscuits.

## PAGE A-18: EXERCISE 6
1. Backup          5. Screen     9. Novice
2. Upgrade         6. Virus     10. Password
3. Cyberphobia     7. Carpal    11. Geek
4. Surge           8. Functionally

## PAGE A-21: EXERCISE 1
**Across**              **Down**
 1. Netware            2. Webmaster
 3. CCNA               4. Certification
 7. Programming        5. Programmer
 8. GIS                6. CNA
10. WAN                9. Cisco
11. LAN               12. MCSE
12. Micro             13. CNE
15. Engineer          14. Aided
16. Debug             17. Bug
18. Language

## PAGE A-21: EXERCISE 2
1. F: An error is called a bug.
2. F: A webmaster creates web pages.
3. F: The "L" stands for local.
4, 5, 6, and 7 are all T.

## PAGE A-21: EXERCISE 3
1, 2, 3, 4, and 5 are all T.
6. F: They are both networks, but one is "wide" and the other is "local"
7. F: GIS stands for Geographic Information Systems.

## PAGE A-22: EXERCISE 4
1. Cisco Certified Network Associate
2. Local Area Network
3. HyperText Markup Language
4. Computer Aided Drafting and Design
5. Microsoft Certified Systems Engineer
6. Certified Novell Administrator
7. Wide Area Network
8. Geographic Information System

9. Certified Novell Engineer
10. Microsoft Certified Systems Administrator

## PAGE A-22: EXERCISE 5
1, 2, 3, and 4 are all T.
5. F: CNE stands for Certified Novell Engineer.
6. F: The W stands for "Wide"
7. F: CADD stands for Computer Aided Drafting and Design.

## PAGE A-22: EXERCISE 6
A CNA performs day-to-day maintenance of elements (e.g., sets up user workstations, manages resources, installs and configures print servers, and handles routine software maintenance). A CNE performs more technical work (e.g., troubleshooting network problems, performing system upgrades, and planning for technological changes, as well as working with network cards, cabling, and routers). The engineer is hardware oriented while the administrator is software oriented. The CNE has advanced skills compared to the CNA.

## PAGE A-22: EXERCISE 7
1. Dozer          8. Drafting
2. NetWare        9. WAN
3. Webmaster     10. Debug
4. Bug           11. Geographic
5. Certification 12. LAN
6. Programmer    13. HTML
7. Cisco         14. Microsoft

## PAGE A-23: EXERCISE 1
1. G      8. A     15. N     22. C
2. T      9. B     16. V     23. U
3. P     10. E     17. X     24. Z
4. H     11. F     18. Q     25. L
5. J     12. I     19. K     26. Y
6. S     13. D     20. W
7. R     14. M     21. O

## PAGE A-23: EXERCISE 2
1. Hardware          5. Multi-tasking
2. Byte              6. Dot Pitch
3. Expansion Cards   7. Refresh Rate
4. System Unit       8. Troubleshooting

## PAGE A-23: EXERCISE 3
1. D    2. A    3. B    4. C

## PAGE A-23: EXERCISE 4
When new software or hardware is available, a system is technologically obsolete. When a system will no longer do what you want it to do, it is functionally obsolete. While you may <u>want</u> to upgrade when technologically obsolete, you only <u>need</u> to upgrade when your system is functionally obsolete. Technological obsolescence deals with what <u>can</u> be done; functional obsolescence deals with what you <u>want</u> to do.

## PAGE A-23: EXERCISE 5
1. F: The F1, F2, F3, keys are function keys, not format keys.
2. F: A computer turns data into information.
3, 4, and 5 are all T.
6. F: A binary digit is called a bit, not a bingit. I invented the word bingit-- it means nothing.
7. F: Places to plug in devices are called ports, not sockets.
8. T

## PAGE A-23: EXERCISE 6
1. Compact Disk-Read Only Memory

2. Compact Disk-ReWritable
3. Certified Novell Administrator
4. Certified Novell Engineer
5. Central Processing Unit
6. Gigabyte
7. Geographic Information Systems
8. Graphical User Interface
9. Kilobyte
10. Local Area Network
11. Megabyte
12. Random Access Memory
13. Read Only Memory
14. Wide Area Network

## PAGE A-24: EXERCISE 7
1. T
2. F: The A is the floppy drive and the C is the hard drive. They are two different drives.
3. F: Since a **dot-matrix is a type** of printer, not a monitor, I doubt that it can cause eyestrain.
4. F: An offline printer is not communicating with a computer; an online printer is.
5. T
6. F: Since a CRT (Cathode Ray Tube) is a type of monitor, not a printer, it does not use toner.
7. T
8. F: A gigabyte is one billion bytes.

## PAGE A-24: EXERCISE 8
1. Novice              5. Anti-static mat
2. Password            6. User interface
3. Pixels              7. Cyberphobia
4. Bootup (launch, start)  8. Piracy

## PAGE A-24: EXERCISE 9
You can convert any photo or image on paper to a digitized image using a scanner (a device that works much like a copy machine in that a hard copy of the data is scanned. However, unlike a copier, instead of producing a paper copy, the data is digitized). On the other hand, if you wanted to directly create a digitized image, you would use a digital camera which works much like a camera. However, instead of developing the film, the image is saved in a digital format.

## PAGE A-24: EXERCISE 10
1. Clock Speed          5. Multimedia
2. Surge Suppressor     6. Upgrading
3. Anti-virus Program   7. Windows
4. Write-protection square  8. Cache

## PAGE A-24: EXERCISE 11
1. P  2. P  3. P  4. P  5. P   6. P  7. T  8. P

## PAGE A-24: EXERCISE 12
1. The speed of the processor (1.2 GHz--1.2 billion cycles per second) and the type of processor (Celeron).
2. The size of the screen (15" diagonally) and the distance between pixels (.28 millimeters).
3. The storage capacity of Random Access Memory (RAM), 256 million bytes.
4. The storage capacity of the hard drive (60 GB--60 billion bytes).
5. The speed of the CD-ROM drive (40 times faster than the original CD-ROM).
6. A modem connects a computer to a phone line to allow for Internet access. 56K (56,000 bits per second) is the maximum speed at which this modem can transfer data.
7. Windows XP is the operating system.

## PAGE A-24: EXERCISE 13
1. AMD    2. Intel    3. AMD    4. Intel

# Dozer's Quintessential Guide to Computer Concepts

**A-drive**: A secondary storage device that writes to and reads from a floppy disk. Also called a floppy drive.

**Access**: A Microsoft database program used to store, organize, and retrieve data.

**alt key**: A key which is often used with other keys to execute commands.

**anti-static mat**: A pad under a chair or the keyboard that protects a computer system by absorbing potentially-harmful static electricity.

**anti-virus program**: Software that detects and eradicates some computer viruses.

**applications software**: Programs that are used for productivity purposes, such as database, word processing, or accounting programs. Also called productivity software.

**arrow keys**: The keys that move the insertion point within a document.

**Athlon**: A processor chip used in some IBM-compatible machines.

**backspace key**: The key that deletes data to the left of the insertion point.

**backup**: A duplicate copy of a file, kept to protect against the possibility that the original file may become corrupted or lost.

**bit**: A binary digit, eight of which form a byte.

**boot up**: To turn on a computer system. Some folks just say "start" it or "turn it on".

**bugs**: Errors in a program.

**bus width**: The number of bits that can be simultaneously transported via the circuitry that connects the various devices in a computer system.

**buses**: The circuitry that connects the various devices in a computer system.

**byte**: A unique sequence of eight bits which together represents a character.

**C-drive**: A secondary storage device that stores programs and files. Also called the hard drive.

**cache**: Very fast memory.

**CADD**: An acronym for Computer-Aided Drafting and Design, which is software used by architects, engineers, and artists to create meticulous drawings and illustrations.

**capacity**: How much can be stored (e.g., the capacity of a diskette is 1.44 MB).

**carpal tunnel syndrome**: A painful wrist condition sometimes caused by the repetitive nature of using a keyboard for extended periods of time.

**CCNA**: An acronym for Cisco Certified Network Associate, which is a person certified as proficient with the hardware, software, and technology used in Cisco networking.

**CD-R**: An acronym for Compact Disk-Recordable, which is a CD to which files can be saved.

**CD-ROM**: An acronym for Compact Disk-Read Only Memory, which is a secondary storage device which permits you to read data from it, but not save data to it.

**CD-RW**: An acronym for Compact Disk-ReWritable, which is a CD to which files can be saved multiple times.

**Celeron**: An Intel processor chip used in some IBM-compatible machines.

**central processing unit**: The primary chip that converts data into information. Also called the processor or the computer (abbreviated as CPU).

**certification**: The validation that a person has achieved a specific level of expertise in some area. He proves this by passing a test or series of tests which are globally recognized as indicative of knowledge and skills acquired.

**Certified Novell Administrator**: A person certified as being proficient in setting up user workstations, installing print servers, and managing resources, etc. associated with a Novell NetWare network (abbreviated as CNA).

**Certified Novell Engineer**: A person certified as proficient in working with network cards, cabling, and routers, etc. associated with a Novell NetWare network (abbreviated as CNE).

**Cisco**: A major producer of the hardware, software, and technology used in LANs and WANs.

**Cisco Certified Network Associate**: A person certified as proficient with the hardware, software, and technology used in Cisco networking (abbreviated as CCNA).

**click**: The act of rapidly pressing the left mouse button one time, generally done to select an on-screen object.

**clock speed**: The rate at which the system beats per second, measured in units called megahertz. Each beat (cycle) can execute one or more instructions. One megahertz is one million cycles per second.

**clone**: A computer system that uses the same type of processor chip as an IBM. Also called an IBM compatible.

**CNA**: An acronym for Certified Novell Administrator, who is a person certified as proficient in setting up user workstations, managing resources, and installing print servers, etc. associated with a Novell NetWare network.

**CNE**: An acronym for Certified Novell Engineer, which is a person certified as proficient in working with network cards, cabling, and routers, etc. associated with a Novell NetWare network.

**computer**: The primary chip that converts data into information. Also called the CPU (central processing unit) or simply the processor.

**computer system**: The processor chip and all the physical components connected to it.

**computer vision syndrome**: A condition with symptoms including eyestrain, blurred vision, and headaches caused by excessive use of a computer under less-than-optimal conditions.

**Corel Presentations**: Software that allows you to create slide-shows, similar to PowerPoint.

**CPU**: An acronym for Central Processing Unit. The primary chip that converts data into information. Also called the processor or the computer.

**CRT**: An acronym for Cathode Ray Tube, which is the type of monitor that is typically used with a desktop machine. It works like a TV.

**ctrl key**: The "control" key. Often used with other keys to execute commands.

**cyberphobia**: The fear of computers in general or the fear of using a computer.

**data**: Raw, unorganized details.

**database**: A program dedicated to the storage, organization, and retrieval of records.

**debug**: The process of finding and eliminating errors (bugs) in a program.

**delete**: To remove (erase) a file, folder, text, or an image.

**delete key**: The key that deletes data to the right of the insertion point.

**density**: The amount of pixels per square inch of screen area on a monitor or the amount of bytes per disk area (i.e., how tightly the pixels or bytes are packed).

**desktop**: The entire area on the screen where windows, documents, programs, folders, and files are displayed.

**desktop publishing**: A program that is dedicated to producing professional-quality ads, newsletters, brochures, etc.

**digital cameras**: An input device that works like any other camera, except instead of generating a paper copy, the image is stored in digital format.

**diskette**: A removable medium for storage of files used in conjunction with a floppy drive. Also called a floppy disk.

**dot-matrix printer**: A printer that constructs characters on paper by striking a ribbon with pins that produce an array of dots, which in turn, form the characters.

**dot-pitch**: The distance between pixels on the screen. The smaller the distance, the higher the resolution.

**double-click**: The act of rapidly pressing the left mouse button two times.

**Dozer**: The smartest cyberdog on the planet.

**drag**: To move the mouse.

**drag and drop**: The act of pointing to an object on the screen, holding down the left mouse button, moving the mouse, and then releasing the mouse button, thereby moving the object. In essence you have dragged and then dropped the object.

**DVD**: Digital Versatile Disc or Digital Video Disc, depending on whom you ask. Very similar to a CD, except it will hold much more data.

**esc key**: The "escape" key. Used to cancel an action.

**Excel**: Software created by Microsoft that permits complex and rapid manipulation of values.

**expansion cards**: Circuit cards that can be added to a system to expand its capabilities. Also called expansion boards, add-on cards, or add-on boards.

**flat-panel monitor**: A thin, light-weight monitor used on laptop computers and recently used on some desktop computer systems.

**floppy disk**: A removable medium for storage of files used in conjunction with a floppy drive. Also called a diskette.

**floppy drive**: A secondary storage device that writes to and reads from a floppy disk. Also called the A drive.

**formatting**: Removing all files from a disk, checking for bad sectors on the disk surface, and creating a File Allocation Table (full format).

**freeware**: Software that is given away free of charge. However, it is copyrighted and its use is restricted.

**function keys**: Keys at the top of a keyboard (F1, F2, F3, etc.) used to execute commands.

**functional obsolescence**: The condition that occurs when your hardware and/or software will no longer do what you want it to do. For instance, you might want to listen to music over the Internet, but your system lacks speakers or headphones.

**GB**: An abbreviation for gigabyte (one billion bytes).

**geek**: A person who knows lots of neat stuff about computers, sometimes called a nerd. The opposite of a novice.

**Geographic Information Systems**: Software that permits you to query a database and have the results appear in the form of a map or graph (abbreviated as GIS).

**GHz**: An abbreviation for gigahertz, the unit of measurement for a computer's clock speed. One hertz is one cycle, which executes one or more instructions per second. Giga (billion) indicates that a billion cycles per second are possible.

**gigabyte**: One billion bytes (abbreviated as GB).

**gigahertz**: The unit of measurement for a computer's clock speed. One hertz is one cycle, which executes one or more instructions per second. Giga (billion) indicates that a billion cycles per second are possible (abbreviated as GHz).

**GIS**: An acronym for Geographic Information Systems, which is software that permits you to query a database and have the results appear in the form of a map or graph.

**graphic artist**: A person who designs logos, documents, advertisements, and brochures requiring the use of visually appealing graphics.

**graphical user interface**: A computer interface using icons, windows, etc. often called a GUI.

**hard copy**: The output received from a printer.

**hard drive**: A secondary storage device that stores programs and files. Also called the C-drive.

**hardware**: The physical components that make up a computer system.

**help desk technician**: A professional who troubleshoots hardware and software problems and provides technical support for customers and other users.

**IBM-Compatible**: A computer system that uses the same type of processor chip as an IBM. Also called a clone.

**icons**: On-screen graphical images that, when selected, execute commands.

**information**: Organized, meaningful data.

**ink-jet printer**: A printer that sprays a mist of ink to form the characters on the paper.

**input**: A device that permits data or programs to be made available to a computer (e.g., a mouse, keyboard, or scanner).

**integrated programs**: A program designed to perform functions normally associated with different programs (e.g., Microsoft includes database, word processing, and spreadsheet capabilities in a single integrated program called Works).

**Internet Explorer**: A web browser distributed by the fine folks at Microsoft. This program enables its users to find, load, view, print, and create web pages.

**KB**: An abbreviation for kilobyte (one thousand bytes).

**keyboard**: An input device used to enter data and to execute commands.

**kilobyte**: One thousand bytes (abbreviated as KB).

**LAN**: An acronym for Local Area Network, which is two or more computers connected together to permit the sharing of files, programs, and hardware devices. The "local" refers to the geographic proximity of the computers (they are in the same building or in the same geographic area as opposed to a WAN, which consists of computers with a greater degree of geographic dispersion).

**laptop**: A light-weight, portable computer.

**laser printer**: A printer that utilizes a laser beam to form the characters on the paper.

**liteware**: A limited version of a program that is distributed to give folks an idea of what the full-fledged version might do. Liteware is usually free; the full-fledged version is not free.

**magnetic tape**: A secondary storage device that stores and retrieves data sequentially. Used mostly for inexpensive backups.

**MB**: An abbreviation for megabyte (one million bytes).

**MCSE**: An acronym for Microsoft Certified Systems Engineer, which is a person certified as proficient in planning, setting up, maintaining, and trouble-shooting networks running under Microsoft Windows server.

**megabyte**: One million bytes (abbreviated MB).

**megahertz**: The unit of measurement for a computer's clock speed. One hertz is one cycle, which executes one or more instructions per second. Mega (million) indicates that a million cycles per second are possible (abbreviated as MHZ).

**memory**: The temporary location where the data and programs currently being used by a processor reside. Also called RAM (an acronym for Random Access Memory).

**MHZ**: An abbreviation for megahertz, the unit of measurement for a computer's clock speed. One hertz is one cycle, which executes one or more instructions per second. Mega (million) indicates that a million cycles per second are possible.

**mice**: More than one mouse.

**Microsoft Certified Systems Engineer**: A person certified as proficient in planning, setting up, maintaining, and trouble-shooting networks running under Microsoft Windows server (abbreviated as MCSE).

**modem**: A device that permits a computer to be connected to a phone line. The modem converts digital data (data understood by a computer) into an analog signal (data understood by a phone line) and vice versa.

**monitor**: An output device that displays the program and data in soft copy form.

**motherboard**: The main circuit board in the system unit. Also called a system board.

**mouse**: Input device that typically has two buttons on the top and a ball on its underside. Used to select, move, and resize objects and to execute commands.

**multimedia**: More than one media (e.g., playing a game that includes video and audio).

**multitasking**: Simultaneously working with more than one program.

**nerd**: A person who knows lots of neat stuff about computers. The opposite of a novice. Sometimes called a geek.

**NetWare**: Software developed by Novell that is often used on computers that are connected to each other.

**network engineer**: A person who is certified as proficient in planning, setting up, maintaining, and trouble-shooting networks (See CNE, MCSE, or CCNA).

**non-volatile**: Permanent. Referring to the nature of secondary storage whereby the data or programs found there are not lost when the power is turned off.

**Novell NetWare**: An operating system often used when computers are connected together.

**novice**: A beginning computer user.

**obsolescence**: The state of being outdated.

**offline**: The condition whereby another device is not in communication with a computer.

**online**: The condition whereby another device is in communication with a computer.

**operating system**: A general category of software that manages the computer resources and communicates with the mouse, printer, keyboard, etc.

**output**: What the computer gives you. It could be sound via a speaker, visual display via a monitor, or a printed document via a printer.

**password**: A secret sequence of characters that prohibits any unauthorized access to a computer, an email account, or a web site.

**Pentium**: An Intel processor chip used in some IBM-compatible machines.

**piracy**: Unauthorized use of software.

**pixels**: The thousands of dots that create the image on the screen.

**ports**: Places to plug in other devices so as to permit an improvement in capabilities.

**PowerPoint**: A program developed by Microsoft that permits us to create dynamic slide shows so as to enhance any audience presentation.

**presentation**: A type of software that permits us to create dynamic slide shows.

**primary storage**: The place where data and programs can be temporarily stored while being used by a computer. Also called RAM (Random Access Memory) or memory.

**processor**: The primary chip that converts data into information. Also called the CPU (central processing unit) or simply the computer.

**productivity software**: Programs used for productivity purposes, such as database or word processing. Also called applications.

**program**: The set of instructions used by a processor to convert data into information. Also called software.

**programmer**: A person who writes the sets of instructions used by a processor to convert data into information.

**programming**: The process of writing the sets of instructions used by a processor to convert data into information.

**public domain software**: Software which is not under any copyright protection. This software can be copied, distributed, or modified freely.

**RAM**: An acronym for Random Access Memory, which is the temporary location where the data and programs currently being used by a processor reside. Often referred to as simply "memory".

**random access memory**: (See RAM).

**reading from disk**: The act of retrieving data from a disk.

**recording window**: The rectangular hole in the hard plastic case under the shutter mechanism through which the disk surface is accessed for reading from or writing to a diskette by the disk drive.

**refresh rate**: The number of times per second that the image is reconstructed on the monitor's

screen. The more times it does this, the better the image will appear.

**repair and maintenance technician**: A person who installs hardware and software, performs maintenance, and troubleshoots and fixes problems on computers, printers, and other peripheral devices.

**resolution**: The clarity of a monitor's image determined primarily by the density of the pixels and the refresh rate.

**right-click**: The act of rapidly pressing the right mouse button one time.

**ROM**: An acronym for Read Only Memory, used when a machine is booted up. Instructions used to activate the machine comes from instructions found on the ROM chip.

**save**: The act of placing a copy of a document that is currently in memory into secondary storage.

**scanner**: An input device that works like a copy machine, except instead of producing a paper copy, it digitizes the image.

**screen saver**: Software that produces random images on the screen after the mouse and keyboard have been idle for a period of time.

**secondary storage**: The place where data and programs can be permanently stored (e.g., hard drive, zip drive, floppy drive, etc.).

**select**: To identify an object, text, or image to which you wish to do something.

**Sempron**: A processor chip used in some IBM-compatible machines.

**shareware**: Software that is provided free for a limited period of time or a limited version is provided. If the borrower likes it, she should pay a fee to continue to use it or to receive the full-fledged version of it.

**shortcut menu**: A context-sensitive menu that appears when I right click. Also called a Quick Menu.

**shutter mechanism**: A spring loaded cover on a diskette that automatically closes when a disk is extracted from the drive, thereby protecting the surface of the diskette.

**site license**: A permit to install software on multiple machines in an organization.

**soft copy**: The output from a monitor.

**software**: The instructions used by a processor to convert data into information. Also called a program.

**spreadsheet**: A program that permits rapid and complex mathematical manipulation of values. Also called a worksheet.

**storage**: A place where data and programs are kept. Generally classified as primary storage (volatile) and secondary storage (non-volatile).

**suite**: A collection of full-fledged programs bundled together and sold at a discount when compared to the individual purchase of each program (e.g., Microsoft bundles Word, Excel, Access, and PowerPoint in a suite called Microsoft Office).

**surge suppressor**: A device that protects computer system components by absorbing potentially-harmful power spikes.

**system board**: The main circuit board in the system unit. Also called a mother board.

**system unit**: The box the monitor typically sits on in which the motherboard, hard drive, floppy drive, etc, reside. Sometimes, this box is not under the monitor, but is an upright box called a tower.

**systems software**: Software that manage the computer resources and communicate with the mouse, keyboard, printer, etc.

**technological obsolescence**: Being outdated due to the development of an improved version of software or more advanced hardware.

**troubleshooting**: The act of diagnosing and fixing problems.

**upgrade**: Obtaining new hardware or software for an existing computer system.

**USB drive**: A small, portable drive that acts like a floppy disk, but holds much more data. Also called a flash drive, mini drive, or keychain drive.

**user**: A person who uses a computer.

**user interface**: The way a program interacts with a user.

**version**: An edition of software. Software that has been improved by the developer is said to be a new version.

**virtual memory**: A method of extending memory by placing parts of the program on the hard drive and reciprocating between the hard drive and RAM as needed.

**virus**: A piece of code that was deliberately designed to maliciously cause unexpected and/or undesirable consequences for the victim (e.g., deletes files, performs pranks, etc.).

**volatile**: Temporary. Referring to the nature of RAM (Random Access Memory) whereby the data and/or programs found there are lost when the power is turned off.

**WAN**: An acronym for Wide Area Network, which is two or more computers connected together to permit the sharing of hardware devices, files, and programs. The "wide" refers to the geographic proximity of the computers (they are separated by more geographic space as opposed to a LAN).

**web browsers**: A program that permits you to find, load, view, print, and create web pages (e.g., Netscape Navigator and Internet Explorer).

**webmaster**: A person who designs, creates, posts, and maintains web pages.

**Windows**: The operating system used on most desktop machines.

**Word**: A very popular word processing program distributed by the fine folks at Microsoft.

**word processor**: A program dedicated to the processing of text-based documents (e.g., WordPad, WordPerfect, and Microsoft Word).

**WordPerfect**: A word processing program that competes with Word.

**Works**: An integrated program (made by the fine folks at Microsoft) consisting of a word processor, a worksheet, and a database.

**write-protection square**: The square hole in the corner of a diskette that has a movable button. If the hole is open, the diskette is write protected, which means you can't save anything to the disk.

**writing to disk**: Saving a file to a disk.

**zip drive**: A portable, secondary storage device that holds up to 100 or 250 MB of data.

# DOZER'S QUINTESSENTIAL GUIDE TO MICROSOFT® WINDOWS

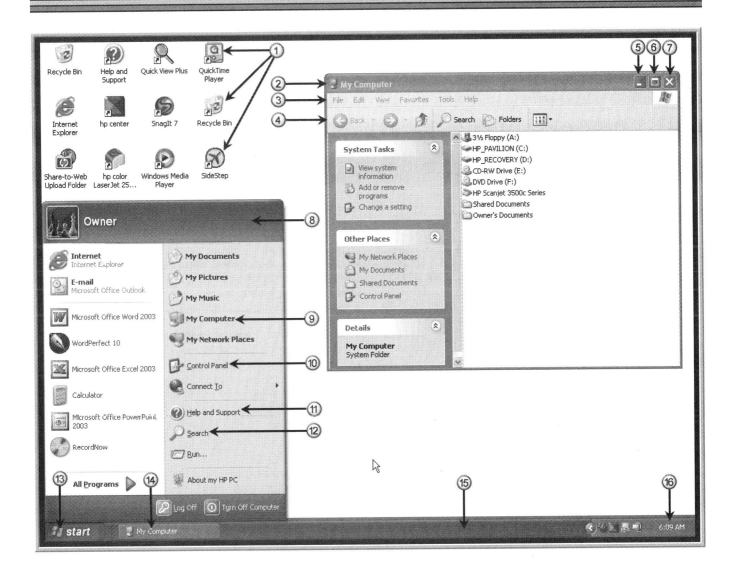

1. Desktop icons (double-click them to open programs and files)
2. Title bar (identifies the window)
3. Menu bar (collection of menu items, each of which contains commands)
4. Toolbar (collection of picture buttons, each of which accesses a command)
5. Minimize button (reduces the window to the size of a taskbar button)
6. Maximize button (enlarges the window to fill the screen)
7. Close button (removes the window from memory)
8. Start menu (displays when the Start button is clicked)
9. My Computer (opens the My Computer window)
10. Control Panel (opens the Control Panel window)
11. Help and Support (a great place to find answers to all your questions)
12. Search (finds files and folders you've lost)
13. Start button (opens the Start menu)
14. Taskbar button (denotes an open window)
15. Taskbar (contains the Start button, open windows buttons, etc.)
16. Time and Date (double click it to access a calendar and a clock)

# Dozer's Quintessential Guide To Microsoft Windows
## TABLE OF CONTENTS

Windows (The primary operating system used on the planet) Is a Graphical User Interface (GUI), which means we will work with windows (boxes displaying information) which appear on a desktop (the entire area of the screen upon which documents, files, folders, and programs are displayed). In addition, a GUI includes icons (graphical images used to execute commands). There are several versions of Windows currently in use (95, 98, Me, NT, 2000, and XP). They all look and operate similarly. While Dozer's Quintessential Guide To Microsoft Windows explains how to use Windows XP, most of what you will learn will apply to whatever version of Windows you might use.

Before you proceed, we need to determine the status of the machine you will be using. First, drag the mouse across the mouse pad a couple of inches and wait 20 seconds. Now, look at the screen. One of three possibilities exist.
1. If the screen displays the desktop (a start button will be visible at the left end of the taskbar-- bottom of the screen), you should skip to the Shut Down Windows section below.
2. If the screen is devoid of any images (it's dark), this means that the machine has been shut down by the prior user. Since your machine is currently shut down, you should skip to the Start Windows section below.
3. If the screen displays a box requesting that you login, skip to the Log On To Windows section below.

### SHUT DOWN WINDOWS
When you are done using a computer, you may want to shut it down. This will allow Windows to write unsaved data to the disk and erase temporary data it has saved. If you merely switched the power off, you may lose some valuable data.

To practice shutting down Windows, do the following:
☞ Close all programs (click the X at the top right corner of each window). Click Start, Turn Off Computer (or Shut Down).
☞ In the Turn Off Computer dialog box, click Turn Off.
☞ In a moment or two, the machine will turn itself off. You can then turn off the monitor's power switch.

### START WINDOWS
To practice starting (booting up) a machine, do the following:
☞ Turn on the computer and monitor (press power buttons).
☞ In a minute or so, the desktop or a login screen will appear.

### LOG ON TO WINDOWS
If you are using a computer owned by someone else (e.g., in a college computer lab), you may need to obtain a username and password before gaining access to the machine and the data on it. If so, ask your instructor for the log on procedures.

### USE A MOUSE
The mouse is an input device that typically has two buttons on the top and a ball on its underside. Basically, a mouse can do six things. The mouse can be clicked (rapidly press the left button), double-clicked (rapidly press the left mouse button twice), or right-clicked (rapidly press the right mouse button). In addition, it can point to on-screen objects, it can be moved across a surface to move the mouse pointer (the on-screen image denoting the location of the mouse), and if you hold down the left mouse button and drag the mouse, you can use a mouse to move objects on the screen.

### How to hold a mouse:
Place your thumb on the left side of the mouse and your fourth finger (the one next to your pinky) on the right side (the mouse won't bite you). Use your index finger (the one next to your thumb) to click and your middle finger to right click. When you are ready to click, right click, or double click, anchor the palm of your hand onto the mouse pad and squeeze the sides of the mouse to hold it steady while you click. If you twitch, the ball on the underside of the mouse will move and the computer will be confused as to what you want to do. So, hold the mouse steady while you click, right-click, or double-click the mouse buttons.

### What a mouse pointer might look like:

| IF POINTER LOOKS LIKE . . . | THIS MEANS THAT . . . |
| --- | --- |
| Arrow pointing up and left | It's waiting for you to click |
| Two pointed arrow | It can resize the object |
| Four- pointed arrow | It can move the object |
| Hourglass | The computer is busy |
| Pointing hand | It's on a hyperlink |

To practice selecting objects using a mouse, do the following:
☞ Point the mouse to the Recycle Bin icon on the desktop.
☞ Click. Notice the icon is highlighted (it has been selected).
☞ Click in any empty space on the desktop. Notice that the icon is no longer highlighted (it is deselected).
☞ Point the mouse to the Start button on the taskbar.
☞ Click. Notice that a menu appears (it is selected).
☞ Click in any empty space on the desktop. Notice that the menu disappears (it is deselected).

To practice opening and closing windows, do the following:
☞ Point the mouse at the Recycle Bin icon. Double-click.
☞ Notice the window opens and its taskbar button appears (if the window did not open, you did not double-click the icon. You either double-clicked too slowly or you twitched between clicks, thereby moving the mouse. Try again).
☞ Click the Close button (X at right end of the title bar).
☞ Notice the window closes and its taskbar button vanishes.
☞ Click Start, Control Panel.
☞ Notice the window opens and its taskbar button appears.
☞ Click the Close button (X at right end of the title bar).
☞ Notice the window closes and its taskbar button vanishes.

To practice resizing and moving windows, do the following:
☞ Open My Computer by clicking Start, My Computer. When the My Computer window opens, notice that it contains icons that represent the drives and resources on your computer.
☞ At the top right corner of the My Computer window, notice the three buttons. The first one has a _ on it and the third one has an X. While the first and the third buttons never change, the middle button will either have a □ or a ⯐ on it.
☞ Put the mouse on the X button and wait two seconds (don't click, just point). A little box (called a screen tip or a tooltip) will appear identifying the button as the Close button.
☞ Point to the other two buttons to see what they are called.
☞ If the middle button is the maximize button, skip to the next step. If the middle button is the restore button, click it.

Notice it changes into the maximize button. We'll learn more about these buttons later in this project.

☞ Point the mouse to the top or bottom border of the window until the pointer looks like a two-pointed arrow ↕. Hold down the left mouse button and drag the mouse until the window is about 3 inches high. Release the button.

☞ Point the mouse to the left or the right border until the pointer looks like a two-pointed arrow ↔. Hold down the left mouse button and drag the mouse until the window is about 5 inches wide. Release the mouse button. The window should now be about the size of the picture of Dozer on the front cover of this book.

☞ Point the mouse at the title bar. Hold down the left mouse button and drag the mouse until the window is at the top right corner of the desktop. Release the mouse button.

☞ Open the Recycle Bin (double click its desktop icon).

☞ Resize the window to be about 3" high and 5" wide. Since a maximized window cannot be manually resize, click the restore button, if it is currently maximized. Then resize the window).

☞ Move the window to the bottom right corner of the desktop.

☞ Maximize the My Computer window (make it fill the screen). To do so, click its maximize button.

☞ Restore the My Computer window (make it the size it was when it was last manually resized). To do so, click its restore button.

☞ Minimize the My Computer window (make it the size of a taskbar button). To do so, click the minimize button (button at the right end of the title bar, which has a _ on it).

☞ Notice that the window collapses into its taskbar button.

☞ To reopen the window, click its taskbar button.

☞ Resize each open window to be about 4" high and 4" wide.

☞ Move both windows to the left side of the desktop.

☞ Close both windows.

To practice opening shortcut menus, do the following:

☞ Point the mouse to an empty space on the taskbar. Right click. A context-sensitive shortcut menu appears. Notice the types of items on the menu.

☞ Click in any empty space on the desktop. The menu disappears (it is deselected).

☞ Point the mouse to the Recycle Bin icon. Right click. A context-sensitive shortcut menu appears. Notice the types of items on the menu. They differ from the ones that were on it a moment ago. Click in any empty space on the desktop. The menu disappears (it is deselected).

☞ Right click on an empty space on the desktop. A shortcut menu appears. Notice the items on it. They differ from the ones that were on it previously. Whenever you right click, the menu you get will contain items that will let you do things to the object you right clicked on. Click in an empty space on the desktop. The menu disappears (it is deselected).

## USE A SCROLL BAR
When a window contains more data than can be displayed, scroll bars appear. A scroll bar works like an elevator. It is a shaft with a box (elevator car). The scroll box indicates your location in a window (e.g., if you have a 100-page document and the box is 25% of the way down the bar, page 25 will be visible in the window). The box also indicates the percentage of the contents visible (e.g., if the box is half the size of the scroll bar, then you can see half the contents of the window). You can move the contents of the window by dragging the box, clicking between the box and a scroll arrow, or by clicking a scroll arrow.

To practice scrolling, do the following:
☞ Open the My Computer window.

☞ To ensure that the following steps work, click View, List.

☞ Resize the height of the window until the scroll box in the scroll bar (right side of window) is about 1/3 the height of the scroll bar.

☞ Click the down scroll arrow a few times. Notice that each time you click, the contents of the window moves one line.

☞ Click the up scroll arrow several times. Notice that each time you click, the contents of the window moves one line.

☞ Click in the scroll bar between the scroll box and the down arrow. Notice that each time you click, the contents of the window moves one window screen at a time.

☞ Click in the scroll bar between the box and the up arrow. Notice that each time you click it, the contents of the window moves one window screen at a time.

☞ Drag the scroll box up and down to move the contents.

☞ Close the My Computer window.

## GET HELP
In the old days, when you purchased software, it came in a box along with a hefty manual. Nowadays, the paper manual has been replaced with an online manual.

To practice using the Help feature, do the following:
☞ Click Start, Help And Support. Wait until the window opens.

☞ In the Search box, type in a word or phrase that describes the desired topic. In this case, type starting programs.

☞ Click the arrow next to the search box (or press Enter on the keyboard). The search results will be provided. Look through the results and find the exact topic you want. In this case, find "Start a Program" and click it. Notice that information on this topic appears on the right side.

☞ Notice that some terms may appear in green, underlined print. Point to the word "taskbar" (it is green and underlined) and notice that the pointer turns into a hand.

☞ Click the "taskbar" term (a definition of the term appears).

☞ Click outside of the definition box (the box disappears).

☞ Notice the Related Topics link (blue ink below instructions).

☞ Click the Related Topics link. Suggestions appear. To view one, click it. Go ahead and click any one of them.

☞ To return to the prior window, click the Back toolbar button (at the top left corner of the window).

☞ To print the steps, click the Print toolbar button (the Print dialog box appears).

☞ Click the Print button. Go to the printer to fetch your printout.

☞ Click the Close button to close Help.

## LOG OFF OF WINDOWS
After a machine has been shut down, it takes several minutes for the next user to bootup. So, while you might shut down your home computer after using it, when you are done using someone else's computer, you can save the next user time by simply closing whatever applications you have been using and logging off. This leaves the machine on for the next user. By the way, if you are using a machine that does not require a login procedure, then simply shut down the machine.

To practice logging off of Windows, do the following:
☞ Close all applications.

☞ Click Start, Log Off.

☞ In the Log Off Windows dialog box, click Log Off.

☞ Click the OK button. The computer will log you off, and will display the Login screen. You have successfully logged off.

## EXERCISE 1: CROSSWORD

Use the clues below to complete the crossword puzzle. (Note: the answers for this and many other exercises can be found in the Answer Key, beginning on page B-25).

### ACROSS

2. When I click a desktop icon (e.g., Recycle Bin), the icon changes color, indicating that the icon has been ___.
5. Inside a scroll bar, between the 2 arrows is a scroll ___.
6. To access a shortcut menu, I would ___ click.
8. To make a window the size it was when I last manually resized it, I would ___ the window.
10. A geeky, nerdy way of saying "turn on" a computer.
11. To ___ a window, I would drag its title bar.
13. Windows is an ___ system.
15. To make a window as big as the screen, I would ___ it.
19. When a window is too small for all the data to be displayed, ___ bars appear which are used to move the data within the window so I can see the other data.
20. To ___ the mouse, I would point to an on-screen object (e.g., an icon or the title bar of a window). Then, I would hold down the left mouse button, and move the mouse.
21. At the far left end of the taskbar is the ___ button.
23. At each end of a scroll bar, you will find an ___ button which, when clicked, moves the content of the window.
25. To open the Recycle Bin window, I would ___ click it.
27. The most widely-used operating system is ___.
29. A graphical image that can execute a command.
30. When you double click the Recycle Bin icon, the window opens and a button for the window appears on the ___.
31. The floppy drive is often called the ___ drive.

### DOWN

1. If I drag a corner or a border of a window, I will ___ the window.
3. The X button found at the top right corner of a window is called the ___ button.
4. If I click an object, such as a desktop icon, it will change color, indicating that it has been selected. If I then click in an empty space on the desktop, the object will be ___.
7. GUI is an acronym for ___ User Interface.
9. At the top of each window is a bar that tells you the name of the window. In addition, if you want to move the window, you can drag this bar. This is the ___ bar.
11. To make a window the size of a taskbar button, I would ___ the window. When I do this, the window's contents are still in memory, it's just that I have reduced the window's size so I can create more space on the desktop.
12. Dozer is a super cyber ___.
14. The ___ is typically located at the bottom of the screen. The Start button resides at the far left end of it and the time of day is displayed at the far right end of it.
16. An Input device that typically has two buttons on the top and a ball on its underside, used to click, right-click, double-click, and drag.
17. The on-screen image that tells me where the mouse is currently located is called the mouse ___.
18. To rapidly press the left mouse button.
20. The entire area on the screen upon which documents, files, folders, and programs are displayed.
21. To ___ a computer, I should click Start, Turn Off Computer.
22. If I right-click, I get a "context-sensitive" menu, which is a fancy way of describing a menu that has items which are most likely needed by me at that time. This menu is sometimes called a quick menu or a ___ menu.
24. If I maximize a window, how many windows will be visible on the desktop?
26. Folks who use computers.
28. Scroll bars appear when a window contains more ___ than can be displayed.

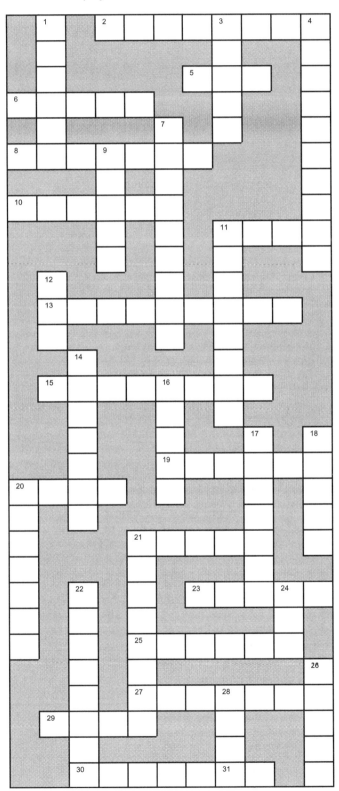

## EXERCISE 2: TRUE-FALSE

For each of the following eight statements, place a T or an F on the line to indicate if the statement is True or False.

1. ___Windows is the most widely used operating system.
2. ___I can close a window by clicking the task bar.
3. ___I can resize a window by dragging any border or corner.
4. ___When I click an icon, it becomes highlighted.
5. ___To move a window, I simply drag its status bar.
6. ___All windows have scroll bars all the time.
7. ___GUI stands for Graphical User Interface.
8. ___To turn off a computer, the first step is to click Start.

## EXERCISE 3: MATCHING

Match each of the following terms with the word or phrase that is its best description by writing the letter of the term on the line next to its description.

| A. Click | B. Double-click | C. Drag | D. Right Click |
| --- | --- | --- | --- |

1. ___ Rapidly press the right button once.
2. ___ Rapidly press the left button once.
3. ___ Rapidly press the left button twice.
4. ___ Hold the left button down and move the mouse.

## EXERCISE 4: IDENTIFY TERMS

Below are eight definitions. Below the definitions are eight lines. In each line, write the word that matches the definition.

1. Another way to say "start" a computer.
2. Area of screen where documents, files, and folders appear.
3. Input device with buttons on the top.
4. On-screen boxes that display information.
5. The X at the top right corner of a window.
6. The thing that appears when I right click.
7. Graphical images used to execute commands.
8. Rapidly pressing the left mouse button twice.

1. _____     5. _____
2. _____     6. _____
3. _____     7. _____
4. _____     8. _____

## EXERCISE 5: MATCHING

A scroll bar appears in any window that is too small for all of its contents to be displayed at once. The scroll bar permits you to move the contents of the window so that you can see the remainder of the contents. Below is a list of three ways to use a scroll bar. Below that list is a list of three things you might want to do in a window. Match each. By the way, between the two buttons, most mice now come with a scrolling wheel that can be used instead of the on-screen vertical scroll bar.

A. Drag the scroll box.
B. Click the scroll bar arrow.
C. Click between the scroll box and the scroll bar arrow.

1. ___Move the contents of the window one line at a time.
2. ___Move the contents of the window one screen at a time.
3. ___Move rapidly through the contents.

## EXERCISE 6: USE HELP

Open the Help and Support feature and use "Glossary" as the search keyword to find the definition of each of these terms?

| TERM | DEFINITION |
| --- | --- |
| 1. Thumbnail | |
| 2. Desktop | |
| 3. Share | |
| 4. Queue | |
| 5. Dock | |

## EXERCISE 7: SHUT DOWN (TURN OFF) AND BOOTUP

☞ Shut down the machine.
☞ Boot up the machine (turn the power on).

## EXERCISE 8: USE A MOUSE

☞ Select the Recycle Bin desktop icon.
☞ What color does the Recycle Bin icon become? _____
☞ What word is used to describe an icon this color? _____
☞ Click in an empty space on the desktop.
☞ Is the Recycle Bin icon still blue? _____
☞ If not still blue, does this mean it has been deselected? ____
☞ Open the My Computer window.
☞ Resize the window so that it is about the size of your thumb.
☞ Move the window to the top right corner of the desktop.
☞ Open the Recycle Bin window.
☞ Resize the window so that it is about the size of your thumb.
☞ Move the window to the bottom right corner of the desktop.
☞ Maximize the My Computer window.
☞ How much of the desktop does the window cover? _____
☞ Minimize the My Computer window.
☞ Where did the window go? _____
☞ Click the My Computer button on the taskbar.
☞ How much of the desktop does the window cover? _____
☞ Restore the My Computer window.
☞ How big is the My Computer window? _____
☞ Resize each window to the size of your favorite candy bar.
☞ Move both windows to the left side of the desktop.
☞ Close the My Computer and the Recycle Bin windows.

## EXERCISE 9: ACCESS SHORTCUT MENUS

This exercise is designed to demonstrate that right clicking produces a customized menu. When asked how many items appear in each menu, count the ghosted items too.

☞ Point to an empty space on the desktop and right click.
☞ How many items appear on the shortcut menu? _____
☞ Point to the Start button on the taskbar and right click.
☞ How many items appear on the shortcut menu? _____
☞ Point to an empty space on the taskbar and right click.
☞ How many items appear on the shortcut menu? _____
☞ Point to the Recycle Bin icon and right click.
☞ How many items appear on the shortcut menu? _____

## EXERCISE 10: SHUT DOWN (TURN OFF) THE MACHINE

☞ When you are done working, shut down the machine. However, if you are using a machine that required you to logon to it, you might want to simply log off instead of shutting it down. By merely logging off, you will leave the machine on for the next user.

## WORK WITH MENUS

An on-screen menu serves the same purpose as a restaurant menu. In either case, a menu contains a list of items from which to choose. A menu bar (located under the title bar) consists of a series of words denoting command groups. To use a specific command in a group, click the menu bar item. Regardless of the program used, certain menu bar conventions exist, such as:

| A COMMAND . . . | MEANS THAT THIS . . . |
|---|---|
| preceded by a check (✔) | feature has been selected |
| preceded by a bullet (●) | mutually-exclusive item is selected |
| followed by an arrow | command leads to a sub-menu |
| that is faded (ghosted) | command is unavailable |
| followed by ellipses (. . .) | command leads to a dialog box |

To practice working with menus, do the following:
☞ Open My Computer and maximize the window.
☞ Click View on the menu bar. Notice that a drop-down menu containing a more detailed list of commands appears and that within this list, groups of related commands are separated by horizontal lines called command separators.
☞ The first group of related items includes Toolbars, Status Bar, and Explorer Bar. The first item, Toolbars, has a small arrow (triangle) after it. This means that, if selected, a submenu will appear. To select a menu item with an arrow after it, you don't need to click it. Simply put the mouse pointer on the item and the submenu will appear. Move the mouse so it points to Toolbars (the submenu appears).
☞ The items on the Toolbars submenu are sometimes referred to as toggles or toggle switches because, like a light switch, each is either on or off. A menu item with a check mark is on (selected). A menu item that does not have a check mark is off (it is deselected). Any of them may have a check mark in front of it. If Standard Buttons has a check mark next to it, click outside of the menu to close it and skip the next step.
☞ If the Standard Buttons item does not have a check mark, click Standard Buttons (the menu disappears). Click View, Toolbars to have the submenu reappear. The Standard Buttons item now has a check mark. Click outside the menu to have the menu disappear.
☞ The Standard Buttons toolbar itself is the line of picture buttons that appears below the menu bar. Look below the menu bar to see it. To turn it off (deselect the toolbar so it does not appear), click View, Toolbars, Standard Buttons. Notice that the Standard Buttons toolbar no longer appears in the window.
☞ To turn the Standard Buttons toolbar on (i.e., to select it so the toolbar will appear at the top of the window), click View, Toolbars, Standard Buttons. Notice that the Standard Buttons toolbar is again visible.
☞ Click View. Notice the second group of related items: Thumbnails, Tiles, Icons, List, and Details. One of them has a bullet (●) in front of it, which means that only one of these items can be selected. It is said to be a "mutually-exclusive" option because to choose one excludes choosing another. The one with the bullet is selected. Later, we'll learn more about this group of items and how they work.

☞ Click outside the menu to have it disappear.
☞ Click File and notice that several items on the menu are in faded type (also called ghosted or dimmed), indicating that these commands are currently unavailable. Click one of the faded items. Nothing happens. Later, they may appear unfaded, at which time they will be usable.
☞ Click Tools and notice that the Folders Options item has an ellipses (three periods) after it. This means that, if selected, a dialog box will appear.
☞ Click Folder Options. A dialog box appears. We'll learn about dialog boxes in the next section of this project. For now, click the Cancel button in the dialog box.
☞ Close all windows.

## WORK WITH DIALOG BOXES

A dialog box is Windows' way of saying "I know you want to do something, but in order to do precisely what you want, I need more information." So, you must have a dialog with the program to specify what you want it to do. A dialog box asks questions in several ways, such as:

| WITH A . . . | YOU NEED TO . . . |
|---|---|
| Folder tab | Click the desired folder tab |
| List box | Select an item from the list |
| Spin box | Click the up or down arrow |
| Command button | Click the appropriate button |
| Radio (option) button | Click one mutually-exclusive option |
| Slider | Drag the slide control |
| Text box | Click in the box and type a response |
| Check box (square box) | Click as many options as wanted |

To practice working with dialog boxes, do the following:
☞ Right click in any empty space on the desktop.
☞ On the shortcut menu, click Properties.
☞ A dialog box appears with tabs (e.g., Themes, Desktop, Screen Saver, etc.), each of which accesses a different page. Click each tab and take a look at each page.
☞ Click the Screen Saver tab.
☞ Click the arrow to the right of the Screen Saver list box.
☞ On the list that appears, click Marquee.
☞ Notice that the list disappears and a preview of the chosen screen saver appears in the dialog box.
☞ Notice the Wait spin box. Click either the up or down arrow to set the wait time at 40 minutes. Now, set it at 10 minutes.
☞ Click the Settings command button. In the Position area, notice the small circles called radio buttons (sometimes called option buttons), which are mutually-exclusive options (i.e., you can only choose one).
☞ Click Random. A dot appears in the radio button. Click Centered. The dot moves from one option to the other.
☞ Notice the slider control in the Speed area. Drag it to Slow and notice how slowly the marquee moves. Now, drag it to Fast and notice how fast the marquee moves.
☞ Click in the Text box. Press the Backspace key and/or the Delete key until the text is deleted. Type your name.

☞ Click the Format Text command button. In the Effects area, notice the Strikeout and Underline options. They each have a check box which means you can pick one, both, or neither of the options.
☞ Click the Strikeout check box. Notice the sample provided.
☞ Click the Underline check box. A sample is provided.
☞ Click the Strikeout box to deselect it. Look at the sample.
☞ Click the Cancel button in this dialog box and in the other dialog boxes that appear to clear the desktop.

## WORK WITH MY COMPUTER

The resources on the computer are displayed as icons (sometimes called objects) in the My Computer window. Once the My Computer window is open, its contents can be displayed in several different ways (e.g., Thumbnails, Tiles, Icons, List, and Details). The window's contents don't change; only how the contents are displayed.

To practice changing the display of objects, do the following:
☞ Open the My Computer window and the C: drive window.
☞ If not already done, maximize the C drive window so you can see more of its contents.
☞ Click View. Notice the second group of related items which includes Thumbnails, Tiles, Icons, List, and Details. Notice that one of the five has a bullet (●) in front of it. Recall from a prior section of this project that this means only one of the items in this group can be selected.
☞ Click Tiles. Notice how the contents appear.
☞ Click View, Icons. Notice that the same contents of the window appear, but they appear as smaller icons.
☞ Click View, List. The contents are organized in a list.
☞ Click View, Details. The contents now appear with details as to the size, type, and modification date of some of the objects (you may need to scroll down to see examples of objects for which all the details are provided).
☞ Click View, Thumbnails. If any of the files are graphic images, a thumbnail (small sample) of the image found in the file will be displayed. Later, we'll see how the thumbnail view will benefit us.
☞ Close all windows.

## ARRANGE WINDOWS

If you want to see the contents of more than one window at the same time, you can open the desired windows and manually move them by dragging their title bars (you learned how to do this in Windows Project 1). In addition, you can have windows arranged automatically by either vertically tiling them (have them appear side-by-side), horizontally tiling them (have them appear on top of each other), or cascading them (have them appear layered, like a deck of fanned cards, with each window's title bar visible).

To practice tiling windows vertically, do the following:
☞ Open the Recycle Bin (double click its desktop icon).
☞ Open My Computer (click Start, My Computer).
☞ Open the Control Panel (click Start, Control Panel).
☞ Notice that there is a taskbar button for each open window.
☞ Right click the taskbar in any empty space (if the taskbar is full of buttons, you will need to carefully click in an empty space between the buttons).
☞ Click Tile Windows Vertically.
☞ Click in one of the windows to make it the active window (it will have a highlighted title bar).
☞ Click in an inactive window to make it the active one.

To practice tiling windows horizontally, do the following:
☞ Right click the taskbar in any empty space.
☞ Click Tile Windows Horizontally.
☞ Click in one of the windows to make it the active window (it will have a highlighted title bar).
☞ Click in an inactive window to make it the active one.

To practice cascading windows, do the following:
☞ Right click the taskbar in any empty space.
☞ Click Cascade Windows.
☞ Click one of the windows to make it the active window (notice that after you click the window, its title bar will be highlighted and it will be in front of the inactive windows).
☞ Click in one of the inactive windows to bring it to the front and make it the active window.
☞ Close all windows.

## FORMAT A DISKETTE

Most diskettes are pre-formatted when you buy them. They are formatted for either IBM-compatibles or for Mac machines. If you buy an unformatted disk or you have a used one that you want to erase and reuse, you will need to format it. If your disk has never been formatted or if you are unsure about its quality, you will need to do a Full Format, which erases all files, creates a File Allocation Table (FAT), and checks for bad sectors on the disk surface. If your disk has previously been formatted, you can do a Quick Format, which simply erases all files on it. In the following steps, you will format your diskette both ways.

To practice performing a full format, do the following:
☞ Insert your diskette (label up, shutter end first. Notice that your diskette has a little arrow at the top left corner which points in the direction to which the diskette should be inserted into the floppy drive).
☞ Open My Computer.
☞ Click the floppy drive icon to select it (don't double-click it).
☞ Click File, Format to have the Format dialog box appear.
☞ Click Start. Read the warning that appears. Click OK.
☞ Notice the progress bar fills with little green boxes to indicate how far along in the process you are.
☞ Wait a minute or so for a dialog box to appear that tells you that the formatting has been completed. Then click OK.
☞ In the Format dialog box, click Close.
☞ Close the My Computer window.
☞ Remove your diskette.
☞ Close all windows.

To practice performing a quick format, do the following:
☞ Insert your diskette into the floppy drive. Even though your disk was fully formatted a moment ago, go ahead and follow these steps to practice performing a quick format on the same diskette.
☞ Open My Computer.
☞ Click the floppy drive icon to select it (don't double-click it).
☞ Click File, Format to have the Format dialog box appear.
☞ In the Format Options area of the Format dialog box, click the Quick Format check box.
☞ Click Start. Read the warning that appears. Click OK.
☞ Wait. This time, it should only take a couple of seconds.
☞ When given the format results, click OK.
☞ In the Format dialog box, click Close.
☞ Close the My Computer window.
☞ Remove your diskette.
☞ Close all windows.

## EXERCISE 1: CROSSWORD

Use the clues below to complete the crossword puzzle.

### ACROSS

2. A ___ bar consists of words (e.g., File, Edit, View) denoting command groups.
3. Before a diskette is useable, someone must ___ it.
5. To arrange multiple windows so that they are layered, like a deck of fanned cards, with each window's title bar visible.
9. Some dialog boxes contain several pages, each of which is accessed by clicking a ___ at the top of the box.
10. A ___ consists of picture buttons denoting commands.
13. A ___ button denotes a mutually-exclusive choice, which means you can pick one option only.
14. The Close button on the title bar has an ___ on it.
15. A ___ format erases all files, creates a File Allocation Table, and checks for bad sectors.
16. To ___ a mouse, I press the left mouse button once.
17. A menu command that is unavailable will appear ___.

### DOWN

1. Unlike 15 Across, a ___ format simply erases all files from the surface of the diskette.
2. The ___ window shows a computer's drives & resources.
3. Another word for 17 across.
4. Windows appearing on the desktop side-by-side are said to be ___.
6. A place in a dialog box where you are asked to enter text.
7. An acronym for File Allocation Table.
8. To move the mouse while holding down the left button.
11. File and folder icons are sometimes called ___.
12. Sometimes when you attempt to execute a command, a ___ box will appear which asks you questions.

## EXERCISE 2: TRUE-FALSE

For each of the following eight statements, place a T or an F on the line to indicate if the statement is True or False.

1. ___An active window will have a highlighted title bar.
2. ___To move a window, I would drag its Status bar.
3. ___File and folder icons are sometimes called objects.
4. ___To use a specific command in a menu, click the item.
5. ___To open a window, I would double-click its icon.
6. ___A menu bar item with a bullet is a toggle.
7. ___The menu bar is typically located under the toolbar.
8. ___I can have three active windows at one time.

## EXERCISE 3: MATCHING

An on-screen menu serves the same purpose as a restaurant menu. In either case, a menu contains a list of items (in the case of a restaurant menu, food items; in the case of a computer menu, command items). A menu bar consists of a series of words denoting command groups. To use a specific command in a group, click the menu bar item. Regardless of the program you use, certain menu bar conventions exist. Below is a list of conventions and another list of what various conventions mean. Match the convention with its meaning.

> A. Preceded by a check mark (✓).
> B. Preceded by a bullet (●).
> C. Followed by an arrow.
> D. Item itself is faded (dimmed, ghosted).
> E. Followed by an ellipses ( . . . ).

1. ___ This command is unavailable.
2. ___ This command leads to a sub menu.
3. ___ This command leads to a dialog box.
4. ___ This non-mutually-exclusive item has been selected.
5. ___ This mutually-exclusive item has been selected.

## EXERCISE 4: IDENTIFY TERMS

Below are six definitions. Below the definitions are six lines. In each line, write the word that matches the definition.

1. The line of picture buttons below the menu bar.
2. Arranging windows so they appear side-by-side.
3. Arranging windows so they appear on top of each other.
4. Arranging windows so they look like a deck of fanned cards.
5. If only one item in a group can be chosen, what is it called?
6. Words at the top of the screen denoting command groups.

1. _____    4. _____
2. _____    5. _____
3. _____    6. _____

## EXERCISE 5: TRUE-FALSE

For each of the following eight statements, place a T or an F on the line to indicate if the statement is True or False.

1. ___FAT stands for Format Access Table.
2. ___A new, unformatted diskette can be Quick Formatted.
3. ___A Full Format checks for bad sectors.
4. ___A Quick Format erases all of the files on the diskette.
5. ___A Full Format creates a new FAT.
6. ___A Full Format erases all of the files on the diskette.
7. ___A Quick Format creates a new FAT.
8. ___To format a diskette, you must have the A window open.

## EXERCISE 6: MATCHING

Dialog boxes ask questions. A question can be asked and answered in many ways. For instance, some questions require a mutually-exclusive answer. That is, if I choose to center text, I can't simultaneously right align the text. It's one or the other, never both. On the other hand sometimes a question can have several answers simultaneously such as having a word appear in bold print and underlined. In such a case, you don't have to choose one or the other, you can choose one, both, or none. Below are eight items, each of which is utilized in various dialog boxes to obtain the answers to questions. Match each of the following items to the description below by placing the letter on the line preceding each description.

| | |
|---|---|
| A. Check Box | E. Radio Button |
| B. Command Button | F. Slider |
| C. Folder Tab | G. Spin Box |
| D. List Box | H. Text Box |

1. ___ Some dialog boxes have so many questions to ask that it takes more than one page to contain the choices. Each page is represented by one of these. To access the desired page, click the appropriate one of these.

2. ___ Sometimes a dialog box will ask you to make a choice from a list of options. In such cases, you would click the arrow to have a collection of options appear. The collection of options from which you make your selection is one of these.

3. ___ Sometimes, a choice can be made by clicking the up or down arrow in one of these. For instance, to change the wait time for the screen saver, one of these is provided.

4. ___ In virtually all dialog boxes, I am given rectangular buttons with names on them. For instance, many dialog boxes have a "Cancel" button and/or an "OK" button. If I click the button, a command is executed. Each of these buttons is one of these.

5. ___ Some questions require a mutually-exclusive answer. That is, only one choice can be made. To make the one choice excludes all other choices. For these type of questions, a dialog box will provide a collection of circles, one of which will have a black dot. Click in the appropriate circle to have the black dot appear there. Each circle is one of these.

6. ___ To speed up a screen saver or mouse speed, or to adjust the volume on my speakers, I might need to drag this object from left to right or up and down to adjust the speed or the volume.

7. ___ Sometimes, a dialog box has no idea what the possible answers are. For instance, when asked to name a file, you are required to type in the filename in one of these.

8. ___ Sometimes, you can select more than one option. To do so, a series of square boxes will be provided. If you click in a square box, a check mark appears in the square box. You can click in one, two, several, or none of these square boxes to make a variety of non-mutually-exclusive choices. Each square is one of these.

## EXERCISE 7: EXPLORE MENUS

☞ Open the My Computer window and the C drive window.

☞ From the menu bar, click View. Does "Status Bar" have a check mark next to it? If yes, then go to the next step. If no, click Status Bar. By doing so, you will be activating the status bar so it will appear at the bottom of the window.

☞ Click View, Tiles. How many icons (objects) are in the window (If no objects are selected, you don't need to count them. Just look at the left end of the Status bar)? _____

☞ Click View. Which item has a bullet next to it? _____ Why does it have a bullet? _____

☞ Click Icons. How many icons (objects) are in the window? _____. Are they the same ones that were in it when you looked at them as Tiles? _____

☞ Click View. Which item has a bullet next to it? _____

☞ Click List. How many icons (objects) are in this window? _____. Are they the same ones that were in it when you looked at them as Icons? _____

☞ Click View. Which item has a bullet next to it? _____

☞ Click Details. How many icons (objects) are in the window? _____. Are they the same ones that were in it when you looked at them as a List? _____

☞ When you view the My Computer contents using Details, what types of information about the objects are we given? _____

☞ Click Tools, Folder Options. A Folder Options box appears. This box is called a _____ box. Close the box.

☞ Click View. Point to Toolbars. What appears? _____ How can you make it disappear? _____

☞ Click File. Some of the items on this list are faded (dim, ghosted). Click a faded item. What happens? _____

☞ Close all windows

## EXERCISE 8: ARRANGE WINDOWS

☞ Open the Recycle Bin and the My Computer windows.

☞ Tile the two windows horizontally.

☞ Click anywhere in the Recycle Bin window.

☞ Which window is the active window? _____

☞ Click anywhere in the My Computer window.

☞ Which window is the active window? _____

☞ Tile the windows vertically.

☞ Click anywhere in the Recycle Bin window.

☞ Which window is the active window? _____

☞ Click anywhere in the My Computer window.

☞ Which window is the active window? _____

☞ Cascade the windows.

☞ Click anywhere in the front window.

☞ Which window is the active window? _____

☞ Click in the back window.

☞ Which window is the active window? _____

☞ Click in the back window to make it return to the front.

☞ Move the top window so it covers the back one entirely.

☞ If you want to activate the back window, you can't click it. So, what can you do? _____

☞ Resize each window to be the size of your big toe (don't take off your shoes! Use your memory about your toes to resize each window). Close both windows.

## EXERCISE 9: FORMAT A DISKETTE

☞ Format a disk using the Full Format method (remember, only format a disk that contains nothing of value--after formatting it, whatever files were on it will be long gone).

☞ Format a disk using the Quick Format method (if you want, just format the disk that you fully formatted in the prior step).

## START (LOAD, LAUNCH, OPEN) A PROGRAM
To use a program, it must be loaded into memory.

To practice starting a program, do the following:
☞ Click the Start button (on taskbar). A menu appears.
☞ Move the mouse until the mouse pointer is on All Programs.
☞ Move the mouse to the right until the pointer is in the sub-menu, then point the mouse on Accessories.
☞ Move the mouse to the right until the pointer is in the sub-menu, then click on WordPad.
☞ When WordPad opens, maximize its window, if necessary.

## ENTER TEXT
To practice entering text, do the following:
☞ Press the Tab key to indent the first line and then type the paragraph below (a collection of proverbs). At the end of each line, don't press the Enter key—let the words automatically wrap. They will wrap differently than below.

> It's better to burn a candle than curse the vast darkness. If you chase two rabbits, you will not catch either one. He who pays the piper, calls the tune. We never know the worth of water until the well is dry. Never dance in a small boat.

☞ Compare the right edge of your paragraph to the right end of the ruler bar. Does the text wrap at the end of the ruler bar? If so, skip to the next step. If not, click View, Options, Rich Text, Wrap To Ruler, OK.
☞ Press Enter to start a new paragraph, press Tab to indent the first line, and type the paragraph below:

> Be happy while you're living, for you're a long time dead. The firm tree does not fear the storm. There's no need to fear the wind if your haystacks are tied down. Do not insult the alligator until after you have crossed the river.

☞ Press Enter to start a new paragraph, press Tab to indent the first line, and type the paragraph below:

> First secure an independent income, then practice virtue. When the student is ready, the teacher appears. The most dangerous food is wedding cake. How beautiful it is to do absolutely nothing, and then rest afterward.

## SAVE A FILE
Your document resides only in memory (temporary storage). To ensure that your document is permanently stored, save it to the hard drive or a diskette. A saved document is called a file.

To practice saving a file to a diskette, do the following:
☞ Insert your diskette into the floppy drive.
☞ Click File, Save.
☞ In the Save As dialog box, click the Save In list box arrow.
☞ In the drop-down list, click the 3½ Floppy A: drive icon.
☞ Click in the File Name box to highlight its contents.
☞ Type Win3-Maxims. Click the Save button. While you wait for the file to be saved, notice that the floppy drive light is on and once it's done being saved, notice the filename now appears in the title bar of your document.

## CHANGE THE FONT
To improve the appearance of a document, you may want to change the font type and/or the font size of the text.

To practice changing the font, do the following:
☞ Select text to be changed (drag over the entire document).
☞ Click Format, Font (the Font dialog box will appear).
☞ Select any font, size, and color you like. Click OK.
☞ Click anywhere outside of the selected text to deselect it.
☞ Save your modified document (click File, Save). Since you have previously saved this file, you don't need to specify where to save it or what to call it. When you click File, Save, the newly-modified file will automatically replace the old one.

## APPLY ENHANCEMENTS
Enhancements (bold, italics, underline) are applied to text to emphasize the title or other key points in a document. You can apply one, any two, or all three of these enhancements to text.

To practice applying enhancements, do the following:
☞ Select the text to be enhanced (select any word).
☞ Click the Bold toolbar button (button with a "B"). If this button is not visible, click View, Format Bar.
☞ Click anywhere outside of the selected text to deselect it.
☞ Select any word. Click the Italic toolbar button ("I").
☞ Click anywhere outside of the selected text to deselect it.
☞ Select any word. Click the Underline button ("U").
☞ Click anywhere outside of the selected text to deselect it.
☞ Select any word. Click the B, I, and U toolbar buttons.
☞ Click anywhere outside of the selected text to deselect it.
☞ Save your modified document (click File, Save).

## CHANGE THE ALIGNMENT
Text can be aligned with the straight edge on the left or the right. Or, the text can be centered between the margins. The toolbar has one button for each alignment style and each of these buttons has an image which shows how the alignment will look.

To practice changing the alignment of text, do the following:
☞ Select the text (select the entire document).
☞ Click the Center alignment toolbar button.
☞ Click anywhere outside of the selected text to deselect it.
☞ Each line of text is now centered between the margins.
☞ Change the alignment of the document back to Align Left.

## EDIT TEXT
To practice editing (modifying) text , do the following:
☞ Select the word "burn" in the 1st sentence (drag over it).
☞ Type light (note that "light" replaces "burn").
☞ Click after "vast" in the 1st sentence.
☞ Press the Backspace key until "vast" is deleted.
☞ Click in front of "absolutely" in the last sentence.
☞ Press the Delete key until "absolutely" is deleted.
☞ Click at the end of the 3rd paragraph, press the Enter key twice to insert two lines, and type your full name.
☞ Save your modified document (click File, Save).

## MOVE TEXT
When you want text to appear in a different location, you can move it. When you move text, the original (source) text will be removed and placed in its new location (the destination).

To practice moving text, do the following:
☞ Select the text to be moved (select the 2nd sentence).
☞ Click Edit, Cut (the text is sent to the clipboard).

☞ Click where you want the text (at end of 2nd paragraph).
☞ Click Edit, Paste (the sentence has been moved). If needed, click in front of that sentence and press the spacebar twice to put two spaces between it and the prior sentence.

## COPY TEXT
If you want text to appear in many places, you could repeatedly type it. However, to save time, copy the text (the text will remain where it was and you will insert a copy of it elsewhere).

To practice copying text, do the following:
☞ Select the text to be copied (select the 3rd sentence).
☞ Click Edit, Copy (a copy of the text is sent to the clipboard).
☞ Click where you want the text (at end of 2nd paragraph).
☞ Click Edit, Paste (the sentence has been copied). If needed, put two spaces between it and the prior sentence.

## USE THE PRINT PREVIEW FEATURE
To see how the printed document will look, you can use the Print Preview feature. By doing so, you will save paper and ink by reducing the number of preliminary copies you make.

To practice previewing a document, do the following:
☞ Click File, Print Preview.
☞ To close Print Preview, click the Close button on the Print Preview bar (not the Close button on the Title bar).

## PRINT A DOCUMENT
To practice printing a document, do the following:
☞ Click File, Print (the Print dialog box will appear).
☞ In the Page Range area, select the pages (select All).
☞ In the Number of Copies Area, select 1.
☞ Click the Print button. Go get your copy from the printer.

## CLOSE A PROGRAM
To practice closing a program, do the following:
☞ Click the Close button (X at end of title bar). If reminded to save the file before the program closes, click Yes.

## OPEN A DOCUMENT
To read, edit, or print a previously-saved document, you will need to open it (i.e., place a copy of it in memory).

To practice opening an existing document, do the following:
☞ Start WordPad. Click File, Open.
☞ Click the Look In list box arrow (a drop-down list appears).
☞ Select the drive and folder in which the document resides (select the 3½ Floppy A: drive).
☞ The files on the diskette appear. Select the desired file (if not already selected, click "Win3-Maxims").
☞ Click the Open button. Now, go ahead and close WordPad

## USE PAINT
To practice using Paint, do the following:
☞ Click Start, All Programs, Accessories, Paint.
☞ If needed, maximize the window.
☞ Draw a small house (the size of your thumb) by clicking a tool from the Toolbox (left of screen) and a color from the Color Box (bottom of screen).
☞ Click a tool and a color and draw a small tree by the house (make the tree about the size of your thumb).
☞ Click a tool and a color and draw yourself in the yard.
☞ Open the Save As dialog box (click File, Save)
☞ In the Save In box, specify 3½ Floppy A: drive

☞ In the File Name box, name the file Win3-House.
☞ In the Save As Type list box, select 256 Color Bitmap (by saving the file this way, less storage space will be required, which is important, since you're saving this file to a diskette).
☞ Click Save. If you see a warning box telling you about the loss of color information, click Yes.
☞ Print this document. Close Paint.

## USE CALCULATOR
To practice using the calculator, do the following:
☞ Click Start, All Programs, Accessories, Calculator.
☞ Click the keys on the calculator to discover that 458 plus 878 plus 667 is _____ and that 122 multiplied by 16 is _____.
☞ Click the Close button to close the Calculator window.

## SWITCH BETWEEN PROGRAMS
You can easily run more than one program simultaneously and you can rapidly switch between them (multitasking).

To practice switching between programs, do the following:
☞ Open Paint. Note that a highlighted Paint button appears on the taskbar indicating that the application is open and active.
☞ Click the Minimize button. Notice that the Paint button is still on the taskbar, but it is no longer highlighted, indicating that the application is running, but is minimized.
☞ Open WordPad. Note that a highlighted WordPad button appears on the taskbar indicating the application is open.
☞ Click the Minimize button. Notice that the WordPad button is still on the taskbar, but it's no longer highlighted, indicating that the application is running, but is minimized.
☞ Click the Paint taskbar button to switch to Paint.
☞ Click the WordPad taskbar button to switch to WordPad.
☞ Notice that WordPad opens on top of Paint.
☞ Click the Close button to close WordPad. Notice that when closed, WordPad has no button on the taskbar.
☞ Click the Close button to close Paint. Notice that when closed, Paint has no button on the taskbar.

## COPY AN IMAGE BETWEEN APPLICATIONS
You can copy or move an image or text from a document in one program and paste it in a document in another program.

To practice copying an image, do the following:
☞ Open Paint and the file you created called "Win3-House"
☞ Click the Select toolbox button (dotted rectangle).
☞ Place the mouse pointer at the top left corner of the image.
☞ Drag the mouse down and to the right until the border contains the picture. Release the mouse button.
☞ If you don't have the entire picture in the dotted box, click the Select toolbox button again and retry.
☞ Click Edit, Copy to send a copy of the image to the clipboard.
☞ Open WordPad and the "Win3-Maxims" file you created.
☞ Put the insertion point on the line between the last paragraph and your name. Click Edit, Paste (the image will appear).
☞ To resize the image, drag any sizing handle (black square around the image). If handles do not appear, click on the image. To remove handles, click outside of image.
☞ Use Print Preview to see if your image will print on the same page as your text. Close the Print Preview screen.
☞ If your image was on the same page as your text, save the document. Otherwise, resize the image and preview it again. When you get it the way you want it, save it.
☞ Print the "Win3-Maxims" document.
☞ Close WordPad. Close Paint.

# EXERCISE 1: CROSSWORD

Use the clues below to complete the crossword puzzle.

## ACROSS

1. Another name for the floppy drive. This is the drive you should use to save all your documents you create on a computer that you don't own.
2. An acronym for File Allocation Table.
3. Another name for the hard drive.
6. If I press the ___ key, the character to the right of the insertion point will disappear.
7. To ensure that my document is permanently stored, I will ___ it to my diskette.
8. In order to indent a line of text at the beginning of a paragraph, I press the ___ key.
10. If I want to modify a document that I previously created , the first thing I would need to do is place it in memory. I can do this by clicking File, ___.
13. Another word for "Launch" or "Start".
14. If I say "boot__" a computer, I mean "turn it on".
15. In WordPad, the "I" on the toolbar button stands for ___.
19. Before you save a document, it only resides in RAM, which is often simply referred to as ___.
21. The art program that comes with Windows that lets me draw pictures is called ___.
23. The Start button is on the ___ bar.
24. If I click Edit, Cut (or if I click Edit, Copy), the selected text, image, or object goes to the ___ board.
25. In WordPad, the "U" on the toolbar button stands for ___.
28. An acronym for "Random Access Memory".
30. Another way to say "Start" a program is to say "___" a program. Doing so, places the program in memory.
31. At the left end of the Taskbar, you can find the ___ button, which is used to start a program.
32. If I am using more than one program at one time, I am doing something called multi ___.
35. The smartest cyberdog on the planet.

## DOWN

1. Paint, WordPad, and Calculator can be found by clicking Start, All Programs, ___.
2. An unavailable menu item is displayed in ___ characters (other words for this are ghosted or dimmed).
4. Another way to say "modify" text is to say "___" the text.
5. The entire area on the screen upon which documents, files, folders, and programs are displayed.
9. In WordPad, the "B" on the toolbar button stands for ___.
11. In WordPad, the B, I, and U buttons allow me to apply ___ to text in my documents, thereby improving the appearance and readability of my documents.
12. The shape and size of the characters.
16. Before I can change fonts or alignment, move or copy text, or apply enhancements, I first ___ the text to be modified.
17. As I type a document and approach the end of each line, I don't need to press the Enter key, because words will automatically ___ (excess text moves to the next line).
18. To obtain a hard copy of my document, I click File, ___.
20. To ___ text, I first must select the text and click Edit, Cut.
22. The way the characters line up at the margins.
25. Folks who use computers are sometimes called ___.
26. If I press the ___ key, the character to the left of the insertion point will disappear.
27. To type an uppercase character, I would hold down the ___ key then I would press the keyboard key for the character.
29. The space along the edge of the paper where text does not appear is the ___.
33. An abbreviation for International Business Machines.
34. Does the Close button on the title bar have a "C" on it?

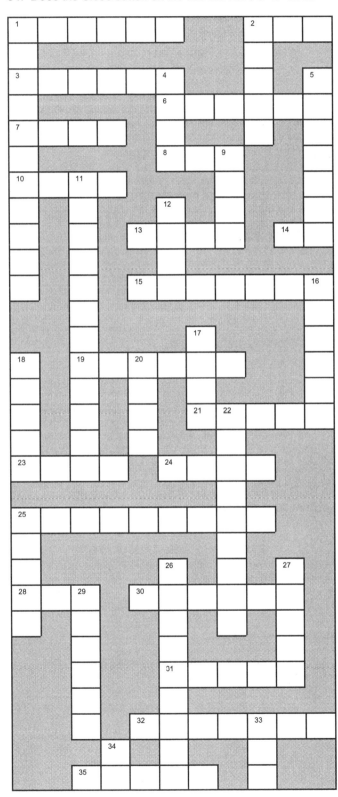

## EXERCISE 2: TRUE-FALSE

For each of the following eight statements, place a T or an F on the line to indicate if the statement is True or False.

1. ___The "B" toolbar button is used to display text in bold.
2. ___Alignment refers to which edge of the text is straight.
3. ___"Start," "load," and "launch" all mean the same thing.
4. ___The "I" toolbar button is used to indent a line.
5. ___The Close button on the title bar has a "C" on it.
6. ___Print Preview shows me how a printed page will look.
7. ___Windows comes with an art program called Paint.
8. ___The "U" toolbar button is used to Undo a prior action.

## EXERCISE 3: IDENTIFY TERMS

Below are eight definitions. Below the definitions are eight lines. In each line, write the word that matches the definition.

1. The key to press to indent a paragraph.
2. To place a copy of a document in a permanent place.
3. Working with more than one program simultaneously.
4. The size and shape of the characters in a document.
5. The key that removes text to the left of the insertion point.
6. The X button at the top right corner of a window.
7. The horizontal bar at the bottom of the screen.
8. The key to press to end one paragraph and start another.

1. _____     5. _____
2. _____     6. _____
3. _____     7. _____
4. _____     8. _____

## EXERCISE 4: USE WORDPAD

☞ Start WordPad.
☞ Look at the list of endorsements found on the back cover of Dozer's Quintessential Guide To Computer Literacy. Type E. A. Poe's endorsement. Do not be concerned if each line in your document wraps in a different place. Also, don't be concerned if the right edge is not as straight as the one shown on the back cover. Just type the text.
☞ Below the statement, insert two blank lines and then type your name.
☞ Save the file to your diskette (name it Win3-Poe).
☞ Print one copy of the document.
☞ Close WordPad.

## EXERCISE 5: USE CALCULATOR

☞ Start the Windows Calculator.
☞ What is 345 divided by 5? _____
☞ What is 679 times 524? _____
☞ What is the sum of 258, 745, 856, and 654? _____
☞ What is 568,754 minus 429,879? _____
☞ Close the Calculator.

## EXERCISE 6: USE PAINT

☞ Start Paint.
☞ Draw a small picture of a birthday cake.
☞ Put four candles on the cake, one blue, one green, one red, and one yellow.
☞ Use the pencil tool to write your name below the cake.
☞ Save the drawing to your diskette using the filename of Win3-Cake (save it as a 256 Color Bitmap).
☞ Print one copy of the drawing.
☞ Close Paint.

## EXERCISE 7: USE ACCESSORIES

☞ To start this exercise with an empty disk, format your disk (Forgot how to format a diskette? See page B-8).
☞ Start WordPad. If necessary, maximize the window.
☞ Start Paint. If necessary, maximize the window.
☞ Start Calculator. Can you maximize this window? _____.
☞ Switch to WordPad. Type the following document*. Don't press the Enter key at the end of each line. Let the words wrap automatically. They will wrap in a different place than they do below. Don't be concerned. Just type the text.

> There is no psychiatrist in the world like a puppy licking your face. Don't accept your dog's admiration as conclusive evidence that you are wonderful. A dog is the only thing that loves you more than he loves himself. I care not for a man's religion whose dog and cat are not the better for it. The average dog is a nicer person than the average person.

☞ Save the document to your disk (call it Win3-Dog Quotes).
☞ Beneath the paragraph, insert a couple of blank lines. Then, type Dozer's Favorite Quotes.
☞ Beneath "Dozer's Favorite Quotes" insert a couple of blank lines. Then, type your name.
☞ Move "Dozer's Favorite Quotes" so it appears as the title on a line above the paragraph. Then center it on that line.
☞ Enhance the title by making it bold and underlined.
☞ Change the font of the title to Arial, size 18.
☞ Dozer thinks he's an artist. In fact, he used the Paint program to draw a picture of himself using a computer. He gave me permission to reproduce his artwork below. Use Paint to draw your own picture of Dozer using a computer.

☞ When you're proud of your artwork, save the drawing to your diskette (name it Win3-Cyberdog and save it as a 256 Color Bitmap).
☞ Copy the picture to the clipboard (remember, use the Select tool from the toolbox).
☞ Switch to WordPad.
☞ Paste the picture below your name in the document.
☞ Resize the image so that it is about the size of a Big Mac.
☞ Click outside of the image to remove the sizing handles.
☞ Save the modified document (it may take a minute).
☞ Switch to Calculator.
☞ Since Dozer takes six naps every day, he wants to know how many naps he takes in a year. So, multiply 6 times 365 to discover how many naps he takes each year. Record the answer here: _____.
☞ Switch to WordPad.
☞ Below your name, type Dozer takes XXX naps each year and he's proud of it (type the answer where the Xs are).
☞ Save the modified WordPad document.
☞ Print the WordPad document. Close all open windows.

* This document contains quotes from Ben Williams, Ann Landers, Josh Billings, Abraham Lincoln, and Andrew Rooney.

## SELECT FILES AND FOLDERS

Before you can move, copy, delete, or rename a file or a folder, you must select the file or folder. Since files are selected in the same way as folders are selected, the practice below will only have you select files. Distinguishing files from folders is difficult for some folks. To avoid confusion, just remember that a folder looks like a folder. A file doesn't. So, if it looks like a folder, it's a folder. Nearly everything else is a file. By the way, both files and folders are sometimes called objects.

To practice selecting objects, do the following:
☞ Open My Computer.
☞ Open the C drive. In the window, there are many objects; some are folders (they look like folders) and some are files (they do not look like folders). You may need to scroll to see the files. If the C drive contains no files, open a folder or two until you find a folder that contains at least four files.
☞ Click View, Details to have each object appear in a line.
☞ To select a single object, click it (click any object).
☞ Notice that the selected object is highlighted.
☞ To deselect the object, click an empty spot on the screen.
☞ Notice the object is no longer highlighted (it is deselected).
☞ Click the 1st file in the list. Notice that the file is highlighted.
☞ Click the 4th file in the list. Notice that the 1st file is deselected and the 4th file is selected. You can select only one file at a time by clicking.
☞ To deselect the file, click an empty spot on the screen.
☞ Notice that the file is no longer selected.
☞ To select adjacent files, click a file, then Shift + Click the last file in the group (to practice, click the 1st file, then Shift + Click the 4th file). Note that "Shift + Click" means to hold down the Shift key while you click. Notice that once done, four selected files are highlighted.
☞ To deselect the files, click an empty spot on the screen.
☞ Notice that the files are no longer selected.
☞ To select non-adjacent files, click one file, then Ctrl + Click each additional file (to practice, click the 1st file and then Ctrl + Click the 4th file). Note that "Ctrl+ Click" means to hold down the Ctrl key while you click.
☞ Notice that both of the selected files are highlighted.
☞ To deselect the files, click an empty spot on the screen.
☞ Notice that the files are deselected.
☞ Close all windows.

## CREATE FOLDERS

You organize and store paper documents in paper folders; on a computer you organize and store files in folders on the hard drive or on disks. As you follow the steps below, notice that the steps for creating folders is consistent (i.e., open the window in which you want the new folder to reside, click File, New, Folder, type a name, and press the Enter key). In Exercise 7 (page B-14), you created a document. You saved it to your diskette under the filename "Win3-Dog Quotes". You will need that file to complete this project. If you don't have that file, redo that exercise. Then do the following.

To practice creating folders, do the following:
☞ Open My Computer.
☞ Insert the diskette with the "Win3-Dog Quotes" file on it.
☞ Open the A: Drive window (double-click its icon).
☞ In the A: drive window, click File, New, Folder (a new folder

will appear). Note: if there are two "new" items on the File menu, point to the one with the arrow pointing to the right.
☞ Type the name of the folder (name it May).
☞ Press Enter.
☞ To deselect the folder, click an empty spot in the window.
☞ To create another folder in the A: drive window, click File, New, Folder (a new folder will appear).
☞ Type a name for the folder (name it June).
☞ Press Enter.
☞ To deselect the folder, click an empty spot in the window.
☞ To create a folder in the May folder, open the May folder.
☞ Notice that the folder opens as a window and that its name, "May" is in the title bar.
☞ In the "May" window, click File, New, Folder.
☞ Type a name for the folder (name it Dozer).
☞ Press Enter.
☞ To deselect the folder, click an empty spot in the window.
☞ Create another folder in the May folder (name it Skooter).
☞ Close all windows.

## COPY FILES AND FOLDERS

From time to time, you will want to copy a file or a folder. When you copy a file or a folder, the source file or folder will remain where it was and an identical copy of the file or folder will be placed where you specify. The process for copying is the same whether you are copying a file or a folder, except that when you copy a folder, you copy it and its contents. By the way, a copy of a file is sometimes referred to as a backup, which will be useful if the original version of the file is lost or damaged.

To practice copying a file, do the following:
☞ Open My Computer and the A drive window.
☞ Select the "Win3-Dog Quotes" file (click it).
☞ Click Edit, Copy (a copy of the file goes to the clipboard).
☞ Open the C drive.
☞ Open the My Files folder (If you don't have a My Files folder, create one on the C drive and then open it).
☞ Click Edit, Paste (the file will be copied to the folder).
☞ To deselect the file, click an empty spot on the screen.
☞ Close all windows.

To practice copying a folder, do the following:
☞ Open My Computer and then open the A drive window.
☞ Open the May folder.
☞ Since you want to copy the Skooter and the Dozer folders so that they appear in both the May and the June folders, click the Skooter folder, then Ctrl + Click the Dozer folder (both folders will be highlighted).
☞ Click Edit, Copy (a copy of the folders goes to the clipboard).
☞ Open the June folder.
☞ Click Edit, Paste. A copy of the Skooter and Dozer folders are each pasted to the June folder. The Dozer and the Skooter folders that once were only in the May folder are now in both the May and the June folders.
☞ Close all windows.

## MOVE FILES AND FOLDERS

From time to time, you will want to move a file or a folder from the hard drive to the floppy drive or vice versa. After you move a file or a folder, the source file or folder will not be where it was, but will only be where you moved it. The process is the same whether you are moving a file or a folder, except that when moving a folder, you move it and its contents.

To practice moving a file, do the following:
- ☞ Open My Computer and then open the A drive window.
- ☞ Select the "Win3-Dog Quotes" file (click it).
- ☞ Click Edit, Cut.
- ☞ Open the May folder, then open the Dozer folder.
- ☞ In the Dozer folder, click Edit, Paste.
- ☞ To deselect the file, click in an empty space in the window.
- ☞ Return to the A drive window. Notice that the "Win3-Dog Quotes" file is gone. It's in the A:/May/Dozer folder where you just moved it.
- ☞ Close all windows.

## RENAME FILES AND FOLDERS
From time to time, you will want to rename a file or a folder. The process is the same whether it is a file or a folder.

To practice renaming files and folders, do the following:
- ☞ Open My Computer and the A drive window.
- ☞ Find the "Win3-Dog Quotes" file (it is in A:\May\Dozer).
- ☞ Select the file (click it).
- ☞ Click File, Rename. Notice that the file name is highlighted.
- ☞ Type the new name (name it Dozer's World). Press Enter.
- ☞ To deselect the file, click in an empty space in the window.
- ☞ Now, go and rename the June folder (name it Summer).
- ☞ Rename the May folder (name it Winter).
- ☞ Now, go to the "Win3-Dog Quotes" file that is in C:\My Files and rename it using your full name as its new file name.
- ☞ Close all windows.

## DELETE FILES AND FOLDERS
When a file or a folder is no longer needed, you may want to delete it. Files or folders deleted from the C drive are placed in the Recycle Bin where they can be restored (retrieved). You will learn all about this later. Files deleted from a diskette are not placed in the Recycle Bin. The process is the same whether you are deleting a file or a folder, except that when you delete a folder, you delete it and any files or folders in it.

To practice deleting files and folders, do the following:
- ☞ Find the "Dozer's World" file (it is in A:\Winter\Dozer).
- ☞ Select it and click File, Delete. If more than one "delete" item appears, click the bold one. The faded one won't work.
- ☞ If asked to confirm your intention to delete the file, click Yes.
- ☞ Find the "Winter" Folder and delete it.
- ☞ If asked to confirm your intention to delete the folder and all its contents, click Yes.
- ☞ Delete the Summer folder from your diskette.
- ☞ Delete the file that has your name as its filename (you can find it in C:\My Files).
- ☞ Close all windows.

## USE THE RECYCLE BIN
Files and folders deleted from the C drive are placed in the Recycle Bin, which looks like a trash can. The files and folders reside in the Recycle Bin until you restore the files and folders, empty the bin, or until the bin gets full. If your Recycle Bin is full and you attempt to delete a file or a folder, the objects that have been in the recycle bin for the longest period of time will be discarded to make room for newly-deleted objects. When the bin has something in it, paper can be seen in the bin; if empty, it looks like an empty trash can.

To restore a deleted file or folder, do the following:
- ☞ Look at the Recycle Bin icon on the desktop. The papers in it indicate that discarded objects are in the bin (the file you previously deleted from the C drive and any other objects recently deleted from the C drive are in the recycle bin).
- ☞ Double-click the Recycle Bin icon on the Desktop.
- ☞ Notice that the Recycle Bin window opens and any objects (files and/or folders) residing therein are displayed. If needed, maximize the window.
- ☞ Select the file you want restored (the file with your name).
- ☞ Click File, Restore. The file is removed from the Recycle Bin and returned to where it was before you deleted it. In this case, it will be returned to C:\My Files.
- ☞ Use My Computer to look in the C:\My Files folder to confirm that the file has been restored there.
- ☞ Now, once again, delete the file from C:\My Files. After you delete it, notice that it is no longer in the My Files window.
- ☞ Close all windows

To practice emptying the Recycle Bin, do the following:
- ☞ Double-click the Recycle Bin icon on the Desktop.
- ☞ Notice that the file with your name is in the Recycle Bin (other objects may also be there, as well).
- ☞ Click File, Empty Recycle Bin.
- ☞ If asked to confirm your intention to delete the items in the Recycle Bin, click Yes. Notice that the objects disappear.
- ☞ Close all windows. Note: there are no papers visible in the Recycle Bin, which indicates that the bin is empty.

## FIND A FILE
From time to time, you will forget where you stored a file, or you will forget its name, thereby making it difficult to locate. The Windows Search feature will help you find it.

To practice doing a simple search, do the following:
- ☞ Click Start, Search.
- ☞ In the What Do You Want To Search For section, click All Files and Folders
- ☞ In the All Or Part Of The File Name box enter what you know about the filename (in this case, type cookies).
- ☞ If you know some of the text in the file, enter it in the A Word Or Phrase In The File box (for now, leave this box empty).
- ☞ In the Look In drop-down list, select the drive where you want the program to look for your file (select the C drive).
- ☞ Click the Search button.
- ☞ Notice that a list of objects (files and/or folders) appear as Windows uses your clues to locate files and folders. Be patient, it may take a few minutes to complete the search.
- ☞ Double-click one of the "cookies" files or folders to open it.
- ☞ Close all windows.

To see how to do an advanced search, do the following:
- ☞ Click Start, Search, All Files and Folders.
- ☞ If you know when the file was last modified, click the When Was It Modified link.
- ☞ If you know the approximate size of the lost file, click the What Size Is It link.
- ☞ If you know the type of program used to create the lost file, click the More Advanced Options link.
- ☞ For now, click each of these links. Look over the options.
- ☞ Close all windows.

# EXERCISES

## EXERCISE 1: CROSSWORD
Use the clues below to complete the crossword puzzle.

### ACROSS
2. To return a file from the recycle bin to its original location.
5. To send text to the ___board, click Edit, Cut.
8. To organize your files, you would create ___ and then you would place related files inside them.
9. To move a folder, select it, then click Edit, ___.
10. To take a file from one place and put it elsewhere.
12. A saved document.
14. To modify a document.
15. To place a duplicate of a file or a folder elsewhere.
16. To move, copy, delete, or rename an object, I first need to click the object to __ it. The object then changes color.
17. In My Computer, to see the size of each file and the last date modified, click the ___ command on the View menu.

### DOWN
1. The best way to open a folder would be to ___ click it.
2. Files and folders deleted from the C drive are put here.
3. To select a group of adjacent files or folders, click the first one in the list and then ___ + click the last one in the list.
4. This button is on the title bar and it has an X on it.
6. To get a hard copy of my document, I ___ it.
7. To change the name of a file or folder, I would select the object and choose the ___ command from the File menu.
11. The ___ Recycle Bin command is used to remove files and/or folders from the recycle bin.
13. If I want to get rid of a file, I would click File, ___.
15. To select a group of non-adjacent files or folders, click the first one and then ___ + click each of the others.

## EXERCISE 2: TRUE-FALSE
For each of the following eight statements, place a T or an F on the line to indicate if the statement is True or False.

1. ___A folder is a place where I can put files.
2. ___To select a single folder, I would double-click it.
3. ___When I copy a file, it will exist in more than one place.
4. ___A folder deleted from the C drive is put in the Recycle Bin.
5. ___Moving a folder is done the same way as moving a file.
6. ___A file is deleted the same way a folder is deleted.
7. ___To select four adjacent files, I would click each file.
8. ___To deselect a file, I would click in any empty space.

## EXERCISE 3: MATCHING
Below is a list of three menu bar items and one taskbar button, each of which is used to access a list of commands that can help me do lots of neat stuff (such as the tasks listed below). For each task, identify the item that you would click to access the commands needed to perform the desired task. Place the letter on the line preceding each description.

| A. EDIT | B. FILE | C. START | D. VIEW |
| --- | --- | --- | --- |

1. ___ Change the way the icons look in a window.
2. ___ Delete a file.
3. ___ Copy a folder to the clipboard.
4. ___ Move a folder.
5. ___ Rename a file.
6. ___ Restore files from the Recycle Bin.
7. ___ Find a lost file.
8. ___ Copy a file to the clipboard.
9. ___ Create a folder.
10. ___ Rename a folder.
11. ___ Empty the Recycle Bin.
12. ___ Delete a folder.
13. ___ Move a file.
14. ___ Find a lost folder.
15. ___ Paste the contents of the clipboard.

## EXERCISE 4: TRUE-FALSE
For each of the following eight statements, place a T or an F on the line to indicate if the statement is True or False.

1. ___To deselect a file, I would click it.
2. ___Copying a file is done the same way as copying a folder.
3. ___To open a folder, I would double-click it.
4. ___I rename a file the same way as I rename a folder.
5. ___A folder deleted from the A drive is put in the Recycle Bin.
6. ___When I open a folder, its contents display in a window.
7. ___To select 3 non-adjacent folders, I would click each folder.
8. ___A file is selected the same way a folder is selected.

## EXERCISE 5: TRUE-FALSE
For each of the following eight statements, place a T or an F on the line to indicate if the statement is True or False.

1. ___To select a single file, I would double-click it.
2. ___If I click two files, two files will be selected.
3. ___A file is a place where I can put folders.
4. ___When I move a file, it will exist in more than one place.
5. ___A folder is represented by an icon of a red file folder.
6. ___A selected file is highlighted.
7. ___The Recycle Bin icon has papers in it if it contains stuff.
8. ___A file deleted from the C drive is put in the Recycle Bin.

## EXERCISE 6: IDENTIFY TERMS

Below are six definitions. Below the definitions are six lines. In each line, write the word that matches the definition.

1. It's yellow and it's where I keep my files.
2. To remove an unwanted file or folder.
3. A saved document or drawing.
4. I do this to change the name of a file or folder.
5. This is what I do to select a file or a folder.
6. Files and folders deleted from the C drive are kept here.

1. _____        4. _____
2. _____        5. _____
3. _____        6. _____

## EXERCISE 7: TRUE-FALSE

For each of the following six statements, place a T or an F on the line to indicate if the statement is True or False.

1. ___To select three non-adjacent files, I would click each file.
2. ___To deselect a folder, I would click in any empty space.
3. ___A file deleted from the A drive is put in the Recycle Bin.
4. ___To select three adjacent folders, I would click each folder.
5. ___To select a single file, I would click it.
6. ___A deselected folder is highlighted.

## EXERCISE 8: EMPTY THE RECYCLE BIN

☞ Look at the Recycle Bin icon located on the desktop.
☞ Does it have pieces of paper in it? _____
☞ If it does, what does that mean? _____
☞ If it has pieces of paper in it, let's remove them. If it doesn't have pieces of paper in it, skip to Exercise 9 below.
☞ Open the Recycle Bin. Click File, Empty Recycle Bin.
☞ If asked to confirm your intention to empty it, click Yes.
☞ Notice that the Recycle Bin icon no longer has paper in it.

## EXERCISE 9: SELECT FILES

In this exercise, you will be practicing selecting various files (objects). By doing so, you will learn how to select one or more objects simultaneously. To select a single file, click it. If you want to select multiple files simultaneously, you will need to use a combination keystroke. This exercise will give you the steps.

☞ Open the My Computer window.
☞ Open the C drive window.
☞ Scroll down until you can see lots of files (you may need to open another folder to find some files).
☞ To see the size of each file, click View, Details.
☞ Click one file. What color does the file icon become? ___
☞ Click anywhere in a blank space in the window.
☞ How does the file icon change? _____
☞ Click any file. Now, click a second file.
☞ How many files are selected? _____
☞ Click anywhere in a blank space in the window.
☞ How many files are selected? _____
☞ Click a file and then Shift + Click the third file down from it.
☞ How many files are selected? _____
☞ Click anywhere in a blank space in the window.
☞ How many files are selected? _____
☞ Click a file and then Ctrl + Click the third file down from it.
☞ How many files are selected? _____
☞ Click anywhere in a blank space in the window.
☞ How many files are selected? _____
☞ Close all open windows.

## EXERCISE 10: FIND A FILE

☞ Search the C drive for objects named "font". How many were found? _____. Hint: the number of objects found is provided in the task pane (left side of the screen).
☞ Remove "font" from the Search box and then search the C drive for all files that were modified within the last week. How many were found? _____

## EXERCISE 11: MANAGE FILES

☞ To start this exercise with an empty disk, format your disk.
☞ Create a folder on your diskette (name it Project 4).
☞ Copy two small files from the C drive.
☞ Paste the files in the "Project 4" folder on your diskette.
☞ Rename one of the files (name it your first name).
☞ If asked to confirm your intention to rename it, click Yes.
☞ Rename the other file (name it your last name).
☞ If asked to confirm your intention to rename it, click Yes.
☞ Copy the first name file to the My Files folder in the C drive (if your C drive does not have a My Files folder, create one).
☞ Start WordPad and type the following paragraph:

> Nothing is so simple that it cannot be misunderstood. If you are sure you understand everything that is going on, you are hopelessly confused. Get to know what you don't know as fast as you can. Chance favors the prepared mind. Learning is discovering that something is possible. Some people will never learn anything, because they understand everything too soon. Practice is the best of all instructors.

☞ Below the last line, type your name.
☞ Above the paragraph, type the title LEARNING.
☞ Right align your name.
☞ Center the title.
☞ Make the title appear bold and underlined.
☞ Change the font of the title to be Arial 20.
☞ Save the document in the Project 4 folder on your diskette. To save it to that folder, click File, Save. Then, in the Save As dialog box, select the floppy drive from the Save In drop down list. The folder in the drive will appear below the Save In drop down list. Double click the Project 4 folder so that its name appears in the Save In box. In the File Name box, name it WinP4-Learning Quotes and click the Save button.
☞ Print one copy of your document.
☞ Close WordPad.
☞ Delete the last name file from your diskette.
☞ Delete the first name file from C:\My Files.
☞ Look at the Recycle Bin. It should have pieces of paper in it which indicates that at least one object resides there.
☞ Open the Recycle Bin.
☞ Which of your deleted files is there? _____
☞ Why aren't both of them there? _____
☞ Restore the first name file from the Recycle Bin.
☞ Open the My Files folder in the C drive.
☞ Has your first name file been restored? _____
☞ Delete the first name file from C:\My Files.
☞ Look at the Recycle Bin. It should have pieces of paper in it which indicates that at least one object resides there.
☞ Open the Recycle Bin. Click File, Empty Recycle Bin.
☞ If asked to confirm your intention to empty it, click Yes.
☞ Open the C:\My Files folder. Is your file there? _____
☞ Open the Recycle Bin. Is your file there? _____
☞ Delete the Project 4 folder from your diskette. Notice that since this folder contains a file, you will be asked to confirm your intention to delete the folder and its contents. Click yes.
☞ Close all open windows.

## CHANGE THE SCREEN SAVER

A screen saver is a program that automatically displays random patterns on the screen after a period of inactivity (i.e., the keyboard and mouse have been idle). Screen savers were originally developed to protect the screen from burn-in damage caused by prolonged use of a static screen display. Nowadays, this is less of a problem and screen savers are mostly used for entertainment value.

To practice changing the screen saver, do the following:
- ☞ Right-click on an empty space on the desktop.
- ☞ On the shortcut menu, click Properties.
- ☞ When the dialog box appears, click the Screen Saver tab.
- ☞ Click the Screen Saver drop-down list arrow.
- ☞ Select a screen saver (select 3D Text).
- ☞ Click the Settings button.
- ☞ In the Text area, click the Custom Text radio button.
- ☞ In the text box, type your name.
- ☞ Select a motion, surface style, resolution, size, and rotation speed.
- ☞ Click OK.
- ☞ To preview the screen saver, click the Preview button.
- ☞ To return to the dialog box, move the mouse.
- ☞ Enter the wait time (1 minute) in the Wait box. Click OK.
- ☞ Don't touch the keyboard or mouse until the screen saver comes on. Since you set it for 1 minute, that's how long you will need to wait. While you wait, think positive thoughts. If you can't think of a positive thought, say "Computers are my friends" over and over to yourself while you wait.
- ☞ Change the screen saver to Mystify (if your machine doesn't have Mystify, select any screen saver you want).
- ☞ Change Wait time to 3.
- ☞ Click OK.
- ☞ Close all windows.

## CHANGE THE BACKGROUND (WALLPAPER)

The background (wallpaper) to the desktop can be a picture or pattern supplied with the computer, or a background found on the Internet, or a picture of your own (e.g., one you took with a camera and then scanned, or one you took with a digital camera, or one you drew using a program like Paint). Your picture can be centered on the desktop, or tiled, or stretched to cover the entire desktop. The purpose is aesthetic (the way the desktop looks) rather than functional (the way it works).

To practice changing the background, do the following:
- ☞ Right-click an empty space on the desktop.
- ☞ On the shortcut menu, click Properties.
- ☞ In the Display Properties dialog box, click the Desktop tab.
- ☞ In the Background list, select a background (select any).
- ☞ Click the Position list box arrow.
- ☞ From the list, select either Center, Tile, or Stretch.
- ☞ Take a look at the sample.
- ☞ Click the Position list box arrow and select a different option.
- ☞ Take a look at the sample.
- ☞ When you find a background and position you like, click OK.
- ☞ Look at the desktop. Sometimes, a specific background might look good in the preview screen, but not so good on the desktop, because it may obscure your desktop icons. If you don't like the background, change it.
- ☞ Close all windows.

## CHANGE THE COLOR SCHEMES (APPEARANCE)

By default, buttons and windows are displayed in a style called Windows XP, a color scheme called Default Blue, and a font size of Normal. You can change the style, the color scheme, and/or the font size of the windows in general or of specific parts of the windows to suit your idea of aesthetics.

To practice changing the color schemes, do the following:
- ☞ Right-click on an empty space on the desktop.
- ☞ On the shortcut menu, click Properties.
- ☞ Click the Appearance tab.
- ☞ Click the Windows and Buttons drop-down list arrow.
- ☞ From the list, select Windows Classic Style (the style used in prior versions of windows) and look at the preview screen.
- ☞ Click the Color Scheme drop-down list arrow.
- ☞ Select a color scheme and take a look at the preview screen.
- ☞ Select several color schemes and take a look at each. When you find a scheme that you like, click OK.
- ☞ Open the Start menu and take a look at how it appears.
- ☞ Open the My Computer window and see what it looks like.
- ☞ Right click on the desktop, click Properties, and change the style back to Windows XP, and experiment with a few color schemes. When you find a combination you like, click OK.
- ☞ Open the Start menu and the My Computer window and see how they look with the new style and color scheme.
- ☞ Return the desktop appearance to Windows XP style with a Default Blue color scheme. Close all windows.

## CHANGE THE MOUSE PROPERTIES

If you are having trouble double-clicking the mouse, you may want to slow down the speed of the mouse. Or, if you are left-handed, you may want to configure the mouse so that the operation of the mouse buttons is reversed.

To practice changing the mouse properties, do the following:
- ☞ Click Start, Control Panel, Printers And Other Hardware, Mouse.
- ☞ In the Mouse Properties dialog box, click the Buttons tab.
- ☞ In the Double-Click Speed area, slide the control to the right to increase the speed. Then, in the Test area, try to double-click the folder. If you can't get the folder to open, reduce the speed. Once you open the folder, double-click it to close it. Be sure to slow it down so that you can make it work.
- ☞ If you wanted to switch the buttons, you would click the box in the Button Configuration area. If you do, the two mouse buttons will switch functions (i.e., the left button will behave like the right; and the right will behave like the left). You might do this if you are a left-handed user. Otherwise don't click that box.
- ☞ Click OK. Close all windows.

## RESIZE THE TASKBAR

When many buttons are on the taskbar, the buttons become smaller. If you enlarge the taskbar, the buttons will get bigger, thus making them easier to read.

To practice resizing the taskbar, do the following:
- ☞ Point the mouse at the top border of the taskbar until the pointer looks like a two-pointed arrow (if the pointer does not look like a two-pointed arrow, your taskbar is locked. To unlock it, right click on it, then click Lock The Taskbar).

☞ Hold down the left mouse button and drag the mouse up or down. When it is the desired size, release the button.
☞ Repeat these steps to have the taskbar disappear.
☞ Repeat these steps to return the taskbar to its original size.

## MOVE THE TASKBAR

By default, the taskbar appears at the bottom of the desktop. You can move the taskbar so that it takes up space on the side of the screen instead of at the bottom.

To practice moving the taskbar, do the following:
☞ Point the mouse to any empty space on the taskbar.
☞ Hold down the left mouse button and drag the mouse to the right side of the desktop. Release the button. The taskbar should now be on the right side of the screen. If not, your taskbar is locked. To unlock it, right click on it, then click Lock The Taskbar. Then drag and drop the taskbar to the right side of the screen.
☞ Point the mouse to any empty space on the taskbar.
☞ Hold down the left mouse button and drag the mouse to the top of the desktop. Release the button.
☞ Point the mouse to any empty space on the taskbar.
☞ Hold down the left mouse button and drag the mouse back to its default location (bottom of desktop).

## HIDE THE TASKBAR

In addition to moving the taskbar, you can also free up desktop space by hiding it. It will still be accessible, but it will not take up screen space until you need to use it.

To practice hiding the taskbar, do the following:
☞ Right click in any empty space on the taskbar.
☞ From the shortcut menu, click Properties.
☞ In the dialog box, click Auto Hide The Taskbar to select it.
☞ Click OK. Notice that the taskbar is hidden.
☞ To access the hidden taskbar, move the mouse pointer to the bottom of the screen. The taskbar will appear. To make it disappear again, click in the screen. Each time you need the taskbar, merely move the mouse pointer to the bottom of the screen to have it temporarily pop up.

To return the taskbar to be visible at all times, do the following:
☞ Right click in any empty space on the taskbar.
☞ From the shortcut menu, click Properties.
☞ In the dialog box, click Auto Hide The Taskbar to deselect it.
☞ Click OK. Notice that the taskbar is visible.

## PRINT A SCREEN SHOT (PRINT SCREEN)

Normally, when you print a document, you print only the information in the document. The printer does not print the title bar, menu bar, scroll bars, etc. On rare occasions (e.g., when taking a test and your instructor needs you to do this), you will want to be able to capture everything on the screen and print it out. This is sometimes called a screen capture or a screen shot. It's like taking a picture of everything on the screen.

To practice taking and printing a screen shot, do the following:
☞ Open the desired windows (in this case, open My Computer and open the C drive). Note: if the My Computer window disappears when you open the C drive window, click Tools, Folder Options, and click the General tab. In the Browse Folders area of the dialog box, click Open Each Folder In Its Own Window. Then click OK. Redo the first step of this exercise and the windows will stay open.

☞ Move and resize these windows on the desktop so that they are not on top of each other.
☞ Press the Print Screen key (the key to the right of the F12 key). This puts an image of the screen in the clipboard.
☞ Open WordPad. If necessary, maximize the window.
☞ Click Edit, Paste (this inserts the clipboard contents).
☞ To preview the document, click File, Print Preview. Notice that the entire image may not appear on one page. If it does not, you will need to resize it. First, close the Print Preview screen by clicking the Close button on the Print Preview feature bar (not the Close button on the title bar).
☞ To resize the image, put the mouse pointer on one of the sizing handles (there's one on each corner and each border of the image). When the pointer looks like a two-pointed arrow, hold down the left mouse button and drag to reduce the size of the image. Release the mouse button.
☞ Now, use Print Preview to see if the image fits on one page. If not, repeat the last step until it will.
☞ Print the document (click File, Print, Print).
☞ Close WordPad.
☞ Close all other open windows.

## CREATE DESKTOP SHORTCUTS

Starting a program and loading a file using a desktop shortcut is faster than starting the program from the Start menu and then loading the file. You can create desktop shortcuts to your programs and files located on your hard drive, CD-ROM, or a floppy. Below, we will practice creating them using a diskette.

To practice creating desktop shortcuts, do the following:
☞ First, create a file using Notepad (to start Notepad, click Start, All Programs, Accessories, Notepad). By the way, Notepad is an extremely simplistic text editing program that is part of the Windows program.
☞ In the document window, just type your name.
☞ Save it to a disk (use Me as the filename).
☞ Close Notepad.
☞ Open My Computer and the A: Floppy Drive.
☞ If necessary, resize the window so you can see part of the desktop behind the window.
☞ Select the Me file icon.
☞ Click File, Create Shortcut (a "Shortcut to Me icon" appears).
☞ Drag the "Shortcut to Me" icon to a space on the desktop.
☞ Close all windows. Notice the Shortcut to Me icon on the desktop. Drag it to another location on the desktop.
☞ Click anywhere on the desktop to deselect the shortcut.
☞ Double-click the desktop shortcut (the Notepad program is launched and the "Me" file is loaded).
☞ Close Notepad.

## DELETE DESKTOP SHORTCUTS

When too many shortcuts clutter up the screen or when the shortcuts are no longer needed, you can delete them. When you delete a shortcut, you are not deleting the program or the file to which it refers. You are just deleting the shortcut icon.

To practice deleting desktop shortcuts, do the following:
☞ Right click on the Shortcut to Me desktop icon. Click Delete.
☞ If asked to confirm your intention to delete the item, click Yes. Notice that the desktop icon is gone.
☞ Open My Computer and the A: Floppy drive.
☞ Notice that the "Me" and the "Shortcut to Me" files still exist. You merely deleted the shortcut that was on the desktop.
☞ Close all windows.

## EXERCISE 1: CROSSWORD

Use the clues below to complete the crossword puzzle.

### ACROSS

1. A background is a picture behind the desktop icons. Another name for this background is ___.
4. To hide (or unhide) the taskbar, right click on an empty space on the taskbar and click Properties. Then, in the dialog box, select Auto____ The Taskbar.
6. A desktop graphical image used to execute a command.
7. If I click on a file and Ctrl + click on another file, how many files will be selected?
9. To change the color of screen elements, click the ___ tab in the Display Properties dialog box.
10. File, Edit, and View are words typically found on a ___ bar.
12. To access a shortcut menu, I would ___ click.
13. The size and shape of text is its ___.
14. When you pick a desktop background, you can choose to center it, tile it, or ___ it.
16. The entire area of the screen upon which documents, files, folders, and programs are displayed.
20. If I put the mouse pointer on the taskbar, hold down the left button, and drag the mouse, an unlocked taskbar will ___.
22. The ___ typically appears at the bottom of the desktop. It has the Start button at the left end, the time at the right end, and a button for every open window.
25. When you paste an image onto a WordPad document, the selected image will have a little box, called a ___ handle at each corner and border.
26. Is Dozer the smartest cyberdog on the planet?
27. If you click on one file and then click on another file, how many files will be selected?
30. If you logged on to a computer, you might want to ___ when you are done, instead of turning off the machine.
32. When you pick a desktop background, you can choose to center it, stretch it, or ___ it.
33. The most popular operating system in the world.

### DOWN

2. To capture everything on the screen and print it out, I would press the ___ key. I could then paste the image of the screen into a document and then print it out.
3. To change mouse settings, click Start, ___ Panel, Printers And Other Hardware, Mouse.
5. Capturing everything on the screen and printing it out as though I took a picture is called a screen capture or a ___.
8. The desktop ___ is a picture behind the desktop icons.
11. A copy of my files is called a back___.
15. Windows is an ___ system.
17. To have a permanent copy of my work, I ___ it to a disk.
18. To change the screen saver, background, or appearance, I would right click on the desktop and then click ___.
19. When you pick a desktop background, you can choose to tile it, stretch it, or ___ it.
21. If a dialog box has multiple pages, each page will be accessible by clicking a ___ at the top of the dialog box.
23. A ___ saver is a program that automatically displays random patterns on the screen if the mouse or the keyboard have been inactive for a specified period of time.
24. To see what a document will look like when printed, I can view it on-screen by clicking File, ___.
27. A printer in communication with a computer is ___.

28. The X at the top right corner of a window is the ___ button.
29. A printer not in communication with a computer is ___.
31. An acronym for Graphical User Interface.

## EXERCISE 2: IDENTIFY TERMS

Below are six definitions. Below the definitions are six lines. In each line, write the word that matches the definition.

1. The horizontal bar found at the bottom of the screen.
2. Software that produces random patterns on the screen.
3. A picture in the center of the desktop or tiled on it.
4. The default style used by Windows.
5. A printout of everything on the screen.
6. Press this key to send the screen's image to the clipboard.

1. _____     4. _____
2. _____     5. _____
3. _____     6. _____

## EXERCISE 3: TRUE-FALSE

For each of the following eight statements, place a T or an F on the line to indicate if the statement is True or False.

1. ___Wallpaper cannot be centered and it cannot be tiled.
2. ___You can change the screen saver wait time.
3. ___You can not add your own desktop shortcuts.
4. ___The double-clicking speed of the mouse can be changed.
5. ___To change the background, click Edit, Properties.
6. ___To move the taskbar, drag it to its new location.
7. ___A background and wallpaper are two different things.
8. ___Mouse buttons can be changed for a left handed user.

## EXERCISE 4: TRUE-FALSE

For each of the following six statements, place a T or an F on the line to indicate if the statement is True or False.

1. ___Wallpaper can be tiled, but not centered.
2. ___The Start button is found in the taskbar.
3. ___Wallpaper can be centered, but not tiled.
4. ___The screen saver wait time is always two minutes.
5. ___Wallpaper can be either centered, stretched, or tiled.
6. ___The time of day can be found on the taskbar.

## EXERCISE 5: FIND A WORD

The answers to the following statements can be found in the matrix below. The answers may be backwards, diagonal, vertical, and/or horizontal. Circle each word in the matrix.

1. A screen ___ is a picture of everything that's on the desktop.
2. A picture placed on the desktop.
3. A desktop ___ is an icon that will open a program and a file.
4. The device with two buttons on top and a ball on the bottom.
5. In the Display Properties dialog box, I would click the ___ tab to change the color scheme or style of windows.
6. A ___ saver is software that produces a random pattern on the screen if I leave the mouse and the keyboard idle.

| R | A | P | P | E | A | R | A | N | C | E |
|---|---|---|---|---|---|---|---|---|---|---|
| W | T | I | P | S | A | V | E | M | T | S |
| W | V | Y | C | B | H | E | L | H | I | U |
| B | A | C | K | G | R | O | U | N | D | O |
| A | E | S | O | C | T | I | T | U | H | M |
| U | A | R | S | H | O | R | T | C | U | T |

## EXERCISE 6: CUSTOMIZE THE DESKTOP

☞ Change the desktop to Windows Classic style and then change the color scheme to Brick. Do you like it? _____
☞ Change the color scheme to Teal. Do you like it? _____
☞ Look at several other color schemes until you find the one you like best. Then, choose the one you like best.
☞ Change the active title bar so that it is red instead of blue.
☞ Open the My Computer window.
☞ Do you like the color of the title bar? _____
☞ Change the color of the active title bar to another color.
☞ Change the background to be a picture you created in Paint (if you don't have a picture on your diskette, go to Paint, draw a picture, and save it to your diskette (use any name you like for the filename). Remember to save it as a 256 bit Bitmap. Then you will have a picture to use as background for the desktop).
☞ Change the background to None.
☞ Change the style to Windows XP
☞ Change the screen saver to a marquee consisting of your name with a wait time of 1 minute. Leave the mouse and keyboard alone until the screen saver comes on.
☞ Change the screen saver to None.
☞ Close all dialog boxes and windows.

## EXERCISE 7: PRINT A SCREEN SHOT

☞ Open the My Computer window.
☞ Resize the window to be about the size of a diskette.
☞ Move the window to the top right corner of the desktop.
☞ Open the Recycle Bin window. Note: if the My Computer window disappears when you open the Recycle Bin window, click Tools, Folder Options, and click the General tab. In the Browse Folders area of the dialog box, click Open Each Folder In Its Own Window, and click OK. Then go back to the first step of this exercise and repeat these steps.
☞ Resize the Recycle Bin window to be the size of a diskette.
☞ Move the Recycle Bin window to the top left corner of the desktop.
☞ Take a screen shot of the desktop.
☞ Paste it on to a WordPad document.
☞ Resize the image so it prints on one page.
☞ Type your name below the image.
☞ Print the document. Close all open windows.

## EXERCISE 8: RESIZE AND MOVE THE TASKBAR

☞ Resize the taskbar so it is twice its current height.
☞ Resize the taskbar so that it covers half the screen.
☞ Resize the taskbar so only its top edge appears at the bottom of the screen.
☞ Return the taskbar to its original size.
☞ Move the taskbar to the top of the screen.
☞ Move the taskbar to the left edge of the screen.
☞ Move the taskbar to the right edge of the screen.
☞ Return the taskbar to its original location along the bottom of screen.
☞ Hide the taskbar.
☞ With the taskbar hidden, make it appear.
☞ Unhide the taskbar.

## EXERCISE 9: USE DESKTOP SHORTCUTS

☞ Create a desktop shortcut to any file on your diskette.
☞ Double click the desktop shortcut to verify that it works.
☞ Close the program that opened.
☞ Delete the desktop shortcut.
☞ If done, log off or shut the machine down.

## WINDOWS COMPREHENSIVE
# E X E R C I S E S

## EXERCISE 1: TRUE-FALSE
For each of the following eight statements, place a T or an F on the line to indicate if the statement is True or False.

1. ___To deselect a file, I would click in any empty space.
2. ___To format a diskette, I must have the A window open.
3. ___I can resize a window by dragging any border or corner.
4. ___When I click an icon, it becomes highlighted.
5. ___To move a window, I simply drag its status bar.
6. ___A Full Format creates a new FAT.
7. ___GUI stands for Graphical User Interface.
8. ___All windows have scroll bars all the time.

## EXERCISE 2: TRUE-FALSE
For each of the following eight statements, place a T or an F on the line to indicate if the statement is True or False.

1. ___I can close a window by clicking the task bar.
2. ___To select a single folder, I would double-click it.
3. ___When I copy a file, it will exist in only one place.
4. ___A folder deleted from the C drive is put in the Recycle Bin.
5. ___Moving a folder is done the same way as moving a file.
6. ___A file is deleted the same way a folder is deleted.
7. ___Windows is the most widely used operating system.
8. ___FAT stands for Format Access Table.

## EXERCISE 3: IDENTIFY TERMS
Below are eight definitions. Below the definitions are eight lines. In each line, write the word that matches the definition.

1. Arranging windows so they look like a deck of fanned cards.
2. Area of screen where documents, files, and folders appear.
3. Input device with buttons on the top.
4. The horizontal bar at the bottom of the screen.
5. The size and shape of the characters in a document.
6. The thing that appears when I right click.
7. To place a copy of a document in a permanent place.
8. Rapidly pressing the left mouse button twice.

1. _____     5. _____
2. _____     6. _____
3. _____     7. _____
4. _____     8. _____

## EXERCISE 4: TRUE-FALSE
For each of the following eight statements, place a T or an F on the line to indicate if the statement is True or False.

1. ___Alignment refers to which edge of the text is straight.
2. ___To move a window, I would drag its title bar.
3. ___The "I" toolbar button is used to indent a line.
4. ___To use specific commands in a menu, click the word.
5. ___Print Preview shows me how a printed page will look.
6. ___A menu bar item with a check mark is a toggle.
7. ___The menu bar is typically located under the toolbar.
8. ___"Start," "load," and "launch" all mean the same thing.

## EXERCISE 5: IDENTIFY TERMS
Below are eight definitions. Below the definitions are eight lines. In each line, write the word that matches the definition.

1. When I double click the Recycle Bin icon, its ___ opens.
2. The key to press to end one paragraph and start another.
3. Arranging windows so they appear on top of each other.
4. Another way to say "start" a computer.
5. If only one item in a group can be chosen, what is it called?
6. Words at the top of the screen denoting command groups.
7. Working with more than one program simultaneously.
8. The line of picture buttons below the menu bar.

1. _____     5. _____
2. _____     6. _____
3. _____     7. _____
4. _____     8. _____

## EXERCISE 6: TRUE-FALSE
For each of the following eight statements, place a T or an F on the line to indicate if the statement is True or False.

1. ___To select three adjacent files, I would click each file.
2. ___A new, unformatted diskette can be Quick Formatted.
3. ___A Full Format checks for bad sectors.
4. ___A Quick Format erases all of the files on the diskette.
5. ___A folder is a place where I can put files.
6. ___A Full Format erases all of the files on the diskette.
7. ___A Quick Format creates a new FAT.
8. ___To shut down Windows, the first step is to click Start.

## EXERCISE 7: IDENTIFY TERMS
Below are eight definitions. Below the definitions are eight lines. In each line, write the word that matches the definition.

1. To take a file and put a duplicate copy of it elsewhere.
2. Graphical images used to execute commands.
3. To take a file from one location and put it elsewhere.
4. The X at the top right corner of a window.
5. The key that deletes text to the left of the insertion point.
6. Rapidly pressing the left mouse button one time.
7. The key to press in order to indent a paragraph.
8. Arranging windows so they appear side-by-side.

1. _____     5. _____
2. _____     6. _____
3. _____     7. _____
4. _____     8. _____

## EXERCISE 8: TRUE-FALSE
For each of the following eight statements, place a T or an F on the line to indicate if the statement is True or False.

1. ___The "B" toolbar button is used to display text in bold.
2. ___An active window will have a dimmed title bar.
3. ___I can have three active windows at one time.
4. ___File and folder icons are sometimes called objects.
5. ___The Close button on the title bar has a "C" on it.
6. ___To open a window, I would double-click its icon.
7. ___Windows comes with an art program called Paint.
8. ___The "U" toolbar button is used to Undo a prior action.

## EXERCISE 9: KNUCKLEHEAD PAINTERS

I have three cousins, Zeke, Zack, and Zeb. They are big fans of the Three Stooges. In fact, they imitate the Three Stooges every chance they get. If you look at the drawings of them below, you will see that they even try to look like the Three Stooges. Anyway, they saw a Stooges episode the other day where Larry, Moe, and Curly were in the house painting business. My cousins decided to do the same.

**ZEKE      ZACK      ZEB**

### PART A: MANAGE FILES

☞ Format a diskette.
☞ On the diskette, create a folder (name it <u>Cousins</u>).
☞ In the Cousins folder, create a folder (name it <u>Zeke</u>).
☞ In the Cousins folder, create a folder (name it <u>Zack</u>).
☞ In the Cousins folder, create a folder (name it <u>Zeb</u>).
☞ Copy a small file from the C drive to the Zeke folder.
☞ Rename the file (use your last name as the filename).
☞ Copy a small file from the C drive to the Zack folder.
☞ Rename the file (use your first name as the filename).
☞ Copy a small file from the C drive to the Zeb folder.
☞ Rename the file (use your month of birth as the filename).
☞ Move the first name file from the Zack to the Zeb folder.
☞ Move the month-of-birth file to C:\My Files (note: if your C drive does not have a My Files folder, create one).
☞ Copy the last name file from the Zeke to the Zack folder.
☞ Delete the month-of-birth file from C:\My Files.
☞ Go to the Recycle Bin and restore the month-of-birth file.
☞ Open C:\My Files to confirm that the file has been restored.
☞ Delete the month-of-birth file again from C:\My Files.
☞ Empty the Recycle Bin.
☞ Open C:\My Files to confirm that the file is not there.
☞ Open the Recycle Bin to confirm that the file is not there.
☞ Close all windows on the desktop.

### PART B: USE PAINT

My cousins have gone into the house painting business. For their first job, they are painting a house for the Chief of Police.

☞ Start Paint and draw a picture of a house being painted by Zeke, Zack, and Zeb.
☞ Use blue, green, and red to color the house.
☞ Since these dudes don't have a clue how to paint a house without painting themselves in the process, they have gotten paint all over themselves. So, color Zeke blue, Zack green, and Zeb red.
☞ Save the drawing as a 256 color bitmap in the Zack folder (use <u>WinC-Knucklehead Painters</u> as the filename). Remember, if you save it as a 24-bit bitmap, the file will require an enormous number of bytes and this picture will take up too much space on your diskette.
☞ Close Paint.

### PART C: USE WORDPAD

☞ Start WordPad. If needed, maximize the window.
☞ Type the following two paragraphs:

> My cousins learned everything they know from the Stooges. For instance, by closely observing these buffoons, my cousins realized that a dude who is suffering from carpal tunnel syndrome could be helped to ignore the pain by merely poking him hard enough in the eyes.
>
> Regardless of the obstacles thrown their way, Larry, Moe, and Curly triumphed over their adversaries by applying common sense. My cousins learned lots from these gentlemen. They are convinced that the Stooges exemplify how folks should conduct themselves as they travel through life.

☞ Save the document to the Zeb folder on your diskette (call the file <u>WinC-Three Wise Men</u>).
☞ Insert two blank lines below the last paragraph and type your name on the third line below the last paragraph.
☞ Insert two blank lines above the first paragraph. On the top line insert the title <u>The Three Wise Men</u> (when done with this step, your title will be at the top of the document and there will be one blank line between your title and the first paragraph of the document).
☞ Center, bold, and underline the title.
☞ Change the font of the title to Arial 24.
☞ Start Paint and open the "Knucklehead Painters" file (you previously saved it in A:/Zack).
☞ Copy the picture to the clipboard.
☞ Paste the picture above the title of your WordPad document.
☞ Resize the picture to be about the size of a diskette.
☞ In the 1st sentence, insert <u>Three</u> in front of "Stooges".
☞ Move the last sentence to appear after the 1st sentence.
☞ Save your modified WordPad document.
☞ Print the WordPad document.

### PART D: USE CALCULATOR

My Cousins don't know much about math. Help them by starting the Windows Calculator and solving these problems:

Q: If they paint 196 houses and charge each homeowner $459, how much will they collect this year?
A: _____.

### PART E: PRINT A SCREEN SHOT

☞ Close all open windows.
☞ Open My Computer, the A drive window, and every window representing a folder (you should have six windows open). Note: if the My Computer window disappears when you open the A drive window, click Tools, Folder Options, and click the General tab. In the Browse Folders area of the dialog box, click Open Each Folder In Its Own Window. Then click OK. Redo the first step of this exercise and the windows will stay open.
☞ Change the view of each window to show objects in a List.
☞ Resize and move the windows so you can see all six windows, all the contents of each window, and the complete title on each window's title bar.
☞ Take a screen shot of the desktop.
☞ Print your document.
☞ Close all documents.
☞ Close all programs.

## PAGE B-5: EXERCISE 1

| Across | Down |
|--------|------|
| 2. Selected | 1. Resize |
| 5. Box | 3. Close |
| 6. Right | 4. **Deselected** |
| 8. Restore | 7. Graphical |
| 10. Bootup | 9. Title |
| 11. Move | 11. Minimize |
| 13. Operating | 12. Dog |
| 15. Maximize | 14. Taskbar |
| 19. Scroll | 16. Mouse |
| 20. Drag | 17. Pointer |
| 21. Start | 18. Click |
| 23. Arrow | 20. Desktop |
| 25. Double | 21. Shut Down |
| 27. Windows | 22. Shortcut |
| 29. Icon | 24. One |
| 30. Taskbar | 26. Users |
| 31. A | 28. Data |

## PAGE B-6: EXERCISE 2

1. T
2. F: I can close a window by clicking the Close button (the X at the top right corner of the window). Clicking the taskbar does nothing. Well, it might prove to be good exercise for my finger, but it probably ain't worth the effort.
3. T
4. T
5. F: To move a window, I simply drag its title bar, not its status bar.
6. F: A window will have scroll bars only when you can't see all the stuff in the window. That is, when the contents of the window can't all be seen at one time, scroll bars appear so that you can scroll through the material that can't be seen.
7. T
8. T

## PAGE B-6: EXERCISE 3

1. D
2. A
3. B
4. C

## PAGE B-6: EXERCISE 4

1. Bootup (or launch)
2. Desktop
3. Mouse
4. Windows
5. Close Button
6. Shortcut Menu
7. Icons
8. Double-clicking

## PAGE B-6: EXERCISE 5

1. B    2. C    3. A

## PAGE B-9 EXERCISE 1

| Across | Down |
|--------|------|
| 2. Menu | 1. Quick |
| 3. Format | 2. My Computer |
| 5. Cascade | 3. Faded |
| 9. Tab | 4. Tiled |
| 10. Toolbar | 6. Text Box |
| 13. Radio | 7. FAT |
| 14. X | 8. Drag |
| 15. Full | 11. Objects |
| 16. Click | 12. Dialog |
| 17. Ghosted | |

## PAGE B-9: EXERCISE 2

1. T
2. F: To move a window, I simply drag its title bar, not its status bar.
3. T
4. T
5. T
6. F: A menu bar item with a check mark (✔) is a toggle. A menu bar item with a bullet (black dot) is a mutually-exclusive choice. The difference is that a toggle will turn an item on or off and you can have many items turned on at once, while a bullet denotes a choice that is mutually exclusive which is a fancy way of saying one, and only one, of the choices can be turned on at one time.
7. F: The menu bar is typically located above the toolbar, not under it.
8. F: While you can have many windows open at any given time, only one of them can be the active window. You will know which one is active because it will be in front on the inactive windows, its title bar will be highlighted, and its taskbar button will be depressed.

## PAGE B-9: EXERCISE 3

1. D
2. C
3. E
4. A
5. B

## PAGE B-9: EXERCISE 4

1. Toolbar
2. Vertically Tiled
3. Horizontally Tiled
4. Cascade
5. Mutually-Exclusive
6. Menu Bar

## PAGE B-9: EXERCISE 5

1. F: FAT stands for File Allocation Table.
2. F: A new, unformatted diskette cannot be quick formatted--you must do a full format. The reason for this requirement is that an unformatted diskette needs to have lots of stuff done to it that has never been done before and the only way for that to happen is to perform a full format on it.
3, 4, 5, and 6 are all T
7. F: A full format will create a new FAT, but a quick format will not.
8. F: **To format a diskette, you must have the A window closed.** You can't format the A drive if its window is open.

## PAGE B-10: EXERCISE 6

1. C  2. D  3. G  4. B  5. E  6. F  7. H  8. A

## PAGE B-13: EXERCISE 1

| Across | Down |
|--------|------|
| 1. A Drive | 1. Accessories |
| 2. FAT | 2. Faded |
| 3. C Drive | 4. Edit |
| 6. Delete | 5. Desktop |
| 7. Save | 9. Bold |
| 8. Tab | 11. Enhancements |
| 10. Open | 12. Font |
| 13. Load | 16. Select |
| 14. Up | 17. Wrap |
| 15. Italics | 18. Print |

| | |
|---|---|
| 19. Memory | 20. Move |
| 21. Paint | 22. Alignment |
| 23. Task | 25. Users |
| 24. Clip | 26. Backspace |
| 25. Underline | 27. Shift |
| 28. RAM | 29. Margin |
| 30. Launch | 33. IBM |
| 31. Start | 34. No |
| 32. Tasking | |
| 35. Dozer | |

## PAGE B-14: EXERCISE 2

1, 2, and 3 are all T.
4. F: The "I" toolbar button is used to italicize text.
5. F: The Close button has an "X" on it, not a "C".
6. T
7. T
8. F: The "U" toolbar button is used to underline text.

## PAGE B-14: EXERCISE 3

| | |
|---|---|
| 1. Tab | 5. Backspace |
| 2. Save | 6. Close Button |
| 3. Multitasking | 7. Taskbar |
| 4. Font | 8. Enter |

## PAGE B-17: EXERCISE 1

| Across | Down |
|--------|------|
| 2. Restore | 1. Double |
| 5. Clip | 2. Recycle Bin |
| 8. Folders | 3. Shift |
| 9. Cut | 4. Close |
| 10. Move | 6. Print |
| 12. File | 7. Rename |
| 14. Edit | 11. Empty |
| 15. Copy | 13. Delete |
| 16. Select | 15. Ctrl |
| 17. Details | |

## PAGE B-17: EXERCISE 2

1. T
2. F: To select a single folder, I would click it. If I double click it, its window will open.
3, 4, 5, and 6 are all T.
7. F: If I merely clicked each file, as I click each file, the previously-clicked file will be deselected. To select four adjacent files, I would click the first file and then Shift + click the fourth one. That way, the first file, the fourth file, and every file in between the first and fourth file will be selected.
8. T

## PAGE B-17: EXERCISE 3

| | | | | |
|---|---|---|---|---|
| 1. D | 4. A | 7. C | 10. B | 13. A |
| 2. B | 5. B | 8. A | 11. B | 14. C |
| 3. A | 6. B | 9. B | 12. B | 15. A |

## PAGE B-17: EXERCISE 4

1. F: To deselect a file, I would click outside of it. I would select a file by clicking on it.
2. T
3. T
4. T
5. F: While a folder deleted from the C drive is put in the Recycle Bin, a folder deleted from the A drive is not put in the Recycle Bin. Instead, it

simply goes bye bye.

6. T

7. F: If I merely clicked each folder, as I click each one, the previously-clicked one will be deselected. To select three non-adjacent folders, I would click the first one and then Ctrl + Click each of the other two folders.

8. T

## PAGE B-17: EXERCISE 5

1. F: To select a single file, I would simply click it. If were to double click it, the file would open.

2. F: If I click two files, only the second file clicked will be selected, because once a file is clicked, the previously-clicked file is deselected. To select more than one file, I would either need to Ctrl + click each file, or I could click one file and Shift + click the last file in an adjacent list of files.

3. F: I put my files into folders. I don't put my folders into files.

4. F: When I move a file, it will exist in one place. On the other hand, if I were to copy a file, it will appear in more than one place. Think of it this way: If I were to move a piece of paper from one place on my desk to another place, the paper will no longer be where it was--it will only be where I moved it. On the other hand, if I were to make a copy of the piece of paper, I would have two of them--the original and the copy.

5. F: A folder is represented by an icon of a yellow folder, not a red folder.

6, 7, and 8 are all T.

## PAGE B-18: EXERCISE 6

1. Folder
2. Delete
3. File
4. Rename
5. Click
6. Recycle Bin

## PAGE B-18: EXERCISE 7

1. F: To select three non-adjacent files, I would click the first one and then Ctrl + Click each of the other two files. If I were to merely click each file, every time I clicked one file, the previously-clicked file would automatically be deselected.

2. T

3. F: A file deleted from the C drive is put in the Recycle Bin; a file deleted from the A drive is not put in the Recycle Bin. Instead, the file will simply vanish.

4. F: To select three adjacent folders, I would click the first one and then Shift + click the third one. If I were to merely click each file, every time I clicked one file, the previously-clicked file would automatically be deselected.

5. T

6. F: A selected folder is highlighted; a deselected folder is not highlighted.

## PAGE B-21: EXERCISE 1

**Across**
1. Wallpaper
4. Hide
6. Icon
7. Two
9. Appearance
10. Menu
12. Right
13. Font
14. Stretch
16. Desktop
20. Move
22. Taskbar
25. Sizing

**Down**
2. Print Screen
3. Control
5. Screen Shot
8. Background
11. Up
15. Operating
17. Save
18. Properties
19. Center
21. Tab
23. Screen
24. Print Preview
27. Online

26. Yes
27. One
30. Logoff
32. Tile
33. Windows
28. Close
29. Offline
31. GUI

## PAGE B-22: EXERCISE 2

1. Taskbar
2. Screen Saver
3. Background (also called wallpaper)
4. Windows XP Style
5. Screen Shot
6. Print Screen

## PAGE B-22: EXERCISE 3

1. F: Wallpaper can be centered or tiled.
2. T
3. F: You can add your own desktop shortcuts.
4. T
5. F: To change wallpaper, right-click the desktop and click Properties from the shortcut menu.
6. T
7. F: They are two names for the same thing.
8. T

## PAGE B-22: EXERCISE 4

1. F: Wallpaper can be tiled or centered.
2. T
3. F: Wallpaper can be centered or tiled.
4. F: The screen saver wait time is not always set at two minutes. You can change the wait time.
5. T
6. T

## PAGE B-22: EXERCISE 5

1. Shot
2. Background
3. Shortcut
4. Mouse
5. Appearance
6. Screen

## PAGE B-23: EXERCISE 1

1. T

2. F: To format a diskette, you must have the A window closed. You can't format the a diskette if the A drive is open.

3. T

4. T

5. F: To move a window, I simply drag its title bar, not its status bar.

6. T

7. T

8. F: A window will have scroll bars only when you can't see all the stuff in the window. That is, when the contents of the window can't all be seen at one time, scroll bars appear so that you can scroll through the material that can't be seen.

## PAGE B-23: EXERCISE 2

1. F: I can close a window by clicking its Close button which can be found on the title bar, not on the taskbar.

2. F: To select a single folder, I would click it. If I were to double-click it, its window would open.

3. F: When I copy a file, it will exist in more than one place (where it was copied from and where it was copied to). On the other hand, if I were to move a file, it will appear in only one place, the place to which it was moved.

4, 5, 6, and 7 are all T.

8. F: FAT stands for File Allocation Table.

## PAGE B-23: EXERCISE 3

1. Cascade
2. Desktop
3. Mouse
4. Taskbar
5. Font
6. Shortcut (quick) Menu
7. Save
8. Double Clicking

## PAGE B-23: EXERCISE 4

1. T
2. T
3. F: The "I" toolbar button is used to italicize text.
4. T
5. T
6. T
7. F: The menu bar is typically located above the toolbar, not under it.
8. T

## PAGE B-23: EXERCISE 5

1. Window
2. Enter
3. Horizontally Tiled
4. Bootup (or Load or Launch)
5. Mutually Exclusive
6. Menu Bar
7. Multitasking
8. Toolbar

## PAGE B-23: EXERCISE 6

1. F: If I were to merely click each file, every time I clicked one file, the previously-clicked file would automatically be deselected. To select three adjacent files, I would click the first file. Then I could Shift + click the last file.

2. F: A new, unformatted diskette can not be quick formatted—you must do a full format. The reason for this requirement is that an unformatted diskette needs to have lots of stuff done to it that has never been done before and the only way for that to happen is to perform a full format on it.

3. T

4. T

5. T

6. T

7. F: A full (not a quick) format creates a FAT.

8. T

## PAGE B-23: EXERCISE 7

1. Copy
2. Icons
3. Move
4. Close Button
5. Backspace
6. Clicking
7. Tab
8. Vertically Tiled

## PAGE B-23: EXERCISE 8

1. T

2. F: An active window will have a highlighted title bar. An inactive window will have a dimmed (also called faded or ghosted) title bar.

3. F: While I can have many windows open at one time, I can have only one active window at one time. I will know which one is the active one because the active window will be in front of the other windows, it will have a highlighted title bar, and its taskbar button will be depressed.

4. T

5. F: The Close button has an "X" on it, not a "C".

6. T

7. T

8. F: The "U" toolbar button will underline text.

☞ *Dozer's Quintessential Guide To Microsoft Windows* ☜

**A drive**: A secondary storage device that writes to and reads from a floppy disk. Also called a floppy drive.

**accessories**: The Windows folder where Paint, WordPad, Calculator, and games reside.

**alignment**: The way the text lines up in relation to the margins.

**anti-static mat**: A pad under a chair or the keyboard that protects a computer system by absorbing potentially-harmful static electricity.

**anti-virus program**: Software that detects and eradicates some computer viruses.

**background**: An image that appears behind the icons or on a desktop. Also called wallpaper.

**backspace key**: The key that deletes data to the left of the insertion point.

**boot up**: The act of turning on a computer. Also called starting or simply turning it on.

**bullet**: A small black dot that appears next to a menu item, indicating the item has been chosen. With a bulleted menu item, you can only choose one of the items in the list.

**C drive**: A secondary storage device that stores programs and files. Also called the hard drive.

**Calculator**: A Windows program that operates like a hand-held calculator.

**cascaded windows**: Windows layered on top of each other in such a way that each window's title bar is visible, like a fanned deck of cards.

**check boxes**: Square boxes in a dialog box that I can click to make my selections.

**click**: The act of rapidly pressing the left mouse button one time, generally done to select an on-screen object.

**clipboard**: A part of memory where cut or copied data or images are kept.

**close**: The process of removing a file or a program from memory.

**close button**: The X at the right end of a title bar that, when clicked, removes the program from memory.

**color box**: In Paint, the collection of colors from which to choose.

**command buttons**: A button, found in a dialog box that, when clicked, executes a command (e.g., Cancel, OK, Apply).

**copy**: To place a file, folder, text or an image elsewhere while maintaining the original item

where it was.

**delete**: To remove (erase) a file, folder, image, or text.

**delete key**: The key that deletes data to the right of the insertion point.

**deselect**: To click outside of a selected image, icon, or text.

**desktop**: The entire area on the screen where programs, windows, documents, folders, and files are displayed.

**desktop shortcut**: An icon appearing on the desktop that, when double clicked, will open a file and its associated program.

**dialog box**: A box that appears on the screen when the program needs to have a "dialog" with you to get the details about what you want to do.

**diskette**: A removable medium for storage of files used in conjunction with a floppy drive. Also called a floppy disk.

**DOS**: An acronym for Disk Operating System, a medieval operating system from the dinosaur era that used command syntax instead of a graphical user interface.

**double-click**: The act of rapidly pressing the left mouse button two times.

**Dozer**: The smartest cyberdog on the planet.

**drag**: To move the mouse.

**drag and drop**: The act of pointing to an object on the screen, holding down the left mouse button, moving the mouse, and then releasing the mouse button, thereby moving the object. In essence you have dragged and then dropped the object.

**edit**: To modify a document.

**ellipses**: Three dots that appear after some menu items which indicate that if that item is clicked, a dialog box will appear.

**enhancements**: Bold, italics, and underline.

**FAT**: An acronym for File Allocation Table, which is the directory on a disk or diskette that keeps track of where files are located.

**file**: A document that has been saved to some sort of secondary storage device such as a hard drive, diskette, zip drive, etc.

**file allocation table**: The directory on a disk or diskette that keeps track of where files are located (abbreviated as FAT).

**filename**: The name given to a file.

**folder**: A place where files are kept on a computer.

**font color**: The color of the characters.

**font size**: The dimension of the characters.

**font type**: The shape of the characters.

**formatting**: Removing all files from a disk (quick format) or removing all files, checking for bad sectors on the disk surface, and creating a File Allocation Table (full format). Or, the process of modifying a document in ways that change its appearance but not its content.

**full formatting**: A method of formatting which erases all files, creates a FAT, and checks for bad sectors on the disk surface.

**graphical user interface**: (See GUI).

**GUI**: An acronym for Graphical User Interface (pronounced "goo-eey"). A computer interface using icons, windows, etc.

**help**: A feature that provides answers to questions about the Windows operating system. To access it, click Start, Help and Support.

**icons**: On-screen graphical images that, when selected, execute commands.

**insertion point**: The on-screen blinking vertical line identifying where entered text will appear. Some folks refer to this as a cursor.

**interface**: The way a person communicates with a computer.

**landscape orientation**: A document printed on paper that is 11 inches wide and 8-1/2 inches high (i.e., sideways).

**launch**: To place a program or document into memory. Also called start, load, or open.

**Linux**: An operating system.

**list boxes**: A list of items found in a dialog box that can be accessed by clicking an arrow next to each box.

**load**: To place a program or document into memory. Also called start, launch, or open.

**locked taskbar**: A taskbar that cannot be moved or hidden.

**log in**: Signing into an account. Also called log on or sign on.

**log off**: Signing out of an account. Also called log out or sign off.

**margins**: The space between the text and the edges of the paper.

**maximize button**: The button (on the title bar) that, when clicked, will make the window fill the entire screen.

**memory**: The temporary location where the data and programs currently being used by a processor reside. Also called RAM (an acronym for Random Access Memory).

**menu bar**: The bar (under the title bar) which consists of a series of command categories. To access specific commands in a category, click the item on the menu bar.

**minimize button**: The button (on the title bar) that, when clicked, will make the window become the size of a taskbar button.

**mouse**: Input device that typically has two buttons on the top and a ball on its underside. Used to select, move, and resize objects and to execute commands.

**move**: To place a file, file, folder, text or an image elsewhere while removing the original item from where it was.

**move handle**: A vertical bar on a toolbar that, when dragged, will allow the user to move the toolbar.

**My Computer**: A Windows feature that displays the resources available to your computer.

**Notepad**: A Windows text editor program.

**open**: To place a program or document into memory. Also called start, load, or launch.

**operating systems**: A general category of software that manages the computer resources and communicates with the mouse, printer, keyboard, etc.

**option button**: A mutually-exclusive choice found in a dialog box. To make your selection you click in the circle (option button). Also called a Radio Button.

**page orientation**: The way the print appears on the page. If 11" wide, the page has a landscape orientation; if 8-12" wide, the page has a portrait orientation.

**Paint**: A Windows accessory that allows us to create artwork.

**password**: A secret sequence of characters that prohibits unauthorized access to a web site, an email account, or a computer.

**portrait orientation**: A document printed on paper that is 8-1/2 inches wide and 11 inches high.

**print preview**: A feature that permits you to see how each page of your document will look before you print the document.

**print screen key**: The key that sends the entire image on the screen to the clipboard.

**programs**: The set of instructions used by a processor to convert data into information. Also called software.

**quick formatting**: A method of rapidly formatting a disk whereby all the files and folders on the disk are deleted.

**quick menu**: A context-sensitive menu that appears when I right click. Often called a shortcut menu.

**radio button**: A mutually-exclusive choice found in a dialog box. To make your selection you click in the circle (radio button). Also called an Option Button.

**Recycle Bin**: The place where files that have been deleted from the C drive are kept. Later, they can be retrieved, if desired.

**redo button**: The toolbar button that, when clicked, will reverse the last undo done. It has a crooked arrow pointing to the right.

**rename**: To change the name of a file or folder.

**restore button**: The button that, when clicked, will restore the window so that it is the size it was when it was last manually resized. It can be found on the title bar.

**right-click**: The act of rapidly pressing the right mouse button one time.

**save**: The act of placing a copy of the document currently in memory into secondary storage.

**screen saver**: Software that produces random images on the screen after the mouse and keyboard have been idle for a period of time.

**screen shot**: A picture of all the contents of the screen.

**scroll arrows**: Buttons on the ends of a scroll bar that, when clicked, scrolls through a window that is too small to simultaneously display all its contents.

**scroll bar**: A horizontal and/or vertical bar that permits movement within a window that is too small to simultaneously display all its contents.

**scroll box**: A box in a scroll bar that permits rapid movement within a window that is too small to simultaneously display all its contents.

**select**: To identify an object, text, or image to which you wish to do something.

**shortcut menu**: A context-sensitive menu that appears when I right click. Also called a Quick Menu.

**shut down**: The act of properly turning a computer off. Also called "turn off computer".

**slider control**: A dialog box feature that lets you select what you want by dragging a switch from left to right or up and down.

**software**: The set of instructions used by a processor to convert data into information. Also

called a program.

**spin box**: A dialog box feature that lets you select what you want by clicking a button that spins through a variety of choices.

**start**: The act of turning on a computer, also called booting up. Or, to place a program or document into memory. Also called launch, load, or open.

**status bar**: The bar at the bottom of many windows that provides information about the contents of the window.

**tab key**: The key used to indent a line in word processing or to move from cell to cell in a table or in a worksheet.

**taskbar**: The horizontal grey bar, typically at the bottom of the desktop, upon which the Start button resides.

**thumbnail**: A miniature version of an image.

**tiled windows**: Two or more windows placed side by side or on top of each other on the screen.

**title bar**: The top bar in a program that identifies the program and the current document being worked on. In addition, the Minimize, Maximize, and Close buttons reside on this bar.

**toolbar**: A collection of picture buttons that, when clicked, execute a command. These buttons typically appear below the menu bar.

**toolbox**: In Paint, the collection of drawing tools (paint brush, pencil, eraser, etc.).

**turn off computer**: The act of properly turning a computer off. Also called "shut down computer".

**undo button**: The toolbar button that, when clicked, will reverse the last action taken. It has a crooked arrow pointing to the left.

**UNIX**: An operating system.

**user interface**: The way a program interacts with a user.

**view**: A menu bar item that lets me choose the way stuff looks on the screen. For instance, in My Computer, the way the icons appear (thumbnails, tiles, icons, list, or details).

**wallpaper**: An image that appears behind the icons or on a desktop. Also called background.

**window**: An on-screen box wherein information is displayed.

**Windows**: The operating system used on most desktop machines.

**word wrap**: A word processor feature that moves excess text to the next line automatically, thereby preventing text from spilling over into the margins.

# DOZER'S QUINTESSENTIAL GUIDE TO THE INTERNET

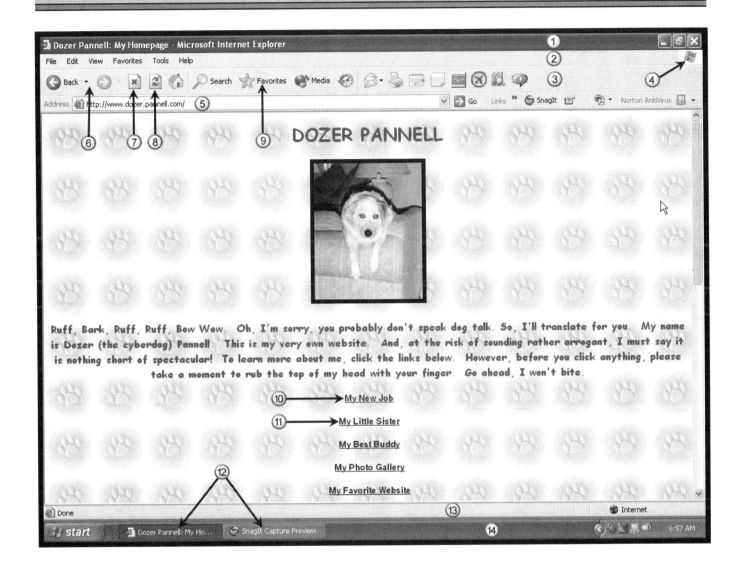

1. Title bar (identifies the program being used and the web page being viewed)
2. Menu bar (collection of menu items, each of which contains commands)
3. Toolbar (collection of picture buttons, each of which accesses a command)
4. IE logo (it is animated during the page-loading process)
5. Address box (displays the URL of the current page)
6. Back and Forward buttons (transports you to previously-viewed pages)
7. Stop button (stops the page-loading process)
8. Refresh button (reloads the current page)
9. Favorites button (contains a list of bookmarked pages called favorites)
10. Previously followed link (you've already been there)
11. Unfollowed link (you haven't been there, but you can go there if you click the link)
12. Taskbar buttons (each denotes an open window)
13. Status bar (provides data on the page-loading progress)
14. Taskbar (contains the Start button, open windows buttons, etc.)

# Dozer's Quintessential Guide To The Internet

## T A B L E   O F   C O N T E N T S

## INTRODUCTION TO THE INTERNET

The Internet is a global system of millions of linked computers. To allow computers with different hardware and software configurations (platforms) to communicate, a common protocol (standard for communicating between computers) is needed. Transmission Control Protocol/Internet Protocol (TCP/IP) has been adopted for the Internet. TCP/IP divides information into units called packets each of which contains routing instructions explaining where the packet should go. Each computer on the network reads the instructions and sends each packet along its way to its ultimate destination. A packet may pass through dozens of computers. This "packet switching" system means that the Internet is decentralized (there is no central location where all packets must go to be sorted and sent out). Therefore, if one routing computer goes down, others take over.

## WEB BROWSERS

The World Wide Web (www) is a series of linked electronic documents called web pages. A web page may have text, pictures, sounds, and/or links to other pages. Web browsers, (e.g., Internet Explorer and Netscape Navigator), are programs that enable us to find, load, view, print, and create web pages.

## LAUNCH INTERNET EXPLORER (Dozer's Favorite Browser)

To launch Internet Explorer (IE), do the following:
- ☞ Click the Start button on the taskbar.
- ☞ On the menu, point to Programs.
- ☞ On the sub-menu, click Internet Explorer (If you don't see it, open additional menus until you find it).
- ☞ The Menu Bar displays items, such as File, Edit, View, etc. The Standard Buttons toolbar displays icons denoting frequently-used commands (If this bar is not displayed, click View, Toolbars, Standard Buttons). The Address Bar displays the address of the current page (If this bar is not displayed, click View, Toolbars, Address Bar).

## ACCESS A WEB SITE WITH A KNOWN ADDRESS

While a page is loading (also called opening), the IE logo near the top, right corner of the window is animated. Be patient. Some pages may take several minutes to load. The first page to load in a website is its homepage. Note: Since the Internet changes often, some of the web sites that you are asked to access in Dozer's Quintessential Guide may no longer exist and some may be modified to appear differently than described in the next few pages. Don't be concerned. Change is all a part of the Internet experience. Also, be careful how you enter a web page address (also known as its URL, which stands for Uniform Resource Locator). If you mistype the URL, one of two things will happen. If the URL does exist, you will be taken to that web page; if the URL does not exist, you will receive a message telling you so. To see such a message, do the following:

- ☞ Go to **www.dozer.pannell.ccsn.com** (type the URL in the address box and press the Enter key). Wait for page to load.
- ☞ In a moment or two, a message will appear telling you that the web page could not be found. This message means there is no web page on the planet with that URL.
- ☞ Now, go to **www.dozer.pannell.com** (or www.pannell.biz). Note: Dozer has two identical websites, so he has two URLs, one for each site.
- ☞ Whose picture is on this web page? _____

## USE HYPERLINKS

A web page may contain links to other places. The other place may be in one of four locations: 1) on the same page on the current site, 2) on a different page on the current site, 3) on a different site, or 4) in the Internet graveyard (i.e., the page to which the link points is either temporarily or permanently not available). If you put the mouse pointer on a word or image and the pointer changes into a pointing hand, you have found a link. When clicked, the browser finds the page using its URL and the link often changes color to indicate it has been selected, providing a marker to keep track of where you have been.

To practice using hyperlinks, do the following:
- ☞ Go to **www.netidentity.com**
- ☞ At the bottom of the page, point to the Support link. Notice that the mouse pointer turns into a pointing hand.
- ☞ To view the page to which the link points, click the link. Notice that after clicking the link, you are taken to another web page on the same web site.
- ☞ When the next page loads, click the Glossary link. Notice that you're taken to another web page on the same web site.
- ☞ On the Glossary page, alphabetic links are provided. Click the "S" link. Notice that you are taken to glossary terms starting with the letter "S". Also, notice that you are still on the same page as you were when you clicked the "S" link.
- ☞ Scroll up to see the link you just clicked. This type of link merely takes you to another place on the same page. Instead of using this type of link, you could just scroll down the page to find the item that interests you. Go ahead and scroll up and down the page to see the items.
- ☞ Go to **www.dozer.pannell.com** (or www.pannell.biz). As you begin to type this URL, Internet Explorer (IE) may remember that you entered it earlier. If so, instead of continuing to type, just click the address provided. Otherwise, you will need to type the URL.
- ☞ On Dozer's homepage, click the My Little Sister link. Notice that you are taken to another web page on the same site.
- ☞ At the bottom of the My Little Sister web page, click the Home button. You will go back to Dozer's homepage.
- ☞ On Dozer's homepage, click the My Favorite Website link.
- ☞ Notice that you are taken to a totally different web site.

## MOVE THROUGH PREVIOUSLY-VIEWED WEB PAGES

After you have viewed many pages, you may want to return to a previously-viewed page. To go back one page, click the Back toolbar button (←). Once you have gone back, you can go forward by clicking the Forward toolbar button (→).

To practice moving through pages, do the following:
- ☞ Click the Back toolbar button. Notice that you were at this page a moment ago. It is a previously-viewed page.
- ☞ Click the Back toolbar button several more times. Notice that each time you click it, you go back one page as if you were reading a book and were turning the pages back.
- ☞ Click the Back toolbar button until it is faded. You are now at the first of a series of previously-viewed pages.
- ☞ Click the Forward toolbar button (you go forward one page).
- ☞ Click the Forward toolbar button several more times. Note that each time you click it, you go forward one page.
- ☞ Click the Forward toolbar button until the button is faded. You are now at the last of the previously-viewed pages.

## ACCESS WEB SITES & FIND INFORMATION

When you know the URL (web page address), it's easy to access a web page. Below is a list of URL's. Go to each web site and find the answers to the questions. Once you load the home page of each web site, you may need to scroll down on that page or you might even need to click on links to load other pages to find each answer. Note: on the day that Dozer's Quintessential Guide To Computer Literacy was printed, all of these web sites were accessible. Since then, it is possible that one or more of these web sites may no longer exist or they may have been modified in such a way that the questions that follow cannot be answered. So, if you are denied access to any specific web site or if you go there and can't find the answer, don't worry. Just move on to the next question.

### DOZER

www.dozer.pannell.com (or www.pannell.biz).
Q: What color is Dozer's left ear?
A: _____

Q: If you click the "My Favorite Website" link, where do you go?
A: _____

Q: If you click the Back toolbar button, where do you go?
A: _____

Q: If you click the Forward toolbar button, where do you go?
A: _____

### TRAVEL

www.peabodymemphis.com
Q: You have decided to take a road trip from Las Vegas, Nevada to Memphis, Tennessee. When you get there, you want to stay at the Peabody, the most famous hotel in Memphis. What is the address of the Peabody?
A: _____

maps.yahoo.com
Q: Your trip will take you from 6375 W. Charleston Blvd. in Las Vegas, NV to the Peabody in Memphis. Use this website to create driving directions. How many miles will you need to drive?
A: _____

www.ask.com
Q: What is the weather for Memphis, Tennessee today?
A: _____

www.ramada.com
Q: Since it is such a long drive from Las Vegas to Memphis. You have decided to rest in Amarillo, Texas. How many Ramada Inns are located in Amarillo?
A: _____

### MOVIES

www.movie-mistakes.com
Q: How many mistakes have been reported in one of Dozer's favorite movies, "Scooby Doo"?
A: _____

www.allmovie.com
Q: While Dozer likes the movie Scooby Doo, his all time favorite movie is "My Dog Skip". Who directed "My Dog Skip"?
A: _____

### LITERATURE

www.amazon.com
Q: What is the #1 Hardcover Best Seller in fiction?
A: _____

www.infoplease.com
Q: In what year was William Shakespeare born?
A: _____

www.annabelle.net
Q: Can you find a Mark Twain quotation?
A: _____

www.promo.net/pg
Q: Here at the Project Gutenberg site, they digitize writings that are in the public domain (pubic domain means that these books can be freely copied and distributed). You can find thousands of free books. Can you find Robinson Crusoe by Daniel Defoe? When you find it, you will see two versions to download (.txt and .zip). Use the one with a ".txt" extension. According to the first sentence of that book, in what year was the narrator born? (hint: you will need to scroll down through 10 pages or so of heading material before the book begins).
A: _____

### GOVERNMENT

www.gksoft.com/govt
Q: What kind of information can be found at this web site?
A: _____

www.usps.com
Q: The zip code for 1600 Pennsylvania Ave., Washington, DC?
A: _____

www.irs.gov
Q: This is the web site for what organization?
A: _____

### COMPUTING

www.whatis.com
Q: What is a "nanosecond"?
A: _____

www.webopedia.com
Q: What is a "flame"?
A: _____

www.smartcomputing.com
Q: What is a "cookie"?
A: _____

### NEWS

www.usatoday.com
Q: What is the headline in today's edition of USA Today?
A: _____

www.variety.com
Q: What is the top story in today's edition of this publication?
A: _____

www.time.com
Q: What is the headline in Time magazine?
A: _____

## EXERCISE 1: CROSSWORD

Use the clues below to complete the crossword puzzle. (Note: the Answer Key can be found beginning on page C-25).

### ACROSS

2. Dozer, the cyberdog, is always looking for a treat. Sometimes he loves to chew on ___.
3. A web page address is often referred to as a ___ which is an acronym for Uniform Resource Locator.
5. A very popular web browser is called Internet Explorer, which sometimes is abbreviated as ___.
7. When on the Internet, I often find text or images called ___, which, when clicked, take me to another web page.
8. A very popular web browser (not Dozer's favorite one).
11. If I click a link, it will change ___. This will remind me later that I have already visited the web page to which it points.
12. To execute a command, sometimes I might double-click an image called an ___.
13. Standard and Address are two types of ___ bars found in Internet Explorer.
14. To launch Internet Explorer, click ___, All Programs, Internet Explorer.
16. While a page is loading (opening), the IE ___ is animated.

### DOWN

1. A web ___ is a program that enables us to find, load, view, print, and create web pages.
2. To return to a previously-viewed page, click the ___ toolbar button.
4. Packet ___ is the process by which individual computers send each packet along its way to its ultimate destination.
6. Dozer's Favorite web browser is Internet ___.
9. TCP/IP divides data into units called ___ each of which contains routing instructions explaining where it goes.
10. If you can't see all of the web page on the screen, you can use the ___ bar to move the contents of the web page.
15. An acronym for Random Access Memory.

## EXERCISE 2: TRUE-FALSE

For each of the following eight statements, place a T or an F on the line to indicate if the statement is True or False.

1. ___ WWW stands for Wait, Watch, and Wonder.
2. ___ Internet Explorer is a popular web browser.
3. ___ A mouse pointer looks like a hand when I point to a link.
4. ___ To access a web page, I type its LUR in the Address bar.
5. ___ Sometimes a link is text and sometimes it is an image.
6. ___ If the Forward button is dimmed, it won't work.
7. ___ All web site addresses begin with "www".
8. ___ URL stands for User Register Login.

## EXERCISE 3: IDENTIFY TERMS

Below are eight definitions. Below the definitions are eight lines. In each line, write the word that matches the definition.

1. Standards for communicating between computers.
2. The global system of millions of linked computers.
3. Programs that enable us to find, view, and create web pages.
4. Individual units of data being transmitted via the Internet.
5. The series of linked electronic documents called web pages.
6. A web page address.
7. An abbreviation for Internet Explorer.
8. The first page to load in a website.

1. _____    5. _____
2. _____    6. _____
3. _____    7. _____
4. _____    8. _____

## EXERCISE 4: EXPLAIN CONCEPTS

Dozer's sister Skooter thinks "packet switching" is what she does on Christmas morning when she gets up early and opens all of Dozer's packages to see what is in them. She then rewraps them and "switches" name tags on the good stuff intended for Dozer so that she gets the good presents. Is this what is meant by "packet switching"? If not, what is a "packet" and how does "packet switching" work? Write your answer in the space provided.

_____
_____
_____
_____
_____
_____
_____
_____
_____
_____
_____

## EXERCISE 5: TRUE-FALSE

For each of the following eight statements, place a T or an F on the line to indicate if the statement is True or False.

1. ___ TCP/IP divides information into units called blocks.
2. ___ When a page is loading, the IE logo is animated.
3. ___ A web page travels to me in one big packet.
4. ___ Internet Explorer is Dozer's favorite web browser.
5. ___ The Back button closes the web browser.
6. ___ URL stands for Uniform Resource Locator.
7. ___ The Internet is a series of connected computers.
8. ___ When clicked, a link changes into an hourglass icon.

## EXERCISE 6: ACCESS WEB SITES

When you know the URL (web page address), it's easy to access the web page. Below is a list of URLs. Go to each web site and find the answers to the questions. Once you load the home page of each web site, you may need to scroll down on that page or you might even need to click on links to load other pages to find each answer. Note: on the day that this edition of Dozer's Quintessential Guide To Computer Literacy was printed, all of these web sites were accessible. Since then, it is possible that one or more of these web sites may no longer exist or they may have been modified in such a way that the questions that follow cannot be answered. So, if you are denied access to any specific web site or if you go there and can't find the answer, don't worry. Just move on to the next question.

### LIFE AND DEATH

**www.findagrave.com**
Each of the deceased folks below were entertainers. Each is well known for a quotation, which appears on his gravestone. What famous quote appears on each person's gravestone?
Jackie Gleason: _____
Mel Blanc: _____
Dean Martin: _____
Sonny Bono: _____

**www.deathclock.com**
Q: According to this web site, when will you die?
A: _____

**www.urban75.com/Mag/dog.html** (Note: Case counts! The "M" in "Mag" must be typed in uppercase as shown).
Q: How old are you, in dog's years?
A: _____

**www.math.berkeley.edu/~galen/popclk.html**
Q: What was the world's population on the day you were born?
A: _____

### FOOD

**www.backofthebox.com**
Q: What is the recipe of the day?
A: _____

**www.foodtv.com**
Q: Who is the host of the TV show called "Unwrapped"?
A: _____

**www.topsecretrecipes.com**
Q: How many recipes are available for Taco Bell foods?
A: _____

**www.whymilk.com**
Q: What kind of milk does Paul Shaffer like (Hint: Paul Shaffer is a celebrity)?
A: _____

### NAMES

**www.babynames.com**
Q: What is the meaning of your first name?
A: _____

**www.namestatistics.com**
Q: What percentage of people in the U.S. share your last name?
A: _____

### DICTIONARIES, ETC.

**www.onelook.com**
Q: What is the definition for the word "netiquette"?
A: _____

**www.acronymfinder.com**
Q: NSPCA is an acronym for what organization?
A: _____

### TRAVEL

**www.kbb.com**
Q: You want to buy a new car and you intend to trade in your current car. What is the used-car trade-in value of a 1999 Pontiac Firebird 2-door coupe in Las Vegas (zip code: 89130)? The car has an automatic transmission, 24,569 miles, and is in excellent condition. In addition, it has the following options:

| | | |
|---|---|---|
| Air Conditioning | Cruise Control | Premium Sound |
| Power Steering | AM/FM Stereo | ABS (4-Wheel) |
| Power Windows | Cassette | Alloy Wheels |

A: _____

**www.mapsonus.com**
Q: You want to drive your new car to visit your cousin who lives in California. How many miles is it from your home to your cousin's home (he lives at 8695 Sierra Avenue in Fontana, CA)?
A: _____

**www.weather.com**
Q: So that you will know what kind of clothing to pack, what is today's weather forecast for Fontana, California?
A: _____

**www.nationalgeographic.com**
Q: When you arrive at your cousin's home, he tells you that over the summer he visited a town called Dozer. What country did he visit?
A: _____

### DOGS AND CATS

**www.citizenlunchbox.com/famous/dogs.html**
Q: What is the name of the last famous dog in the list. That is, the last dog whose name begins with a "Z"?
A: _____

**www.citizenlunchbox.com/famous/cats.html**
Q: In what TV show did Pequita appear?
A: _____

**www.lyricsrobot.com**
Q: The other day, Dozer heard a Donny Osmond song on the radio called "Puppy Love". He liked the song and wants to know what is the last line in this song?
A: _____

**www.puppyfinder.com**
Q: If you were going to get a puppy, according to this website, what breed of dog would be best for you to get? To find out, complete the Breed Selector survey.
A: _____

**www.thepuppyplace.org**
Q: What kind of dogs are featured on this website?
A: _____

## USE A SEARCH ENGINE

In Internet Project 1, you learned how to access a web page when you know its URL. But, what do you do if you don't know the URL? You can use a search engine. Dozens of different search engines exist, such as Excite, Yahoo, and Google. Each is merely a web site that keeps a database that permits you to search for information on the millions of web sites worldwide. In a search engine, you search for information in one of two ways. You can enter words in a search text box describing the topic or you can click one of the subject links to access a narrower choice of links and continue to narrow the search by clicking additional links until you find what you want.

To practice using a search engine text box, do the following (assume we want information about training dogs to do tricks):

☞ Go to **www.google.com** (Dozer's favorite search engine).
☞ In the Search box, type <u>dogs</u> and click the Google Search button (or, simply press the Enter key).
☞ Notice that the first ten citations appear. Each citation (also called a hit, result, or match) identifies a web page having something to do with the word "dogs" and each provides a link to the site, a brief description of the site, and its URL.
☞ Record the number of citations here: _____ (it should appear between the search box and the actual citations).
☞ Read some of the citations. Scroll to the bottom of the list.
☞ Click the Next link (the next 10 citations are displayed).
☞ Scroll until you reach the bottom of the list.
☞ Click the Next link (the next 10 citations are displayed).
☞ Scroll until you reach the bottom of the list.
☞ Click the Previous link to return to the previous 10 citations.
☞ We could continue to read citations until we found some related to training dogs to do tricks, but given the large number of citations, this might take a long time. In fact, some of the web sites found have nothing to do with dogs (canines), but are all about food (hot dogs). To speed up the search, we could narrow the search.
☞ Scroll to the top of the page. In the Search box, enter a word that will narrow the search (in this case, click after the word "dogs" and insert a space, then type <u>training</u>). Then click the Google Search button (or, simply press the Enter key).
☞ Google will look for web sites about dogs and training.
☞ Record the number of hits here: _____. Since you are finding web sites about dogs and training, instead of merely about dogs, you should have fewer citations than before.
☞ Read some of the citations.
☞ Now, let's narrow the search further to find web sites dealing with not just training dogs, but training dogs to do tricks. To do so, scroll to the top of the page. In the Search box, enter a word that will narrow the search (in this case, click after the word "training" and insert a space, then type <u>tricks</u>). Then click the Google Search button (or, press the Enter key).
☞ Google will look for sites about dogs, training, and tricks.
☞ Record the number of hits here: _____. Since you are finding web sites about dogs, training, and tricks instead of merely about dogs and training, you should have fewer citations than before.
☞ Find a citation that looks promising and click its link. If the web site that opens does not contain the information you want, click the Back button to return to the citations and click another one. Continue until you find a nice document that tells you how to teach a dog to do tricks.

## PRINT A WEB PAGE

To practice printing a web page, do the following:
☞ Go to **www.google.com**
☞ Find a biography about William (Bill) Gates.
☞ Click File, Print (if a dialog box does not appear, click anywhere in the web page and then click File, Print).
☞ In the Print Range area, select Pages and print only page 1.
☞ Specify the number of copies (select 1).
☞ Click the Print button. Go get your printout from the printer.
Note: you could also print the web page by simply clicking the Print button on the toolbar. But, when you do this, the printer will print one copy of the web page and a web page may be one, two, two dozen, or two hundred printed pages long. So, be careful with the Print toolbar button. Using File, Print will give you the Print dialog box which will let you choose how many paper pages to print from the web page.

## COPY AND PASTE TEXT FROM A WEB PAGE

If you print the page, you will print the graphics on the page along with the text. And, the formatting may not be what you like. To avoid these problems, copy and paste the text into another program that permits you to change the formatting.

To practice copying and pasting text, do the following:
☞ Go to **www.dozer.pannell.com** (or www.pannell.biz).
☞ Click the "My Thoughts On Doing The Deed" link.
☞ When the next page loads, drag the mouse over the text in the "Doing The Deed" paragraph. Don't drag over Dozer's name, or the title at the top, or the Home button at the bottom. Just drag over the paragraph you want.
☞ Click Edit, Copy (the text is sent to the clipboard).
☞ Start Word, not WordPad (the next 3 steps tell you how).
  ☞ To start Word, click the Start button on the taskbar.
  ☞ On the start menu, point to Programs.
  ☞ On the sub-menu, click Microsoft Word (If you don't see it, open additional menus until you find it).
☞ At the right side of the screen, a Task Pane will appear. To close it, click the X at the top right corner of the Task Pane.
☞ Click Edit, Paste. The paragraph appears in the document. Below the paragraph, a Paste Options button appears. Click it and then from the menu, click Keep Text Only to remove the formats from the web page and keep just the text.
☞ Type your name below the paragraph.
☞ Save the document to your diskette (call it <u>Deed</u>).
☞ Print one copy. Get your printout. Close Word.

## FIND, SAVE, AND INSERT IMAGES FROM A WEB PAGE

Most Internet images can be saved to your hard drive or diskette. When saved, you can send them via email or you can insert them into your documents.

To practice finding and saving images, do the following:
☞ Go to **www.google.com** and click the Images link.
☞ In the Search box, type a search term (type <u>puppies</u>).
☞ Click the Google Search button (or, simply press the Enter key). Notice that a collection of images appears. Scroll to find puppies you think would make good friends for Dozer. If you don't see a good image on the first page, click the Next link at the bottom of the page to see other images.
☞ When you find some puppy friends for Dozer, point to the image and right click. On the menu, click Save Picture As.

- In the Save Picture box, indicate that you want to save the image on your diskette.
- Notice that a filename is supplied. In the future, when you want to find this image, you'll need to recall it by its name. So, the filename should make sense to you. In the File Name box enter a new name for the file (call it puppies).
- Click the Save button (the image is saved to your diskette).
- Now, go to **www.dozer.pannell.com** (or www.pannell.biz).
- Right click on Dozer's image and, from the shortcut menu, select Save Picture As.
- Indicate that you want to save the image on your diskette.
- Notice that a filename is supplied. In the File Name box enter a new name for the file (name it Dozer).
- Click the Save button (the image is saved to your diskette).
- Go to **www.clipartconnection.com**
- Find an image of a dog that would make a good friend for Dozer and the puppies. Save it (name it Friend).

To practice inserting an image from a disk, do the following:
- Start Word, not WordPad. At the right side of the screen, a Task Pane will appear. To close it, click the X at the top right corner of the Task Pane.
- Click Insert, Picture, From File.
- In the Look in box, select the 3½ Floppy (A:) drive.
- Select the file to be inserted (the "Dozer" file). If you can't see that file, select All Files from the Files of Type list box.
- Click the Insert button to insert the picture.

To practice selecting a graphics box, do the following:
- Click the image (sizing handles appear around the image and the Picture toolbar should appear. If the Picture toolbar does not appear, click View, Toolbars, Picture).
- Click outside of the graphics box to deselect it.

To practice resizing an image, do the following:
- Click on the image to select it. Sizing handles appear.
- Point to any corner sizing handle until the mouse pointer looks like two-pointed arrow.
- Drag the handle until the image is the desired size (make the image the size of your thumb). Release the mouse button.
- Click outside of the image to deselect it.

To practice moving an image, do the following:
- Click the image and point to it. If the mouse pointer does not look like a four-pointed arrow, click the Text Wrapping button on the Picture toolbar (this button has a picture of a dog on it), then click Behind Text. Now, when you point to the image, the mouse pointer will look like a four-pointed arrow.
- Drag and drop the image to its new location.
- Click outside of the image to deselect it.
- Now, insert the "puppies" and "Friend" images.
- Resize each image to be about the size of your thumb.
- Move the three images to be across the top of the page. Remember, to move an image the mouse pointer must look like a four-pointed arrow. If it does not, click the image, then click the Text Wrapping button on the Picture toolbar, then click Behind Text. Now, you will be able to move the image.
- Type your name below the images.
- Save your document (name it Dozer and His Pals).
- Print your document. Close the document. Close Word.

## USE FAVORITES
To save a hit (valuable web page) for future reference, mark it as a favorite. You would do this because it's too hard to memorize most URLs. In addition, even if you memorized the URLs of your favorite sites, it's too time consuming and annoying to have to type in the URL every time you want to access one of your favorite websites.

To practice marking pages as favorites, do the following:
- Go to **www.abc.com**. From IE's menu bar, click Favorites, Add To Favorites. In the Add Favorite box, change the name to ABC TV, and then click OK.
- Go to **www.nbc.com**. From IE's menu bar, click Favorites, Add To Favorites. In the Add Favorite box, change the name to NBC TV, and then click OK.
- Go to **www.cbs.com**. From IE's menu bar, click Favorites, Add To Favorites. In the Add Favorite box, change the name to CBS TV, and then click OK.

To practice viewing your Favorites, do the following:
- Click Favorites. Click ABC TV. The web page appears.
- Click Favorites. Click NBC TV. The web page appears.
- Click Favorites. Click CBS TV. The web page appears.

## UNDERSTAND COOKIES
Sometimes when you access a web site, the site places a cookie on your hard drive. A cookie contains information of interest to the web site (it lets the site remember certain things about you). For example, a television network might ask you for your zip code (this would identify your general location). The next time you accessed that web site, they could use that information to provide you with local news and weather reports. They don't want to ask for your zip code every time you access their web page (and, you don't want them to either). So, they store that information as a cookie on your machine. You can prevent web sites from putting cookies on your hard drive by disabling cookies. However, if cookies are disabled, some web sites will not let you access their web pages. So, Dozer recommends that you not worry too much about cookies.

## LISTEN TO AUDIO
Many web pages provide audio (sound) as well as video (sight).

To practice listening to audio, do the following:
- Go to **www.expage.com/dozerdog**
- Do you hear the music? If not, do the following.
- First adjust the volume controls on the headphone wires or on the speakers. If that doesn't work, do the following.
- Click the icon of the speaker (on the taskbar).
- Drag the volume slide control to increase the volume and make sure the Mute box does not have check mark in it.

## DOWNLOAD THE GOOGLE TOOLBAR (OPTIONAL)
Besides being the most popular search engine on the planet, Google has a lot of other valuable features. For instance you can download the Google Toolbar so you can do searches without having to go to www.google.com. And, best of all, when you download the toolbar, you get a free pop-up blocker that stops web sites from annoying you with all those nasty pop-up ads. To get it, go to www.google.com and click the More link. Then, click the Google Toolbar link and download the toolbar.

## A WORD ABOUT INTERNET MISINFORMATION
Any fool can disseminate information on the Internet. Some information is inaccurate because its author is ignorant; some is intentionally a spoof (joke or intentional deception). Beware. Seek information from reliable sources.

# EXERCISES

## EXERCISE 1: CROSSWORD
Use the clues below to complete the crossword puzzle.

### ACROSS

3. After I enter a search term in the Google text box, Google provides a list of web sites. Each includes a description of the site, its URL, etc. Each item on the list is a ___.
5. To return to a previously-viewed page, click the ___ toolbar button.
6. A web page address is often referred to as a ___.
8. Followed links are a different ___ than unfollowed links, which help me to remember which web sites I've already visited.
12. Each corner and border of a selected image has a ___ handle which can be dragged to resize the image.
13. When saving an image from the Internet, enter a filename that makes sense to you. To do so, just change the file's name in the File ___ box of the Save Picture dialog box.
14. While a page is loading, the IE ___ is animated.
17. When I find a web page that I like and I think I will want to revisit it at a later time, I mark it as a ___.

### DOWN

1. With Google, in addition to searching for text, I can use the Directory to find a ___ to information.
2. To launch IE, click ___, All Programs, Internet Explorer.
4. Another name for 3 across.
7. Some web sites will place a ___ on your hard drive (it contains information of interest to the web site).
9. Dozer's favorite search engine.
10. Dozer's last name.
11. To save an image from a web site, right click on the image and then, from the shortcut menu, click Save ___ As.
15. A printer not communicating with a computer is ___ line.
16. An abbreviation for Internet Explorer.

## EXERCISE 2: TRUE-FALSE
For each of the following eight statements, place a T or an F on the line to indicate if the statement is True or False.

1. ___A muffin is data put on my hard drive by a web site.
2. ___The boxes around a selected image are sizing handles.
3. ___Another word for "citation" is "ticket".
4. ___Excite, Yahoo, and Google are search motors.
5. ___To select an image in Word, I click in the image.
6. ___ To deselect an image in Word, click outside of the image.
7. ___I can copy, but I can't print a web page.
8. ___When I do a word search, I get 10 citations to the page.

## EXERCISE 3: EXPLAIN CONCEPTS
Dozer has been trying to tell his little sister Skooter that cookies are not evil (he ain't talkin' about chocolate chip cookies). How would you describe "cookies" to Skooter and how might you try to convince her that cookies are not so evil?

_____
_____
_____
_____
_____
_____
_____
_____
_____

## EXERCISE 4: TRUE-FALSE
For each of the following eight statements, place a T or an F on the line to indicate if the statement is True or False.

1. ___Excite, Yahoo, and Google are search engines.
2. ___The boxes around a selected image are moving handles.
3. ___I can save a valuable web page as a "favorite".
4. ___To insert an image into Word, I click File, Open.
5. ___If I disable cookies, some web sites will deny me access.
6. ___I can copy text from a web page and paste it into Word.
7. ___Another word for "citation" is "hit".
8. ___All the information on the Internet is factually accurate.

## EXERCISE 5: FIND A WORD
The answers to the following statements can be found in the matrix. The answers may be backwards, diagonal, vertical, or horizontal. Circle each answer.

1. Information placed on your hard drive by a web site.
2. Dozer's favorite search engine.
3. The first page in a web site.
4. A marker that helps me rapidly find a valuable web page.
5. The address of a web page.
6. Another word for a citation, result, or a match.

| H | C | G | E | T | A | S | F | U | U | G |
|---|---|---|---|---|---|---|---|---|---|---|
| C | H | O | M | E | P | A | G | E | R | K |
| R | L | O | O | O | G | I | J | U | D | L |
| N | W | G | R | K | U | H | T | L | R | V |
| E | A | L | E | T | I | R | O | V | A | F |
| T | H | E | M | T | P | E | L | E | X | A |

## EXERCISE 6: COPY TEXT FROM THE INTERNET

To make sure your disk has enough space to save the work you will do in this and the next few exercises, format your diskette.

☞ Start Internet Explorer and go to **www.google.com**
☞ Find a biography about Walt Disney and copy the first three paragraphs of the biography to the clipboard.
☞ Start Microsoft Word. At the right side of the screen the Task Pane will appear. Since you don't need it, close it by clicking the X at the top right corner of the Task Pane.
☞ Paste the biography onto the document. Click the Paste Options button (it appears below the biography) and then from the Paste Options menu, click Keep Text Only to remove the formats from the web page, keeping just the text.
☞ Save the document to your diskette (call it cartoon).

## EXERCISE 7: SAVE IMAGES FROM THE INTERNET

☞ Using Internet Explorer, go to **www.google.com**
☞ Find pictures of three of the following characters (pick one character from each column).

| A | B | C |
|---|---|---|
| Elmer Fudd | Mickey Mouse | Fred Flintstone |
| Porky Pig | Minnie Mouse | Popeye |
| Bugs Bunny | Snoopy | Bart Simpson |
| Yosemite Sam | Donald Duck | George Jetson |
| Tweety Bird | Hank Hill | Garfield |

☞ Save each of the three images to your disk. When you right click on each image and click Save Picture As, a dialog box will provide a name for each picture. In the File Name box, enter a new name for each picture. For instance, if you are saving a picture of Snoopy, call it "Snoopy".
☞ At the top of the "cartoon" document that you created in Exercise 6, insert the three cartoon images. Note: When you go to Insert, Picture, From File and open the A Drive, if you cannot see the files you saved a few moments ago, select All Files from the Files of Type list box.
☞ Resize each image so that each is the size of your thumb.
☞ Move the images to be across the top of the page.
☞ Type your name on a line between the images and the text.
☞ Save the modified document (that is, save the current version of your document so that your changes will be permanently stored on your diskette).
☞ Print the document. Close the document. Close Word.

## EXERCISE 8: FIND INFORMATION

Start Internet Explorer and answer the following questions. In each instance, you will need to use Google to actually find a phone book, map maker, etc. that will help you find the answers.

### PHONE BOOK

Go to **www.google.com** and use the phrase "phone book" to find a web site that will permit you to answer these questions.

Q: A business called "Dozer, Inc" is located in Natchez, Mississippi. What is the phone number of that company?.
A: _____

Q: Elvis Presley lives in San Francisco, California. What is his street address?
A: _____

Q: What is the address of your college campus?
A: _____

### MAPS

Go to **www.google.com** and use the term "maps" to find a web site that will permit you to answer these questions.

Q: Find a map of the neighborhood surrounding your college campus. Is the map accurate?
A: _____

Q: Find a map of your home neighborhood. Print one copy of the map. Is the map of your neighborhood accurate?
A: _____

### TRANSLATORS

Go to **www.google.com** and use the phrase "text translator" to find a web site that will permit you to answer these questions.

Q: If you translate "ordinateurs sont mes amis" from French to English, what does it say?
A: _____

Q: Translate **www.dozer.pannell.com/dozersjob.html** (or www.pannell.biz/dozersjob.html) from English to Spanish. What three words are on the line under Dozer's name? (Hint: use the Web Page translator feature).
A: _____

### WEIGHT CONVERSION

Go to **www.google.com** and use "weight conversion" to find a web site that will permit you to answer this question.

Q: Dozer weighs 32 kilograms. How many pounds is that?
A: _____

## EXERCISE 9: LISTEN TO AUDIO

☞ Go to **www.expage.com/dozerpannellsmostfavoritesong**
☞ Can you hear the music? If you don't hear it, you may need to increase the volume.

## EXERCISE 10: MARK A WEB PAGE AS A FAVORITE

If you liked the sounds from the web site you visited in Exercise 9, you could return there anytime. The only problem is that the URL for that page is too long to remember. So, to be able to return to this page later, mark the page as a favorite. Go ahead and mark it now and name it Tunes. Later, we'll come back to this page and hear the music again.

## EXERCISE 11: PRINT A WEB PAGE

☞ Go to **www.dozer.pannell.com** (or www.pannell.biz).
☞ Click the My Thoughts On Doing The Deed link.
☞ Print one copy of the document. By the way, this document contains the secret to college success. It clearly identifies the one and the only person who is responsible for learning. Keep this document. You may want to read it from time to time. Note that the background does not print.

## EXERCISE 12: VIEW A FAVORITE PAGE

In Exercise 10, you marked a page as a favorite. Since then, you have visited another site. To return to the favorite page (the one with the music that you marked in Exercise 10), click Favorites, and click "Tunes" from the list. The browser will load the web page for you.

## INTRODUCTION TO EMAIL

Email is the most popular service on the Internet. Its popularity is due to the following characteristics.

☞ COST: Email is cheaper than a stamp and an envelope and much cheaper than a long distance phone call.

☞ CONVENIENCE: You can write and send email anytime. In addition, you can send it simultaneously to lots of different people (recipients).

☞ SPEED: While snail mail (postal service mail) may take days, email typically takes seconds.

## NETIQUETTE

Netiquette refers to common rules of Internet etiquette. For example, as you explore a newsgroup or web site, most of your questions have already been asked by prior visitors. These questions and their answers have been compiled in a list called a FAQ (Frequently Asked Questions). You should read the list before you ask a question. Otherwise, you will rudely waste the time of the person to whom you direct your inquiry. Listening to an ongoing chatroom conversation before you jump in, or reading newsgroup postings before you post a message, is called lurking. By lurking, you will discover what the group is interested in and you will not rudely change the subject. Spam (generally useless information sent to many people at once) should be avoided. Your impulse might be to send each of your messages to everyone in your address book, but it's more efficient to send it to the person to whom you wish to communicate. A message that incites others to anger is a flame. A free-for-all is a flame war. Text in capital letters may be interpreted by the recipient as shouting. Pretending to be someone else (e.g., using someone else's userid or deceiving others in a similar way) is spoofing. Punctuation symbols that represent human faces if turned sideways are smileys (also called emoticons), which are used to communicate feelings. Some examples of smileys include:

| smiling :-) | smiling with glasses 8-) |
| scuba diver (:)- | baseball fan d:-) |
| laughing :-D | frowning :-( |

## EMAIL ADDRESSES

An address follows the pattern of username@domainname. The username is an electronic mail box for a specific person using the domain (the computer system upon which the email resides). The best way to understand the structure of an email address is to look at an example. In the email address president@whitehouse.gov, president is the username (also called a login name or userid) identifying a mailbox at the whitehouse.gov domain (also called a host). By the way, we would pronounce this address as "president at whitehouse dot gov." Do not confuse URLs with email addresses. A URL seldom, if ever, has a "@" in it and an email address virtually never starts with "www".

## OBTAIN A YAHOO EMAIL ACCOUNT

Many free Internet mail services exist. Since Dozer's favorite is Yahoo, we'll follow his lead and use Yahoo email. Yahoo is supported mostly by firms who pay to have their ads placed on the screen. To obtain a free email account with Yahoo, you are required to fill out a brief form. Since Yahoo is financially supported, not by you, but by advertisers, Yahoo is unable to process registration forms that do not have complete

information. The information you will supply is used to match advertising on the service to your interests. For example, if you tell Yahoo during the registration process that you are interested in sports, you are more likely to see ads for sporting events and athletic equipment.

To register for a free Yahoo email account, do the following:

☞ Start Internet Explorer and go to **www.yahoo.com**

☞ When the Yahoo home page loads, click the Mail link.

☞ When the next page loads, click Sign Up Now.

☞ When the next page loads, click Sign Up Now (Free Mail).

☞ In the next page, click in the Yahoo ID text box, then type an ID (use your name with no spaces between your first and last name, followed by your class code. For example, if Dozer Pannell's class code is S3, his Yahoo ID would be dozerpannellS3. How will you know what your class code is? Ask your instructor and write it on the bottom right corner of page C-29.

☞ Click in the Password text box. Type a password.

☞ Write your password here _____. Record it EXACTLY the way you entered it on the screen. Take your time and do this with great care. If you don't, you will not be able to use your email. IDs and passwords must be entered precisely. Passwords are case sensitive, which means that dozer, Dozer, and DOZER are three distinctly different passwords.

☞ Click in the Re-type Password text box. Type the password exactly as you wrote it on the line above.

☞ Continue to provide the information requested (you will need to scroll down from time to time to see the questions).

☞ Click the Submit This Form button. If there's anything wrong with the information you provided, you will be told what the problem is and will be given instructions as to what to do to correct the problem. After correcting the problem, click the Submit This Form button. When you successfully register, click the Continue To Yahoo Mail button (bottom of page).

☞ Notice the Mail, Addresses, Calendar, and Notepad tabs at the top of the screen. Each provides access to a different resource in your Yahoo account.

## COMPOSE MAIL

To practice composing mail, do the following:

☞ Click the Mail tab. Then click the Compose button.

☞ In the "To:" box, enter the email address of the recipient. In this case, since you are merely practicing, enter your email address in that box. Be sure to enter your entire email address which consists of your username and the domain name (e.g., dozerpannellS3@yahoo.com).

☞ In the "Subject:" box, enter <u>Compose Practice</u>.

☞ In the message box, type your message (in this case, type <u>computers are my friends</u>).

☞ If you were sending this message to someone other than yourself, you might want to save a copy of your message. To do so, you could CC yourself or you could save a copy to your Sent folder. In this practice, let's save a copy to your Sent folder. Before you actually send the message, make sure that a check mark appears in the Save A Copy In Your Sent Items Folder box (below the message box). Now, sending a message to yourself AND saving a copy in your Sent folder may seem silly, but we are just practicing now.

☞ Click the Send button. Your message was sent to you and a copy was placed in your Sent folder.

## READ MAIL

To practice reading mail, do the following:

☞ Click the Check Mail button to see if you have a message (you should have two: one from the fine folks at Yahoo with the subject of Welcome To Yahoo Mail and another from yourself).

☞ The subject of a message is a link to the message. Click on the Welcome To Yahoo Mail link to open the message. When you are done reading a message, you can choose to delete it or keep it. To delete it, click the Delete button; to keep it, simply click Check Mail. For now, don't delete it.

## REPLY TO MAIL

Sometimes, you will receive a message to which you want to respond. You could compose a new message to the person. However, it would be more efficient to reply to the message.

To practice replying to mail, do the following:

☞ Click Check Mail to see if you have a message (find the message you previously sent to yourself).

☞ Click on the subject of the message to read the message.

☞ Click the Reply button. A screen appears with the original sender's address in the "To" field (which in this case is your address) and the original subject in the "subject" field with the letters "Re:" (Reply) in front of it.

☞ In the Mail body area, click on a blank line above the original message and type I Love Computers!  Click Send.

☞ Click Check Mail to open the Inbox. You should have three messages (the Welcome To Yahoo Mail, the Compose Practice, and the Reply to the Compose Practice). It is possible that you only have two messages in your Inbox. Perhaps, you clicked Check Mail before the last message arrived. If so, wait a few seconds and click Check Mail again to reopen the Inbox. Once the Reply message arrives, notice that the subject of the unread message appears in bold type; the subject of any read message is faded.

## BOUNCED MAIL

If you address a postal letter incorrectly and send it via the U.S. Postal Service (snail mail), one of two things will happen. If the address belongs to someone, the letter will be delivered to them, not to the person you intended to get the letter. If the address does not exist, the letter will be marked "Return To Sender: Address Unknown" and the postal service will send it back to you. Likewise, if you enter an email address incorrectly, one of two things will happen. If the email address you entered belongs to someone, they, not the person you intended, will receive the message. If the email address does not belong to anyone, the message will "bounce" back to you. In such a case, you will have a message in your Inbox telling you about the situation. Compare the address in the bounced message with the correct address. The most likely reason for non-delivery is that you mistyped the address. After you find the error, resend the message using the correct address.

To see what a bounced message looks like, do the following:

☞ Send a message to dozer@dozerpannell.com.

☞ Notice that after you click the Send button, you are told that your message was sent.

☞ Wait a few seconds for the message to be delivered.

☞ Click Check Mail and look for a message from the Mailer Daemon. Read the message. It will tell you that your mail was not delivered. It was sent, but not delivered (i.e., your message bounced). The Mailer Daemon will provide you

with the undeliverable address you used.

☞ Dozer's email address is not dozer@dozerpannell.com. It is dozer@pannell.com. There's no need to send him email now. Just remember that when you do send a message to him or to anyone else, you must address it precisely.

## GET HELP

The fine folks at Yahoo want you to be satisfied and successful in using your Yahoo email account. Therefore, they provide lots of neat features for you to use. And, they provide instructions on how to use those features. To access Help, click the Help link. Click the relevant links to get answers to your questions.

To practice using Help, find answers to these questions.

Q: What does "Bcc" stand for?
A: _____

Q: What is Spam and what is Yahoo's policy on Spam?
A: _____

Q: What is a filter?
A: _____

Q: What is a bulk mail folder?
A: _____

Q: Does Yahoo provide a spelling checker?
A: _____

## SIGN OUT

To prevent others from accessing your account, sign out at the end of each session.

To practice signing out, do the following:

☞ Click Sign Out (top of screen).

☞ Wait for the next page to load.

☞ When you see the "You Have Signed Out of The Yahoo Network" message, close Internet Explorer.

## LOG IN

To practice logging in, do the following:

☞ Start Internet Explorer and go to **www.yahoo.com**

☞ Click the Email link.

☞ When the next page appears, enter your ID in the Yahoo ID text box. This is the ID you specified when you requested the account. It must be entered precisely. If you registered as previously instructed, your ID is your name with no spaces between the first and last name followed by your class code (e.g., dozerpannellS3). Note: Don't enter the "@yahoo.com" part of your address. Yahoo already knows that part.

☞ Enter your password in the Password text box. It must be entered precisely the way you entered it when you registered for the account--it is case-sensitive. Forgot your password? Look on page C-11 where you wrote it down. Didn't write it down? Yahoo will help you find it. Under the Password text box, click "Password Lookup" and follow the on-screen directions to attempt to discover your ID or password. If unsuccessful, you must register for a new Yahoo account by returning to the "Obtain a Yahoo Email Account" on page C-11 and signing up for a new account.

☞ Click the Sign In button.

☞ Read any mail you have received.

☞ Sign Out.

# EXERCISES

## EXERCISE 1: CROSSWORD
Use the clues below to complete the crossword puzzle.

### ACROSS
3. If I want to respond to a message, I would click the ___ button so my message would immediately be addressed to the person who sent me the original message.
4. An acronym for the World Wide Web.
7. If I send email to a non-existent address, the ___ daemon will inform me of non-delivery.
11. In the address dozer@pannell.com, "dozer" is the ___.
14. Proper behavior on the Internet.
16. In Yahoo, I click ___ to get answers to my questions.
17. Email in capital letters can be interpreted as ___.
20. Is a spoof and an emoticon the same thing?

### DOWN
1. To get a hard copy of a web page, I click File, ___.
2. Useless information sent to many people at once.
5. Folks exchange hostile messages in a flame ___.
6. A message that incites others to anger.
8. Listening to an ongoing conversation before speaking.
9. Punctuation marks that create faces if turned sideways.
10. If you send an email message to a non-existent address, the message will ___, whIch means It will return to you.
12. To read a message in your Inbox, click the ___ link.
13. dozer@pannell.com is read "dozer ___ pannell dot com".
15. In the email address dozer@pannell.com, "pannell" is the domain (sometimes this is called the ___).
18. In Yahoo, incoming messages are kept in the ___box.
19. Does FAQ stand for Frequently Accessed Quotations?

## EXERCISE 2: IDENTIFY TERMS
Below are eight definitions. Below the definitions are eight lines. In each line, write the word that matches the definition.

1. Internet etiquette.
2. Pretending to be someone else.
3. A message that incites others to anger.
4. Useless information sent to many people.
5. Listening to a chatroom conversation before you jump in.
6. Text in capital letters may be interpreted as this.
7. A free-for-all where insults are exchanged between folks.
8. A list of commonly-asked questions and their answers.

1. _____    5. _____
2. _____    6. _____
3. _____    7. _____
4. _____    8. _____

## EXERCISE 3: TRUE-FALSE
For each of the following eight statements, place a T or an F on the line to indicate if the statement is True or False.

1. ___ A smiley is sometimes called an emoticon.
2. ___ The Mailer Daemon tells me when messages bounce.
3. ___ A "bounced" letter is one that could not be delivered.
4. ___ In Yahoo, to write a message, I click the Compose link.
5. ___ A URL has an "@" in it.
6. ___ "Case sensitive" means that "bob" & "Bob" are the same.
7. ___ :-) and 8-) are called smileys.
8. ___ In Yahoo, to reply to a message, click the Respond link.

## EXERCISE 4: MATCHING
Below is a list of terms associated with proper behavior on the Internet. Below the list are some statements. For each statement, identify the term to which it refers by placing the letter of the term on the line preceding each statement.

| | | |
|---|---|---|
| A. Flame | D. Lurking | G. Smiley |
| B. FAQ | E. Netiquette | H. Spam |
| C. Flame war | F. Shouting | I. Spoofing |

1. ___ Listening before entering a conversation.
2. ___ A list of questions that have been asked before.
3. ___ Common rules of Internet etiquette.
4. ___ When folks exchange a barrage of insults.
5. ___ Text in capital letters can be interpreted as this.
6. ___ Useless information sent to many people at once.
7. ___ Pretending to be someone else.
8. ___ A group of punctuation symbols that look like a face.
9. ___ A message that incites the recipient to anger.

## EXERCISE 5: TRUE-FALSE
For each of the following eight statements, place a T or an F on the line to indicate if the statement is True or False.

1. ___ :-) and 8-) are called sideshots.
2. ___ An email address always starts with "www".
3. ___ FAQ stands for "Forward Another Question".
4. ___ If I "CC" myself, a copy of the message will be sent to me.
5. ___ In Yahoo, to open my Inbox, I click the Check Mail link.
6. ___ Yahoo charges $10 per month for each email account.
7. ___ Postal Service mail is sometimes called "snail mail".
8. ___ If I pretend to be someone else, I am lurking.

## EXERCISE 6: EXPLAIN CONCEPTS

Skooter sent a message to her brother Dozer. When she sent it, Yahoo told Skooter that the "mail was sent", but Dozer said he never got the message and suggested that perhaps it "bounced." If Yahoo "sent it", Skooter wants to know how could Dozer have not gotten it? And, what is a "bounced" message? How can Skooter know if a message "bounces"?

_____

_____

_____

_____

_____

_____

_____

_____

_____

_____

## EXERCISE 7: IDENTIFY EMAIL ADDRESSES VS URLS

Which addresses are email addresses and which are web page addresses (URLs)? Indicate by writing either Email or URL on the line for each item.

| EMAIL | URL |
|-------|-----|
| 1. _____ www.dozer.pannell.com | |
| 2. _____ dozer@pannell.com | |
| 3. _____ dog.com | |
| 4. _____ beauaugustusbitter@yahoo.com | |
| 5. _____ home.switchboard.com/dozerpannell | |
| 6. _____ president@whitehouse.gov | |
| 7. _____ www.whitehouse.gov | |
| 8. _____ www.math.berkeley.edu/~galen/popclk.html | |
| 9. _____ skooterpannell@yahoo.com | |

Based on what you have noticed, answer these two questions.
1. What does every email address have in it? _____
2. Do all URL's start with a "www"? _____

## EXERCISE 8: EXPLAIN CONCEPTS

Skooter doesn't understand what all the big fuss over email is. After all, she can send a letter via the U.S. Postal service. Could you explain to Skooter why email is better than snail mail? Please provide three characteristics of email that make it much better than snail mail.

_____

_____

_____

_____

_____

_____

_____

_____

_____

_____

_____

## EXERCISE 9: OPEN AN EMAIL ACCOUNT

On page C-11, you were instructed to obtain a Yahoo email account. If you have not done that yet, follow the instructions found on page C-11 to open an account. Then do Exercise 10.

## EXERCISE 10: SEND A MESSAGE

☞ Address a note to your instructor (your instructor's address should be on the bottom right corner of page C-29).
☞ The subject should be address.
☞ The message should be please add my email address to your address book. CC yourself. Send the message.

## EXERCISE 11: SIGN OUT OF YOUR ACCOUNT

☞ Sign out of your Yahoo account. Close Internet Explorer.

## EXERCISE 12: LOG INTO YOUR ACCOUNT

☞ Start Internet Explorer and go to www.yahoo.com
☞ Sign into your Yahoo email account.

## EXERCISE 13: COPY & PASTE TEXT TO A MESSAGE

Dozer heard a rumor that hot dogs are made from dim-witted dogs. Since he is dim-witted, he is understandably worried.

☞ Go to www.google.com to find a web page that tells you what kinds of meats are used to make hot dogs. That is, what are the ingredients used to make hot dogs.
☞ Copy the information to the clipboard.
☞ Paste the information about hot dogs to an email message.
☞ Address the message to yourself.
☞ The subject should be hot dogs.
☞ Send the message.
☞ Go to your Inbox, open the message you sent to yourself, and print out one copy.
☞ Sign out of your Yahoo email account.

## EXERCISE 14: CREATE A FILM

☞ Go to www.dfilm.com
☞ Click the DFilm Moviemaker link (at top of screen).
☞ Click the Start link.
☞ Select the type of background and sky (at the bottom of each column, there is an arrow which can be clicked to access additional backgrounds and skies). When done making these selections, click the Next link.
☞ Select a plot. Then click the Next link.
☞ Select your character(s) by clicking them (at the bottom of each column of characters, there is an arrow which can be clicked to access additional characters). When you're done making these selections, click the Next link.
☞ Click in the text boxes and type the dialog (Note: when you click in the text boxes, the insertion point may not appear there. Don't be concerned, just click and type). Click Next.
☞ Select your music. Click Finish Movie.
☞ Click a title design from the selection on the left and then click in the text boxes and type the title for your movie and your name. Click the Preview & Send Movie link.
☞ Wait for your movie to load (it may take several minutes).
☞ If you don't like something about your movie, click the Back link and fix it. If it's so beautiful that Steven Spielberg would be envious of it, send it to a friend and be sure to enter your email address as the sender so that a copy of it will be sent to you. Click the Send link.
☞ Go to your email and open the dfilm message.
☞ Click the link to view your film the way your friend will.
☞ Close the dfilm windows.
☞ Log off of your Yahoo email.

## USE A SIGNATURE

A signature is text at the end of a message. It is commonly used for a favorite quotation or to give contact information (e.g., URL, telephone number, postal address, etc.).

To practice creating a signature, do the following:
☞ Using Internet Explorer, log into your Yahoo account.
☞ Click Mail Options (top of screen). Then click Signature.
☞ In the box, type a signature. In this case, type a favorite quotation. Which quotation, you ask? Any one you like. Can't think of one? Then, use Dozer's favorite, as follows: A Child Denied A Puppy Is A Child Denied A Childhood.
☞ Make sure that the Add Signature To All Outgoing Messages check box is selected. Then click the Save button.
☞ Click Compose and send yourself a message.
☞ Click Check Mail and look at the message you just sent to yourself. Notice the signature you just created.

## ADD ADDRESSES TO YOUR ADDRESS BOOK

In the same way that you need an address book to keep track of postal addresses of friends and relatives, you will want to have an address book to keep track of email addresses. If someone gives you his or her email address, you can manually enter it into your address book. On the other hand, when you receive an email message, you can choose to have Yahoo enter the address.

To practice adding addresses given to you, do the following:
☞ Click the Addresses tab (top of screen) and then click Add Contact.
☞ Type the person's first name, last name, and email address (in this case, use your instructor's name and email address (it's on the bottom right corner of page C-29). In addition to the required fields, there are optional fields (e.g., nickname, home phone, work phone). For now, leave them empty.
☞ Click the Save Contact button. Then click the Done button.
☞ Repeat the above steps to add your own address to your address book. This may seem silly, but it is very common for folks to write messages to themselves and it's easier and faster to do so when the address is in the address book.
☞ Add Dozer Pannell's address (dozer@pannell.com).
☞ Add Skooter Pannell (skooterpannell@yahoo.com). By the way, in case you forgot, Skooter is Dozer's little sister.

To practice adding addresses using the link that comes with incoming mail, do the following:
☞ Open your Inbox (click the Mail tab, then click Check Mail). Read any message. Hey, if you don't have any messages from friends, you need to get some better friends. Without messages from them, you won't be able to add their addresses to your address book. You'll need to do this later.
☞ If you do have a message from a friend, click the Add To Address Book link (in the "From" line).
☞ Click the Add Checked Contacts button (the address is added to your address book and you return to the message).
☞ Click Addresses (top of the screen) and confirm that the address has been added to your address book.

## SEND MESSAGES USING THE ADDRESS BOOK

Using an address book serves two purposes. First, it is difficult to remember hundreds of email addresses, especially when they must be remembered exactly. An address book solves this problem by keeping an accurate record of addresses. Second, by having an address book, you won't need to type the address every time a message is written. Since typing addresses takes time and increases the likelihood of a mistake, you can save time (and increase accuracy) by using an address book.

To practice emailing with an address book, do the following:
☞ Click the Mail tab and then click Compose.
☞ Click Insert Addresses (above the "To:" box).
☞ From your address book, find the person to whom you want to send the message (in this case, find your own address).
☞ Click in the "To" check box next to your name. Note that you can click more than one "To" check box and your message will be sent to each selected person.
☞ You can also click the "Cc:" (Carbon Copy) check box to designate that a person is to receive a copy of the message (in this case, send a copy to yourself. This may sound silly, but you are merely practicing, so it doesn't matter if you end up sending this message "To" you and a "CC" to you).
☞ Click the Insert Checked Contacts button (your address is inserted in the "To:" box and your address is also inserted in the "Cc:" box).
☞ Type the subject Address Book Practice.
☞ Compose your message. Write anything you like.
☞ Send the message. Once sent, you will be told to whom the message was sent (You!).

## EDIT AN ADDRESS BOOK ENTRY

A person may change her email address (e.g., she changes jobs and her employer-provided email account is closed) or she may change her name (e.g., she gets married). In such cases, you can edit the address book entry for that person.

To practice editing an address book entry, do the following:
☞ Click the Addresses tab (top of screen).
☞ Click the Edit link to the right of the entry (in this case, click Dozer Pannell's Edit link).
☞ In the Add Contact screen, modify any text box desired (in this case, specify his company is Dozer Security Services, his home phone number is 555-3214, and his home address is 1234 Dog Bone Road, Dogtown, NV 89122).
☞ Click the Save Contact button. Then click the Done button.
☞ Click Dozer's name in your address book and notice that his entry now displays the information you provided.

## DELETE AN ADDRESS BOOK ENTRY

When someone closes her email account or when a friend is no longer a friend and you no longer wish to communicate with her, you will want to delete her entry from your address book.

To practice deleting an address book entry, do the following:
☞ Click the Addresses tab (top of screen).
☞ Click the box to the left of the entry to be deleted (in this case, click the box next to Skooter's name) and click the Delete button).
☞ When asked to confirm your intention, click Delete Checked.

## FORWARD A MESSAGE

When you receive a message that would be of interest to someone else, you can forward the message to her.

To practice forwarding a message, do the following:
☞ Open the message to be forwarded (open any message).
☞ Click Forward. A screen appears with the original subject and "Fwd" (Forward) in the subject line.
☞ Enter a recipient in the "To" field (forward it to yourself--this may sound silly, but if you forward it to yourself, you will be able to read it to see what a forwarded message looks like).
☞ Add some text in the Mail Body area. Click Send.
☞ Go read the message you just forwarded to yourself.

## SEND ATTACHMENTS
To practice sending text attachments, do the following:
☞ Start Word (to do so, click Start, All Programs, Microsoft Word. (if you don't see it, open other menus until you find it).
☞ Create a document (just type your name in the document).
☞ Save the document to your diskette (name it hello).
☞ Close Microsoft Word.
☞ In your Yahoo account, address a message to yourself.
☞ Type Text Attachment for the subject.
☞ Click the Attach Files link (below the Subject Box).
☞ Click the File 1 Browse button.
☞ In the Choose File dialog box, select the Floppy Drive.
☞ Select the "Hello" file that you just created. Click Open.
☞ Click the Attach Files button.
☞ Wait until you see your file listed in the Files Attached box (you may wait a few seconds or a few minutes for this).
☞ Click the Done button. Wait until the Compose Message screen reappears. Click the Send button.

To practice sending image attachments, do the following:
☞ Go to www.animfactory.com
☞ Find an animated image you like and right click it.
☞ On the shortcut menu, click Save Picture As.
☞ Indicate where to save it (save it on your floppy disk).
☞ Type a filename (give it a name that describes the image).
☞ Click the Save button.
☞ Repeatedly click the browser's Back button until you return to your email.
☞ In your Yahoo account, address a message to yourself.
☞ For the subject, type Image Attachment.
☞ Click the Attach Files link (below the Subject Box).
☞ Click the File 1 Browse button.
☞ In the Choose File dialog box, select the Floppy Drive.
☞ Select the image you saved from the web site. Note: If you cannot see the file you saved a few moments ago, select All Files from the Files of Type list box. Click Open.
☞ Click the Attach Files button.
☞ Wait until you see your file listed in the Files Attached box.
☞ Click the Done button. Wait until the Compose Message screen reappears and then click the Send button.

## VIEW ATTACHMENTS
If you receive a message with an attachment, there will be an image of a paper clip next to the subject of the message. The attachment will either appear below the message box (if it is an image) or it will be represented by a link (if it is text). By the way, you should know that your computer may not recognize all file types. So, you may be unable to read some attachments.

To practice viewing attachments, do the following:
☞ Click Check Mail. Notice that the two messages you just sent to yourself each have a paper clip next to the message subject. This indicates that they each have an attachment.
☞ Open the message with the "Text Attachment" subject.

☞ Scroll down to see the Attachment box.
☞ Click Scan With Norton Antivirus.
☞ When told "no virus detected," click Download File.
☞ When the File Download dialog box appears, click Open.
☞ Notice that Word is launched and the file is opened.
☞ Close Word.
☞ Open the Image Attachment message. Notice the image appears (you may need to scroll down to see it).

## USE FOLDERS
To organize messages, put them in folders. When you opened your Yahoo account, Yahoo gave you four folders (in addition to these four, you can create as many folders as you wish):
☞ INBOX: where incoming mail is stored.
☞ DRAFT: where partially-completed letters can be kept.
☞ SENT: where copies of sent messages can be saved.
☞ TRASH: where deleted messages are temporarily kept.

## DELETE MESSAGES
While Yahoo lets you store thousands of messages (100MB), if folks send you lots of mail with attachments, you may reach the storage limit. To avoid this, you should periodically delete unneeded mail. However, merely deleting the messages is not sufficient, because all deleted messages are put in the Trash folder, which still takes up storage space. So, after deleting the messages, be sure to empty the Trash folder.

To practice deleting mail, do the following:
☞ In your Inbox, click the check box to the left of a message you want to delete (in this case, choose any unwanted message). A check mark will appear in the box.
☞ Click the Delete button. The message is put in the Trash folder where it will stay until the trash is emptied. Until then, messages can be retrieved by clicking the Trash link.
☞ To empty the Trash folder, click the Empty link (next to the Trash folder link). Notice that after you do this, you are told that your Trash folder has been emptied.

## CHANGE YOUR PASSWORD
If you think someone has learned your password, change it. To do so, click Mail Options (top of screen) and then click Account Information (left of screen). Enter your current password and then follow the on-screen instructions to create a new password.

## FIND EMAIL ADDRESSES
If you don't know someone's phone number, you can look it up in a telephone directory. If you don't know someone's email address, you can look it up in an email directory. There are dozens of email directories to use. If you can't find the person you are looking for at one, try another. If all else fails, call the person on the phone and ask her for her email address.

To practice finding email addresses, do the following:
☞ Go to www.yahoo.com and click the People Search link.
☞ In the Email Search boxes, enter the name to be searched (in this case, enter Dozer Pannell).
☞ Click the Search button. How many entries were found? __.
☞ Go to www.switchboard.com and click the Find Email Address link. Search for Dozer Pannell. How many entries were found? __.
☞ Go to www.bigfoot.com. In the Find People box, search for Dozer Pannell. How may entries were found? __.
☞ Now, use these directories to try to find yourself or a friend.
☞ If done for now, log off of the machine.

# EXERCISES

## EXERCISE 1: CROSSWORD
Use the clues below to complete the crossword puzzle.

### ACROSS
3. Useless, unsolicited, unwanted information sent to many people at once.
5. If you create a document using another program, you can email it as a ___ attachment.
6. A ___ is a few lines of text at the end of a message (e.g., postal address, favorite quote, or a web site address).
9. When I receive a message that I feel would be of interest to someone else, I can ___ the message to her.
11. A very popular directory service is www.___foot.com.
12. In Yahoo, deleted messages are kept in the ___ folder.
13. Inbox, Sent, Draft, and Trash are names of ___ in Yahoo.
14. In the address dozerpannell@yahoo.com, the "yahoo.com" part identifies the domain. Another word for domain is ___.

### DOWN
1. Before I send a message, if I click the box in front of "Save Copy To ___ Folder", a copy of the message will be saved.
2. The time is displayed at the right end of the taskbar and the ___ button is at the left end.
4. A ___ is a secret code used to open your Yahoo account. Folks who don't know the code, can't access your mail.
7. In the same way that you need an ___ book to keep track of postal addresses of friends and relatives, you will want one to keep track of email addresses.
8. Sending an ___ attachment is similar to 5 Across except, with this type of attachment, the recipient will most likely be able to see the picture in the message.
10. If you are in the middle of typing an email message and aren't ready to mail it yet, you could save it in the ___ folder, which is where partially-completed letters are kept until you are ready to complete and mail the message.
11. A very popular directory service is www.switch___.com.

## EXERCISE 2: TRUE-FALSE
For each of the following eight statements, place a T or an F on the line to indicate if the statement is True or False.

1. ___A deleted email message is put in the Recycle Bin.
2. ___I can edit contacts in my address book.
3. ___In email, "CC" stands for Community College.
4. ___Text at the end of each message is called an emoticon.
5. ___A collection of addresses are kept in the Address Book.
6. ___Using a password restricts access to an email account.
7. ___Copies of sent messages can be kept in the Sent folder.
8. ___To send a file attachment, I click the Send File link.

## EXERCISE 3: IDENTIFY TERMS
Below are eight definitions. Below the definitions are eight lines. In each line, write the word that matches the definition.

1. A few lines of text at the end of a message.
2. "CC" is an abbreviation for this.
3. The image that indicates a message contains an attachment.
4. The location where my addresses are stored.
5. To respond to a message received.
6. To send a received message to someone else.
7. Inbox, Sent, Draft, and Trash are examples of these.
8. A file that is sent along with the email message.

1. _____    5. _____
2. _____    6. _____
3. _____    7. _____
4. _____    8. _____

## EXERCISE 4: MATCHING
To get you started, Yahoo provided you with four folders when you opened your email account. (You can, of course, create additional folders into which you could organize your mail). Below is a list of the four folders that were automatically provided by Yahoo. Below the list are some statements which describe these folders. For each statement, identify the folder to which it refers by placing the letter of the folder on the line preceding each statement.

| A. Draft | B. Inbox | C. Sent | D. Trash |
| --- | --- | --- | --- |

1. ___ Incoming mail is stored here.
2. ___ Copies of sent messages can be saved here.
3. ___ To create space for new messages, I empty this.
4. ___ Partially-completed letters can be kept here.
5. ___ Deleted messages are temporarily kept here.
6. ___ To see the messages here, I click the Check Mail link.

## EXERCISE 5: TRUE-FALSE
For each of the following eight statements, place a T or an F on the line to indicate if the statement is True or False.

1. ___Text at the end of each message is called a signature.
2. ___I cannot put links to web sites in my email messages.
3. ___A "CC" is a copy of a message sent to someone.
4. ___You will be able to view all attachments you receive.
5. ___I can find email addresses at www.switchboard.com.
6. ___I can change my Yahoo password as often as I like.
7. ___I must read a message before I can delete it.
8. ___In email, "CC" stands for Carbon Copy.

## EXERCISE 6: ADD ENTRIES TO AN ADDRESS BOOK

☞ Exchange email addresses with five different people. Ask each person to send you an email message.

☞ While they are writing messages to you, you should open your Yahoo email account and write them each a message.

☞ When you are done writing the five messages, open your Inbox and read a message from one of dudes who wrote you. Add his email address to your address book. Reply to his message.

☞ Read a message from another dude. Add his email address to your address book. Reply to his message.

☞ Read the other messages, reply to them, and add addresses until you have all five email addresses in your address book.

## EXERCISE 7: ATTACH AN IMAGE TO EMAIL

☞ Using Internet Explorer, go to **www.dozer.pannell.com** (or www.pannell.biz).

☞ Click the My Photo Gallery link.

☞ From the pictures provided, choose one and save it to your diskette.

☞ Address an email message to yourself.

☞ The subject of the email message should be Dozer.

☞ Attach the picture to the email.

☞ Send the message.

## EXERCISE 8: ATTACH A TEXT FILE TO EMAIL

☞ Using Internet Explorer, go to **www.google.com**

☞ Find out how to teach a dog to do tricks.

☞ Copy the information to the clipboard.

☞ Start Microsoft Word.

☞ Paste the information to the document.

☞ Save the file to your diskette (call it Dog Tricks).

☞ Close Microsoft Word.

☞ Address an email message to yourself.

☞ The subject of the email should be Tricks.

☞ Attach the "Dog Tricks" file.

☞ Send the message.

## EXERCISE 9: READ EMAIL WITH AN IMAGE

☞ Open the message with the subject of "Dozer" (in Exercise 7, you sent it to yourself).

☞ Scroll down to see the image of Dozer. If you don't see the picture, go back to Exercise 7 and find out what you did wrong and redo it.

## EXERCISE 10: READ EMAIL WITH A TEXT FILE

☞ Open the "Tricks" message (in Exercise 8, you sent this message to yourself).

☞ Scan the attached file for viruses. If safe, open it.

☞ Notice that Microsoft Word (the program you used to create the file) is started and the "Dog Tricks" file is opened.

☞ Close the document. Close Microsoft Word.

## EXERCISE 11: SEND A YAHOO E-GREETING CARD

In Exercise 6, you added some email addresses to your address book. Use an address from your address book to send a Yahoo e-greeting card to one of those folks. To do so, click the Greetings link found at the bottom of the Yahoo screen. Then, follow the on-screen instructions to create a card. When asked for the recipient's name, click the Insert From Address Book link. Then, choose one (or several) people to receive your card. Your card will be sent to the designated recipients and Yahoo will send you a message confirming the delivery of the card to those folks.

## EXERCISE 12: FIND EMAIL ADDRESSES

☞ Go to **www.yahoo.com** and click the People Search link.

☞ Do an Email Search (not a Telephone search). Find an email address for each of the following folks. You will find several listings for each person. Pick just one of the folks found for each name and record his email address in the table below:.

| PERSON | EMAIL ADDRESS |
|---|---|
| Santa Claus | |
| Uncle Sam | |
| Easter Bunny | |
| Tooth Fairy | |
| Bugs Bunny | |
| Scooby Doo | |

## EXERCISE 13: ADD ENTRIES TO AN ADDRESS BOOK

In Exercise 12, you found several email addresses. Please add each of those addresses to your address book.

## EXERCISE 14: EDIT AN ADDRESS BOOK ENTRY

In Exercise 13, you added some addresses to your address book. Edit the entry for Santa Claus to include his home phone number of 555-4358.

## EXERCISE 15: DELETE EMAIL MESSAGES

Find a message in your Inbox that you no longer need. It may be a message that you have already read and do not need to keep, or it may be junk mail you have received that you never intend to read. When you find the unwanted email, delete it.

## EXERCISE 16: RETRIEVE DELETED EMAIL MESSAGES

In Exercise 15, you deleted a message. However, now you have decided that you need to read that message again. When you deleted it, you merely told Yahoo to put it in the Trash. When you throw a postal letter in the trash, you can go and retrieve the postal letter from the trash. Likewise, you can retrieve the email message from the trash. Click Trash (left of screen), and click the subject link of the message you previously deleted. Read the message and then click Check Mail to return to your Inbox.

## EXERCISE 17: EMPTY THE TRASH FOLDER

All deleted messages are put in the Trash folder, which still takes up space in your Yahoo account. So, after deleting the messages, be sure to empty the Trash folder. Periodically, Yahoo will empty your Trash folder for you. However, to create more space in your Yahoo account for incoming messages, you might want to empty the Trash folder yourself. Go ahead and empty your Trash folder.

## EXERCISE 18: DELETE ADDRESS BOOK ENTRIES

In Exercise 13, you added several addresses to your address book. Dozer did the same thing the other day. He was real excited about his new list of friends. However, he has since learned that these folks are imposters. For instance, the Santa Claus, ain't the real Santa Claus. He's a fake, a fraud, a phoney. So are all of the others. So, go to your address book and delete each of these rascals from your address book.

## INTRODUCTION TO WEB PAGES

A home page is the first page seen when a site is accessed. The web site itself consists of the home page and its associated web pages. To have a web site, after creating the pages via HTML (HyperText Markup Language), it must be posted to a server. By the way, the person who creates web pages is called a webmaster. Many web hosting services will, for a fee, post your pages to their servers. These fee-based services are used by folks who do not want to be limited as to the size of their sites and those who want to have a web page devoid of ads (other than their own). For those of us who need a small web site and are unconcerned about ads being placed on the pages, there are free web hosting services. These services are financially supported by selling ad space which appears on each page. Every time someone goes to one of these pages, she will see an ad. This is a minor inconvenience. We will use a free service to create, post, and maintain a home page.

On page C-8, you read about the Google toolbar and how it blocks pop-up ads. If you want to block the pop-up ads at Expage.com, go to www.google.com and click the More link. Then, click the Google Toolbar link and download the toolbar.

## REGISTER FOR AN EXPAGE WEB PAGE

To register for a web page, do the following:
- ☞ Start Internet Explorer and go to **www.expage.com**
- ☞ Expage offers two different web hosting services. Expage Ultra is fee based; Expage Basic is free. Since we want the free stuff, click the Let's Create My Basic Website link (near the bottom right corner of the Expage Basic section).
- ☞ Click the Create/Update Homepage link (left side of screen).
- ☞ In the Page Name box, type a name for the page. Use what you used for your Yahoo ID (i.e., the part before the @).
- ☞ In the Password text box, type a password (use the same password you use for your Yahoo email account).
- ☞ In the Email Address box, type your email address.
- ☞ Click the I Have Read And Agree To All Of The Rules button.
- ☞ In the Welcome To The Express Page box, click OK.

## SELECT A STYLE AND A BACKGROUND

To select a style and a background, do the following:
- ☞ Click the Style button and, from the samples, click the desired style. Each style determines where the various elements (title, slogan, graphics, etc.) will appear in the page).
- ☞ Click the Background button.
- ☞ Click the Additional Backgrounds list box arrow.
- ☞ In the drop-down list, select a category. Click Go.
- ☞ Click the background you like or return to the Additional Backgrounds list box and select other categories until you find a background you like.
- ☞ If you don't like the background, click the Background button and repeat the last few steps to select another one.

## ENTER TEXT

To enter a title, do the following:
- ☞ Click the Title button.
- ☞ Click in the text box and type a title (type your name).
- ☞ Select a text color and a text size.
- ☞ From the Animated area, select Yes or No (Yes will make the first letter of your name dance).
- ☞ Click the Save Your Title button.

- ☞ If you dislike the results, repeat the last few steps. If the text can't be seen, change the background or the text color.

To enter a slogan (a subtitle), do the following:
- ☞ Click the Slogan button. Click in the text box.
- ☞ Type Welcome to My Home Page (or a similar slogan).
- ☞ Select a text color and a text size.
- ☞ From the Animated area, select Yes or No.
- ☞ Click the Save Your Slogan button.
- ☞ If you don't like the results, repeat the last few steps.

To enter text for the body (middle) of the page, do the following:
- ☞ Click the Body button.
- ☞ Click in the text box and type the desired text (type a couple of lines of whatever you want).
- ☞ Select a text color and a text size.
- ☞ Click the Save Middle Section button.

## INSERT HYPERLINKS

To have the URL appear as the link, do the following:
- ☞ Click the Body button to open the middle section of the page.
- ☞ Below your text in the text box, type a description of a web site followed by its URL (in this case, type To learn about the ASPCA, click HERE http://www.aspca.org).
- ☞ Click the Save Middle Section button.
- ☞ Look at the URL. Note that it is highlighted.
- ☞ Click it. You will be taken to www.aspca.org.
- ☞ Click the Back toolbar button to return to the prior page.

To have a word appear as the link, do the following:
- ☞ Click the Controls button.
- ☞ In the Display Links As area, select Prior Word. This will hide the URL and use the word that appears in front of the URL as the link (in this case, it will make a link out of the word "HERE").
- ☞ Click the Save Your Controls button.
- ☞ Look at the link. Note that "HERE" is highlighted and the URL is hidden. This is much better, don't you agree?
- ☞ Click the link. You will be taken to www.aspca.org.
- ☞ Click the Back toolbar button to return to the prior page.

## INSERT LINES AND IMAGES

To insert a horizontal line, do the following:
- ☞ Click the Lines button.
- ☞ Click the Additional Lines list box arrow.
- ☞ In the drop-down list, select a category. Click Go.
- ☞ In the samples, click the one you like or if you want to view more lines, return to the Additional Lines list box and select other categories until you find a line you like.
- ☞ If you want the line to appear in designated locations, click the Title, Slogan, Body (middle), or Footer (bottom) button. Then in the text box, type *L where the line is to appear.
- ☞ If you don't like the lines, click the Lines button and repeat the last few steps to select another one.

To insert a graphic image, do the following:
- ☞ Click the Graphics button.
- ☞ Click the Additional Graphics list box arrow.
- ☞ In the list box select a category of graphic. Click Go.
- ☞ In the samples, click the one you like or view more graphics by returning to the Additional Graphics list box and select

other categories until you find a graphic you like.
- ☞ If you want the graphic to appear in designated locations, click the Title, Slogan, Body (middle), or Footer (bottom) button. In the text box, type *G where you want the graphic.
- ☞ If you don't like the graphic, repeat the last few steps.

To insert an animated image, do the following:
- ☞ Click the Animate button.
- ☞ Click the Additional Animations list box arrow.
- ☞ In the drop-down list select a category. Click Go.
- ☞ In the samples, click the one you like or if you want to view more animations, return to the Additional Animations list box and select other categories until you find one you like.
- ☞ If you want the animation to appear in certain locations, click the Title, Slogan, Body (middle), or Footer (bottom) button. In the text box, type *A where you want the animation.
- ☞ If you don't like the animation or where it appears, repeat the relevant steps above to make the desired changes.

## EXIT FROM EXPAGE
To end a session, click the Log Off button.

## VIEW YOUR WEB PAGE
To view your web page the way others will, do the following:
- ☞ Go to **www.expage.com/YOUR PAGE** (www.expage.com/ followed by the name you gave the page).

## EDIT YOUR WEB PAGE
To edit your web page, do the following:
- ☞ Go to **www.expage.com**
- ☞ Click the Expage Basic System log in link.
- ☞ In the Page Name text box, type the name of your page.
- ☞ In the Password text box, type your password.
- ☞ In the Email Address box, type your email address.
- ☞ Click the I Have Read And Agree To All Of The Rules link.
- ☞ Click the button for the feature you want to modify (in this case, click the Features button and select some type of music. Try several tunes until you find one you like.
- ☞ When done, click the Log Off button.
- ☞ To see your web page the ways other folks will see it, simply type its URL in the Address bar and go there. Since you just modified your page, in order to see the newly-modified page, you may need to click the Reload toolbar button when you get there. On occasion, you may even need to close your web browser and restart it before going to your page.

## USE YOUR OWN PHOTOS (OPTIONAL)
You can have photos on your Expage web page if you are willing to pay a fee. Since a fee is required, the following information is provided for folks who wish to upload their own photos to their web pages. The following instructions can be ignored if you do not want to use your photos on your web page. As noted earlier, there are many sites that will let you create web pages, some of which will let you use your photos. If you are interested in using your photos on a web page and you do not wish to pay a fee, you might want to create a web page elsewhere (www.geocities.com or www.switchboard.com). This is not something you NEED to do; it is something you might WANT to do.

To digitize a photo using a scanner, do the following:
- ☞ Open the scanner lid. Lay the photo face down on the glass (Look around the rim of the glass for an indication as to which corner you should use). Close the scanner lid.
- ☞ Click Start, All Programs, and look for the scanner software installed on your machine. When you find it, click it.

- ☞ Since not all scanners operate the same, at this point it is virtually impossible to provide any additional guidance as to the steps to take to scan an image on the scanner you are currently using. So, you should consult the Help feature of your scanner software to obtain step-by-step instructions.
- ☞ When you are done scanning your image, be sure to save your file to your diskette and don't forget to remove your photo from the scanner before leaving.

To post a photo to a web site, do the following:
- ☞ Log on to your web page. Since Expage will only permit you to upload your pictures if you pay a fee, you might want to create a web page where they don't charge a fee (e.g., www.switchboard.com).
- ☞ Once you've logged onto your website, look for a link called "Upload Photos" or "Post Pictures" or "Load Pictures" or something similar. Then, click the link.
- ☞ Follow the directions provided by the web hosting service to upload your photos to your web page.

## ADDITIONAL FEATURES (OPTIONAL)
To add a joke page, games, etc., click the Features button.

## PROMOTE YOUR WEB PAGE (OPTIONAL)
To entice others to visit your web site, do the following:

ANNOUNCE YOUR WEBSITE. Email all of your friends (and enemies) telling them about your site. Also, place a signature in your email that is a hyperlink to your web site. Also, be sure to print your URL on your business cards and letterheads.

BUY ADVERTISING. Go to a search engine and look for a link that says something like "Advertise on" or "Advertise with us" to find out how you can pay for advertising.

FORM ALLIANCES. Finds friends or business people who have web sites and tell them that if they provide a link to your web site on their web site, you will provide a link from your web site to their web site. This is especially helpful if you and your friends' web sites share similar topics (e.g., pet care, gardening, etc.)

REGISTER WITH SEARCH ENGINES. Add your web site to search engine listings. To do so, go to a search engine and look for a link called "Add URL" or "Submit Site" and click it. Fill out the form. It might take a week or two for the search engine to list your site (hey, they may never list it). Every day or so, go to the search engine and type your name or key words and see if your web page is included in the list of hits.

Before you register your website, make your site search-engine friendly by incorporating some of the following suggestions. Use keywords in the title that define what your page is all about and pepper the entire web page with these words. For instance, if you want folks to find your page with your name as the search term, your title should be your name and your name should be repeated throughout the page. By the way, variations of your name may adversely affect a search engine's ability to point someone to it. For instance, if the title of your page is "Dozer's Home Page" and someone uses a search engine to find "Dozer" that person will be less successful than the person who uses "Dozer's" as a search term. Since most folks would search for Dozer with a search term of "Dozer", the home page should have a title that says something like "Dozer Welcomes You To His Home Page."

## EXERCISE 1: CROSSWORD
Use the clues below to complete the crossword puzzle.

### ACROSS

1. A professional who designs and creates web pages is a web___.
5. A few lines of text that appears at the end of every email message that I send, commonly used to give contact information (telephone number, postal address, web site address, or a favorite quotation).
8. After creating the pages for a web site, the pages must be posted to a server. Many web hosting ___ will post my pages to their servers. Some charge a fee, while others will post my pages free of charge.
9. When you are done creating an Expage web page or when you are done with your Yahoo email, you need to exit the account. Another way of saying "exit" is to say "sign off" or ___ off.
12. The ___ page is the first page seen when a web site is accessed. It generally has a collection of links to other pages on the web site.
13. A web site consists of a collection of linked documents called web ___.
15. A __ is text or an image that, when clicked, takes you to another place on the current page, to another page at the current website, or to another page on another website.
16. Behind the text and images on a web page, you will frequently see some sort of color or pattern. Its purpose is totally aesthetic. If you printed the web page, these elements would not appear on the printout. This color or pattern is the ___.
20. To promote your web site, you might want to notify search engines of its existence with the hope that they will index it. To do so, go to various search engines and click a link called ___ (some search engines have this link, while some have the link referred to in 3 Down).
21. In an Expage web page, I place most of the important text in the Body of the page, which is found in the ___ of the web page.
23. When I access a web site, I am really accessing files that have been placed on someone else's computer. Each file appears to me in the form of a web ___.
24. Google is Dozer's favorite search ___.

### DOWN

2. A device that permits you to convert a photograph into digital format so that you can then post it to a web site, send it via email, or insert it into any other document.
3. To promote your web site, you might want to notify search engines of its existence with the hope that they will index it. To do so, go to various search engines and click a link called Submit ___ and provide the requested information.
4. A ___ engine is a web site that maintains a database that permits folks to search for web sites worldwide.
6. A ___ consists of the home page and some associated web pages.
7. A web site address is often referred to as a ___.
10. In an Expage web page, a vast collection of images are provided for me to use. These images can be found by clicking the ___ button on the Expage toolbar.
11. Is the global collection of millions of connected computers called the Internet?

12. Web pages are often constructed using HyperText Markup Language, which is the code behind the pages. Most folks refer to HyperText Markup Language as ___.
14. Since we don't have time to learn HyperText Markup Language, we created web pages at www.__.com, where simplified software helped us build a page.
16. An Expage web page is divided into four sections. To put information in the ___ section, I would click the Footer button on the Expage toolbar.
17. One obvious way to promote a web site would be to put its address on your business ___.
18. In an Expage web page, you can have a line of text under your title. At Expage, this sub-title is called a ___.
19. A collection of characters that, when viewed sideways, represent a human face is called a ___.
22. Dozer is the world's smartest cyber ___.

### EXERCISE 2: FIND OTHER FREE WEB PAGE SITES
Go to **www. google.com** and search for other web sites (other than Expage) that permit you to create free web pages. On each line below, write the URL of each web site you find.

_____

_____

_____

_____

## EXERCISE 3: TRUE-FALSE

For each of the following eight statements, place a T or an F on the line to indicate if the statement is True or False.

1. ___In an Expage page, "*A" identifies an address location.
2. ___In Expage, a slogan and a subtitle are the same thing.
3. ___A "title page" is the first page seen when a site is loaded.
4. ___I must pay a fee to place my pictures in an Expage page.
5. ___A password restricts access to a web page account.
6. ___Each web page is actually just a file on another computer.
7. ___In Expage, "*G" identifies the location of an graphic image.
8. ___I can change the color of text in my Expage page.

## EXERCISE 4: IDENTIFY TERMS

Below are eight definitions. Below the definitions are eight lines. In each line, write the word that matches the definition.

1. A global collection of millions of connected computers.
2. The person who creates web pages.
3. The code behind the pages.
4. A web page address.
5. The first page seen when a web site it accessed.
6. The subtitle in an Expage web page.
7. The common way to refer to HyperText Markup Language.
8. The place where I type in the URL of the page I want to load.

1. _____    5. _____
2. _____    6. _____
3. _____    7. _____
4. _____    8. _____

## EXERCISE 5: EXPLAIN CONCEPTS

Skooter's web page (at Expage) has a link that is the entire URL. Skooter has noticed that some folks have links on their web pages that consist of a single word instead of the whole URL. She thinks these folks are very clever and she wants to know how they did that? Can you explain how they did that?

_____
_____
_____
_____
_____
_____
_____
_____
_____
_____

## EXERCISE 6: TRUE-FALSE

For each of the following eight statements, place a T or an F on the line to indicate if the statement is True or False.

1. ___Expage Basic charges a $5 fee to host a webpage.
2. ___I can change the size of text in my Expage page.
3. ___A background is the pattern behind the text and images.
4. ___A hosting service lets me post (store) my web pages.
5. ___The first line of text on a web page is typically the title.
6. ___A web site always consists of only one page.
7. ___Web page backgrounds print along with text and images.
8. ___To create an Expage web page, go to www.expage.com.

## EXERCISE 7: EXPLAIN CONCEPTS (OPTIONAL)

Skooter has created a spectacular web site for which she is very proud. How can she promote her web site so that is doesn't just sit in cyberspace with no traffic?

_____
_____
_____
_____
_____
_____
_____
_____
_____
_____

## EXERCISE 8: CREATE WEB PAGES

You can create as many web pages as you like at Expage. The only rule is that you must have a different URL for each page. In this exercise, you will create two web pages, each of which will have the same look and sound. And, you will link the two pages so that you have a multi-page web site. First, think of two page names that you want to use. Remember, you will need to think of two page names that do not currently exist. So, if your name is Bob, forget about using Bob1 and Bob2. These page names are probably already taken. Regardless of your page name, your URL will begin with "www.expage.com/" and will end with your chosen page name. My suggestion: use your first and last name followed by 1 and 2. For example, Dozer would use dozerpannell1 for his first web page and dozerpannell2 for his second web page. So that you don't forget your URLs later, write them down here:

www.expage.com/_____
www.expage.com/_____

☞ Go to **www.expage.com**. Register for a Basic (free) page.
☞ Select a style, a background, a graphic, and lines.
☞ Use your name in the title.
☞ Put an animation in front of and at the end of your name.
☞ In the Body (middle) section, insert a Prior Word hyperlink that points to the second page (the one you will create after you create this page). It won't work yet, because the second page does not exist yet. However, when you create the second page, the link will work. To create the link, type <u>My Favorite Websites http://www.expage.com/XXX</u>. Replace XXX with the name of your second web page. Since it's a prior word link, the word "Websites" will be the link.
☞ Click the Features button. Select music. When done, log off from this web page.
☞ Create the second web page, using the same style, background, music, etc. you used in the prior page. This will make your two pages look like a single web site.
☞ In the Body (middle) section of your web page, create links to at least six of your favorite web sites (if you can't think of any, take a look at pages C-4 and C-6 for ideas).
☞ In the Footer (bottom) section, create a link to your homepage that says <u>Return to Homepage</u> so that "Homepage" is the link.
☞ Log off.
☞ Type the URL of your first page in the Address bar to access your home page.
☞ Use the links on both pages to be sure they work properly.
☞ Print one copy of your magnificent webpage.

## INTERNET COMPREHENSIVE
# E X E R C I S E S

### EXERCISE 1: TRUE-FALSE
For each of the following eight statements, place a T or an F on the line to indicate if the statement is True or False.

1. ___To select an image in Word, I click the image.
2. ___Dozer's favorite search engine is Google.
3. ___A web page travels to me in one big packet.
4. ___An email address always starts with "www".
5. ___A deleted email message is put in the Trash folder.
6. ___When clicked, a link changes into an hourglass icon.
7. ___The mouse pointer looks like a ring when I point to a link.
8. ___To access a web page, I type its URL in the Address bar.

### EXERCISE 2: IDENTIFY ACRONYMS
In the computing world, lots of terms are referred to by an acronym. What do each of the following acronyms stand for?

| ACRONYM | FULL NAME |
|---------|-----------|
| 1. CC | |
| 2. HTML | |
| 3. WWW | |
| 4. URL | |
| 5. FAQ | |

### EXERCISE 3: TRUE-FALSE
For each of the following eight statements, place a T or an F on the line to indicate if the statement is True or False.

1. ___Another word for "citation" is "hit".
2. ___A collection of related web sites is called a web browser.
3. ___I can change my Yahoo password as often as I like.
4. ___I can save a valuable web page as a "favorite".
5. ___All the information on the Internet is factually accurate.
6. ___TCP/IP divides information into units called blocks.
7. ___If I disable cookies, some web sites will deny me access.
8. ___To resize an image, I drag one of its sizing handles.

### EXERCISE 4: IDENTIFY TERMS
Below are eight definitions. Below the definitions are eight lines. In each line, write the word that matches the definition.

1. Pretending to be someone else.
2. A small file put on my hard drive by a web site.
3. A global series of connected computers.
4. The first page in a web site.
5. Useless information sent to many people.
6. Common rules of Internet etiquette.
7. A message that incites the recipient to anger.
8. Postal Service mail.

1. _____   5. _____
2. _____   6. _____
3. _____   7. _____
4. _____   8. _____

### EXERCISE 5: TRUE-FALSE
For each of the following eight statements, place a T or an F on the line to indicate if the statement is True or False.

1. ___Sometimes a link is text and sometimes it is an image.
2. ___To deselect an image in word, I click outside of the image.
3. ___A Favorite is a web page I've marked for future use.
4. ___You will be able to view all attachments you receive.
5. ___A URL has an "@" in it.
6. ___If the Forward button is dimmed, it won't work.
7. ___All web site addresses begin with "www".
8. ___I can copy text from a web page and paste it into Word.

### EXERCISE 6: MATCHING
Below is a list of 21 terms associated with the Internet. Below the list are 21 statements, each of which is a description for one of the terms. For each descriptive statement, identify the term to which it refers by placing the letter of the term on the line preceding each statement.

| | | |
|---|---|---|
| A. Address Bar | H. Inbox | O. Sizing Handles |
| B. Bounce | I. Internet | P. Smiley |
| C. FAQ | J. Lurking | Q. Snail Mail |
| D. Flame | K. Netiquette | R. Spam |
| E. Flame war | L. Search Engine | S. Spoofing |
| F. Home Page | M. Shouting | T. URL |
| G. Hyperlink | N. Signature | U. Web Browser |

1. ___Squares around a selected image used to resize it.
2. ___Text that, when clicked, takes me elsewhere.
3. ___Listening before entering a conversation.
4. ___The global collection of millions of linked computers.
5. ___A web site database that lets me find stuff.
6. ___A list of questions that have been asked before.
7. ___Where my incoming email messages are kept.
8. ___This is what Postal Service mail is sometimes called.
9. ___Common rules of Internet etiquette.
10. ___Undelivered mail will do this.
11. ___The first page seen when a web site is accessed.
12. ___When folks exchange a barrage of insults.
13. ___Text found at the end of some email messages.
14. ___Text in capital letters can be interpreted as this.
15. ___Where I enter the web site address I want to load.
16. ___Useless information sent to many people at once.
17. ___Pretending to be someone else.
18. ___Punctuation symbols that look like a human face.
19. ___A web site address.
20. ___The type of software used to access the Internet.
21. ___A message that incites the recipient to anger.

### EXERCISE 7: TRUE-FALSE
For each of the following eight statements, place a T or an F on the line to indicate if the statement is True or False.

1. ___To insert an image into Word, I click File, Open.
2. ___The boxes around a selected image are sizing handles.
3. ___Another name for a smiley is an emoticon.
4. ___If I "CC" myself, a copy of the message will be sent to me.
5. ___:-) and 8-) are called mugshots.
6. ___Excite, Yahoo, and Google are search motors.
7. ___When a page is loading, the IE logo is animated.
8. ___I must pay a fee to place my pictures in an Expage page.

## EXERCISE 8: CAN YOU HELP MY FRIEND?

Beau Augustus Bitter is always coming up with some get-rich-quick scheme. Personally, I think his get-rich-quick schemes are more like go-broke-fast schemes. But, Beau is a true believer in miracles and he insists that one day he will hit the jackpot. As usual, he needs help in his current project.

### PART A: COPY & PASTE INTERNET INFORMATION

Beau Augustus Bitter wants to brew beer in his garage (he plans to name the beer after himself and call it "Bitter Beer"). I've tried to tell him that this would be a bad name for his beer, but he insists on naming it after himself. At least he admits to knowing nothing about brewing beer. Perhaps, you can help him. Please start Internet Explorer and go to **www.google.com** to search for a web site about brewing beer at home (by the way, people who brew beer are involved in zymurgy). When you find a site that you think Beau would like to see, write its URL on the line below:

_____

Copy a couple of paragraphs from the web site and paste them into a Word document. Fix any formatting errors. Type your name a couple of lines below the last paragraph. Save the document to your diskette (call it zymurgy). Close Word.

### PART B: FIND A BOOK

Beau wants to find some books about beer brewing. Use the search feature at **www.amazon.com** to find a book on zymurgy. Write the title of the book on the line below:

_____

### PART C: FIND SOME WEB PAGES

Beau wants to market his beer on the Internet. But, he needs some ideas. So, he wants to see some examples of web pages that feature beer. Go to **www.google.com** and find two different brewers. Write the URL of each on a line below:

_____
_____

### PART D: CREATE A WEB PAGE

After viewing some professionally-created pages, Beau wants to see a page created by you. Go to **www.expage.com** and create a Basic (free) web page which tells folks about Bitter Beer. Use a graphic and an animation. Include a link to the web site you found in Part A. Write the URL of your newly-created web site on the line below and then log off from Expage:

_____

### PART E: ADD AN ADDRESS BOOK ENTRY

Since you expect Beau (beauaugustusbitter@yahoo.com) and his cousin Bert (bertaugustusbitter@yahoo.com) to become your friends, add their addresses to your Yahoo address book.

### PART F. MODIFY A WEB PAGE

In Part D, you created a web page. Modify that web page so that its title is Bitter Beer is Better Beer. Exit from Expage.

### PART G: FIND THE VALUE OF A CAR

To finance his brewery, Beau will sell his 2004 Chevrolet Corvette. He needs to know its private party value. It's a coupe 2-D, with automatic transmission and 9,157 miles. His zip code is 89146. It has air conditioning, power steering, power windows, power door locks, tilt wheel, cruise control, AM/FM stereo, single compact disc, ABS, leather, and dual power seats. The car is in excellent condition. Go to **www.kbb.com**. How much is the car worth? Write its value here: _____

### PART H: FIND SOMEONE'S ADDRESS

Beau's cousin, Bert, is willing to pay an extra $500 for the car if Beau will deliver it to Bert's home. Beau is uncertain if it would be worth his time to drive the car to Bert's house. Help him decide. First, go to **www.switchboard.com** and find the address of Bert Bitter (he lives in California). Write Bert's home address on the line below:

_____

### PART I: FIND THE DISTANCE BETWEEN TWO PLACES

Go to **www.mapsonus.com** and find out how far it is from Beau's home (6330 W. Charleston Blvd., Las Vegas, NV) to Bert's home via the fastest route. Write the mileage here: ___

### PART J: FIND & SAVE A MAP

Beau can drive to Bert's hometown without a map, but once he arrives, he does not know how to find Bert's house. Go back to **www.mapsonus.com**. Find a map of Bert's neighborhood. Save the image of the map to your diskette (call it Bert's Map).

### PART K: OBTAIN A WEATHER REPORT

If Beau drives the car to Bert, he wants to know what weather conditions he will encounter. Please go to **www.weather.com.** What is tomorrow's weather forecast for Bert's home town?

_____

### PART L: SAVE IMAGES FROM THE INTERNET

Beau needs help designing the label for Bitter Beer. He wants to look at other beer labels to get some ideas. Use Google to find images of beer bottles from two different beer brands. Save each image to your disk.

### PART M: INSERT IMAGES INTO A DOCUMENT

Open Word and the "zymurgy" document you created in Part A. Insert the image of the map of Bert's neighborhood, from Part J. Resize the map to be about the size of a diskette. Move the image to the top center of the page. Save the modified document. Print the document. Close Word.

### PART N: EMAIL ATTACHMENTS

Address an email to yourself. Include three attachments (the two images of beer bottles you saved in Part L and the "zymurgy" document you completed in Part M). In the message box, insert a link to the web page created in Part D.

### PART O: DELETE AN ADDRESS BOOK ENTRY

In part E, you thought that Beau and Bert were going to become your good friends. Since then, they have both turned out to be idiots. Consequently, you have decided that you no longer want to associate with either of them. So, delete Beau's and Bert's addresses from your address book.

### PART P: PRINT A WEB PAGE

Go to the web page that you created in Part D. Print it.

### PART Q: OPEN A TEXT ATTACHMENT

In Part N, you sent a message to yourself. Open that message. Do the images of beer bottles appear? Open the "zymurgy" attachment. Print it out. It should be identical to the printout you made in Part M.

### THANK YOU

On behalf of my friend, I thank you for your assistance. If you ever see Bitter Beer at the store, take pride in knowing that you helped make the dreams of Beau Augustus Bitter come true.

# Dozer's Quintessential Guide To The Internet

## A N S W E R   K E Y

### PAGE C-5: EXERCISE 1

**Across**
2. Bones
3. URL
5. IE
7. Links
8. Netscape
11. Color
12. Icon
13. Tool
14. Start
16. Logo

**Down**
1. Browser
2. Back
4. Switching
6. Explorer
9. Packets
10. Scroll
15. RAM

### PAGE C-5: EXERCISE 2
1. F: WWW stands for World Wide Web.
2. T
3. T
4. F: To access a web page, I type its URL in the Address bar. I don't have a clue what a "LUR" is.
5. T
6. T
7. F: All web site addresses do not begin with "www". Most do, but some don't.
8. F: URL stands for Uniform Resource Locator.

### PAGE C-5: EXERCISE 3
1. Protocols
2. Internet
3. Web browsers
4. Packets
5. World wide web
6. URL
7. IE
8. Homepage

### PAGE C-5: EXERCISE 4
TCP/IP (the Internet protocol) splits information into packets each of which contains routing instructions explaining where the packet should go. Each computer on the network reads the instructions and sends each packet along its way to its ultimate destination. A packet may pass through dozens of computers. This "packet switching" system means that the Internet is decentralized. Therefore, if one routing computer goes down, others take over.

### PAGE C-5: EXERCISE 5
1. F: TCP/IP divides information into units called packets, not blocks.
2. T
3. F: A web page travels to me in many packets of data. These packets of data are then assembled on my monitor upon arrival.
4. T
5. F: The Back button takes me to the previously-viewed web page. It does not close the browser. To close the web browser, I would click its Close button, the X at the top right corner of the window.
6. T
7. T
8. F: When clicked, a link does not change into an hourglass icon. A clicked link changes color to indicate that I have been to that page. This helps me to remember where I've been so I don't waste time going there again.

### PAGE C-9: EXERCISE 1

**Across**
3. Citation
5. Back
6. URL
8. Color
12. Sizing
13. Name
14. Logo
17. Favorite

**Down**
1. Link
2. Start
4. Match
7. Cookie
9. Google
10. Pannell
11. Picture
15. Off
16. IE

### PAGE C-9: EXERCISE 2
1. F: Data put on my hard drive by a web site is called a cookie, not a muffin. A muffin is a delicious food product.
2. T
3. F: Other words for "citation" are "hit" or "match" or "result". A "ticket" is something you earn for running a red light.
4. F: Excite, Yahoo, & Google are search engines, not search motors.
5. T
6. T
7. F: I can copy and I can print a web page.
8. T

### PAGE C-9: EXERCISE 3
Sometimes when you access a web site, the site places a cookie on your hard drive which contains information of interest to the web site (it lets the site remember certain things about you). Some folks don't like cookies because they feel they are an invasion of their privacy. But cookies can be valuable time savers in that the web site can "remember" some things about you so that you don't have to tell them the same thing every time you access their web site.

### PAGE C-9: EXERCISE 4
1. T
2. F: The boxes around a selected image are sizing handles, not moving handles.
3. T
4. F: To insert an image into Word, I click Insert, Picture. Then I click From File if the picture is saved to a disk. Or, I click Clip Art if it is in the Clipart Gallery.
5, 6, and 7 are all T.
8. F: Information on the Internet is just like information you get from other sources. Some of it is accurate; some of it is completely false.

### PAGE C-9: EXERCISE 5
1. Cookie
2. Google
3. Homepage
4. Favorite
5. URL
6. Hit

### PAGE C-13: EXERCISE 1

**Across**
3. Reply
4. WWW
7. Mailer
11. Username
14. Netiquette
16. Help
17. Shouting
20. No

**Down**
1. Print
2. Spam
5. War
6. Flame
8. Lurking
9. Smileys
10. Bounce
12. Subject
13. At
15. Host
18. In
19. No

### PAGE C-13: EXERCISE 2
1. Netiquette
2. Spoofing
3. Flame
4. Spam
5. Lurking
6. Shouting
7. Flame war
8. FAQ

### PAGE C-13: EXERCISE 3
1, 2, 3, and 4 are all T.
5. F: A URL is a web site address. It seldom, if ever, will have an "@" in it. Email addresses have an "@" in them; web site addresses do not.
6. F: "Case sensitive" refers to whether or not the characters are in uppercase or lowercase. Being "sensitive" means it matters. Therefore, if something is identified as being "case sensitive" that means that "bob" & "Bob" are not the same.
7. T
8. F: In Yahoo, to reply to a message, click the Reply link, not the Respond link. In fact, there is no Respond link in Yahoo email.

### PAGE C-13: EXERCISE 4
1. D
2. B
3. E
4. C
5. F
6. H
7. I
8. G
9. A

### PAGE C-13: EXERCISE 5
1. F: :-) and 8-) are called smileys or emoticons.
2. F: While many web site addresses start with "www" an email address rarely starts with "www".
3. F: FAQ is Frequently Asked Questions
4. T
5. T
6. F: The basic Yahoo email account is free. You can buy more mailbox space or other services via Yahoo, but the basic Yahoo email account is free to open and free to use.
7. T
8. F: If I pretend to be someone else, I am spoofing. When I read prior postings or listen in on chatrooms before I enter the discussions, I am lurking. Spoofing is bad; lurking is good.

### PAGE C-14: EXERCISE 6
If an email address is incorrectly entered, one of two things will happen. If the email address entered belongs to someone, that person, not the intended recipient, will receive the message. If the email address does not belong to anyone, the message will "bounce" back to the sender. In such a case, the sender will have a message in her Inbox telling her about the situation. The most likely reason for non-delivery is that she mistyped the address. Compare the address in the bounced message with the correct address. After the error is found, resend the message using the correct address.

### PAGE C-14: EXERCISE 7
1. URL
2. Email
3. URL
4. Email
5. URL
6. Email
7. URL
8. URL
9. Email

☞ Dozer's Quintessential Guide To The Internet ☜          C-25

1. Every email address has a "@" in it.
2. No. Many URLs do not contain a "www".

**PAGE C-14: EXERCISE 8**
COST: Email is cheaper than a postage stamp.
CONVENIENCE: You can write and send email anytime and you can send it simultaneously to lots of different people (recipients).
SPEED: While snail mail (postal service mail) may take days, email typically takes seconds.

**PAGE C-17: EXERCISE 1**

| Across | Down |
|---|---|
| 3. Spam | 1. Sent |
| 5. Text | 2. Start |
| 6. Signature | 4. Password |
| 9. Forward | 7. Address |
| 11. Big | 8. Image |
| 12. Trash | 10. Draft |
| 13. Folders | 11. Board |
| 14. Host | |

**PAGE C-17: EXERCISE 2**
1. F: A deleted email message is put in your Yahoo Trash folder, not in the Recycle Bin.
2. T
3. F: In email, "CC" stands for Carbon Copy.
4. F: Text at the end of each message is called a signature, not an emoticon.
5, 6, and 7 are all T.
8. F: To send a file attachment, I click the Attach Files link, not the Send File link. In fact, I don't think that a Send File link exists in Yahoo mail.

**PAGE C-17: EXERCISE 3**
1. Signature
2. Carbon Copy
3. Paper clip
4. Address book
5. Reply
6. Forward
7. Folders
8. Attachment

**PAGE C-17: EXERCISE 4**
1. B  2. C  3. D  4. A  5. D  6. B

**PAGE C-17: EXERCISE 5**
1. T
2. F: I can put links to web sites in my messages. By doing so, the recipient of the message can click the link to access the web page to which it points.
3. T
4. F: You may not be able to view all attachments you receive. Sometimes, your computer will not have the required software to permit you to view the attachment.
5. T
6. T
7. F: I do not need to read a message before I can delete it. In fact, the first thing many people do when they look at their Inbox is delete messages that obviously are junk mail (spam). They don't even bother to read the junk stuff. Life is too short to waste it reading junk mail. Smart folks are too busy reading Dozer's Quintessential Guide To Computer Literacy to waste their time reading piles of junk mail.
8. T

**PAGE C-21: EXERCISE 1**

| Across | Down |
|---|---|
| 1. Master | 2. Scanner |
| 5. Signature | 3. Site |
| 8. Services | 4. Search |
| 9. Log | 6. Website |
| 12. Home | 7. URL |
| 13. Pages | 10. Graphics |

15. Hyperlink
16. Background
20. Add URL
21. Middle
23. Page
24. Engine
11. Yes
12. HTML
14. Expage
16. Bottom
17. Card
18. Slogan
19. Smiley
22. Dog

**PAGE C-21: EXERCISE 2**
By using search words such as "free web pages" you might find dozens and dozens of web sites that permit you to create free web pages. While your list might differ from mine, some popular places are www.angelfire.com, www.tripod.com, www.geocities.com, and www.freeyellow.com.

**PAGE C-22: EXERCISE 3**
1. F: In an Expage page, "*A" marks the location of an animation, not an address.
2. T
3. F: A "home page" is the first page seen when a site is loaded, not a "title page".
4, 5, 6, 7, and 8 are all T.

**PAGE C-22: EXERCISE 4**
1. Internet
2. Webmaster
3. HTML
4. URL
5. Homepage
6. Slogan
7. HTML
8. Address Bar

**PAGE C-22: EXERCISE 5**
To have a word appear as the link, type the word, enter one space, and type the URL. Then click the Controls button. In the Display Links As area, select Prior Word (this will hide the URL and use the word that appears in front of the URL as the link).

**PAGE C-22: EXERCISE 6**
1. F: While Expage does have a premium web-hosting service that charges a fee, Expage Basic charges nothing to host a webpage.
2, 3, 4, and 5 are all T.
6. F: A web site can consist of one page or hundreds or even thousands of web pages.
7. F: Web page backgrounds do not print along with text and images.
8. T

**PAGE C-22: EXERCISE 7**
There are many ways to promote your web site, including: Send an email message to all your friends (and enemies) telling them about your site. Place a signature in your email that is a link to your site. Go to a search engine and find a link that says something like "Advertise with us" to find out how you can pay for advertising. Hire an Internet marketing service. Find folks who have web sites and tell them that if they provide a link to your site on their site, you will provide a link from your web site to their web site. Register with various search engines so they will add your web site to their database. Make your web site search-engine friendly by using key words in the title and throughout your web site. Print your URL on your business cards and letterheads.

**PAGE C-23: EXERCISE 1**
1. T
2. T
3. F: A web page travels to me in many packets of data. As the individual packets arrive, they are assembled to form the web page.

4. F: While many web site addresses start with a "www", few email addresses will.
5. T
6. F: When clicked, a link does not change into an hourglass icon. A clicked link changes color to indicate that I have been to that page. This helps me to remember where I've been so I don't waste time going there again.
7. F: The mouse pointer looks like a pointing hand when I point to a link, not a ring.
8. T

**PAGE C-23: EXERCISE 2**
1. Carbon Copy
2. HyperText Markup Language
3. World Wide Web
4. Uniform Resource Locator
5. Frequently Asked Questions

**PAGE C-23: EXERCISE 3**
1. T
2. F: A collection of related web pages is called a web site. A web browser is the type of software that is used to find, print, or create web pages.
3. T
4. T
5. F: Information on the Internet is just like information you get from other sources. Some of it is accurate; some of it is completely false. One must be cautious as to what one believes.
6. F: TCP/IP divides information into units called packets, not blocks.
7 and 8 are T.

**PAGE C-23: EXERCISE 4**
1. Spoofing
2. Cookie
3. Internet
4. Homepage
5. Spam
6. Netiquette
7. Flame
8. Snail mail

**PAGE C-23: EXERCISE 5**
1, 2, and 3 are all T.
4. F: You may not be able to view all attachments you receive. Sometimes, your computer will not have the required software to permit you to view the attachment.
5. F: A URL is a web site address. An email address has an "@"; web site addresses do not.
6. T
7. F: While many web site addresses start with a "www", few email addresses will.
8. T

**PAGE C-23: EXERCISE 6**
1. O
2. G
3. J
4. I
5. L
6. C
7. H
8. Q
9. K
10. B
11. F
12. E
13. N
14. M
15. A
16. R
17. S
18. P
19. T
20. U
21. D

**PAGE C-23: EXERCISE 7**
1. F: To insert an image into Word, I click Insert, Picture. Then I click From File if the picture is saved to a disk. Or, I click Clip Art if it is in the Clipart Gallery.
2, 3, and 4 are all T.
5. F: :-) and 8-) are called smileys or emoticons.
6. F: Excite, Yahoo, & Google are search engines, not search motors.
7 and 8 are T.

**A drive**: A secondary storage device that writes to and reads from a floppy disk. Also called a floppy drive.

**address book**: A list of email addresses.

**attachment**: A text or an image file that is sent with an email message.

**audio**: Sound.

**background**: The color or image behind the text and images on a web page.

**backspace key**: The key that deletes data to the left of the insertion point.

**bookmark**: In Netscape, saving the location of a favorite web site so that returning to it will be easier. Internet Explorer calls them favorites.

**bounced email**: An email message that has been sent to a non-existing address and returned to its sender.

**citations**: A list of these appear after doing a search with a search engine. Each citation contains a brief description, the posting date, and the URL of a web site that conforms to your search term. Also called a hit, a match, or a result.

**click**: The act of rapidly pressing the left mouse button one time, generally done to select an on-screen object.

**clipart**: Artwork that can be viewed on screen, inserted into a document, or sent via email.

**close**: The process of removing a file or a program from memory.

**compose**: In Yahoo, to write an email.

**cookie**: A small amount of information placed on your hard drive by web sites that you visit. Its purpose is to allow the web site to "remember" certain things about you.

**copy**: To place a file, folder, text or an image elsewhere while maintaining the original item where it was.

**delete**: To remove (erase) a file, folder, image, or text.

**delete key**: The key that deletes data to the right of the insertion point.

**disable cookies**: To set your web browser so that visited web sites will not be able to leave cookies on your hard drive.

**domain**: The server (computer) upon which a website exists.

**double-click**: The act of rapidly pressing the left mouse button two times.

**Dozer**: The smartest cyberdog on the planet.

**draft folder**: The folder in Yahoo email wherein partially-completed messages can be kept.

**drag**: To move the mouse.

**drag and drop**: The act of pointing to an object on the screen, holding down the left mouse button, moving the mouse, and then releasing the mouse button, thereby moving the object. In essence you have dragged and then dropped the object.

**edit**: To modify a document.

**email**: Electronic mail.

**email addresses**: The address of a mailbox at a server where the recipient's mail is kept.

**emoticons**: Punctuation symbols that, when turned sideways, resemble a human face. Sometimes, these are called emoticons.

**enable cookies**: To set your web browser so that visited web sites can leave cookies on your hard drive.

**enhancements**: Bold, italics, and underline.

**Expage**: One of many websites that permit folks to create and maintain free web pages.

**FAQs**: Frequently Asked Questions, which is a list of questions and associated answers that have previously been asked so many times that the website administrator is too busy to continue to answer the same questions over and over again. So, she develops a FAQ so that I can find the answer myself. Before I ask a question, I should consult the FAQ to see if the answer is there.

**favorites**: In Internet Explorer, saving the location of a favorite web site so that returning to it will be easier.

**flame**: An email message that is intended to anger the recipient.

**flame war**: When two or more people flame each other.

**folders**: A place where something is kept. In Yahoo email, you have several folders in which you can store your messages for future retrieval.

**font color**: The color of the characters.

**font size**: The dimension of the characters.

**font type**: The shape of the characters.

**forward**: To send a received email message to someone else. Also, a button in a web browser that, when clicked, takes you to a previously-viewed web page from which you have retraced your steps by clicking the back toolbar button.

**Google**: Dozer's favorite search engine, which is a web site that keeps a database that permits folks to search worldwide for desirable web pages.

**hits**: A list of these appear after doing a search with a search engine. Each hit contains a brief description, the posting date, and the URL of a web site that conforms to your search term. Also called a citation, a match, or a result.

**host**: A server (computer) that stores a web page, a program, or data that is available to folks using another computer.

**HTML**: An acronym for HyperText Markup Language, which is the code (consisting of a collection of tags) from which web pages are produced.

**hyperlinks**: A connection to another place on the current web page, to another page on the current web site, or to another page on a different web site. When clicked, you are taken elsewhere. Also referred to simply as links.

**IE**: An abbreviation for Internet Explorer.

**inbox**: The place where incoming mail is kept in a Yahoo email account.

**Internet**: A global collection of millions of linked computers.

**Internet Explorer**: A web browser distributed by the fine folks at Microsoft. This program enables its users to find, load, view, print, and create web pages.

**Internet Explorer logo**: The image at the top right corner of the Internet Explorer screen that is animated while a web page is loading.

**insertion point**: The on-screen blinking vertical line identifying where entered text will appear. Some folks refer to this as a cursor.

**landscape orientation**: A document printed on paper that is 11 inches wide and 8-1/2 inches high.

**launch**: To place a program or a document into memory. Also called start, load, or open.

**links**: A connection to another place on the current web page, to another page on the current web site, or to another page on a different web site. When clicked, you are taken elsewhere. Also referred to as hyperlinks.

**load**: To place a program, document, or a web page into memory. Also called open.

**log in**: Signing into an account. Also called log on or sign on.

**log off**: Signing out of an account. Also called log out or sign off.

**lurking**: Listening to an ongoing chatroom conversation before joining the conversation so that you will be discussing the same subject they are.

**mailer daemon**: A program that manages electronic mail and sometimes bounces it (returns undeliverable mail to its sender).

**margins**: The space between the text and the edges of the paper.

**matches**: A list of these appear after doing a search with a search engine. Each match contains a brief description, the posting date, and the URL of a web site that conforms to your search term. Also called a hit, a citation, or a result.

**maximize button**: The button (on the title bar) that, when clicked, will make the window fill the entire screen.

**memory**: The temporary location where the data and programs currently being used by a processor reside. Also called RAM (Random Access Memory).

**menu bar**: The bar (under the title bar) which consists of a series of command categories. To access specific commands in a category, click the item on the menu bar.

**minimize button**: The button that, when clicked, will make the window become the size of a taskbar button.

**move**: To place a file, file, folder, text or an image elsewhere while removing the original item from where it was.

**move handle**: A vertical bar on a toolbar that, when dragged, will allow the user to move the toolbar.

**netiquette**: Proper behavior on the Internet.

**Netscape**: A program that enables us to find, load, view, print, and create web pages.

**office assistant**: A Microsoft help feature that displays a character in the form of a paper clip that asks you to pose a question for him to answer.

**open**: To place a program, document, or a web page into memory. Also called load.

**option button**: (See radio button).

**packet switching**: The process occurring when each computer reads the instructions on each packet and sends the packet along its way to its ultimate destination on the Internet.

**packets**: The clusters of data created by TCP/IP that are sent when a web page is loading. Each packet has an address indicating where its desired destination.

**password**: A secret sequence of characters that prohibits unauthorized access to a web site, an email account, or a computer.

**platform**: The specific collection of software and hardware being used by a computer system.

**protocols**: Standards that allow different types of computers to communicate with each other.

**redo button**: The toolbar button that, when clicked, will reverse the last undo done. It has a crooked arrow pointing to the right.

**reply**: To read an incoming message and then to send a response to the person who sent it.

**results**: A list of these appear after doing a search with a search engine. Each result contains a brief description, the posting date, and the URL of a web site that conforms to your search term. Also called a hit, a match, or a citation.

**right-click**: The act of rapidly pressing the right mouse button one time.

**save**: The act of placing a copy of the document currently in memory into secondary storage.

**search engine**: A web site that keeps a database that permits you to search for desirable web pages worldwide.

**select**: To identify an object, text, or image to which you wish to do something.

**sent folder**: The folder in Yahoo where a copy of my outgoing mail will be kept if I click the Save Copy of Outgoing Message To Sent Folder check before I send the message.

**server**: A computer that stores data or programs that can be accessed from another computer.

**shortcut menu**: A context-sensitive menu that appears when I right click. Also called a Quick Menu.

**shouting**: Writing an email message using capital letters. Some folks will interpret the capital letters as an indication that the writer is angry.

**signature**: A few lines of text at the end of an email message, usually consisting of a web site address, phone number, or favorite quotation.

**smiley**: Punctuation symbols that, when turned sideways, resemble a human face. Sometimes, these are called emoticons.

**snail mail**: Standard postal service mail (which is as slow as a snail) as compared to email (which is faster than Dozer running for supper).

**spam**: Generally useless, unsolicited, obnoxious information sent to thousands (or millions) of people at once.

**spoofing**: Pretending to be someone else. For instance, using an email address to send a message that would give the recipient the idea that you were someone you are not.

**taskbar**: The horizontal bar, typically at the bottom of the desktop, upon which the Start button resides.

**toolbar**: A collection of picture buttons that, when clicked, execute a command. These buttons typically appear below the menu bar.

**trash folder**: The place where deleted Yahoo email is temporarily kept.

**undo button**: The toolbar button that, when clicked, will reverse the last action taken. It has a crooked arrow pointing to the left.

**URL**: An acronym for Uniform Resource Locator, a web site address.

**userid**: The specific identification of the person using an account. Also called a Username.

**username**: (See UserId).

**web browser**: A program that permits you to find, load, view, print, and create web pages (e.g., Netscape Navigator and Internet Explorer).

**web page**: A file on the Internet.

**website**: A series of related, linked electronic documents maintained by an individual or organization.

**webmaster**: A person who designs, creates, posts, and maintains web pages.

**world wide web**: (See WWW).

**WWW**: An acronym for World Wide Web, a massive collection of web pages.

**Yahoo**: A popular search engine used to locate web sites with desired information or images. Also a very popular free email provider.

| Instructor's Email Address |
|---|
|  |

| Class Code |
|---|
|  |

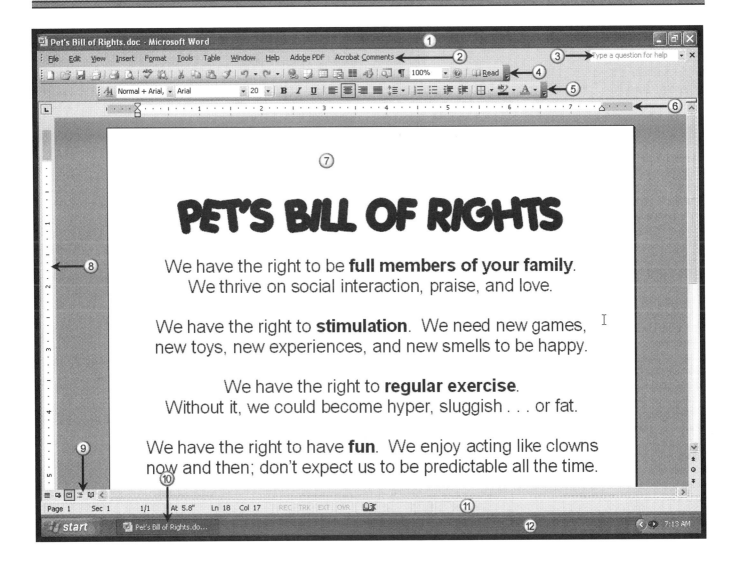

1. Title bar (identifies the program and the document being used)
2. Menu bar (collection of menu items, each of which contains commands)
3. Help (a great place to find answers to all your questions)
4. Standard toolbar (collection of picture buttons, each of which accesses a command)
5. Formatting toolbar (collection of picture buttons, each of which accesses a command)
6. Horizontal Ruler bar (displays the margin and tab settings)
7. Document Area (where your documents reside)
8. Vertical Ruler bar (provides information about margins)
9. View toolbar (changes the appearance of the on-screen document)
10. Taskbar button (denotes an open window)
11. Status bar (displays location of insertion point and provides other information)
12. Taskbar (contains the Start button, open windows buttons, etc.)

# Dozer's Quintessential Guide To Microsoft Word
## T A B L E   O F   C O N T E N T S

## START (LOAD, OPEN, LAUNCH) WORD
To use Word, the program must be placed into memory (RAM).

To start Word, do the following:
☞ Click the Start taskbar button.  Point to All Programs.
☞ On the sub-menu, click Microsoft Word (or Microsoft Office Word).

## SURVEY THE WORD SCREEN
The Word screen contains elements that are common to many Window-based programs, including:
☞ Title bar (top of screen) identifies the current program and document.  In addition, the Close, Minimize, Maximize, and Restore buttons reside on the title bar.
☞ Menu bar (below title bar) contains command categories. When one is clicked, a list of commands appears.  If all the commands on a list are not visible, click the double-down arrow at the bottom of the list to see the complete list.
☞ Toolbars (below menu bar) consist of picture buttons.  If clicked, a command is executed.  Each toolbar has a Move handle (vertical bar) at its left edge.  If you point the mouse to a Move handle, the pointer will become a four-pointed arrow.  If the Standard and Formatting toolbars appear in one line, drag the Move handle of the Formatting toolbar down so that the Formatting toolbar occupies its own line. Otherwise, you won't be able to see all the toolbar buttons.
☞ Document window (space where your document resides). The document window can be viewed in several ways.  To ensure that it is in normal view, click View, Normal.
☞ Insertion point (the blinking, vertical bar at top left corner of the document window) marks where text will be inserted.
☞ End of Document Marker (the small horizontal line below the insertion point) denotes the bottom of the document.
☞ Scroll bars (right and bottom of document window) permit you to move in long documents.
☞ Task Pane (right side of screen), will be described next.  If the task pane is not visible, click View, Task Pane.

## USE THE TASK PANE
From time to time, the task pane will appear along the right side of the screen.  Its contents change, depending on what you are doing.  For instance, since you just started Word, a task pane appears that wants to know what you want to do (if the task pane is not visible, click View, Task Pane to have it appear). Later, as you attempt other tasks, different task panes will appear, from which you can select items.  Since you want to create a new document, the easiest way to do that is to simply close the task pane.  So, click the X at the top right corner of the task pane.  The task pane disappears, but it will appear later as you attempt other tasks.

## ENTER TEXT
With a typewriter, when you approach the end of a line at the right margin, a bell rings warning you that you need to press the Return (Enter) key to move to the next line.  With word processing, there is no bell and you do not need to press Return (Enter).  Instead a feature called word wrap will automatically move the insertion point to the next line.  In fact, you must remember NOT to press the Enter key at the end of each line. Just keep typing and the word processor will automatically move excess text to the next line.

To practice entering text, do the following:
☞ To indent the first line of the paragraph, press the Tab key. Note: the insertion point moves half-an-inch to the right.
☞ As you type the paragraph below, don't press the Enter key at the end of each line.  Let the words wrap automatically. They will wrap in different places than they do below.  If you misspell a word, don't worry.  Just type the paragraph.

> Work is for people who don't know how to fish.  Women who seek to be equal to men lack ambition.  I used to think I was indecisive, but now I'm not too sure.  Nothing is impossible for those who don't have to do it.  According to my calculations, the problem doesn't exist.

## SAVE A DOCUMENT
While you are creating a document, it resides in memory.  If the power goes out or the machine crashes, you will lose what is in memory.  To avoid this, save your document (a saved document is called a file).  By saving your document, you will be able to retrieve it later.  If you are using a computer that does not belong to you, all your work should be saved to a diskette.

To practice saving a document to a diskette, do the following:
☞ Insert a diskette into the floppy drive.
☞ Click File, Save.  Since your document has not been previously saved, the Save As dialog box appears.
☞ Click the Save In list box arrow (a drop-down list appears).
☞ Select the drive and folder where you want the document to reside (in this case, specify 3 ½ Floppy (A:) drive).
☞ Since the document consists of bumper sticker quotes, in the File Name box, replace the suggested filename with the filename WP1-Bumper Stickers.
☞ Click the Save button.  Notice that the floppy drive indicator light comes on and you can hear the sound of the drive as it saves the document to your diskette.
☞ When it is done saving the file to the diskette, notice that the filename appears in the title bar.

## INSERT ADDITIONAL TEXT
One great benefit to using a computer is that once a document is created, additional text can be inserted.

To practice inserting additional text, do the following:
☞ If the insertion point is not to the right of the period at the end of the last sentence, click there to put it there.
☞ Since you will be typing a new paragraph, press the Enter key to move the insertion point to the next line.
☞ Press Tab to indent the first line of the new paragraph.
☞ Type the paragraph below.  At the end of each line, do not press the Enter key.  If you misspell a word, do not worry about it.  We'll fix mistakes later.  Just type the paragraph.

> Your honor student cheated off my child.  I started out with nothing and I still have most of it left.  A bad day fishing beats a good day at work.  The more people I meet, the more I like my dog.  He who laughs last, thinks slowest.  Always remember that you are unique: just like everyone else.

☞ Save the document.  Since this document has previously been saved, click File, Save (or click the Save toolbar button).  The current version of the document will be saved to the disk using its current filename.   Note: if you ever want to save an existing file using a different name or you want to save it to another place, you can click File, Save As to access the Save As dialog box where you can specify a new name or a different location. For now, let's not do this. Later, you will need to know how to do this.

## MOVE THE INSERTION POINT IN A DOCUMENT

Text is entered at the insertion point location. Therefore, in order to edit a document, you will need to move the insertion point to the place where the editing is to take place.

To practice moving the insertion point, do the following:
- ☞ Press the left arrow key one time. Notice that the insertion point moved one character to the left.
- ☞ Press the left arrow key four times. Notice that the insertion point moved four more characters to the left.
- ☞ Look at the insertion point while you hold down the left arrow key. Notice that the insertion point rapidly moves to the left until you release the left arrow key.
- ☞ The right arrow key works the same as the left, except the insertion point moves to the right. The up arrow key moves the insertion point up one line and the down arrow key moves the insertion point down one line. Experiment with each of the arrow keys until you understand them.

You just learned how to move the insertion point one character or one line at a time using the arrow keys. Sometimes, you will want to move the insertion point over a large body of text. In such cases, using the arrow keys will be very time consuming. So, there are faster ways to move the insertion point.

To practice moving over a large body of text, do the following:
- ☞ Press the Home key. Notice that the insertion point moved to the beginning of the line.
- ☞ Press the End key. Notice that the insertion point moved to the end of the line.
- ☞ Click in front of "people" in the first paragraph (the insertion point will appear there).
- ☞ While holding down the Ctrl key, press the End key (the insertion point will move to the end of the document).
- ☞ While holding down the Ctrl key, press the Home key (the insertion point will move to the top of the document).

## CLOSE A DOCUMENT

When you are done working on a document, you will want to close it. Closing it removes it from memory. Note: Closing a document is different from closing a program. There is more than one Close button. The one on the title bar closes the program; the one on the menu bar closes the document. Also, when the task pane appears, it also has a close button.

To practice closing a document, do the following:
- ☞ Click the Close button (the X at the right end of the menu bar). If you have modified the document since you last saved it, you will be asked if you want to save the changes. If you see this message, click Yes. The document will be saved and closed, but, the program will remain open.

## OPEN A DOCUMENT

To read, edit, or print an existing document, you will need to open it (i.e., place a copy of it in memory, also called RAM).

To practice opening an existing document, do the following:
- ☞ Click File, Open (the Open dialog box appears).

- ☞ Click the Look In list box arrow (a drop-down list appears).
- ☞ Select the drive and folder in which the document resides (select the 3 ½ Floppy (A:) drive).
- ☞ The files on the diskette appear. Select the desired file (if not already selected, click "WP1-Bumper Stickers").
- ☞ Click the Open button (the document will open).
- ☞ Now that the document is open, let's add a paragraph.
- ☞ Place the insertion point at the end of the last paragraph.
- ☞ Press Enter to move the insertion point to the next line.
- ☞ Press Tab to indent the first line of the new paragraph.
- ☞ Type the paragraph below.

> Folks who drive like hell are bound to get there. CAUTION! I drive like you do! Forget about world peace; visualize using your turn signal. If you don't like my driving, stay off of the sidewalk. I brake for no apparent reason. Honk if you love peace and quiet.

- ☞ Press Enter to move to the next line.
- ☞ Press Tab to indent the line. Type your full name.
- ☞ Save the document (click the Save toolbar button).

## PRINT A DOCUMENT

To obtain a hard copy of your document, you will want to print it. There are two common ways to do this. You could click the Print toolbar button (looks like a printer). This will print one copy of the entire document. If your document is long and you only want to print out a portion of it, or if you want to print out more than one copy of it, you should use the Print option on the File menu to access the Print dialog box. Since your document is only one page in length, press the Print toolbar button to print one copy of your document.

## GET HELP

In the old days, when you bought software, it would come in a box with a hefty manual. Nowadays, you won't get the hefty manual, but the information that once was found in the manual can now be found online. This on-line manual will answer most any question you have. This feature normally appears as a cartoon character in the form of a paper clip.

To practice using the Office Assistant, do the following:
- ☞ To access the Office Assistant, click Help, Show the Office Assistant. An animated paper clip will appear on the screen.
- ☞ To ask it a question, click the paper clip. Once clicked, he provides a box in which you can ask your question.
- ☞ Type your question in the text box (in this case, type How do I display a toolbar?).
- ☞ Click the Search button. A series of topics will appear. Click the topic you want information about (click Show Or Hide A Toolbar). You will then receive instructions or additional subtopics from which to choose.
- ☞ Close the Help dialog box.
- ☞ You can leave the Office Assistant on all the time. If you do, it will sometimes automatically offer a suggestion on how to do something. If this feature is annoying you or is taking up too much space on the screen, close it. To do so, click Help, Hide the Office Assistant.

## CLOSE WORD

When you are done with a program, you'll want to remove it from memory by closing the program. Remember, closing a program is different from closing a document.

To close Word, click the Close button (X at right end of title bar).

# EXERCISES

## EXERCISE 1: CROSSWORD

Use the clues below to complete the crossword puzzle. (Note: the Answer Key can be found beginning on page D-25).

### ACROSS

1. When in normal view, the End of Document ___ denotes the bottom of the document.
5. If I have a question about how to do something in Microsoft Word, I can click Help, Show The Office ___, to access a friendly paper clip character who will provide guidance.
8. The ___ point is the blinking, vertical bar that marks where text will be inserted.
9. Word provides an extensive ___ feature that will answer most any question you may have about the program.
10. Is closing a document and closing a program the same thing?
11. To have a permanent copy of a document I am currently creating, I will ___ it to a diskette or to the hard drive.
14. While you are creating a document, it resides in ___.
15. I can save my files to the 3 ½ ___ (A) Drive.

### DOWN

2. When I create a document with a typewriter, I press the ___ (Enter) key at the end of each line. However, with a computer-generated document, I will only do this to start a new paragraph or to insert a blank line.
3. Formatting and Standard are two types of tool___.
4. If you ___ in a document, the blinking, vertical bar (mentioned in 8 Across) will be inserted.
6. If I have a document that is so long that it cannot all be displayed at one time on the screen, ___ bars can be found at the right and bottom of the document window.
7. A collection of picture buttons used to execute commands.
9. To have the blinking, vertical bar (mentioned in 8 Across) move to the beginning of a line, press the ___ key.
12. To have the blinking, vertical bar (mentioned previously) move to the end of a line, press the ___ key.
13. Word ___ automatically moves text to the next line.

## EXERCISE 2: TRUE-FALSE

For each of the following eight statements, place a T or an F on the line to indicate if the statement is True or False.

1. ___ "Load", "start", and "open" a program all mean the same.
2. ___ A toolbar Move handle has a picture of a truck on it.
3. ___ The Office Assistant normally looks like a paper clip.
4. ___ The menu bar has picture buttons on it.
5. ___ While I type a document, it resides in memory.
6. ___ The title bar is at the top of the window.
7. ___ Once I create a document, I can't modify it.
8. ___ The Start button is found on the status bar.

## EXERCISE 3: IDENTIFY TERMS

Below are eight definitions. Below the definitions are eight lines. In each line, write the word that matches the definition.

1. A blinking, vertical bar marking where typed text will appear.
2. The company that makes the Word program.
3. The help feature that normally looks like a paper clip.
4. A line of commands such as File, Edit, View, and Help.
5. A line of commands in the form of picture buttons.
6. The feature that automatically moves text to the next line.
7. The vertical bar on a toolbar, used to move the toolbar.
8. The small horizontal line marking the bottom of the document.

1. _____     5. _____
2. _____     6. _____
3. _____     7. _____
4. _____     8. _____

## EXERCISE 4: MATCHING

Below is a list of ten commonly-used keystrokes. Below that list is a list of what happens when you use each keystroke. Match the keystroke with the results.

| | | |
|---|---|---|
| A. Up Arrow | E. End | I. Ctrl + End |
| B. Down Arrow | F. Enter | J. Ctrl + Home |
| C. Left Arrow | G. Home | |
| D. Right Arrow | H. Tab | |

1. ___ Insertion point moves to the top of the document.
2. ___ Insertion point moves to the bottom of the document.
3. ___ Insertion point moves to the beginning of the line.
4. ___ Insertion point moves to the end of the line.
5. ___ Insertion point moves to beginning of next line.
6. ___ Insertion point moves one tab space to the right.
7. ___ Insertion point moves to the right one character.
8. ___ Insertion point moves up one line.
9. ___ Insertion point moves to the left one character.
10. ___ Insertion point moves down one line.

## EXERCISE 5: TRUE-FALSE

For each of the following eight statements, place a T or an F on the line to indicate if the statement is True or False.

1. ___ To open an existing document, I click File, Open.
2. ___ To indent a line, I press the Indent key.
3. ___ A toolbar Move handle has a vertical bar on it.
4. ___ Text is inserted at the location of the mouse pointer.
5. ___ To find answers to questions about Word, I click FAQ.
6. ___ The word wrap feature moves text to the next line.
7. ___ The Close button on the title bar has an "X" on it.
8. ___ Closing a document means that I remove it from memory.

## EXERCISE 6: CREATE A LIST

Dozer has been planning the annual family vacation. He has compiled a list of places to visit and a list of places to avoid. Please start Word and recreate the lists below. At the end of each line, press the Enter key to have the insertion point move to the next line. When you want a blank line between printed lines, press the Enter key. Note: as you type some of these words, red wavy lines may appear under them. Don't be concerned. We'll learn about red wavy lines later.

---

Places to Visit:

Pleasure Beach, Connecticut
Niceville, Florida
Mt. Healthy, Ohio
Happy Valley, Oregon
Opportunity, Washington
Hometown, West Virginia
Kinder, Louisiana
Friendly, Maryland
Welcome, Minnesota
Doolittle, Missouri

Places to Avoid:

Weed, California
Kill Devil Hills, North Carolina
Devil's Lake, North Dakota
Scalp Level, Pennsylvania
Peculiar, Missouri
Savage, Montana
Weedville, Pennsylvania
Hurt, Virginia
Hurricane, West Virginia
Crook, New York

---

☞ Save the document to your disk (call it WP1-Vacation).
☞ Close the document. Close Word.

## EXERCISE 7: CREATE AND SAVE A DOCUMENT

Yesterday, Dozer read a paragraph that struck him as being rather interesting. He wants to have the paragraph typed. Please help Dozer by creating the document below.

☞ Start Word and type the following paragraph. Do not press the Enter key at the end of each line. Instead, at the end of each line, let the words wrap automatically. They will wrap in different places than they do below. Don't be concerned. To indent the first line of the paragraph, press the Tab key.

---

This is the true joy in life, the being used for a purpose recognized by yourself as a mighty one; the being a force of nature instead of a feverish, selfish little clod of ailments and grievances complaining that the world will not devote itself to making you happy.

---

☞ Insert two blank lines above the paragraph. To do so, click in front of the first line and press Enter twice.
☞ Type your name in the topmost blank line so that there is a blank line between your name and the paragraph.
☞ Save the document to your diskette (name it WP1-Life). By the way, you may have noticed that when you save a document for the first time, a suggested filename appears in the Filename box of the Save As dialog box. If you don't like the suggested name, an easy way to change it is to triple click the suggested name and just type the desired name.
☞ Close the document.
☞ Close Word.

## EXERCISE 8: OPEN AND MODIFY A DOCUMENT

☞ In Exercise 7 you typed a paragraph and saved your document (you called it "WP1-Life"). Open "WP1-Life".
☞ Under the paragraph, type the following paragraph:

---

I am of the opinion that my life belongs to the whole community, and as long as I live it is my privilege to do for it whatever I can. I want to be thoroughly used up when I die, for the harder I work the more I live.

---

☞ Save the modified document.
☞ Under the second paragraph, type this paragraph:

---

I rejoice in life for its own sake. Life is no "brief candle" to me. It is a sort of splendid torch which I have got hold of for the moment, and I want to make burn as brightly as possible before handing it on to the future generations.

---

☞ After typing the last paragraph, press the Enter key a few times to move the insertion point below the paragraph.
☞ Type George Bernard Shaw (Since he's the dude who wrote these words, it is proper that we acknowledge him).
☞ Save the modified document (you will use it later).
☞ Close the document. Close Word.

## EXERCISE 9: SAVING A FILE UNDER A NEW NAME

If there is any one computer-related task that will cause the most sadness, it is incorrectly saving a document. Folks often make the mistake of saving the document to the wrong place. For instance, they want to save it to a diskette, but somehow the document ends up on the hard drive. Later, they can't find the document, because they will look in the wrong place. In addition to being careful "where" you save it, you must be careful "what" you call it. This exercise will let you practice.

☞ Look at the list of endorsements found on the back cover of Dozer's Quintessential Guide To Computer Literacy.
☞ Start Microsoft Word and type B. Franklin's endorsement.
☞ Save the document to your diskette (call it Franklin).
☞ Close Microsoft Word.
☞ Start Microsoft Word and open the Franklin file.
☞ Save the Franklin file again, but this time change its name to Franklin2. To do so, click File, Save As.
☞ In the Save As dialog box indicate that you want the file to be saved to your diskette and that you want to save the file under the name "Franklin2".
☞ Click the Save button. The original Franklin file will still be on your diskette and you will have a second, duplicate file called Franklin2.
☞ Close Microsoft Word.
☞ Open My Computer and the floppy drive window to confirm that your diskette contains both Franklin files.

## EXERCISE 10: GET SOME HELP

Word provides an on-line manual that will answer questions about Word. In this exercise, you will use the Help feature to find the answers to a couple of questions.

**Q:** If you wanted to know how many words are in a document, how would you do a word count?
**A:** _____

**Q:** Using the knowledge you learned in the prior question, open your "WP1-Life" document. How many words are in it?
**A:** _____

☞ Close the document. Close Word.

Few writers can produce a perfect document without editing it. Editing includes such activities as inserting, deleting, moving and copying text, as well as correcting spelling and grammar errors. Start Word and type the paragraphs below. This document will be used throughout this project. Notice that the last paragraph contains spelling and grammar errors. Type the paragraph with the errors. Later, we will fix them. Note: as you type some of these words, wavy lines will appear under them. Don't be concerned. We'll learn about wavy lines later.

> A dude goes to the butcher shop. Upon seeing a big sign that reads "T-bone steak $4 per pound" he puts $20 on the counter and tells the butcher, "Here's my payment for 5 pounds, but please give me less than I am paying for."
>
> A dude goes to Disneyland. He pays the entrance fee. But, instead of taking advantage of the opportunity to ride as many rides as possible and observe as many shows as possible, he sits on a chair outside of the park.
>
> These dudes is displaying irasional behavior. Likewise, some college students pays tuition, computer lab fees, and technology fees. Then, instead of making the very best use of their invessment, they do as little as possible and avoid the computer lab. They often want less than they paid for.

☞ Save the document. Call it <u>WP2-Irrational Behavior</u>.

## SELECT TEXT
To move, copy, delete, or modify text, you must first select the relevant text. There are a number of ways to accomplish this.

To practice selecting text, do the following:
☞ Double-click any word. The word is selected.
☞ Click elsewhere to deselect the text.
☞ Triple-click in the 1st paragraph to select the paragraph.
☞ Click elsewhere to deselect the text.
☞ Drag over parts of a word, sentence, or paragraph to select portions of a word, sentence, or paragraph.
☞ Click elsewhere to deselect the text.
☞ Click Edit, Select All to select the entire document.
☞ Click elsewhere to deselect the text.

## DELETE TEXT
There are three commonly-used methods for deleting text.

To practice deleting text with the Delete key, do the following:
☞ Click in front of the undesired text (in this case, click in front of the word "big" in the 2nd sentence).
☞ Press the Delete key four times (a character or space to the right of the insertion point is deleted each time you press the Delete key).

To delete text using the Backspace key, do the following:
☞ Click at the end of the undesired text (in this case, click at the end of the word "often" in the last sentence).
☞ Press the Backspace key six times (a character or space to the left of the insertion point is deleted each time you press the Backspace key).

To practice deleting a large body of text, do the following:
☞ Select the text (in this case, select the last sentence).
☞ Press the Delete key. The entire sentence is deleted.
☞ Save the document (click the Save toolbar button).

## MOVE TEXT
When you find that a sentence or a paragraph would work best if it were in a different location, you will want to move it to its preferred place. When you move text, the original text (source) will be removed and placed in its new location (destination).

To practice moving text, do the following:
☞ Select the text (select the 1st paragraph).
☞ Click Edit, Cut (the text is placed in the clipboard). By the way, you can also do this by right clicking on the selected text and then clicking Cut from the shortcut menu or you can click the Cut toolbar button (it has a pair of scissors on it).
☞ Put the insertion point where you want the text inserted (put it after the word "park").
☞ Press the Enter key to move to the next line.
☞ Click Edit, Paste. By the way, you can also do this by right clicking and then click Paste from the shortcut menu or you can click the Paste toolbar button (it has a clipboard on it).
☞ When you cut the text, you sent it to the clipboard along with any formats that had been applied to that text. After you paste, the Paste Option button appears. You can choose to keep the source formats, match the destination formats, or remove all formats (keep text only). To make any of these choices, you would click the Paste Option button and make your selection. For now, ignore the Paste Option button. We'll use it later.
☞ If needed, indent the newly-pasted paragraph.
☞ Save the document (click the Save toolbar button).

## COPY TEXT
If a word or phrase needs to appear in numerous places, you could type it repeatedly. However, to save time, copy the text. When this is done, the source text will remain where it was and you will be inserting a copy of it elsewhere. The steps involved in copying text are identical to the steps involved in moving text with one exception. When you move text, you send it to the clipboard by clicking Edit, Cut. To copy text, you send it to the clipboard by clicking Edit, Copy. Since all other steps are the same, there's no need to practice copying text now.

## UNDO & REDO ACTIONS
When you do something and immediately realize it was a mistake, you can reverse the action by using the Undo feature. This feature will undo the last action taken. If you then click the Undo button again, the second-to-last action will be undone. You can, therefore, backtrack through a series of actions, undoing each action by clicking the Undo button. If you find that you undid something you did not want to undo, you can restore the action by clicking the Redo button. Think of these buttons as operating like the Back and Forward buttons on a web browser. The Back button takes you back in a series of previously-viewed web pages (the Undo button takes you back through previous actions); the Forward button takes you forward in a series of previously-viewed web pages (the Redo button takes you forward through previous actions).

To practice using Undo and Redo, do the following:
☞ Click the Undo toolbar button (left-pointing curved arrow). The last action taken is undone.
☞ Click the Undo button again. Notice that the second to last action taken is undone.

☞ Click the Redo button (right-pointing curved arrow). The last action undone is restored.
☞ Click Redo again. The first action undone is redone.
☞ Save the document (click the Save toolbar button).

## REPLACE TEXT

Suppose you are writing a novel in which a character named Skooter is frequently mentioned and you decide to change the name to Corky. You could read through the novel to find each instance of "Skooter" and replace it with "Corky". This may be time-consuming and you might miss an instance or two of the name. To save time and enhance accuracy, have Word find every instance of "Skooter" and replace it with "Corky".

To practice replacing text, do the following:
☞ Click in front of the 1st paragraph to start the search there.
☞ Click Edit, Replace.
☞ The Find and Replace dialog box appears. In the Find What text box, enter the text to be found (enter dude).
☞ In the Replace With text box, enter the text that will replace the word "dude" (enter gentleman).
☞ Click Find Next. The first instance of "dude" is found.
☞ Click Replace. This instance of "dude" is replaced with "gentleman" and the second instance of "dude" is found.
☞ Click Replace. The word "gentleman" replaces "dude" and the word "dudes" is found (it includes "dude"). Since you don't want to replace it, click Find Next. You are told that Word has finished searching the document (no further instances of "dude" were found).
☞ If needed, click OK. Click the Close button in the dialog box.
☞ Save the document (click the Save toolbar button).

## USE AUTOCORRECT

AutoCorrect corrects common errors automatically. For instance, if you type the first word in a sentence without a capital letter, AutoCorrect will capitalize it. If you misspell a word in a way that AutoCorrect recognizes, it will correct it.

To see how this feature works, do the following:
☞ Click at the end of the last paragraph and press Enter a few times to move the insertion point to a blank space.
☞ Type each word in the following sentence exactly how it appears. When you press the space bar after each word, notice how each word is automatically corrected. The sentence to type is: i willbe recieving teh shiped boxs.
☞ Now type :) and notice that it changes to a smiley face.

You can add entries to AutoCorrect. By doing so, it will replace a "misspelled" word with any phrase. For instance, you could have AutoCorrect replace a short "misspelled" word with your full name, so you will never have to type your name again.

To practice adding an AutoCorrect entry, do the following:
☞ Click Tools, AutoCorrect Options.
☞ In the Replace box, enter the text to find (enter xxx).
☞ In the With box, enter the text to substitute (in this case, enter your full name). Click Add, Ok.
☞ At the bottom of the document, type xxx and press the spacebar. Notice that the xxx becomes your full name.

To practice deleting an AutoCorrect entry, do the following:
☞ Click Tools, AutoCorrect Options.
☞ Find the undesired entry (in this case, find the "xxx" you created). You can find it by scrolling down the list, but this

will be time-consuming. So, instead, type xxx in the Replace box. The list box below scrolls up and highlights that entry.
☞ With the entry selected, click Delete, OK.
☞ At the bottom of the document, type xxx and press the spacebar. Notice that xxx doesn't become your name. Since you deleted the AutoCorrect entry, every time you type "xxx" it will appear as "xxx" not as your name.
☞ Save the document (click the Save toolbar button).

## CORRECT SPELLING AND GRAMMAR ERRORS

The Check-Spelling-As-You-Type feature identifies what it believes to be spelling errors (by underlining each word with a wavy red line) and provides suggestions for correcting the error. Any word that is not an AutoCorrect entry and is not in the spelling dictionary will be identified as an error. Similarly, the Check-Grammar-As-You-Type feature marks what it believes to be grammar errors (by underlining each phrase with a wavy green line) and provides suggestions for correcting the error. Since these features can be turned off, we need to first be sure they are turned on.

To be sure these features are turned on, do the following:
☞ Click Tools, Options, Spelling & Grammar.
☞ If not selected, click the Check Spelling As You Type box.
☞ If not selected, click the Check Grammar As You Type box.
☞ Click OK.

To practice checking the spelling of a word, do the following:
☞ Right click on any word with a wavy red line (right click on the word "irasional"). At the top of the shortcut menu, a suggestion for improvement is provided.
☞ Click the suggestion ("irrational"). The word is corrected.
☞ Right click on "invessment" and change it to "investment".
☞ If any other word has a wavy red line under it, right click on it and correct its spelling. If the word is correctly spelled, click Ignore All on the shortcut menu.

To practice checking grammar, do the following:
☞ Right click a word or phrase with a wavy green line (right click on "These dudes is").
☞ Click the desired suggestion ("These dudes are"). Notice that the phrase is corrected.
☞ Right click on "pays" and change it to "pay".
☞ If any other words have a wavy green line under them, right click on them and correct the grammar.
☞ Save the document (click the Save toolbar button).

## USE THE THESAURUS

A thesaurus is a dictionary of synonyms (words with similar meanings) and antonyms (words with opposite meanings). Word has an online thesaurus that will help you find the exact word to describe what you are writing about.

To practice using the thesaurus, do the following:
☞ Right click on a word (in this case, right click on "observe").
☞ From the shortcut menu, point to Synonyms to have a list of synonyms appear.
☞ From the list of synonyms provided, click the one you like best (in this case, click "watch").
☞ Notice that your original word (observe) is replaced with your chosen synonym (watch)
☞ Save the document (click the Save toolbar button).
☞ Close the document.
☞ Close Word.

## EXERCISE 1: CROSSWORD

Use the clues below to complete the crossword puzzle.

### ACROSS

1. The ___ point is the blinking, vertical bar where newly-entered text will appear.
5. To move text, would I click Edit, Move?
6. A red wavy line identifies a possible ___ error.
9. If I click between the "z" and the "e" in the word "Dozer" and then press the ___ key, the letter "z" will disappear.
13. The ___ feature automatically corrects common errors and automatically capitalizes the first word of each sentence.
14. An antonym for "down".
17. If you undid something you did not want to undo, you can restore the action by clicking the ___ button (it has a crooked arrow on it that points to the right).
18. A synonym for "mother".
19. To rapidly and accurately substitute a specific word in your document with another word, use the ___ feature.

### DOWN

2. To move, copy, or delete text, I would first ___ the text.
3. A device is __line if it is communicating with a computer.
4. Are "move" and "copy" synonyms?
7. A dictionary of synonyms and antonyms.
8. If I click between the "z" and the "e" in the word "Dozer" and then press the ___ key, the letter "e" will disappear.
10. To rapidly select a word, I would ___click the word.
11. A good way to select parts of words, sentences, or paragraphs would be to ___ over the text with the mouse.
12. When you start Word, you put the program into ___.
15. When you ___ text, the source text will be removed and placed in its new location (the destination).
16. To have a permanent copy of a document I ___ it.
17. Another name for 12 Down.

## EXERCISE 2: TRUE-FALSE

For each of the following six statements, place a T or an F on the line to indicate if the statement is True or False.

1. ___The blinking, vertical bar is the scroll bar.
2. ___To select a word, I could click it.
3. ___Red wavy lines identify possible spelling errors.
4. ___After I copy and paste text, it will appear in two places.
5. ___The Undo button has a crooked arrow pointing to the left.
6. ___To move text, I would click Edit, Move.

## EXERCISE 3: TRUE-FALSE

For each of the following six statements, place a T or an F on the line to indicate if the statement is True or False.

1. ___To select a word, I could double-click it.
2. ___Red wavy lines identify possible grammar errors.
3. ___I can add entries to the AutoCorrect list.
4. ___The blinking, vertical bar is the insertion point.
5. ___The words "true" and "false" are synonyms.
6. ___To move or copy text, I would first select the text.

## EXERCISE 4: IDENTIFY TERMS

Below are eight definitions. Below the definitions are eight lines. In each line, write the word that matches the definition.

1. A collection of antonyms and synonyms.
2. To remove text from one place and put it elsewhere.
3. The toolbar button that lets me reverse a prior action.
4. Words with opposite meanings.
5. The feature that corrects common errors automatically.
6. The toolbar button that lets me reverse a prior reversal.
7. The type of possible error with a red wavy underline.
8. Words with similar meanings.

1. _____     5. _____
2. _____     6. _____
3. _____     7. _____
4. _____     8. _____

## EXERCISE 5: TRUE-FALSE

For each of the following six statements, place a T or an F on the line to indicate if the statement is True or False.

1. ___The Redo button has a crooked arrow pointing to the left.
2. ___Green wavy lines identify possible spelling errors.
3. ___AutoCorrect capitalizes the first word in a sentence.
4. ___The words "big" and "large" are synonyms.
5. ___To select parts of sentences, drag over the text.
6. ___AutoCorrect corrects common errors automatically.

## EXERCISE 6: MATCHING

Below is a list of four menu bar items. Below that list is another list of tasks. Match each task to the menu bar item you would use to accomplish the task.

| A. File | B. Edit | C. Tools | D. Help |
|---|---|---|---|

1. ___ Add an AutoCorrect entry.
2. ___ Use the Replace feature to replace a word.
3. ___ Save a document.
4. ___ Find a synonym
5. ___ Copy text to the clipboard.
6. ___ Find out how to do something in Microsoft Word

## EXERCISE 7: COPY & PASTE TEXT FROM A WEB SITE
☞ Start Internet Explorer and go to **www.dozer.pannell.com** (or www.pannell.biz) and click the My New Job link.
☞ Copy the paragraphs (not the picture) to the clipboard.
☞ Start Microsoft Word.
☞ Paste the paragraphs into the document (if the ActiveX warning box appears, click Yes). After you paste, the Paste Option button appears beneath the pasted text (it looks like a clipboard). You can choose to keep the source formats, match the destination formats, or keep text only. If you ignore the Paste Option button, the pasted text will have the same formats as those in the source text. If you want to change that, click the Paste Option button and make your selection. In this case, the pasted text appears in brown ink and it has some other formats in it. To remove those formats, click the Paste Option button, and click Keep Text Only. The text should then look like you typed it yourself.
☞ Save the document to your disk (call it WP2-Dozer's Job).

## EXERCISE 8: EDIT TEXT
☞ In the first sentence, insert the word beautiful so that it appears in front of the word "picture".
☞ In the second sentence, delete "would say that I".
☞ In the fifth sentence, replace "100%" with the words "one-hundred percent".
☞ Insert two blank lines above the first paragraph (to do so, you may recall that you need to click in front of the first paragraph and press the Enter key twice).
☞ Type your name in the topmost blank line so that there is a blank line between your name and the first paragraph.
☞ Save your modified document.

## EXERCISE 9: CORRECT SPELLING AND GRAMMAR
☞ Correct any spelling errors. It is possible that some of the words identified as being misspelled are, in fact, correctly spelled. You must use your judgment as to whether or not each identified word is indeed misspelled.
☞ Correct any grammar errors.

## EXERCISE 10: USE THE REPLACE FEATURE
☞ Use the Replace feature to replace each instance of the word "lie" with "fib" (do not replace words containing the character string "lie", such as "belief").

## EXERCISE 11: COPY AND PASTE AN INTERNET IMAGE
If you only want to use the image in a Word document, you don't need to save it to your diskette. You can simply copy it from the Internet and paste it into your document. To see how this works, do the following:
☞ Start Internet Explorer and go to **www.dozer.pannell.com** (or www.pannell.biz).
☞ Click the My Quintessential Guide To Computer Literacy link.
☞ Right click on the image of Dozer using the computer.
☞ From the shortcut menu, click Copy.
☞ Go to your Word document (WP2-Dozer's Job).
☞ Click where you want to paste the image (in this case, click between your name and the first paragraph).
☞ Click Edit, Paste (if the ActiveX warning box appears, click Yes). The image appears.
☞ Center the image between the left and right margins (to do so, click the image and click the Center alignment button).
☞ Will the document print on one page?. If not, resize the image so the document will be only one page long.
☞ Save your document. Print the document. Close Word.

## EXERCISE 12: USE THE THESAURUS
A thesaurus, as you know, is a dictionary of synonyms (words with similar meanings) and antonyms (words with opposite meanings). In this exercise, you will use the Microsoft Word thesaurus to find some synonyms. First, start Word and type the terms found in the table below. Then, find a synonym for each term. Complete the table by writing the synonym below.

| TERM | SYNONYM |
|---|---|
| Frugal | |
| Laconic | |
| Mammoth | |
| Obtuse | |
| Impertinent | |

## EXERCISE 13: CORRECT THE SPELLING
As you know, the Check-Spelling-As-You-Type feature identifies what it believes to be spelling errors (by underlining each word with a wavy red line) and provides suggestions for correcting the error. In this exercise, you will find the correct spelling for some misspelled words. Type the terms found in the table below. Then, find the correct spelling for each term. Complete the table by writing the correctly spelled word.

| MISSPELLED TERM | CORRECT SPELLING |
|---|---|
| Funkshunal | |
| Albatrose | |
| Abstreperous | |
| Teknowlogical | |
| Obselescance | |

## EXERCISE 14: CORRECT THE GRAMMAR
As you know, the Grammar-As-You-Type feature identifies what it believes to be grammar errors (by underlining each phrase with a wavy green line) and provides suggestions for correcting the errors. In this exercise, you will correct some grammatically-incorrect statements. Type the sentences below. Then, correct the grammar and write the grammatically-correct sentences in the space provided.

| GRAMMATICALLY INCORRECT | GRAMMATICALLY CORRECT |
|---|---|
| We am here today. | |
| He gone there for the party. | |
| We is home. | |
| Who's car is it? | |
| Its my car. | |
| Dozer's toy missing. | |

☞ Close the document.
☞ Close Word.

When you start Word, the appearance of the document is defined by the default settings. A default is something that happens in the absence of any action. That is, if you don't change anything, the default settings will be applied. In Word, the default settings include line spacing, font size, font type, margins, etc. Therefore, when you begin to type a document, these settings, by default, will prevail. However, to customize your document, you can change these settings. This project will demonstrate a variety of ways to format a document. First, start Word, click View, Normal, and type the paragraphs below. Remember, don't press the Enter key at the end of each line in each paragraph. Let each line wrap automatically.

> Proverbs to Ponder
>
> A fish wouldn't get into trouble if it kept its mouth shut. Bad news rides a fast horse. A wise head keeps a shut mouth. Don't let your tongue cut your throat. Don't say everything you want to say lest you hear something you would not like to hear. Don't tell a secret even to a fence.
>
> A good beginning is half the work. It is no time to go for the doctor when the patient is dead. The blacksmith's horse and the cobbler's wife are the last to have shoes. A postponement till morning is a postponement forever. You'll never plow a field by turning it over in your mind.
>
> It is no secret that is known to three. It's often a man's mouth broke his nose. Least said soonest mended. Leave the bad tale where you found it. Little talk is easy to cure. The person of the greatest talk is the person of the least work. There are two sides to every story.

☞ Save the document to your disk (name it WP3-Proverbs).
☞ Copy and paste the three paragraphs six times to the end of the document (hint: you'll have one "Proverbs to Ponder" title and 21 paragraphs). Later, you will need a long document.
☞ Type your name on the line below the 21st paragraph.
☞ Save the document (click the Save toolbar button).

### APPLY TEXT ENHANCEMENTS
Enhancements include bold, italics, and underline. These are applied to text to emphasize key points. You can apply one, any two, or all three of these enhancements to text.

To practice applying enhancements, do the following:
☞ Select the text to be enhanced (select the title).
☞ Click the Bold toolbar button (button with a "B").
☞ Click anywhere outside of the selected text to deselect it.
☞ Select the word "mouth" in the first sentence.
☞ Click the Italic toolbar button (button with an "I").
☞ Click anywhere outside of the selected text to deselect it.
☞ Select the word "trouble" in the first sentence.
☞ Click the Underline toolbar button (button with a "U").
☞ Click anywhere outside of the selected text to deselect it.
☞ Select the word "fish" in the first sentence.
☞ Click the B and the U toolbar buttons.
☞ Click anywhere outside of the selected text to deselect it.

To practice removing enhancements, do the following:
☞ Select the text with unwanted enhancement (select "fish"). Notice that the B and the U toolbar buttons are highlighted.
☞ Click the "U" toolbar button to turn it off.
☞ Click anywhere outside of the selected text to deselect it.
☞ Save the document (click the Save toolbar button).

### CHANGE FONTS
The font type (shape of the characters) and the font size (dimension of the characters) can be changed for the entire document or for parts of it, such as titles and headings.

To practice changing the font, do the following:
☞ Select the text (select the title "Proverbs to Ponder").
☞ Click Format, Font. The Font dialog box appears. Choose the desired font and font size (choose the Arial font and size 14). Notice that a variety of other font-related choices are also available in this dialog box. Click OK. Note: you could also change the font via the Font list boxes on the Formatting toolbar.
☞ Click outside the selected text to deselect it.
☞ Save the document (click the Save toolbar button).

### ALIGN TEXT
Text can be aligned so that the straight edge is on the left margin (align left), or on the right margin (align right), or with the straight edges on the left and the right margins (justify), or centered between the margins (center). The toolbar has one button for each alignment style and each of these buttons has an image which shows how the alignment will look.

To practice changing the alignment of text, do the following:
☞ Select the text (select the title "Proverbs to Ponder").
☞ Click the desired alignment toolbar button (click Center).
☞ Click outside the selected text to deselect it.
☞ Select the 21 paragraphs by dragging over them.
☞ Click the desired alignment toolbar button (click Justify).
☞ Click outside the selected text to deselect it.
☞ Save the document (click the Save toolbar button).

### CHANGE LINE SPACING
In Word, the default line spacing is single. However, most manuscripts, including college papers, need to be double spaced, which places a blank line between each line of text.

To practice changing line spacing, do the following:
☞ Select the text (in this case, select the entire document by clicking Edit, Select All or by dragging over the text).
☞ Click Format, Paragraph. The Paragraph dialog box opens. In the Line Spacing list box, select Double. Note: you could also do this by using the Line Spacing toolbar button.
☞ Click OK. Click outside the selected text to deselect it.
☞ Save the document (click the Save toolbar button).

### SET THE MARGINS
The space on the paper between the edges and where the document resides is referred to as the margins. By default, Word sets the top and bottom margins (at 1") and the left and right margins (at 1.25"). Of course, you can change these.

To practice changing the margins, do the following:
☞ Click File, Page Setup. Click the Margins tab.
☞ Specify the margins (in this case, change the top, bottom, left and right margins to .75"). Click OK.
☞ To see the margins, click File, Print Preview (or click the Print Preview toolbar button which looks like a piece of paper with a magnifying glass on it).
☞ Click Close on the Print Preview feature bar.

## INSERT PAGE NUMBERS

Long documents need page numbers so that readers can be directed to specific portions of the manuscript.

To practice inserting page numbers, do the following:
☞ Click on the page where you want the page numbering to begin (in this case, click on the first page).
☞ Click Insert, Page Numbers.
☞ From the Position and Alignment lists, select where you want the numbers to appear (in this case, have them appear at the bottom center of each page). Note that if you wanted to have the numbers start at some value other than 1, you would click the Format button in this dialog box and you would specify the preferred starting page. You would also do this if you wanted to specify the type of page numbers. For example, sometimes you will want the page number to appear as roman numerals (I, ii, iii, etc.).
☞ Click OK. The view may automatically change from Normal to Print Layout. Don't be concerned. In Normal view, page numbers can't be seen, so Word switched views for you.
☞ Scroll down to see the page numbers on each page.
☞ Save the document (click the Save toolbar button).

## FORMAT WITH COLUMNS

By default, a Word document appears in a single column that spans from the left to right margins. Sometimes, a document will look better, and will more efficiently utilize paper space, if it is formatted in more than one column (like this document).

To practice formatting with columns, do the following:
☞ Put the insertion point where the change in columns will begin (in this case, put it on the line below the title).
☞ Click Format, Columns. A dialog box appears.
☞ Specify the number of columns (in this case, set it at 2).
☞ In the Width and Spacing area, notice that the width of the columns along with the width of the spacing between the columns is shown. If you ever want to change the width of these elements, you can do so here. For now, just leave these settings as they are.
☞ In the Apply To list box (at the bottom of the dialog box), select This Point Forward to tell Word that the new columns should start at the location of the insertion point.
☞ Click OK. The 21 paragraphs appear in two columns.
☞ Save the document (click the Save toolbar button).

## INSERT HEADERS & FOOTERS

You can have information appear at the top of each page (header) and/or at the bottom of each page (footer, like at the bottom of this page). For instance, you might want your name or the date to appear on each page. Regardless of the type of information, a header and/or footer can make a document look more professional and can provide needed information.

To practice inserting a header or a footer, do the following:
☞ Click View, Header and Footer. The Header box and the Header and Footer toolbar appear).
☞ In the Header box, type the desired text (type your full name).
☞ Click the Switch Between Header And Footer button on the Header and Footer toolbar (the button looks like a sheet of paper with a yellow rectangle above and below it). The Footer box appears.
☞ In the Header and Footer toolbar, click the Insert Date button (has a picture of a calendar on it). Notice that the current date appears in the footer.

☞ Click the Close button on the Header and Footer toolbar.
☞ Scroll to see what the header and footer look like.
☞ Save the document (click the Save toolbar button).

## USE THE FORMAT PAINTER

If you have a format that needs to be applied to other places in your document (e.g., chapter titles, headings, etc.), you can select each instance of the text and individually apply the formats. This would be time consuming. The Format Painter will copy a set of formats with greater speed and accuracy.

To practice using the Format Painter, do the following:
☞ Select the text that has the desired formats (select the title "Proverbs to Ponder"). Notice that this title has several formats (i.e., it is centered, 14-point Arial, and bold).
☞ Double-click the Format Painter toolbar button (looks like a paint brush).
☞ Select the text to have formats applied (select your name at the end of the document).
☞ Click the Format Painter toolbar button to turn it off.
☞ Click outside the text to deselect it. Notice your name now has the same appearance as the title.

## INSERT & DELETE PAGE BREAKS

We previously learned that when we approach the end of a line, Word automatically places a soft return at the end of the line and moves the insertion point to the next line upon which the additional text will appear. That is, when there is more text than can fit on the line, an additional line is created. Similarly, when we approach the end of a page, Word automatically places a soft page break at the end of the page and moves the insertion point to the next page upon which the additional text will appear. Word will display a horizontal line on the screen indicating where the pages separate. This line is called a soft page break. It is similar to the soft return which Word inserts automatically at the end of each line as you type. Sometimes, you will want to control where a page breaks. For instance, if you were writing a novel, you would probably want each chapter to appear on a new page. Likewise, if you were writing a college paper, you would want the bibliography to start on a new page. You will recall that if you want to force Word to insert text on a new line, you press the Enter key. This places a hard return at the end of the line and moves the insertion point to the next line. Similarly, when you want to force Word to insert text on a new page, you press Ctrl + Enter (to do so, hold down the Ctrl key and then press the Enter key for a moment, then release both keys). When you print the document, these page breaks (both soft and hard page breaks) will indicate to the printer when to load another sheet of paper.

To practice using page breaks, do the following:
☞ Put the insertion point where you want the page break (in this case, click at the end of the third paragraph).
☞ Press Ctrl + Enter. Notice that the page break is inserted. Note: if you wanted to delete a hard page break, you would put the insertion point below the page break and press the Backspace key or above the page break and press the Delete key.
☞ Since you have decided that you don't want a page break here, go ahead and remove the page break.
☞ Change the font of the 21 paragraphs (not the title or your name) to Arial 8.
☞ Save the document (click the Save toolbar button).
☞ Print the document. Close the document. Close Word.

## EXERCISE 1: CROSSWORD

Use the clues below to complete the crossword puzzle.

### ACROSS

1. To change the amount of space between the edge of the paper and the text, I would click File, ___ Setup.
6. The dimension of the characters is the font _____.
7. If you want to change the space between lines, one way to do this would be to click Format, ___ to open a dialog box that will permit you to change the line spacing.
8. When you begin to type a document, the ___ settings (e.g., line spacing, margins, font, etc.) automatically determine the appearance of the document.
10. At the bottom of this page, "Dozer's Quintessential Guide To Microsoft Word" appears. This text is a ___.
11. Do footers appear at the top of a page?
14. The spaces between the edge of the paper and the text.
15. Learning how to use a computer is lots of ___.
16. To change the amount of space between lines, you would click Format, Paragraph, Line ___.

### DOWN

2. The way text lines up vertically in relation to the left or right edge of a document.
3. To ___ text is to make the right edge of the characters line up vertically straight.
4. Before you can copy or move text, you must first ___ it.
5. Information that appears at the top of each page.
9. You can format documents in multiple ___ so there will be more than one vertical arrangement of text on the page.
12. If the left edge of characters line up vertically straight, the text is said to be ___ aligned.
13. If you press Ctrl + Enter, you will insert a page ___.

## EXERCISE 2: TRUE-FALSE

For each of the following seven statements, place a T or an F on the line to indicate if the statement is True or False.

1. ___The "U" on the toolbar button stands for "Undo".
2. ___The "B" on the toolbar button stands for "Bullets".
3. ___WordPad and Word are the same program.
4. ___Font type refers to the shape of the characters.
5. ___To insert a footer, click Insert from the menu bar.
6. ___To insert page numbers, I click Insert, Page Numbers.
7. ___A footer appears at the bottom of each page.

## EXERCISE 3: TRUE-FALSE

For each of the following seven statements, place a T or an F on the line to indicate if the statement is True or False.

1. ___If I press Ctrl + Enter, I go to the top of the document.
2. ___12-point type is smaller than 10-point type.
3. ___The "I" on the toolbar button stands for "Italic".
4. ___Font size refers to the dimensions of the characters.
5. ___I can insert page numbers at the top or bottom of pages.
6. ___The Format Painter button has a paint brush on it.
7. ___To set margins, click File, Page Setup.

## EXERCISE 4: IDENTIFY TERMS

Below are eight definitions. Below the definitions are eight lines. In each line, write the word that matches the definition.

1. Information appearing at the top of each page.
2. Information appearing at the bottom of each page.
3. The empty space around the edges of a printed page.
4. The settings that you get if you don't change them.
5. The dimensions of the characters.
6. The shape of the characters.
7. The toolbar button with the picture of the paint brush on it.
8. The way the text lines up in relation to the margins.

1. _____   5. _____
2. _____   6. _____
3. _____   7. _____
4. _____   8. _____

## EXERCISE 5: TRUE-FALSE

For each of the following seven statements, place a T or an F on the line to indicate if the statement is True or False.

1. ___A footer is data appearing at the bottom of each page.
2. ___The "B" on the toolbar button stands for "Back".
3. ___The way text lines up with the margin is called alignment.
4. ___A default is what happens in the absence of any action.
5. ___The Format Painter button has a paint can on it.
6. ___10-point type is smaller than 12-point type.
7. ___The "U" on the toolbar button stands for "Underline".

## EXERCISE 6: TRUE-FALSE

For each of the following six statements, place a T or an F on the line to indicate if the statement is True or False.

1. ___Justified text is straight at the left and the right margins.
2. ___The "B" on the toolbar button stands for "Bold".
3. ___To set margins, click Format, Margins.
4. ___The "I" on the toolbar button stands for "Indent".
5. ___A header is data that appears at the top of each page.
6. ___If I press Ctrl + Enter, I insert a page break.

## EXERCISE 7: CREATE A RESUME

Open Word, set all margins to 1", and recreate this resume.

---

# George L. Costanza
### 1344 Queens Blvd., Flushing, NY 11351
### Phone: 555-8695

#### EDUCATION
**1973-1977**: JFK High School, New York, NY 10121.
#### EMPLOYMENT
**1992-1993**: NBC, 30 Rockefeller Plaza, New York, NY
Achievements: Co-Creator and Co-Writer of sitcom about "nothing".

**1994-1995**: New York Yankees, 245 Roosevelt Ave., Bronx, NY
Achievements: Took naps under my desk, initiated the use of 100%
cotton uniforms for team players, taught upper management how to
eat candy bars with a fork and knife, and introduced Mr. Steinbrenner
to calzones.

**1996**: Play Now Toy Company, 362 W. 42nd St., New York, NY
Achievements: Withstood management's attempts to terminate my
employment contract.  Faked a disability.

**1997**: Costanza & Son, 1344 Queens Blvd, Flushing, NY
Achievements: Sold computers to myself via telemarketing system.

**1998**: Kruger Industrial Smoothing, 112 W. 11th St., New York, NY
Achievements: Went to meetings.  Campaigned to be called "T-Bone".
#### PERSONAL INTERESTS
Architecture---Rock Climbing---Marine Biology

#### COMMUNITY SERVICE
Big Brother--The Human Fund-- The Susan Ross Foundation

---

☞ Type your name at the bottom of the resume.
☞ Save the resume (call it WP3-Costanza's Resume).
☞ Print one copy of the resume.  Close Word.

## EXERCISE 8: COLUMNS, HEADERS, & PAGE NUMBERS

For this exercise, you will need a long document.  Instead of having you type a multiple-page document, do the following:

☞ Start Internet Explorer and go to **www.dozer.pannell.com** (or www.pannell.biz).
☞ Click the "My Guide To Computer Careers" link.
☞ Copy the entire document except the Dozer Pannell title that appears at the top of that page.
☞ Start Word and paste the document.
☞ Click the Paste Options button (found below the pasted text).
☞ From the Paste Options menu, click Keep Text Only.
☞ Save the document to your disk (call it WP3-Careers).
☞ Change the top, bottom, left, and right margins to be .8"
☞ Change the font of all of the text to Arial 8.
☞ Change the alignment of all of the text to justify.
☞ Center the "Dozer's Guide To Computer Careers" title.
☞ Change the title to be Arial 12 and make it bold and italicized.
☞ Starting below the first paragraph, format the remaining text to appear in two columns with .4" space between columns.
☞ Go to **www.google.com**.  Find three images of people using computers.  Copy and paste each image in the document.
☞ Insert a header that reads Computer Careers and a footer that contains your name.
☞ Insert page numbers (at bottom right) beginning on page one.
☞ Underline and bold the "Getting The Job" heading.
☞ Use the Format Painter to make all other headings appear in bold print and underlined.
☞ Move and/or resize your images so your document is two full pages long (i.e., if it's 1-1/2 pages long, make your images bigger; if more than 2 pages long, make your images smaller).
☞ Save your document.  Print the document.  Close Word.

## EXERCISE 9: FORMAT THE "LIFE" DOCUMENT

In this exercise, you will be using a document you created in Exercises 7-8 on page D-6.  If you don't still have that file, go back to page D-6 and do Exercises 7-8.  Then, you will be ready to do this exercise.

☞ Open the "WP1-Life" file and save it as "WP3-Life".
☞ Notice that your name is at the top of the document and George Bernard Shaw's name (the author of the text) is at the bottom of the document.  Move his name to the top and move your name to the bottom.  If the Clipboard Task Pane opens, click its Close button to make it go away.
☞ Center Shaw's name.
☞ Change the font of Shaw's name to Arial 16.
☞ Make Shaw's name appear in bold print and underlined.
☞ Right align your name.
☞ Change the font of your name to Arial 10.
☞ Make your name appear italicized.
☞ Change the font of the three paragraphs to Arial 16.
☞ Change the line spacing of the paragraphs to be 1.5.
☞ Save your modified document.
☞ Print one copy of the document.
☞ Close Word.
☞ If asked if you want to save the document, click the Yes button.

## EXERCISE 10: CREATE DOZER'S RESUME

Dozer wants to earn some extra money.  He thinks he can get a job as a guard dog.  Information about Dozer's education and experience are below.  Please arrange the data in the form of a professional resume.  Use any formats you think appropriate.

Dozer's address is 1234 Dog Bone Road, Dogtown, NV 89122.  His phone number is 555-3214.  He was educated at Ashleigh's Academy, Las Vegas, NV where, in 1997, he graduated at the top of his class (in your resume, don't mention that he was the only student).  His hobbies (personal Interests) include barking at butterflies, taking naps, and chasing his sister Skooter.

Previously, Dozer never wanted to work for anyone else.  Instead he has always been self-employed.  Whenever he wanted to earn some money, he simply created his own business, which he operated from his home.  Therefore, he has the following employment history:

• From 1996-1997 he operated the Dozer Fish Watching Service, where he was responsible for guarding 17 goldfish.  While under his care, not one fish went missing.
• From 1997-1998 he operated the Dozer Lawn Maintenance Company, where he faithfully fertilized and watered a wide assortment of backyard shrubs and plants.
• From 1998-1999 he performed services as Dozer Document Shredding, Inc., where he shredded sensitive and not-so-sensitive documents his owner had placed in the home office trash can.
• From 1999-2001 Dozer did business as Dozer Disposal Services, where he disposed of excess table food at the conclusion of every meal and removed cookie crumbs from his owner's whiskers.

Save Dozer's resume (name it WP3-Dozer's Resume).

## EXERCISE 11: CREATE YOUR OWN RESUME

Create a resume for yourself.  Copy the format found in Costanza's resume (from Exercise 7) or use any style you wish.
☞ Save your resume (name it WP3-My Resume).
☞ Print one copy of your resume.
☞ Close Word.

## CREATE A TABLE
Some data is best organized by placing it in a table (a matrix of columns and rows). The intersection of each row and column forms a cell, a location where data is placed. A horizontal collection of cells is a row; a vertical collection is a column.

To practice creating a table, do the following:
- ☞ Start Word. Click Table, Insert, Table.
- ☞ Specify how many rows and columns (in this case, specify 3 columns and 11 rows). Click OK (the table is created).

## ENTER DATA INTO A TABLE
Since entered data appears at the insertion point, the first step is to place the insertion point in the desired cell. To do so, click in the cell or use the arrow keys to move the insertion point. When data is entered in adjacent cells, the insertion point can be moved rapidly to the next logical cell by pressing the Tab key. Or, if you prefer, you could click in the another cell or use the arrow keys to move the insertion point to another cell.

To practice entering data in a table, do the following:
- ☞ Click in the cell located at the intersection of the first row and the first column (the cell at the top, left corner of the table).
- ☞ Type FIRST NAME.
- ☞ Press Tab. The insertion point moves to the next cell.
- ☞ Type LAST NAME.
- ☞ Press Tab. The insertion point moves to the next cell.
- ☞ Type CITY.
- ☞ Press Tab. The insertion point moves to the first column of the second row. Note: there is a tendency to want to press the Enter key after entering data in the last column. If you do, you will heighten the row, not return to the next row. So, press the Tab key instead of the Enter key.
- ☞ Type HANK and continue to enter the data shown below:

| FIRST NAME | LAST NAME | CITY |
|---|---|---|
| HANK | HILL | ARLEN |
| AL | BUNDY | CHICAGO |
| BART | SIMPSON | SPRINGFIELD |
| COSMO | KRAMER | NEW YORK |
| MIMI | BOBECK | CLEVELAND |
| WALTER | O'REILLY | OTTUMWA |
| OPIE | TAYLOR | MAYBERRY |
| DOUG | FUNNY | BLUFFINGTON |
| NILES | CRANE | SEATTLE |
| BARNEY | RUBBLE | BEDROCK |

- ☞ Save the document to your disk (call it WP4-My Friends).

## SELECT PARTS OF A TABLE
Sometimes, you will need to select a table or parts of a table. To practice selecting elements of a table, do the following:
- ☞ Put the insertion point in any cell. Click Table, Select, Cell. Notice that the cell is selected.
- ☞ Click elsewhere to deselect the cell.
- ☞ Put the insertion point in any cell and click Table, Select, Row. Notice that the entire row is selected.
- ☞ Click elsewhere to deselect the row.
- ☞ Put the insertion point in any cell and click Table, Select, Column. The column is selected.
- ☞ Click elsewhere to deselect the column.
- ☞ Put the insertion point in any cell and click Table, Select, Table. The entire table is selected.
- ☞ Click elsewhere to deselect the table.

## ADD ROWS OR COLUMNS
If you determine that your table requires additional rows or columns, you can easily add them. Since columns are added the same way as rows, you will only practice adding rows.

To practice adding rows, do the following:
- ☞ Click anywhere in the row where you want to insert a new row (In this case, click in the row with Opie's name).
- ☞ Click Table, Insert, Rows Below. A new row is inserted.
- ☞ Click elsewhere to deselect the row.
- ☞ In that new row, enter your name and city.
- ☞ Add a row at the top of the table by clicking in the top row and then clicking Table, Insert, Rows Above.
- ☞ Click elsewhere to deselect the row.
- ☞ Save the document (click the Save toolbar button).

## ADJUST COLUMN WIDTHS
When you create a table, it spans from the left to the right margin, allocating equal horizontal space to each column. You may need columns to vary in width. For instance, a zip code column can be narrower than a phone number column. You can adjust the widths manually or automatically.

To practice manually adjusting column widths, do the following:
- ☞ Put the mouse pointer on the wall of the column to be adjusted until the pointer becomes a two-pointed arrow (in this case, put it on the right wall of the first column).
- ☞ Drag the border to the desired size (in this case, drag to the left about ½" and release the mouse button).
- ☞ Repeat the above steps to reduce the width of the other two columns by about ½" each.

To practice automatically adjusting column widths so that the column widths adjust to accommodate the widest entry in each column, do the following:
- ☞ Put the mouse pointer on the wall of the column to be adjusted until the pointer becomes a two-pointed arrow.
- ☞ Double click. The column width changes.
- ☞ Repeat the above steps to adjust the other two columns.
- ☞ Save the document (click the Save toolbar button).

## MERGE CELLS
Sometimes, you will want to merge several cells into a single cell. For instance, you may want a title to appear in the first row. You don't want the title in one of the little cells in the first row. Instead, you want the title to be centered across the width of all the columns in the first row. To accomplish this, you will merge the existing cells into one. By the way, you can also split a single cell so that it becomes multiple cells. While you will not practice this technique now, to do so you would simply click in the cell to be split, then click Table, Split Cells, specify the number of columns or rows, and click OK.

To practice merging cells, do the following:
☞ Select the cells to merge (select the cells in the top row).
☞ Click Table, Merge Cells.
☞ Click elsewhere to deselect the row.
☞ In the top row, type ME & MY FRIENDS.

## APPLY TEXT ENHANCEMENTS IN A TABLE
Enhancements include bold, italics, and underline. These are often applied to text to emphasize key points in a document.

To practice applying enhancements, do the following:
☞ Select the text to be enhanced (select the title).
☞ Click the Bold toolbar button (button with a "B").
☞ Select the column headings (in the 2nd row).
☞ Click the Italic toolbar button (button with an "I").
☞ Click elsewhere to deselect the text.
☞ Save the document (click the Save toolbar button).

## CHANGE FONTS IN A TABLE
The font type and the font size can be changed for the entire table or for specific parts of it, such as titles and headings.

To practice changing the font, do the following:
☞ Select the text (in this case, select the title).
☞ Click Format, Font. In the Font dialog box, choose the desired font type and font size (choose Arial 18). Notice that a variety of other font-related choices are also available. Click OK. You may recall that you can also change fonts by using the Font list boxes on the Formatting toolbar.
☞ Select the column headings in the 2nd row and the data in rows 3 to 13 (to do so, drag over the cells).
☞ Click Format, Font.
☞ In the Font dialog box, choose the desired font type and font size (choose Arial 10). Click OK.
☞ Click elsewhere to deselect the text.
☞ Save the document (click the Save toolbar button).

## ALIGN TEXT IN A TABLE
Text can be aligned in the cells so that the straight edge is on the left side of the cell (align left), or on the right side of the cell (align right), or with a straight edge on both sides (justify), or centered within the cell. The toolbar has one button for each alignment style and each of these buttons has an image which shows how the alignment will look.

To practice changing the alignment of text, do the following:
☞ Select the text to be aligned (in this case, select the text found in rows 1 and 2).
☞ Click the desired alignment toolbar button (click Center).
☞ Click elsewhere to deselect the text.
☞ Save the document (click the Save toolbar button).

## FORMAT A TABLE
To enhance the appearance of a table or to emphasize data within a table, you can apply borders and/or shading. By doing so, you can customize the appearance of the table. If you just want to improve its appearance rapidly, you might want to apply a set of automatic formats to the table.

To practice applying a border, do the following:
☞ Select the table.
☞ Click Format, Borders and Shading.
☞ Click the Borders tab. Select a desired border, style, color, and width (select the All setting, Double style, and 3/4 width).

☞ Click OK. Click elsewhere to deselect the table.

To practice applying shading, do the following:
☞ Since we want to apply different shadings to different rows, select the first row.
☞ Click Format, Borders and Shading.
☞ Click the Shading tab.
☞ Select the desired shading (select Gray-30% shading).
☞ Click OK.
☞ Repeat the above steps to apply 20% gray shading to row 2.
☞ Repeat the above steps to apply 10% gray shading to the remaining rows.
☞ Click elsewhere to deselect the rows.

To practice applying preset formats, do the following:
☞ Put the insertion point in any cell.
☞ Click Table, Table AutoFormat.
☞ Select a format (a sample appears).
☞ When you find one you like, click Apply. The AutoFormat feature applies its formats. Note that any prior formats you applied are gone.
☞ If you don't like way your table looks, either apply another AutoFormat style or click the Undo button to return to the way your table looked before you used AutoFormat.
☞ Print one copy of your document.
☞ Save the document (click the Save toolbar button).
☞ Close the document. Close Word

## INSERT BULLETS
As you have seen, one way to organize data is to create a table. Another good way to organize data, is to use bullets to separate and highlight each item on a list (like the bullets used on in this book). A variety of images can be bullets.

To practice inserting bullets, do the following:
☞ Start Word.
☞ Type Dozer's Quintessential Guide to Microsoft Word.
☞ Since you want your list of items to start on the next line, press the Enter key to move the insertion point to the next line. Then, click Format, Bullets and Numbering.
☞ Click the Bulleted tab and select any bullet type you like.
☞ Click OK. Notice that a bullet appears.
☞ Type Project 1: Creating a Document and press Enter. A bullet appears on the next line.
☞ Type Project 2: Editing a Document and press Enter.
☞ Type Project 3: Formatting a Document and press Enter.
☞ Type Project 4: Tables and press Enter.
☞ Type Project 5: Graphics and press Enter.
☞ To stop inserting the bullets, backspace over the last bullet.
☞ To change the type of bullet in a previously-typed list, select the list (select the five items you just entered) and click Format, Bullets and Numbering.
☞ Click the Bulleted tab and select another bullet type. By the way, if you were to click the Customize button and then click the Character button, you would find thousands of other symbols that you could use for bullets.
☞ Click OK. Then, click elsewhere to deselect the list.
☞ If you want to change the amount of indentation of the bullets, select the bullets and click either the Increase Indent toolbar button (looks like a few lines of text with a right pointing arrow) or the Decrease Indent toolbar button (looks like a few lines of text with a left pointing arrow).
☞ Save the document. Name it WP4-Dozer's Guide To Word.
☞ Print the document. Close Word.

## EXERCISE 1: CROSSWORD
Use the clues below to complete the crossword puzzle.

### ACROSS
2. To move to the next cell in a table, press the ___ key.
5. Are ♫, ☺, ✂, and ✎ examples of tokens?
7. A good way to organize data is to use symbols as ___ to separate each item on a list.
9. A web page address is sometimes referred to as its ___.
10. The intersection of a row and a column in a table.
11. Dozer is Steve Pannell's ___.
14. To have a set of predefined formats applied to a table, click Table, Table ___.
15. This crossword puzzle is a table. Some of its cells are grey. Each of the grey cells have had ___ applied.
17. A horizontal collection of cells in a table.
18. To make two or more cells become a single cell, select the cells and then click Table, ___ Cells.
19. Ten merged cells become how many cell(s)?

### DOWN
1. A vertical collection of cells in a table.
2. A matrix of columns and rows used to organize data.
3. To have text appear ___, click the "B" toolbar button.
4. The dude who wrote Dozer's Quintessential Guide.
6. The ___ button has an "X" on it.
8. If you want to move, copy, edit, or enhance data in a table, you will first need to ___ the data.
12. Is a horizontal collection of cells called a column?
13. To select from a variety of lines to frame a table or the cells in a table, click Format, Borders And Shading, ___.
14. To manually adjust column widths, put the mouse pointer on the wall of the column to be adjusted until the pointer becomes a two-pointed ___. Then drag the wall.
16. To move the insertion point to the beginning of the line, press the ___ key.

## EXERCISE 2: TRUE-FALSE
For each of the following six statements, place a T or an F on the line to indicate if the statement is True or False.

1. ___After a table has been created, I can add a new row.
2. ___The "U" on the toolbar button stands for "Undo".
3. ___In a table, a vertical collection of cells is a column.
4. ___I can delete a column in a table.
5. ___To create a table, click Create, Table.
6. ___After a table has been created, I can add a new column.

## EXERCISE 3: IDENTIFY TERMS
Below are eight definitions. Below the definitions are eight lines. In each line, write the word that matches the definition.

1. The way text lines up within the cell.
2. To change multiple cells into a single cell.
3. The intersection of a row and a column.
4. In a table, a vertical collection of cells.
5. To change one cell into multiple cells.
6. Symbols (or numbers) next to items in a list.
7. A matrix of horizontal rows and vertical columns.
8. In a table, a horizontal collection of cells.

1. _____    5. _____
2. _____    6. _____
3. _____    7. _____
4. _____    8. _____

## EXERCISE 4: TRUE-FALSE
For each of the following seven statements, place a T or an F on the line to indicate if the statement is True or False.

1. ___I can split a single cell so that it becomes multiple cells.
2. ___Once a table has been created, I can't add a new column.
3. ___I can put a border around a single cell.
4. ___To move to the next cell in a table, press the Tab key.
5. ___To create a table, click Insert, Table.
6. ___The "B" on the toolbar button stands for "Bookmark".
7. ___A vertical collection of cells is a row.

## EXERCISE 5: TRUE-FALSE
For each of the following seven statements, place a T or an F on the line to indicate if the statement is True or False.

1. ___To move to the next cell in a table, press the Enter key.
2. ___Font type refers to the shape of the characters.
3. ___The "I" on the toolbar button stands for "Index".
4. ___A bullet is a symbol placed after each item on a list.
5. ___I can put shading in a single cell.
6. ___A table is a matrix of columns and rows.
7. ___Once a table has been created, I can't add a new row.

## EXERCISE 6: TRUE-FALSE
For each of the following seven statements, place a T or an F on the line to indicate if the statement is True or False.

1. ___I can merge multiple cells into one cell.
2. ___To create a table, click Table, Create.
3. ___I can delete a row in a table.
4. ___You can adjust the width of columns in a table.
5. ___I can put a border around my table.
6. ___In a table, the data resides in the cells.
7. ___The "B" on the toolbar button stands for "Bold".

## EXERCISE 7: CREATE A TABLE

In some ways, Dozer's really smart (like being able to use a computer), but in other ways, he's not too bright. For instance, Dozer watches lots of TV and he doesn't understand the difference between TV folks and REAL folks. He has created a list of his friends and some gifts he wants to get them. Please help Dozer organize his list into a table.

☞ Recreate the table below.

| GIFTS FOR MY FRIENDS | |
|---|---|
| FRIEND | GIFT |
| Popeye The Sailor | Can of Spinach |
| Sylvester | A Yellow Canary |
| Bugs Bunny | Bunch of Carrots |
| Soupy Sales | Cream Pies |
| Skooter Pannell | Rawhide Bone |

☞ Save the table to a diskette (name it WP4-Gift List).
☞ Close the document. Close Word.

## EXERCISE 8: FORMAT A TABLE

In Exercise 7, you created a table for Dozer and saved it to your diskette under the name "WP4-Gift List." Open that file. If you don't have it, redo that exercise and then return to this exercise. Follow the steps below to format your table.

☞ Merge the cells in row 1.
☞ Change the font of the text in row 1 so that it is 18-point Arial.
☞ Enhance the text in row 1 so that it is bold and italicized.
☞ Align the text in row 1 so it is centered within the row.
☞ Change the font of the text in row 2 so that it is 12-point Arial.
☞ Enhance the text in row 2 so that it is bold.
☞ Center the text in row 2 so it is centered within each cell.
☞ Change the font of the text in rows 3-7 to be 10-point Arial.
☞ Resize the columns and table to the size as shown below.
☞ Apply 25% gray shading to row 1 and 10% to row 2.
☞ Apply a 1½-point double-line border around the table and around each cell as shown.
☞ After doing the above steps, your table should look like this:

| GIFTS FOR MY FRIENDS | |
|---|---|
| **FRIEND** | **GIFT** |
| Popeye The Sailor | Can of Spinach |
| Sylvester | A Yellow Canary |
| Bugs Bunny | Bunch of Carrots |
| Soupy Sales | Cream Pies |
| Skooter Pannell | Rawhide Bone |

☞ Insert a new row between Bugs Bunny and Soupy Sales.
☞ In the new row, insert your name and a gift you want.
☞ Save the modified table.
☞ Print one copy.
☞ Get the printout from the printer.
☞ Close the document. Close Word.

## EXERCISE 9: CREATE A BULLETED LIST

In Exercise 7, you created a table containing the names of Dozer's friends along with a gift for each friend. Now Dozer wants you to create a shopping list of the gifts he wants to buy for his friends. The following steps provide the details.

☞ Start Word and recreate the list below (use any type of bullet you like).

Things I want to buy for my friends:
- Spinach
- Canary
- Carrots
- Cream Pies
- Rawhide Bone

☞ Save the document to your disk (call it WP4-Gifts To Buy).
☞ Modify the text to be 12-point Arial and bold.
☞ Type your name below the list.
☞ In Exercise 8, you added your name and gift to the table. Did you remember to add your gift to Dozer's shopping list. If not, add your gift so that it appears between "Carrots" and "Cream Pies."
☞ Save your modified document.
☞ Print one copy of your list. Get it from the printer.
☞ Close the document.
☞ Close Word.

## EXERCISE 10: CREATE AND FORMAT A TABLE

Dozer has compiled a list of family vacation destinations he wants to visit next summer (and places he wants to avoid). He has organized the information into a table. Please recreate the table below and format it as shown.

| VACATION DESTINATIONS | |
|---|---|
| VISIT | AVOID |
| Pleasure Beach, CN | Weed, CA |
| Niceville, FL | Kill Devil Hills, NC |
| Mt. Healthy, OH | Devil's Lake, ND |
| Happy Valley, OR | Scalp Level, PA |
| Opportunity, WA | Peculiar, MO |
| Hometown, WV | Savage, MT |
| Kinder, LA | Weedville, PA |
| Friendly, MD | Hurt, VA |
| Welcome, MN | Hurricane, WV |
| Doolittle, MO | Crook, NY |

☞ Below the table, type your name.
☞ Save the table (name it WP4-Dozer's Vacation Places).
☞ Print one copy.
☞ Get the printout from the printer.
☞ Close the document.
☞ Close Word.

The appearance of a document can be enhanced by utilizing symbols, clipart, pictures, and borders along with the text.

## INSERT A SYMBOL

Word comes with an extensive array of symbols (non-keyboard characters) that can be treated like keyboard characters (i.e., they can be moved, copied, resized, and deleted).

To practice inserting a symbol, do the following:
☞ Start Word, set the font to Arial 16, and recreate this table:

| ITEM | SYMBOL | ITEM | SYMBOL |
|------|--------|------|--------|
| Airplane | | Book | |
| Scissors | | Clock | |
| Candle | | Sad Face | |
| Globe | | Diskette | |
| Telephone | | Cat | |
| Postal Letter | | Bell | |
| Computer | | Eye Glasses | |
| Happy Face | | Spider | |

☞ Save the document to your disk (name it WP5-Symbols).
☞ Put the insertion point where you want the symbol inserted (put it in the cell next to the word airplane).
☞ Click Insert, Symbol.
☞ Click the Font list arrow (a list of fonts appears).
☞ Click a font. The dialog box displays the symbols. Look for a symbol of an airplane. If the selected font does not have that picture, click other fonts until you find an airplane. Note: all of the symbols you will need can most likely be found in either the webdings or wingdings font lists.
☞ When you find an airplane, click it. Then click Insert, Close. The airplane appears in the cell.
☞ Repeat the above steps for each of the items in your table so that you have a symbol for each item. It is possible that your computer will not have a symbol for each item on the list. If you can't find a specific symbol, don't worry.
☞ Insert a new row at the top of the table.
☞ Merge the cells in the top row and type your name.
☞ Center your name in the top row.
☞ Select the symbol of the book. Click the Font Color toolbar button arrow (it has a large "A" on it) and select a color.
☞ Click to deselect the symbol. It becomes the color chosen.
☞ Make each of the other symbols a different color.
☞ Save the document (click the Save toolbar button).
☞ Close the document, but leave Word open for the next task.

## INSERT IMAGES FROM THE MICROSOFT GALLERY

You can enhance a document with images. Once inserted, they can be moved, copied, resized, edited, or deleted.

To practice inserting clip art, do the following:
☞ First, open a blank document in Word. To do so, click the New toolbar button (this button looks like a blank sheet of white paper and normally is the first button on the toolbar).
☞ Click Insert, Picture, Clip Art. The Clip Art task pane opens.
☞ Enter a word in the Search Text box that describes the clipart you want. In this case, enter the word dog. Then, press the Enter key.
☞ Be patient. It may take awhile for the images to appear. Look at the images. If you don't find an image you like, then do another search, using a different search term (e.g., cat, animal) until you find an image of a critter that you think would be a good friend for Dozer and Skooter. Then, click the image to have it inserted into your document.
☞ Save the document to your disk (name it WP5-Buddies).

To practice selecting a graphics box, do the following:
☞ Click the image (sizing handles appear around the image and the Picture toolbar should appear. If the Picture toolbar does not appear, click View, Toolbars, Picture).
☞ Click outside of the graphics box to deselect it.

To practice resizing an image, do the following:
☞ Click on the image to select it. Sizing handles appear.
☞ Point to any corner sizing handle until the mouse pointer looks like two-pointed arrow.
☞ Drag the handle until the box is the desired size (in this case, the size of your thumb). Release the mouse button.

To practice moving an image, do the following:
☞ With the image selected, put the mouse pointer inside of the box so the pointer looks like a four-pointed arrow. If it does not change shape, click the Text Wrapping button on the Picture toolbar (has a dog on it), then click Behind Text.
☞ Drag and drop the image to its new location.
☞ Click outside of the graphics box to deselect it.

To practice editing an image, do the following:
☞ Click on the image to select it. Sizing handles appear.
☞ Experiment with various Picture toolbar buttons to modify the image. You can't hurt anything, so play around for awhile with these editing features. If you ruin the image, just use the Undo button to reverse any changes.
☞ When done, click outside of the graphics box to deselect it.

To practice deleting an image, do the following:
☞ Click on the image to select it. Sizing handles appear.
☞ Press the Delete key. The image disappears.
☞ Click the Undo toolbar button to have the image reappear.
☞ Click outside of the graphics box to deselect it.
☞ Save the document (click the Save toolbar button).

## INSERT IMAGES FROM YOUR DISKETTE

In addition to inserting images from the Microsoft Gallery, you can insert images from your disk (or, from a CD or the C drive). Once inserted, an object can be moved, copied, resized, edited, and deleted. First, you need to save some images to your disk.

To save images to your diskette, do the following:
☞ Start Internet Explorer (Dozer's favorite web browser).
☞ Go to **www.dozer.pannell.com** (or www.pannell.biz).
☞ Point to the picture of Dozer and right click.
☞ On the shortcut menu, click Save Picture As.
☞ Indicate where to save it (save it on your floppy disk).
☞ Change the filename to Dozer.
☞ Click the Save button. The picture is saved to your disk.
☞ Now, click the My Little Sister link (on Dozer's homepage).

☞ When the page loads, point to the image of Skooter, right click, and save the image to your diskette (name it Skooter).
☞ Close the web browser.

To practice inserting an image from a disk, do the following:
☞ Put the insertion point where you want the image inserted.
☞ Click Insert, Picture, From File.
☞ In the Look in box, select the 3 ½ Floppy (A:) drive.
☞ Select the "Dozer" file. Note: if you cannot see the file, select All Files from the Files of Type list box.
☞ Click the Insert button to insert the picture.
☞ Repeat the above steps to insert the "Skooter" image.
☞ Resize and move the images so they are each the size of your thumb and appear at the top of the page.
☞ Somewhere on the page, type your full name.
☞ Save the document (click the Save toolbar button).
☞ Print the document and close the document.

## USE WORDART

With WordArt, the image is not clipart or a photo—it's text. Once inserted in a document, you can move, copy, resize, edit, and delete the text as if it were an image. For the remainder of this project, you'll be creating a poster announcing the time and place of Dozer's birthday party.

To practice using WordArt, do the following:
☞ Open a new blank document.
☞ Click Insert, Picture, WordArt.
☞ Click a style for the WordArt (pick any style you like).
☞ Click OK.
☞ The Edit WordArt Text dialog box appears. In it, the words "Your Text Here" are highlighted. To have the words "Your Text Here" replaced with your words, type You Are Invited To Attend.
☞ Click OK.
☞ Notice that "You Are Invited To Attend" appears in the WordArt style you previously picked.
☞ Click on one of the characters in the WordArt text. Sizing handles appear around the image and the WordArt toolbar should appear. If the WordArt toolbar does not appear, click View, Toolbars, WordArt to make it appear.
☞ Resize the WordArt (drag a sizing handle).
☞ Point to one of the characters in the WordArt image so the pointer looks like a four-pointed arrow. If the mouse pointer does not look like a four-pointed arrow when you point to the WordArt, then click the Text Wrapping button on the WordArt toolbar (the text wrapping button has an image of a dog on it), then click Behind Text.
☞ Move the WordArt so that it is at the top of the page and centered across the page (drag and drop the WordArt).
☞ Save the document to your disk (name it WP5-Birthday).
☞ Move the insertion point to a place below the WordArt.
☞ Below the "You Are Invited To Attend" line, insert a picture of Dozer at his previous birthday party (you can find this picture at **www.dozer.pannell.com/myphotogallery.html** or at www.pannell.biz/myphotogallery.html.
☞ Move and resize the picture so that it is centered on the page and below the "You Are Invited To Attend" line.
☞ Place the insertion point below the picture and use WordArt to insert the words Dozer's Birthday Party into the poster (again, select any style of WordArt you like).
☞ Move the "Dozer's Birthday Party" WordArt so that it is centered across the page.
☞ Use the Internet to find a picture of some party balloons.

Then copy and paste them into the poster wherever you think looks best.
☞ At the very bottom of the poster, use WordArt to insert the words 2PM Saturday @ Sweetwater Park.
☞ Move and resize the text and images, if necessary to balance out the poster.
☞ Save the document (click the Save toolbar button).

## APPLY A BORDER TO A PAGE

You can apply a border to the poster (or to any other page).

To practice applying a line border to a page, do the following:
☞ Click Format, Borders And Shading.
☞ Click the Page Border tab, if necessary.
☞ Pick the setting, style, color, and width (samples appear).
☞ When you find a sample you like, click OK.
☞ To see the entire poster, click File, Print Preview.
☞ Click the Close button on the Preview feature bar.

To practice applying an art border to a page, do the following:
☞ Click Format, Borders And Shading.
☞ Click the Page Border tab, if necessary.
☞ From the Art list box, select the image for the border (choose any type of border you like). Then Click OK.
☞ To see the entire poster, click File, Print Preview.
☞ Click the Close button on the Preview feature bar.
☞ If you dislike the border, repeat these steps to change it.
☞ Save the document (click the Save toolbar button).

## CHANGE THE PAGE ORIENTATION

By default, Word documents are printed vertically (called portrait orientation--the way an artist would paint a portrait of someone). Your document may be better if printed horizontally (landscape orientation--the way an artist paints a landscape). You can print your documents either way.

To practice changing the page orientation, do the following:
☞ Click File, Page Setup. Click the Margins tab.
☞ In the Orientation area, click Landscape. Click OK.
☞ To see the poster, click File, Print Preview. Since you are now in landscape orientation, some of the poster may be off-center and some may be on page 2. Let's fix all that. But, you can't make changes from the Print Preview screen.
☞ Click the Close button on the Preview feature bar.
☞ Move and resize the text and the image for the landscape orientation (Hint: if you select Whole Page from the Zoom box (on toolbar), you will be able to move and resize the objects while looking at the entire page).
☞ At the bottom of the poster, type your full name (if you changed the Zoom to Whole Page, change it back to 100% so you can see what you are typing).
☞ Save the document (click the Save toolbar button).
☞ Print your document. If you are using an ink-jet printer, the bottom border may not print properly. Don't be concerned.
☞ Close the document. Close Word.

## USE A TEMPLATE

You don't need to construct each document from scratch. Word provides templates of some documents. To view the templates, click File, New. The New Document task pane appears. Click General Templates (or Templates, On My Computer). From this collection you can rapidly create a memo, report, or a resume. Take a moment and look at some of the templates available. Someday, you may need them.

## EXERCISE 1: CROSSWORD

Use the clues below to complete the crossword puzzle.

### ACROSS

1. When you save a document for the first time, the Save As dialog box requests that you type in the name of the file in the ___ box.
4. Word provides ___ (patterns) for many commonly-needed documents, such as memos, reports, and resumes. To use one, click File, New.
6. Is Dozer a cat?
7. If you have an image saved and you want to insert that image into a Word document, you would click Insert, Picture, ___. Then you would find the place where you had saved the image.
9. Word is produced by the fine folks at ___soft.
14. Word___ is an image in the form of text.
15. Documents printed on the paper in ___ orientation will be 11" wide and 8 ½" high.
16. The ___ of a document relates to how the text is printed on the paper (e.g., 8½" or 11" width).
20. Dozer's favorite web browser is Internet ___.
22. The collection of characters mentioned in 25 Across are so extensive that they are organized into groups. Each group is called a ___.
24. To save paper and toner, you can preview a document before your print it. To do so, click File, ___ Preview. By previewing it, you might find that something needs to be fixed before you actually print the document.
25. Are non-keyboard characters such as ♫, ☻, ☞, and ✈ called symbols?
28. The world's smartest cyberdog.
29. The words File, Edit, View, and Help are typically found on a ___ bar.
30. Can symbols be resized, moved, and copied like text?
31. To move text, after selecting it, I click Edit ___.

### DOWN

1. A saved document is called a ___.
2. To take text (or an image) that is in one location and put it elsewhere so that it then appears in only one place.
3. If I do something that didn't turn out so well, I can reverse the action by clicking the ___ toolbar button. Don't you wish all of life's mistakes could be so easily corrected?
4. After I copy and paste text, the text will appear in ___ place(s).
5. Documents printed on the paper in ___ orientation will be 8 ½" wide and 11" high.
6. To open a new blank document, I click the ___ toolbar button, which looks like a blank sheet of paper.
8. Learning how to use a computer is lots of ___.
10. Arial, Times New Roman, Comic Sans, and Impact are all types of ___.
11. Word comes with a collection of images that I can insert into my documents. To access this collection of images, click Insert, Picture ___.
12. The collection of images mentioned in 11 Down reside in the Microsoft Clip ___.
13. To place a border around the entire page, click Format, Borders And Shading. Then, if you click the ___ tab, you will be able to choose a border from a vast collection.
17. A selected image (or text) will disappear if you press the ___ key.
18. To load a document into memory, I click File ___.
19. A graphic image that is not clipart or a photo, but is text.
21. When you are done using a program, you will want to take it out of memory. To do so, you would click the ___ button, which has an "X" on it.
23. To insert an image into a document, I do not "open the file." Instead, I click ___, Picture.
26. If I want to move or copy text (or an image), I must first ___ the text (or image) as the first step.
27. To take text that is in one location and put it elsewhere so that it then appears in both places.

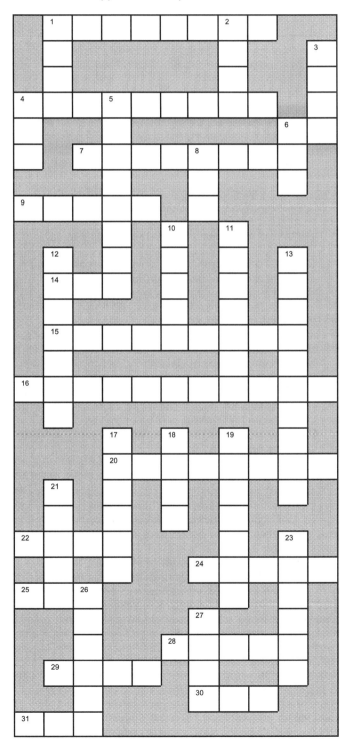

## EXERCISE 2: TRUE-FALSE

For each of the following seven statements, place a T or an F on the line to indicate if the statement is True or False.

1. ___♫, ✈, and ✄ are examples of clipart.
2. ___To select a graphic image, I right click in it.
3. ___Documents printed 11" wide are landscape.
4. ___The New toolbar button has a little puppy on it.
5. ___To deselect an image, click outside of the image.
6. ___To resize an image, I drag a sizing handle.
7. ___The Microsoft Gallery contains WordArt.

## EXERCISE 3: TRUE-FALSE

For each of the following eight statements, place a T or an F on the line to indicate if the statement is True or False.

1. ___To insert an image into Word, click File, Open.
2. ___I can resize WordArt.
3. ___The Microsoft Gallery contains clipart.
4. ___To move an image, I drag a moving handle.
5. ___To view templates, click View, Templates.
6. ___♫, ✈, and ✄ are examples of symbols.
7. ___I can apply a border around the entire page.
8. ___To insert a ♫, ✈, or ✄ I would click Insert, Clipart.

## EXERCISE 4: INSERT AN IMAGE

In this exercise, you will insert an image into a document that you created in Exercise 9 on page D-14.

☞ Start Word and open the "WP3-Life" document.
☞ Save the file as "WP5-Life".
☞ Start Internet Explorer and go to **www.google.com**
☞ Find a picture of George Bernard Shaw.
☞ Right click on the picture and save it to your disk.
☞ Insert the picture anywhere in your "WP1-Life" document.
☞ Resize the picture to be the size of a diskette.
☞ Move the picture so it appears between the title "George Bernard Shaw" and the first paragraph and center it between the left and right margin.
☞ Save your modified document.
☞ Use Print Preview to see what the document will look like when printed. Will it all print on one page? If not, resize the image so that it will all print on one page.
☞ Print one copy of the document and get it from the printer.
☞ Close the document.

## EXERCISE 5: ADD A PAGE BORDER TO A DOCUMENT

In Exercise 4, you inserted an image into the "Life" document and saved it as "WP5-Life. Open that file and add a page border consisting of candles. Preview you document. If you like the way the document looks, save it. Then, print one copy.

## EXERCISE 6: CREATE A BUSINESS ANNOUNCEMENT

On page D-14, Exercise 10, you created a resume for Dozer. At the time, he wanted to get a job as a weekend guard dog at the Yummy Dog Biscuit Company. His plan was to guard the premises and nibble on dog biscuits between naps while getting paid to keep out intruders. In fact, he got the job, but lost it after the first weekend. It seems he paid too much attention to nibbling and napping, and not enough to nabbing intruders. So, he's decided to go into business for himself. Please create a flyer for him to give to his neighbors announcing his desire to guard their homes? Include a picture of him (find one at **www.dozer.pannell.com** (or www.pannell.biz). His phone number and other information is in Exercise 10 (page D-14).

## EXERCISE 7: EDIT IMAGES

This exercise will have you experiment with various methods of editing images. When done, you'll have a one-page document that contains two pictures at the top (Dozer and his sister Skooter) and six images of various types of food.

### PART A: INSERT AN IMAGE FROM YOUR DISKETTE

☞ Start Internet Explorer and go to **www.dozer.pannell.com** (or www.pannell.biz) and click the My Photo Gallery Link.
☞ Save the "Skooter and Me" image (name it Pannell Kids).
☞ Start Word and insert the image anywhere in the document.
☞ Resize the image to be about the size of a diskette.
☞ You now have a picture of Dozer and Skooter. But, you want a picture of Dozer and one of Skooter, not one picture of both. The following steps will show you how to fix that.
☞ Cut off the unwanted parts. To do so, select the image and click the Crop button on the Picture toolbar (if the Picture toolbar does not appear on the screen, click View, Toolbars, Picture). After you have selected the crop tool, the mouse pointer will change shape. Drag the sizing handle on the right border of the picture until Dozer's image is removed. Then, remove the other unneeded parts of the picture until only a headshot of Skooter remains (like the one below).
☞ Resize Skooter's picture to be about the size of a diskette.
☞ Move Skooter's picture to the right side of the document.
☞ Now, insert the Pannell Kids image again. And crop out the image of Skooter and the unneeded other parts of the image until only a headshot of Dozer remains (like the one below).
☞ Resize Dozer's image to be about the size of a diskette.
☞ Move Dozer's image to be at the left side of the page about ½" in from the left margin and Skooter's image to be at the right side of the page about ½" in from the right margin.
☞ Put a double border around each image.
☞ Your images should like these, (except your's are larger):
☞ Save your document to your disk (call it WP5-Treats).

### PART B: INSERT CLIPART

☞ Find and insert six different clipart images of food that you think Dozer and Skooter would like to eat (hint: they are not picky about what they eat--they will eat anything!).
☞ Move the six images so they appear beneath the images of Dozer and Skooter. If desired, resize each of the images.

### PART C: INSERT WORDART

☞ Select any WordArt style you like and put a title on your poster (the title should be, "Dozer & Skooter Treats").
☞ Type your name at the bottom right corner of the poster.

### PART D: APPLY A BORDER TO YOUR PAGE

☞ Apply a Page Border (pick some type of food).
☞ Use Print Preview to see what your poster looks like.
☞ If you are satisfied that the poster will print on one page and that the elements on it are balanced, then print one copy. Otherwise, fix what you don't like before printing.
☞ Save your modified poster.

## WORD COMPREHENSIVE
# E X E R C I S E S

### EXERCISE 1: TRUE-FALSE
For each of the following eight statements, place a T or an F on the line to indicate if the statement is True or False.

1. ___I can insert page numbers at the top or bottom of pages.
2. ___To indent a line, I press the Indent key.
3. ___The Office Assistant normally looks like a paper clip.
4. ___The menu bar has picture buttons on it.
5. ___While I type a document, it resides in memory.
6. ___The title bar is at the top of the window.
7. ___Once I create a document, I can't modify it.
8. ___The Start button is found on the status bar.

### EXERCISE 2: IDENTIFY TERMS
Below are eight definitions. Below the definitions are eight lines. In each line, write the word that matches the definition.

1. A blinking, vertical bar marking where typed text will appear.
2. The empty space around the edges of a printed page.
3. The help feature that normally looks like a paper clip.
4. A line of commands such as File, Edit, View, and Help.
5. The feature that corrects common errors automatically.
6. The feature that automatically moves text to the next line.
7. A collection of antonyms and synonyms.
8. The toolbar button with the picture of the paint brush on it.

1. _____     5. _____
2. _____     6. _____
3. _____     7. _____
4. _____     8. _____

### EXERCISE 3: MATCHING
Below is a list of six commonly-used keystrokes. Below that list is a list of what happens when you use each keystroke. Match the keystroke with the results.

| A. End | C. Home | E. Ctrl + Home |
| B. Enter | D. Ctrl + End | F. Tab |

1. ___ Insertion point moves to the top of the document.
2. ___ Insertion point moves to the end of the document.
3. ___ Insertion point moves to the beginning of the line.
4. ___ Insertion point moves to the end of the line.
5. ___ Insertion point moves to beginning of next line.
6. ___ Insertion point moves one tab space to the right.

### EXERCISE 4: TRUE-FALSE
For each of the following eight statements, place a T or an F on the line to indicate if the statement is True or False.

1. ___"Load", "start", and "open" a program all mean the same.
2. ___A toolbar Move handle has a picture of a truck on it.
3. ___The Format Painter button has a paint brush on it.
4. ___Text is inserted at the location of the mouse pointer.
5. ___To find answers to questions about Word, I click FAQ.
6. ___The word wrap feature moves text to the next line.
7. ___If I press Ctrl + Enter, I go to the bottom of the document.
8. ___Closing a document means that I remove it from memory.

### EXERCISE 5: DOZER'S GUIDE TO CANINE CARE
Dozer is an activist for dog's rights. He wants to encourage humans to take good care of their canine companions. So, to promote better care for canines, Dozer created the poster on the next page. Use the details below to recreate the poster.

#### PART A: SPECIFY DOCUMENT SETTINGS
☞ Set the top, bottom, left, and right margins at 0.8"
☞ Save your document as WC-Dozer's Guide To Canine Care.

#### PART B: INSERT, MOVE, AND RESIZE WORDART
☞ Use WordArt style D4 for the title as shown (that's the style in Column D and Row 4 of the WordArt Gallery table).
☞ Resize and move the WordArt title as shown.

#### PART C: INSERT AND FORMAT TEXT
☞ Go to **www.dozer.pannell.com** (or www.pannell.biz) and click the My Guide To Canine Care link.
☞ Copy and paste the seven paragraphs to the document.
☞ Click the Paste Options button and click Keep Text Only.
☞ Set the paragraphs (not the WordArt) to appear in 2 columns with 0.3" between the columns.
☞ Change the font of the seven paragraphs to Arial 8.
☞ Change the alignment of the seven paragraphs to Justify.
☞ Change each paragraph's title (FOOD, WATER, SHELTER, etc.) to be underlined and bold, as shown.

#### PART D: CREATE AND FORMAT A TABLE
☞ Create a table in the poster, where shown.
☞ Merge the cells in row 1 and enter the table's title in row 1.
☞ Center the table's title across the top row
☞ Change the font of the table's title to Arial 12, Bold.
☞ In rows 2-8, enter the data, center the data, and change the font of the data to Arial 10.
☞ Insert a smiley face symbol in front of & at end of the title.
☞ Apply 40% gray shading to the first row and 20% gray shading to the remaining rows.
☞ Apply a border to the table as shown (1½ pt. double line).
☞ Move and resize the table and its columns so that the table looks like the one on the sample poster.

#### PART E: INSERT A BULLETED LIST
☞ Create a bulleted list at the location shown on the sample poster. You can use any type of bullet you like.

#### PART F: INSERT, MOVE AND RESIZE AN IMAGE
☞ Insert the image of Dozer where shown (you can find the image on the web page where you found the paragraphs).
☞ Move and resize the image as shown.

#### PART G: ENTER AND ENHANCE YOUR NAME
☞ At the bottom right corner, replace Dozer's name with your's.
☞ Change the font of your name to Arial 12 and italicize it.

#### PART H: APPLY A PAGE BORDER
☞ While Dozer used a simple line page border, you should use some sort of "art" page border (pick any kind you like).

#### PART I: CORRECT ERRORS
☞ Correct all grammar and spelling errors.

#### PART J: USE PRINT PREVIEW AND PRINTING
☞ Use the Print Preview feature to compare your poster with the sample poster. When your poster and the sample poster are the same, print your poster. Save your work.

# Dozer's Guide To Canine Care

**FOOD**: Since young puppies need lots of food to grow up healthy, you should feed them several times each day. For adult dogs, many people feed them once a day, but experts believe that dividing the one meal into two meals per day will prevent your dog from getting too full and will make him feel better. Besides, he'd enjoy having two meals a day instead of one. Dog food contains ingredients needed by dogs. Don't feed your dog people food. Some people food can harm your pet. For instance, chocolate, in small quantities, can make your dog sick; in large quantities it can make your dog dead. Also, while your dog may want to chew on leftover chicken bones, these bones often break up into splinters that can cause serious harm to your dog. Instead, give your dog a rawhide chew bone. He'll love the bone; he'll love you; and, he is less likely to injure himself.

**WATER**: You should see to it that your dog has access to clean water at all times. He needs water to quench his thirst and to help him cool off. So, the water should be both clean and cool. On cold winter days, water kept outside may freeze; on hot summer days, water will get warm. The warmer it gets, the less it will cool him off. So, to keep his water cool, change the water often and keep the water bowl in the shade.

**SHELTER**: Your pet needs shelter to protect him from harsh weather (heat, cold, wind, rain, etc.). If your dog lives outside, a doghouse or access to the garage would help keep him healthy and happy. His shelter should be a safe place. Make sure that you puppy-proof his space by removing anything that can cause him harm. Dogs like to chew. If given the opportunity, a dog may chew a container containing harmful chemicals, or he may chew a piece of wood and ingest splinters. Make the shelter a safe place for your friend.

**EXERCISE**: To ensure that your dog is healthy and happy, regular exercise is needed. Going for long walks, chasing a tennis ball, or simply playing vigorously will help keep your dog healthy. His heart, muscles, and lungs will benefit from the activity. And, since dogs can get bored just like people, exercise can make them happy.

**GROOMING**: Grooming involves four activities: bathing, brushing fur, brushing teeth, and cliping nails. Regular attention to grooming will help keep your pet healthy and happy. Give him a bath once a week and brush his fur once a day. If his nails get too long, they may interfere with his ability to walk. Use a pair of toenail clippers made especially for dogs to clip his nails, making sure that you don't clip them too short. To alleviate any fears your dog may have, talk to him while you clip his nails. Giving your dog a rawhide bone to chew on not only makes him happy, but it helps clean his teeth. But, more dental care is needed. You should brush your dog's teeth weekly, especially the side teeth, using a dog toothbrush and toothpaste formulated for dogs.

Remember, grooming involves:
- ❖ Bathing (weekly)
- ❖ Brushing fur (daily)
- ❖ Clipping toenails (as needed)
- ❖ Brushing teeth (weekly)

**HEALTH CARE**: Soon after you get your puppy; take him to the vet for a checkup and vaccinations. The checkup will give the doctor the opportunity to see if your friend needs any special care; the vaccinations will protect your puppy from illnesses. Your vet will tell you when to return for additional vaccinations and/or his rabies shot. Once a year, thereafter, you should return to the vet so your dog can get his annual checkup. Anytime your pet appears to be ill, behaves differently than normal, or loses his appetite, your friend is trying to tell you something. Seek help from the vet.

**FRIENDSHIP**: Perhaps, the most important thing your dog needs is your friendship. Your dog will greatly appreciate your time and attention. Spend time with him. Sit with him. Pet him. Talk to him. Dogs, like people, gets lonely when left alone. Your buddy will never forget the time you spend with him.

| ☺ SEVEN THINGS A DOG NEEDS ☺ | |
|---|---|
| 1 | Food |
| 2 | Water |
| 3 | Shelter |
| 4 | Exercise |
| 5 | Grooming |
| 6 | Health Care |
| 7 | Friendship |

Dozer Pannell

## PAGE D-5: EXERCISE 1

| Across | Down |
|---|---|
| 1. Marker | 2. Return |
| 5. Assistant | 3. Bars |
| 8. Insertion | 4. Click |
| 9. Help | 6. Scroll |
| 10. No | 7. Toolbar |
| 11. Save | 9. Home |
| 14. Memory | 12. End |
| 15. Floppy | 13. Wrap |

## PAGE D-5: EXERCISE 2

1. T
2. F: A toolbar Move handle has a vertical bar on it, not a truck.
3. T
4. F: The menu bar has words on it. A toolbar has picture buttons on it.
5. T
6. T
7. F: Once I create a document, I can modify it as often as I want.
8. F: The Start button is found on the taskbar, not the status bar.

## PAGE D-5: EXERCISE 3

1. Insertion Point
2. Microsoft
3. Office Assistant
4. Menu bar
5. Toolbar
6. Word Wrap
7. Move Handle
8. End-of-Document Marker

## PAGE D-5: EXERCISE 4

1. J
2. I
3. G
4. E
5. F
6. H
7. D
8. A
9. C
10. B

## PAGE D-5: EXERCISE 5

1. T
2. F: To indent a line, I press the Tab key.
3. T
4. F: Text is inserted where the insertion point is located, not where the mouse pointer is located.
5. F: To find answers to questions about Word, I click Help on the menu bar, or I could click the Office Assistant toolbar button, but I do not click FAQ.
6. T
7. T
8. T

## PAGE D-9: EXERCISE 1

| Across | Down |
|---|---|
| 1. Insertion | 2. Select |
| 5. No | 3. On |
| 6. Spelling | 4. No |
| 9. Backspace | 7. Thesaurus |
| 13. AutoCorrect | 8. Delete |

14. Up
17. Redo
18. Mom
19. Replace

## PAGE D-9: EXERCISE 2

1. F: The blinking, vertical bar is the insertion point, not the scroll bar.
2. F: To select a word, I could double-click it. If I were to merely click in the word, the insertion point would be placed where I clicked.
3. T
4. T
5. T
6. F: To move text, I would click Edit, Cut, not Edit, Move. In fact, if I click Edit, there is no "move" command available.

## PAGE D-9: EXERCISE 3

1. T
2. F: Red wavy lines identify possible spelling errors. Possible grammar errors are identified with green wavy lines
3. T
4. T
5. F: The words "true" and "false" are antonyms (opposites), not synonyms (same meaning).
6. T

## PAGE D-9: EXERCISE 4

1. Thesaurus
2. Move
3. Undo
4. Antonyms
5. AutoCorrect
6. Redo
7. Spelling
8. Synonyms

## PAGE D-9: EXERCISE 5

1. F: The Redo button has a crooked arrow pointing to the right. The Undo button has a crooked arrow pointing to the left.
2. F: Green wavy lines identify possible grammar errors. Possible spelling errors are identified with red wavy lines.
3. T
4. T
5. T
6. T

## PAGE D-9: EXERCISE 6

1. C
2. B
3. A
4. C
5. B
6. D

## PAGE D-13: EXERCISE 1

| Across | Down |
|---|---|
| 1. Page | 2. Alignment |
| 6. Size | 3. Right align |
| 7. Paragraph | 4. Select |
| 8. Default | 5. Header |
| 10. Footer | 9. Columns |
| 11. No | 12. Left |

10. Double
11. Drag
12. Memory
15. Move
16. Save
17. RAM

14. Margins
15. Fun
16. Spacing

13. Break

## PAGE D-13: EXERCISE 2

1. F: The "U" toolbar button is for "Underline".
2. F: The "B" toolbar button stands for "Bold".
3. F: WordPad and Word are not the same program. While they are both word processors made available by the fine folks at Microsoft, they are very different. WordPad is a simplistic word processor that is part of the Windows operating system and, therefore, comes with most computers. On the other hand, Word is a very sophisticated word processor that most folks have to buy independent from the purchase of a computer system. Once a person has experienced the power of Word, he or she will seldom, if ever, want to use WordPad.
4. T
5. F: To insert a footer, click View from the menu bar. Then click Header and Footer from the menu.
6. T
7. T

## PAGE D-13: EXERCISE 3

1. F: If I press Ctrl + Enter, I will insert a hard page break. To go to the top of the document, I would press Ctrl + Home.
2. F: 12-point type is larger than 10-point type.
3. T
4. T
5. T
6. T
7. T

## PAGE D-13: EXERCISE 4

1. Header
2. Footer
3. Margins
4. Default
5. Font Size
6. Font Type
7. Format Painter
8. Alignment

## PAGE D-13: EXERCISE 5

1. T
2. F: The "B" on the toolbar button stands for "Bold".
3. T
4. T
5. F: The Format Painter button has a paint brush on it, not a paint can.
6. T
7. T

## PAGE D-13: EXERCISE 6

1. T
2. T
3. F: To set margins, click File, Page Setup.
4. F: The "I" on the toolbar button stands for "Italic".
5. T
6. T

## PAGE D-17: EXERCISE 1

| Across | Down |
|---|---|
| 2. Tab | 1. Column |
| 5. No | 2. Table |
| 7. Bullets | 3. Bold |
| 9. URL | 4. Steve |
| 10. Cell | 6. Close |
| 11. Son | 8. Select |
| 14. AutoFormat | 12. No |
| 15. Shading | 13. Borders |
| 17. Row | 14. Arrow |
| 18. Merge | 16. Home |
| 19. One | |

## PAGE D-17: EXERCISE 2
1. T
2. F: The "U" on the toolbar button stands for "Underline".
3. T
4. T
5. F: To create a table, click Table, Insert, Table.
6. T

## PAGE D-17: EXERCISE 3
1. Alignment
2. Merge
3. Cell
4. Column
5. Split
6. Bullets
7. Table
8. Row

## PAGE D-17: EXERCISE 4
1. T
2. F: Once a table has been created, I can add a new column.
3. T
4. T
5. F: To create a table, click Table, Insert, Table.
6. F: The "B" on the toolbar button stands for "Bold".
7. F: A vertical collection of cells is a column. A row is a horizontal collection of cells.

## PAGE D-17: EXERCISE 5
1. F: To move to the next cell in a table, press the Tab key, not the Enter key. Pressing the Enter key while in a Word table will increase the height of the current row.
2. T
3. F: The "I" on the toolbar button stands for "Italic".
4. F: A bullet is a symbol placed in front of (not after) each item on a list.
5. T
6. T
7. F: Once a table has been created, I can add a new row.

## PAGE D-17: EXERCISE 6
1. T
2. F: To create a table, click Table, Insert, Table.
3. T
4. T
5. T
6. T
7. T

## PAGE D-21: EXERCISE 1

| Across | Down |
|---|---|
| 1. File Name | 1. File |
| 4. Templates | 2. Move |
| 6. No | 3. Undo |
| 7. From File | 4. Two |

9. Micro
14. Art
15. Landscape
16. Orientation
20. Explorer
22. Font
24. Print
25. Yes
28. Dozer
29. Menu
30. Yes
31. Cut

5. Portrait
6. New
8. Fun
10. Fonts
11. ClipArt
12. Gallery
13. Page Border
17. Delete
18. Open
19. WordArt
21. Close
23. Insert
26. Select
27. Copy

## PAGE D-22: EXERCISE 2
1. F: ♫, ✈, and ✄ are examples of symbols, not clipart.
2. F: To select a graphic image, I click in it. If I right click, I will get what I always get when I right click--a shortcut menu.
3. T
4. F: The New toolbar button has a blank sheet of paper, not a puppy, on it.
5. T
6. T
7. F: The Microsoft Gallery contains clip art, not WordArt.

## PAGE D-22: EXERCISE 3
1. F: To insert an image into Word, I click Insert, Picture. Then I click From File if the picture is saved to a disk. Or, I click Clip Art if it is in the Clipart Gallery.
2. T
3. T
4. F: To move an image, I would drag the image to its new location. To resize an image, I would drag a sizing handle.
5. F: To view templates, click File, New.
6. T
7. T
8. F: To insert a ♫, ✈, or ✄ I would click Insert, Symbol.

## PAGE D-23: EXERCISE 1
1. T
2. F: To indent a line, I press the Tab key.
3. T
4. F: The menu bar has words on it. A toolbar has picture buttons on it.
5. T
6. T
7. F: Once I create a document, I can modify it as often as I please.
8. F: The Start button is found on the Taskbar, not on the status bar.

## PAGE D-23: EXERCISE 2
1. Insertion Point
2. Margins
3. Office Assistant
4. Menu Bar
5. AutoCorrect
6. Word Wrap
7. Thesaurus
8. Format Painter

## PAGE D-23: EXERCISE 3
1. E
2. D
3. C
4. A
5. B
6. F

## PAGE D-23: EXERCISE 4
1. T
2. F: A toolbar Move handle has a vertical bar on it, not a picture of a truck.
3. T
4. F: Text is inserted where the insertion point is located, not where the mouse pointer is located.
5. F: To find answers to questions about Word, I click Help on the menu bar, or I could click the Office Assistant toolbar button, but I do not click FAQ.
6. T
7. F: If I press Ctrl + Enter, I insert a hard page break. To go to the bottom of the document, I would press Ctrl + End.
8. T

**A drive**: A secondary storage device that writes to and reads from a floppy disk. Also called a floppy drive.

**address**: The location of a cell in a table.

**alignment**: The way the text lines up in relation to the margin.

**antonyms**: Words with opposite meanings. For instance, "temporary" and "permanent".

**AutoCorrect**: A feature that automatically corrects commonly-misspelled words and capitalizes the first word in each sentence.

**AutoFormat**: A feature that applies a preset collection of formats to a table.

**backspace key**: The key that deletes data to the left of the insertion point.

**bullet**: A symbol (e.g., a dot, check mark, or star) used to separate and highlight items in a list.

**cell**: The intersection of a row and a column in a table.

**click**: The act of rapidly pressing the left mouse button one time, generally done to select an on-screen object.

**clipart**: Artwork that can be viewed on screen, inserted into a document, or sent via email.

**close**: The process of removing a file or a program from memory.

**column**: A vertical collection of cells in a table. Or, the vertical arrangement of text (e.g., this page is printed in three columns).

**copy**: To place text elsewhere while maintaining the original text where it was.

**default settings**: The settings that prevail if the user does not specify other settings.

**delete**: To remove (erase).

**delete key**: The key that deletes data to the right of the insertion point.

**double-click**: The act of rapidly pressing the left mouse button two times.

**Dozer**: The smartest cyberdog on the planet.

**drag**: To move the mouse.

**drag and drop**: The act of pointing to an object on the screen, holding down the left mouse button, moving the mouse, and then releasing the mouse button, thereby moving the object. In essence you have dragged and then dropped the object.

**edit**: To modify a document.

**enhancements**: Bold, italics, and underline.

**font color**: The color of the characters.

**font size**: The dimension of the characters.

**font type**: The shape of the characters.

**footer**: Text that appears at the bottom of each page of a document.

**format painter**: A feature that will copy the formats residing in text and will apply those same formats to other text.

**hard return**: A code placed in a document whenever the Enter key is pressed. This code forces the insertion point to move to the next line.

**header**: Text that appears at the top of each page of a document.

**insertion point**: The on-screen blinking vertical line identifying where entered text will appear. Some folks refer to this as a cursor.

**landscape orientation**: A document printed on paper that is 11 inches wide and 8-1/2 inches high.

**launch**: To put a program or data into memory. Also called start, load, or open.

**load**: To place a program or data into memory. Also called start, launch, or open.

**margins**: The space between the text and the edges of the paper.

**maximize button**: The button (on the title bar) that, when clicked, will make the window fill the entire screen.

**memory**: The temporary location where the data and programs currently being used by a processor reside. Also called RAM (an acronym for Random Access Memory).

**menu bar**: The bar (under the title bar) which consists of a series of command categories. To access specific commands in a category, click the item on the menu bar.

**Microsoft Gallery**. A collection of clipart.

**minimize button**: The button that, when clicked, will make the window become the size of a taskbar button.

**move**: To place text elsewhere while removing the original text from where it was.

**move handle**: A vertical bar on a toolbar that, when dragged, will allow the user to move the

toolbar.

**office assistant**: A Microsoft help feature that displays a character in the form of a paper clip that asks you to pose a question for him to answer.

**open**: To place a program or data into memory. Also called start, load, or launch.

**page breaks**: The location in a document where the printer will cease to print one page and will load another sheet of paper before continuing to print. Page breaks are automatically inserted whenever your document contains more data than can be printed on one page. In addition, you can insert additional page breaks where you want them to appear (e.g., to start a chapter in a book or a bibliography).

**page orientation**: The way the print appears on the page. If 11" wide, the page has a landscape orientation; if 8-12" wide, the page has a portrait orientation.

**paste options button**: A button that appears below text that has been copied and then pasted into a document. If you click the Paste Options button you will be able to select how you want to paste the text.

**portrait orientation**: A document printed on paper that is 8-1/2 inches wide and 11 inches high.

**print preview**: A feature that permits you to see how each page of your document will look before you print the document.

**redo button**: The toolbar button that, when clicked, will undo the last undo done. It has a crooked arrow pointing to the right.

**right-click**: The act of rapidly pressing the right mouse button one time.

**row**: A horizontal line of cells in a table.

**save**: The act of placing a copy of the document that is currently in memory into secondary storage.

**select**: To identify an object, text, or image to which you wish to do something.

**shortcut menu**: A context-sensitive menu that appears when I right click. Also called a Quick Menu.

**Skooter**: Dozer's little sister.

**symbols**: Non-keyboard characters that can be placed in documents (e.g., ♫, ✎, and ❀).

**synonyms**: Words with similar meanings (e.g., "program" and "software").

**tab key**: The key used to indent a line in word processing or to move from cell to cell in a table or in a worksheet.

**table**: A collection of columns and rows forming cells into which data is entered.

**task pane**: A pane that sometimes appears at the right side of the screen which provides for rapid selection of features.

**taskbar**: The horizontal grey bar, typically at the bottom of the desktop, upon which the Start button resides.

**template**: A document file with customized format, content, and features, usually accessed by clicking File, New in the program.

**thesaurus**: A list of synonyms and antonyms.

**toolbar**: A collection of picture buttons that, when clicked, execute a command. These buttons typically appear below the menu bar.

**undo button**: The toolbar button that, when clicked, will reverse the last action taken. It has a crooked arrow pointing to the left.

**view**: A menu bar item that lets me choose the way stuff looks on the screen. For instance, in My Computer, the way the icons appear (thumbnails, tiles, icons, list, or details).

**word wrap**: A word processor feature that moves excess text to the next line automatically, thereby preventing text from spilling over into the margins.

**WordArt**: A graphic image in the form of text.

# DOZER'S QUINTESSENTIAL GUIDE TO MICROSOFT® EXCEL

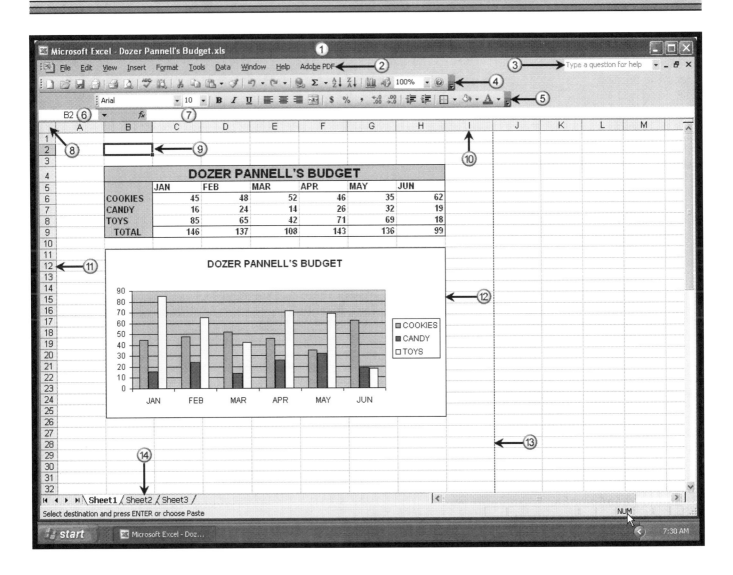

1. Title bar (identifies the program and workbook being used)
2. Menu bar (collection of menu items, each of which contains commands)
3. Help (a great place to find answers to all your questions)
4. Standard toolbar (collection of picture buttons, each of which accesses a command)
5. Formatting toolbar (collection of picture buttons, each of which accesses a command)
6. Name box (displays the address of the active cell)
7. Formula bar (displays the content of the active cell)
8. Select All button (click it to select the entire worksheet)
9. Active cell (selected cell ready for data input, also called the current cell)
10. Column header (displays the name of the column)
11. Row header (displays the name of the row)
12. Chart (a graphical representation of your data)
13. Page Break (denotes the division between printed pages)
14. Sheet tabs (click a tab to move to another sheet in the workbook)

# Dozer's Quintessential Guide To Microsoft Excel
## TABLE OF CONTENTS

A workbook is a collection of worksheets. Each worksheet is a collection of rows and columns. The intersection of each row and column forms a cell. A vertical collection of cells is a column; a horizontal collection of cells is a row. Columns have alphabetic names (e.g., A, B, C); rows have numeric names (e.g., 1, 2, 3). Each cell has an address which is composed of the column name and the row name. For instance, the cell located at the intersection of column D and row 6, is cell D6.

## START (LOAD, OPEN, LAUNCH) EXCEL
To use Excel, the program must be placed into memory (RAM).

To start Excel, do the following:
☞ Click the Start taskbar button. Point to All Programs.
☞ On the sub-menu, click Microsoft Excel (If you don't see it, open additional menus until you find it).

## SURVEY THE EXCEL SCREEN
While the Excel screen contains elements that are common to many Window-based programs, some are unique to Excel.
☞ Title bar (top of screen) identifies the program and the workbook being used. In addition, the Close, Minimize, Maximize, and Restore buttons reside on the title bar.
☞ Menu bar (below title bar) contains command categories (when one is clicked, a list of commands appears. To see all the commands, click the double-down arrow on the list).
☞ Toolbars (below menu bar) consist of picture buttons. If clicked, a command is executed. Each toolbar has a Move handle (vertical bar) at its left edge. If you point the mouse to a Move handle, the pointer will become a four-pointed arrow. If the Standard and Formatting toolbars appear in one line, drag the Move handle of the Formatting toolbar down so that the Formatting toolbar occupies its own line. Otherwise, you won't be able to see all the toolbar buttons.
☞ Name box (above the column A header) displays the location of the active cell.
☞ Formula Bar (to the right of the Name Box) displays the contents of the active cell.
☞ Worksheet area, the space where your worksheet resides which is composed of 256 columns and 65,536 rows which form a matrix of over 16 million cells including one active cell (the cell with the bold outline).
☞ Worksheet frame which provides column headers across the top of the screen and row headers along the left side.
☞ Scroll bars (right and bottom of window).
☞ Worksheet tabs (at bottom, left side of worksheet area). By default a workbook has 3 worksheets. You can add more.

## USE THE TASK PANE
From time to time, the task pane will appear on the right side of the screen. Its contents change, depending on what you are doing. Since you just started Excel, the task pane wants to know what you want to do (if the task pane is not visible, click View, Task Pane to have it appear). Since you want to create a new worksheet, just close the task pane (click the X at the top right corner of the task pane). The task pane disappears, but it will appear later as you attempt other tasks.

## ENTER DATA IN A WORKSHEET
With a worksheet, data is inserted in the active cell (current cell). A cell can contain a label identifying what's in other cells.

Or, it can contain a value (a number to be mathematically manipulated), and/or a formula (how the values will be mathematically manipulated), and/or formats (how the stuff looks). Since entered data appears in the active cell, the first step is to select the desired cell. To do so, click in the cell or use the arrow keys to move to the desired cell. When data is entered in adjacent cells, the next logical cell can be activated by pressing the Tab key.

To practice entering data, do the following:
☞ Click in the cell located at the intersection of column A and row 1 (this cell is called A1). Notice that its border is bold.
☞ Type JAN. Press Tab (Cell B1 becomes the active cell).
☞ Type FEB. Press Tab. (Cell C1 becomes the active cell).
☞ Type MAR and continue to enter the data shown below: As you enter the data, notice that alphabetic labels are left aligned in each cell and numeric values are right aligned. These are the default settings. For now, just enter the data. Later, we will see how to change these settings.

| JAN | FEB | MAR | APR | MAY | JUN |
|-----|-----|-----|-----|-----|-----|
| 272 | 222 | 23  | 275 | 298 | 361 |
| 856 | 856 | 856 | 856 | 856 | 856 |
| 125 | 98  | 136 | 62  | 126 | 88  |

☞ Click in cell A20 and type your name.
☞ Save this workbook (name it EP1-Dozer's Budget).

## USE AUTOCORRECT
AutoCorrect will automatically correct many errors. To add or delete items from AutoCorrect, click Tools, AutoCorrect Options.

## CHECK THE SPELLING
To check the spelling in a worksheet, select cell A1, then click Tools, Spelling. Excel will find and identify each misspelled word and will provide suggestions for correction.

## UNDO & REDO
When you make a mistake, you can fix it by clicking the Undo toolbar button which will undo the last action taken. If you then click the Undo button again, the second-to-last action will be undone. If you undid something you did not want to undo, you can restore the action by clicking the Redo toolbar button.

## COPY AND MOVE CELL CONTENTS
To copy data, select the cells containing the data and click Edit, Copy. Then click where you want the data pasted and click Edit, Paste. Follow the same steps to move data, except, click Cut instead of Copy from the Edit menu.

## CLOSE A WORKBOOK
When you are done working on a workbook, you will want to close it. Closing a workbook removes it from memory (RAM).

To practice closing a workbook, do the following:
☞ Click the Close button (the X at the right end of the menu bar). If you have modified the workbook since you last saved it, you will be asked if you want to save the changes. If you see this message, click Yes. The workbook will be saved and closed, but the program will remain open.

## OPEN A WORKBOOK
To read, edit, or print an existing workbook, you will need to open it (i.e., place a copy of it in memory)

To practice opening a workbook, do the following:
- ☞ Click File, Open (the Open dialog box appears).
- ☞ Click the Look In list box arrow (a drop-down list appears).
- ☞ Select the drive and folder in which the file resides.
- ☞ Select the "EP1-Dozer's Budget" file.
- ☞ Click the Open button (the workbook will open).

## SELECT PARTS OF A WORKSHEET
Before you can move, copy, enhance, modify, or delete data, you must first select the data so that Excel will know which data you want the changes to impact.

To practice selecting cells, do the following:
- ☞ To select a cell, click the cell (click any cell and notice that it becomes the active cell. Click another cell and notice that it becomes the active cell).
- ☞ To select adjacent cells, drag over the cells (point to cell A1 and hold down the left mouse button and drag the mouse down and to the right until you get to cell F4. Release the mouse button. Notice that the range of cells from A1 to F4 is selected). Click outside of the range to deselect it.
- ☞ To select a column, click its header (click any header).
- ☞ To select a row, click its header (click any row header).
- ☞ To select the entire sheet, click the Select All button (at the corner of the worksheet frame, above the row 1 header).
- ☞ Click in the worksheet to deselect it.

## INSERT A COLUMN OR A NEW ROW
You can insert new columns or rows in your worksheets.

To practice inserting a column, do the following:
- ☞ Click the header where you want a new column (in this case, click the column A header).
- ☞ Click Insert, Columns. To deselect the column, click elsewhere. The data that was in that column and that was in every column to the right of that column moved to the right to make room for the new column.

To practice inserting a row, do the following:
- ☞ Click the row header where you want the new row (in this case, click the row 1 header).
- ☞ Click Insert, Rows. Click elsewhere to deselect the row. The data that was in that row and that was in every row below that row moved down to make room for the new row.
- ☞ Click the row 3 header.
- ☞ Click Insert, Rows. Notice that the row is moved down to make room for the new row.
- ☞ Click elsewhere to deselect the row.

## DELETE A COLUMN OR A ROW
Since columns and rows are deleted the same way, you will only practice deleting a row.

To practice deleting a row, do the following:
- ☞ Click the header of the row you want to delete. In this case, click the header for row 3 (the row you just inserted).
- ☞ Click Edit, Delete. Notice that the row disappears and all the rows below that row move up to fill the gap.
- ☞ Save your workbook (simply click the Save toolbar button).

## EDIT DATA
You can edit data (replace existing data or add new data).

To practice inserting data in empty cells, do the following:
- ☞ Activate cell A3 and then type Fritos.
- ☞ Activate cell A4 and then type Candy.
- ☞ Activate cell A5 and then type Bones.

To practice replacing existing data, do the following:
- ☞ Activate the cell containing the unwanted data by either clicking the cell or using the arrow keys to select it (in this case, activate cell A3 which contains "Fritos").
- ☞ Type the new data (type Cookies).
- ☞ Click any other cell to deselect the current cell. Notice that "Fritos" has been replaced with "Cookies".

To practice inserting additional data, do the following:
- ☞ Double-click the cell containing the data to be modified (in this case, double-click cell D3).
- ☞ Notice that the insertion point is placed in the cell.
- ☞ If necessary, put the insertion point between the 2 and 3.
- ☞ Type 1. It is inserted at the insertion point location.
- ☞ Click the Enter button to the left of the Formula Bar (it has a green check mark (✔) on it). By the way, if you decide that you don't want to have your modification accepted, you would click the Cancel button (it has a red X on it).
- ☞ Save your workbook (simply click the Save toolbar button).

## USE THE PRINT PREVIEW FEATURE
To see how the printed worksheet will look, you can use the Print Preview feature. By doing so, you will save paper and toner by reducing the number of preliminary copies you make.

To practice previewing a worksheet, do the following:
- ☞ Click File, Print Preview (or, click the Print Preview toolbar button which looks like paper with a magnifying glass on it).
- ☞ Click on the worksheet to magnify the sheet.
- ☞ To exit the Preview, click the Close button on the Print Preview feature bar. Notice the vertical dotted line on the worksheet. It appears after you do a Print Preview. This line marks the edge of the printed page. Any data on the right side of the line will print out on a different page. If you scroll down, you can see a dotted horizontal line that denotes the bottom of the printed page.

## PRINT A WORKSHEET
There are two ways to print a worksheet. You could click the Print toolbar button (looks like a printer). This will print one copy of the entire worksheet. If your worksheet is long and you only want to print out a portion of it, or if you want to print out more than one copy of it, you should use the Print option on the File menu to access the Print dialog box. Since your worksheet is only one page in length, press the Print toolbar button to print one copy of your worksheet. Notice that the gridlines that appeared on the screen do not print out.

## GET HELP
The Office Assistant will answer your questions. If you see the paper clip dude on the screen, click him. If you don't see him, click Help, Show The Office Assistant to have him appear.

## CLOSE EXCEL
To close Excel (remove it from memory), click the Close button (the X at the top right corner of the window).

## EXERCISE 1: CROSSWORD

Note: the Answer Key can be found beginning on page E-25.

### ACROSS
2. Worksheets in a workbook are identified with ___.
4. The ___ bar displays the contents of the active cell.
6. The ___ button has a green check mark (✔) on it.
7. The Name ___ displays the location of the active cell.
8. A series of columns and rows forming millions of cells.
11. A ___ identifies the data in a row or column.
12. A number that will be mathematically manipulated.
13. The column and row headings form the worksheet ___.
15. The intersection of a row and a column.
19. The ___ feature corrects common errors automatically.

### DOWN
1. A collection of worksheets that, when saved, is a file.
3. To select the entire sheet, click the ___ button.
5. When I click a cell, it becomes the ___ cell.
9. Pressing the ___ key takes me to the cell to the right.
10. The ___ button has a red X on it.
11. Labels, by default, are ___ aligned when typed in a cell.
14. Values, by default, are ___ aligned when typed in a cell.
15. A vertical collection of cells.
16. The vertical bar at the left end of a toolbar is a ___ handle.
17. A horizontal collection of cells.
18. To place a duplicate of data elsewhere.

## EXERCISE 2: TRUE-FALSE
For each of the following seven statements, place a T or an F on the line to indicate if the statement is True or False.

1. ___A vertical collection of cells is a row.
2. ___I can delete a column, but not a row.
3. ___The Name box displays the location of the active cell.
4. ___Each column has an alphabetic name (A, B, C, etc).
5. ___I can edit data in a cell by double-clicking the cell.
6. ___To select a column, I would click its column header.
7. ___The address at the intersection of 3 and C is 3C.

## EXERCISE 3: TRUE-FALSE
For each of the following seven statements, place a T or an F on the line to indicate if the statement is True or False.

1. ___I can delete a row or a column.
2. ___To select an entire worksheet, click the Select All button.
3. ___The Formula Bar displays the location of the active cell.
4. ___I cannot add entries into the AutoCorrect feature.
5. ___To select a range of cells, I drag over the cells.
6. ___I can enter labels, values, or formulas in a cell.
7. ___Unless I create more, a workbook will have 2 worksheets.

## EXERCISE 4: IDENTIFY TERMS
Below are eight definitions. Below the definitions are eight lines. In each line, write the word that matches the definition.

1. A vertical collection of cells.
2. A collection of worksheets that I will save as a single file.
3. A horizontal collection of cells.
4. A matrix of columns and rows.
5. Each of these has an alphabetic name (A, B, C . . .).
6. The place where the address of the active cell is displayed.
7. Each of these has a numeric name (1, 2, 3 . . .).
8. The intersection of a row and a column.

1. _____    5. _____
2. _____    6. _____
3. _____    7. _____
4. _____    8. _____

## EXERCISE 5: TRUE-FALSE
For each of the following seven statements, place a T or an F on the line to indicate if the statement is True or False.

1. ___A worksheet is a collection of workbooks.
2. ___I can add a column, but not a row.
3. ___An active cell is the same thing as the current cell.
4. ___To move to the next cell to the right, press the Tab key.
5. ___The width of columns can be adjusted.
6. ___To select a row, I would click its row header.
7. ___Excel does not have a spelling correction feature.

## EXERCISE 6: TRUE-FALSE
For each of the following six statements, place a T or an F on the line to indicate if the statement is True or False.

1. ___I can add a row or a column.
2. ___A horizontal collection of cells is a column.
3. ___Each column has an numeric name (1, 2, 3, etc).
4. ___The Formula Bar displays the contents of the active cell.
5. ___The Name box is where I type my name.
6. ___Data is inserted in the active cell.

## EXERCISE 7: ENTER DATA IN WORKSHEET

☞ Launch Excel, close the task pane, and recreate the worksheet below. Make sure you put the title in cell A1.

| 15TH PRECINCT ANNUAL ARRESTS REPORT | | | | |
|---|---|---|---|---|
| | | | | |
| | 1996 | 1997 | 1998 | 1999 |
| Andy | 112 | 89 | 96 | 101 |
| Bobby | 97 | 86 | 69 | 96 |
| Diane | 75 | 86 | 94 | 93 |
| James | 36 | 85 | 45 | 22 |
| Jill | 96 | 58 | 29 | 57 |
| | | | | |
| This Annual Arrest Report was created by Arthur Fancy | | | | |

☞ Save the sheet to your diskette (call it EP1-NYPD).
☞ In cell A10, replace Arthur's name with your name.
☞ Since you have mistakenly omitted the data for Greg, insert a new row where James' data resides (row 7).
☞ Enter the data shown below in the new row.

| Greg | 53 | 68 | 29 | 98 |
|---|---|---|---|---|

☞ Change Andy's 1997 arrests from 89 to 91.
☞ Save the modified sheet (you will use this worksheet later).
☞ Use Print Preview to see what your sheet will look like.
☞ Print your worksheet.
☞ Close the workbook. Close Excel.

## EXERCISE 8: CREATE AN EXPENSE SUMMARY

☞ Start Excel, close the task pane, and recreate the worksheet below. Make sure the title is in cell A1.

| CONNER CONSTRUCTION CO. EXPENSE SUMMARY | | | | |
|---|---|---|---|---|
| | | | | |
| | JAN | FEB | MAR | APR |
| Drywall | 569 | 325 | 745 | 157 |
| Lumber | 3569 | 2563 | 1254 | 6321 |
| Paint | 256 | 652 | 324 | 456 |
| | | | | |
| This Expense Summary was created by Darlene Conner | | | | |

☞ Save the sheet to your disk (call it EP1-Conner).
☞ In cell A8, replace Darlene's name with your name.
☞ Change the January lumber expense to from 3569 to 2354.
☞ Since you have mistakenly omitted one of the expenses, insert a new row where the Paint data resides (row 6).
☞ Enter the data shown below in the new row.

| Nails | 25 | 32 | 42 | 13 |
|---|---|---|---|---|

☞ Save the modified sheet (you will use this worksheet later).
☞ Use Print Preview to see what your sheet will look like.
☞ Print your worksheet.
☞ Close the workbook. Close Excel.

## EXERCISE 9: USE AUTOFILL TO ENTER DATA

Please recreate the ER schedule. The title is in cell A1. Notice that much of the data is repetitious or sequential. To save time and increase accuracy when entering such data, use AutoFill. How does AutoFill work? After entering "Sun" in B2, point to the little square box (fill handle) at the bottom right corner of cell B2. When your mouse pointer turns into a small **+** sign, drag to the right. Release the mouse button when you complete the list of days. After entering 1:00 in cell A3, drag its fill handle down until the times are completed. After entering MG, LK, CW, etc., do the same (If the AutoFill Options button appears, you could click it to select the type of format desired. For now, ignore it).

| COUNTY GENERAL WORK SCHEDULE FOR THE ER | | | | | | | |
|---|---|---|---|---|---|---|---|
| | Sun | Mon | Tue | Wed | Thu | Fri | Sat |
| 1:00 | MG | LK | CW | JC | LK | JC | MG |
| 2:00 | MG | LK | CW | JC | LK | JC | MG |
| 3:00 | MG | LK | CW | JC | LK | JC | MG |
| 4:00 | MG | LK | CW | JC | LK | JC | MG |
| 5:00 | MG | LK | CW | JC | LK | JC | MG |
| 6:00 | MG | LK | PB | JC | LK | JC | MG |
| 7:00 | MG | LK | PB | EC | LK | JC | MG |
| 8:00 | MG | JC | PB | EC | CW | JC | MG |
| 9:00 | MG | JC | PB | EC | CW | PB | MG |
| 10:00 | MG | JC | PB | EC | CW | PB | MG |
| 11:00 | CW | JC | PB | EC | CW | PB | EC |
| 12:00 | CW | JC | PB | EC | CW | PB | EC |
| 13:00 | CW | JC | PB | EC | CW | PB | EC |
| 14:00 | CW | JC | PB | EC | CW | PB | LK |
| 15:00 | CW | JC | PB | EC | CW | PB | LK |
| 16:00 | CW | JC | MG | EC | JC | PB | LK |
| 17:00 | CW | JC | MG | EC | JC | PB | LK |
| 18:00 | CW | JC | MG | EC | JC | PB | LK |
| 19:00 | CW | CW | MG | EC | JC | PB | LK |
| 20:00 | CW | CW | MG | EC | JC | PB | LK |
| 21:00 | CW | CW | MG | EC | JC | PB | LK |
| 22:00 | CW | CW | MG | EC | JC | PB | LK |
| 23:00 | LK | CW | MG | LK | JC | PB | LK |
| 0:00 | LK | CW | MG | LK | JC | MG | LK |
| This Work Schedule was created by Carrie Weaver | | | | | | | |

☞ In cell A27, replace Carrie's name with your name.
☞ Save the worksheet (name it EP1-ER). (you will use this worksheet later). Print your worksheet. Close Excel.

The feature that distinguishes a worksheet program is its ability to manipulate numerical data. Excel can perform many complex calculations instantaneously. Your only concern is that you provide accurate data upon which the calculations will be made and that you use the proper formulas. If you still have the "EP1-Dozer's Budget" worksheet from Project 1, open it. Save it as "EP2-Dozer's Budget". If you do not still have it, recreate it as shown below. Make sure that the "JAN" label is in cell B2 and that your full name is in cell B21.

|          | JAN | FEB | MAR | APR | MAY | JUN |
|----------|-----|-----|-----|-----|-----|-----|
| Cookies  | 272 | 222 | 213 | 275 | 298 | 361 |
| Candy    | 856 | 856 | 856 | 856 | 856 | 856 |
| Bones    | 125 | 98  | 136 | 62  | 126 | 88  |

## USE THE AUTOSUM FEATURE
AutoSum will calculate the sum of values residing in a column.

To practice using the AutoSum feature, do the following:
☞ Activate the cell directly below the column to be summed (in this case, click in cell B6).
☞ Click the AutoSum toolbar button (∑). Excel will "guess" that you want to sum the values in B3 to B5. Since this is correct, click the Enter button (✔) on the Formula Bar. The sum will be displayed in B6 and the formula will be displayed in the Formula Bar. Note: you could also sum a column of values by double-clicking the AutoSum button, but you need to be careful because any label that it thinks is a value, such as the years 2001, 2002 will be included in the calculation).
☞ Since you want to sum the values in the remaining five columns, repeat the above steps for each column.
☞ Label these values by clicking in cell A6 and typing TOTAL so that row 6 looks like this:

| TOTAL | 1253 | 1176 | 1205 | 1193 | 1280 | 1305 |
|-------|------|------|------|------|------|------|

☞ Change B3 to be 275 and G5 to be 89. A new total is automatically generated after each change.

## USE FUNCTIONS
In addition to the AutoSum feature, Excel provides hundreds of other formulas useful for manipulating numerical data. You can use them to calculate a simple average, depreciation of a fixed asset, or future values. Don't panic. In Dozer's Quintessential Guide To Microsoft Excel, we will only use simple functions.

To practice using a function, do the following:
☞ Activate the cell where you want the result of the calculation to appear (in this case, you want to average the values in each row. So, activate cell H3).
☞ Click the arrow next to the AutoSum button. A drop down list will appear. From the list, select the desired function (In this case, select the Average function).
☞ Excel will "guess" that you want to average the contents of cells B3 to G3. Since this is correct, click the Enter button (✔) on the Formula Bar.
☞ Notice that the result of the formula (274) appears in cell H3 (274 is the average of the values in the B3 to G3 range).
☞ Repeat the above steps for rows 4 and 5. Make sure that the range of cells is correct each time–Excel will NOT guess each one correctly. When Excel guesses wrong, drag over the correct cells before clicking the Enter button (✔).
☞ Label these values by clicking in cell H2 and typing AVG.
☞ If you entered the formulas correctly, the averages should be as follows: Cookies (274), Candy (856), and Bones (106). If you generated different averages, find and fix your error before continuing.
☞ Save the modified workbook. Close Excel.

## USE FORMULAS
While built-in formulas (e.g., AutoSum, functions) provide fast ways to perform some rather complex calculations, many times, you will need to create a customized formula to obtain the desired results. Start Excel, close the task pane, and recreate the worksheet below. Be sure to place "Item" in cell A1.

| Item   | Quantity | Price    | Total |
|--------|----------|----------|-------|
| A-1256 | 265      | 1.31     |       |
| D-4563 | 2369     | 5.26     |       |
| E-2365 | 758      | .68      |       |
| H-1487 | 752      | 3.11     |       |
| J-6598 | 45       | 12.25    |       |
|        |          | Subtotal |       |
|        |          | Sales Tax|       |
|        |          | Total    |       |

☞ Save the worksheet to your diskette (name it EP2-Invoice).

To practice creating formulas, do the following:
☞ Activate the cell where you want the result of the calculation to appear (in this case, activate cell D2).
☞ Since all formulas (and functions) begin with an equal sign, press the Equal key (=) on the keyboard. Otherwise, Excel will not know you want a formula in the cell. For instance, if you merely typed B2*C2, Excel would place "B2*C2" in the cell. So, to notify Excel of your intention to create a formula, you must start each formula with an equal sign.
☞ Enter each cell reference followed by an operator (in this case, enter B2*C2). By the way, the four operators you'll use most are add (+), subtract (-), multiply (*), and divide (/).
☞ Click the Enter button (✔) on the Formula Bar (or press the Enter key). The formula result (347.15) appears in D2.
☞ Activate the next cell where you want the result of a calculation to appear (in this case, activate cell D3).
☞ Press the Equal key (=) on the keyboard.
☞ Enter each cell reference followed by an operator (B3*C3).
☞ Click the Enter button (✔) or press the Enter key.
☞ Save the modified workbook.
☞ Before entering any more formulas, proceed to the next topic where you will learn how to speed up this process.

## COPY FORMULAS
You could repeat the above steps to calculate a value for cells D4, D5, and D6. But, it would be faster to copy and paste the formula into those cells. As long as the formula in the copied cell is correct, the formula in the pasted cell will be correct (assuming that the cell references in the original formula were relative references--we'll discuss this matter later in this project).

To practice copying formulas, do the following:
- ☞ Select the cell containing the formula (select cell D3).
- ☞ Click Edit, Copy. A marquee (a blinking dotted border which looks like a theater marquee) appears around cell D3. The marquee identifies the cell as the one containing the formula that has been placed in the clipboard. Cell D3 will have a marquee around it until other data is placed in the clipboard or until the clipboard is emptied by pressing the Escape (Esc) key on the keyboard. For now, ignore the marquee.
- ☞ Click in the cell where you want the formula inserted (D4).
- ☞ Click Edit, Paste. Excel will know to copy the contents of the cell and that the cell contains a formula. Excel will adjust the new formula so its references are in the same places in relation to the location of the new formula as they were to the old formula. This is because addresses are relative, which means that instead of using a cell address, Excel marks the location of the referenced cells as they relate to the location where the formula resides (e.g., Excel will take the value in the cell two cells to the left of the formula cell and multiply it by the value in the cell one cell to the left of the formula cell). All this is rather difficult to understand. To illustrate, think of a chess board. Where a knight can move is "relative" to where it is. Its new location is always relative to its old location. Still confused. That's OK for now. Later, when you learn about absolute addresses, this matter will become crystal clear. Or, at least less murky. For now, don't worry.
- ☞ Since the formula you copied is still in the clipboard, you can continue to paste it into the other cells (another way to copy formulas is to drag the D4 AutoFill button down to D6).
- ☞ Paste the formula into cell D5 and then into cell D6.
- ☞ Type your name in cell A20.

## FORMULAS, CONTINUED
To continue practicing with formulas, do the following:
- ☞ Activate the cell where you want the result of the calculation to appear (in this case, click cell D7).
- ☞ You could click the AutoSum button. But, instead, create a customized formula by typing =D2+D3+D4+D5+D6.
- ☞ Press Enter. Notice that cell D7 displays the result of the formula which is the sum of the values in the column.
- ☞ To compute a 6% tax, click in cell D8 and type =D7*.06.
- ☞ Press Enter. Notice that cell D8 displays the result of the formula which is the sales tax on the subtotal.
- ☞ Activate cell D9 and type the formula =D7+D8.
- ☞ Press Enter. Notice that cell D9 displays the result of the formula which is the sum of the subtotal and the sales tax.
- ☞ If your worksheet does not look like this, check your data and your formulas for errors. Go to the next topic to learn a good way to view all your formulas simultaneously.

| ITEM | QUANTITY | PRICE | TOTAL |
|------|----------|-------|-------|
| A-1256 | 265 | 1.31 | 347.15 |
| D-4563 | 2369 | 5.26 | 12460.94 |
| E-2365 | 758 | .68 | 515.44 |
| H-1487 | 752 | 3.11 | 2338.72 |
| J-6598 | 45 | 12.25 | 551.25 |
| | | Subtotal | 16213.50 |
| | | Sales Tax | 972.81 |
| | | Total | 17186.31 |

## VIEW FORMULAS
As you have seen, a cell displays the result of the formula, not the formula. To see a formula, you can click the cell where the formula resides to have the formula appear in the Formula bar. By doing so, you can check the accuracy of the formula. However, sometimes it's helpful to see all the formulas at once.

To practice viewing formulas, do the following:
- ☞ Press Ctrl + ~ (hold down the Ctrl key and press the ~ key. The ~ key is above the tab key).
- ☞ Now that you can see the formulas in the worksheet, print one copy of the worksheet.
- ☞ Press Ctrl + ~ to return to the normal view which displays the results of the formulas in the cells, not the formulas.
- ☞ Save the workbook. Close Excel.

## USE ABSOLUTE ADDRESSES
As stated earlier, the cell references in a formula are relative, which means that if the formula is copied and pasted to another location, the references change to reflect the location of the new formula in relation to the location of the old formula. This is a magnificent feature, without which formulas could not be efficiently copied. By the way, if you never intended to copy a formula, the distinction between relative and absolute references would be of no concern to you. However, sometimes, you will want to copy a formula and you will not want the cell references to change. To have the formula or parts of the formula copied without this adjustment, you need to create the original formula using absolute addresses. Then, when you copy the formula, the cell addresses will remain unchanged. To create an absolute address, place a dollar sign ($) in front of the column and/or row part of the cell reference. To practice, start Excel, close the task pane, and recreate the worksheet below. Be sure to place the "RATE" label in cell A1.

| RATE | | .05 | |
|------|--|-----|--|
| PERSON | SALES | | BONUS |
| Levene | 12547 | | |
| Roma | 45845 | | |
| Moss | 26985 | | |
| Aaronow | 6325 | | |

- ☞ Type your name in cell A12.
- ☞ Save the worksheet to your diskette (name it EP2-Bonus).

To practice using absolute addresses, do the following:
- ☞ Activate cell C3, which is where you want a formula that multiples the bonus rate in cell B1 with the value in B3.
- ☞ Type =$B$1*B3. The dollar signs identify B1 as an absolute reference, while B3 is a relative reference.
- ☞ Click the Enter button (✔) on the Formula Bar. The result of the formula appears in C3.
- ☞ Copy the formula in C3 to cells C4, C5, and C6.
- ☞ View the formulas (Ctrl + ~). In each case, the formula points to B1 for the bonus rate, but changes to point to the cell to the left of the formula cell for the sales value.
- ☞ Return to Normal view (Ctrl + ~).
- ☞ The results should be: Levene (627.35), Roma (2292.25), Moss (1349.25) and Aaronow (316.25). If your results differ, check the data and formulas for errors and fix them.
- ☞ Save the worksheet. Print the worksheet.
- ☞ Close the Workbook. Close Excel.

## EXERCISE 1: CROSSWORD
Use the clues below to complete the crossword puzzle.

### ACROSS
3. =C4*G6 is a ___.
5. To have a permanent copy of a worksheet, I ___ it.
6. A file consists of how many workbooks?
8. The ___ toolbar button has a ∑ on it.
11. All formulas begin with an ___ sign.
13. $B$2 is a(n) ___ reference.
15. G5 is a(n) ___ reference.
17. The ___ button has a green check mark (✔) on it.
18. When I open Excel, I get a work___ which is a collection of worksheets.

### DOWN
1. The ___ box displays the location (address) of the active cell.
2. To use Excel, the program must be placed into ___.
3. A ___ is a formula created by Excel.
4. Each letter at the top of a column is called a column ___.
7. To have a marquee disappear, click the ___ (Esc) key.
9. When data is in the clipboard, the data is circled by a series of moving dots called a ___.
10. A vertical collection of cells.
12. To create an absolute reference, use a ___ sign.
14. A work___ is a series of columns and rows forming millions of cells.
16. Pressing the ___ key takes me to the cell to the right.

## EXERCISE 2: TRUE-FALSE
For each of the following eight statements, place a T or an F on the line to indicate if the statement is True or False.

1. ___Unless I instruct otherwise, cell references are relative.
2. ___To view formulas instead of the results, press Ctrl + F.
3. ___The Formula Bar Enter button has a "E" on it.
4. ___Relative cell references don't change when copied.
5. ___All formulas start with a "=" sign.
6. ___AutoSum is used to sum a column or row of values.
7. ___The Formula Bar Enter button has a "✔" on it.
8. ___A file consists of three workbooks.

## EXERCISE 3: MATCHING
Match the mathematical operators with the proper symbol.

| A. /   B. *   C. -   D. + |
|---|
| 1. ___ Add.      3. ___ Multiply. |
| 2. ___ Divide.      4. ___ Subtract. |

## EXERCISE 4: IDENTIFY TERMS
Below are six definitions. Below the definitions are six lines. In each line, write the word that matches the definition.

1. The toolbar button with an "∑" on it.
2. A cell reference that does not change when it is copied.
3. A cell reference that does change when it is copied.
4. All formulas begin with this sign.
5. The box that displays the location of the active cell.
6. The symbol used to create an absolute cell reference.

1. _____    4. _____
2. _____    5. _____
3. _____    6. _____

## EXERCISE 5: USE SIMPLE FORMULAS
In Exercise 7 (page E-6), you created an Arrest Report. You saved it to your diskette under the filename of "EP1-NYPD". Open that file. Save it as "EP2-NYPD". If you don't have it, redo that exercise and then do the following:

☞ In the cell below Jill's name, type Total.
☞ Use AutoSum to sum the values in each column.
☞ If you entered all the data and formulas correctly, the totals should be as follows: 1996 (469), 1997 (474), 1998 (362), and 1999 (467). If your answers differ from these, check the cell references in your formulas. A common problem in using AutoSum is that it adds values in cells and it will not know that the numbers in the top row are labels, not values. Therefore, AutoSum will add the years to the total. Fix the formulas. To do so, double-click in B10 and change the range of cells to B4:B9, thereby eliminating any reference to B3). Copy the corrected formula to the other cells. Then, if your totals still differ from mine, check to be sure the cells contain the correct data. Remember, anytime your answers differ from my answers, you are wrong and I am right. So, fix your mistake.
☞ In the cell to the right of the 1999 label, type Average.
☞ Insert a function to calculate the average number of arrests for each person over the four-year period covered by this Arrest Report. The answers are: Andy (100), Bobby (87), Diane (87), Greg (62), James (47), and Jill (60).
☞ Save your document (you will use this worksheet later).
☞ Print your worksheet. Close the workbook. Close Excel.

## EXERCISE 6: USE ABSOLUTE REFERENCES

When formulas are copied from one cell to another, the references within the formula typically change. Sometimes, we don't want that to happen. To prevent the references from changing, you would construct the formula so that it contains absolute cell references. To practice doing this, start Excel and follow the steps below to recreate the worksheet.

☞ The title is in cell A1.

| WONDER FURNITURE COMPANY WEEKLY PAYROLL | | | | |
|---|---|---|---|---|
| | | | | |
| HOURLY PAY: | | 3.52 | | |
| TAX RATE: | | .25 | | |
| | | | | |
| HOURS WORKED BY EACH EMPLOYEE: | | | | |
| | | | | |
| | KEVIN | WAYNE | PAUL | WINNIE |
| MON | 6 | 0 | 8 | 3 |
| TUE | 4 | 5 | 0 | 8 |
| WED | 8 | 0 | 7 | 6 |
| THU | 0 | 3 | 5 | 0 |
| FRI | 0 | 3 | 3 | 8 |
| SAT | 4 | 2 | 0 | 6 |
| SUN | 6 | 8 | 4 | 0 |
| HOURS | | | | |
| GR. PAY | | | | |
| TAXES | | | | |
| NET PAY | | | | |
| This Payroll Summary was created by Jack Arnold | | | | |

☞ Save the sheet to your diskette (call it EP2-Wonder).
☞ In the Hours row, insert a formula to sum each column.
☞ In the Gr. Pay row, use an absolute cell reference to compute gross pay (multiply hourly pay by hours).
☞ In the Taxes row, use an absolute cell reference to compute payroll taxes (multiply gross pay by the tax rate).
☞ In the Net Pay row, subtract taxes from gross pay.
☞ If you entered all the data and the formulas correctly, the Net Pay should have the following figures: Kevin (73.92), Wayne (55.44), Paul (71.28), and Winnie (81.84).
☞ In cell A20, replace Jack's name with your name.
☞ Change Winnie's Monday hours from 3 to 6 (notice that her gross pay, taxes, and net pay are automatically updated).
☞ Change the hourly pay to 4.08 (notice that gross pay, taxes, and net pay are automatically updated for each worker). The net pay is now Kevin (85.68), Wayne (64.26), Paul (82.62), and Winnie (104.04).
☞ Save the worksheet (you will use this worksheet later).
☞ Print one copy of your worksheet.
☞ Close the worksheet. Close Excel.

## EXERCISE 7: USE SIMPLE FORMULAS

In Exercise 8 (page E-6), you created a summary for Conner Construction Company. You saved it to your disk as "EP1-Conner". Open that file and save it as "EP2-Conner". If you don't have it, redo that exercise. Then do the following:

☞ In the cell below the Paint label, type Total.
☞ Use AutoSum to sum the values in each column.
☞ If you entered all the data and formulas correctly, the totals should be as follows: JAN (3204), FEB (3572), MAR (2365), and APR (6947). If your answers differ from these, check to be sure the cells contain the correct data. Then, if you find no errors, check the cell references in each of your formulas. Fix the errors before proceeding.
☞ In the cell to the right of the APR label, type Average.
☞ Insert a function to calculate the average expense for each type of material over the 4-month period covered by this Expense Summary. The answers should be: Drywall (449), Lumber (3123), Nails (28), and Paint (422).
☞ Save the worksheet (you will use this worksheet later).
☞ Print one copy of your worksheet.
☞ Close the workbook. Close Excel.

## EXERCISE 8: USE "COUNTIF" FUNCTION

In Exercise 9 (page E-6), you created a Work Schedule for the ER. You saved it to your diskette under the filename of "EP1-ER". Open that file and save it as "EP2-ER". If you don't have it, redo that exercise. Then create a schedule that calculates how many hours each doctor is scheduled to work during the week. To do so, follow the instructions below:

☞ Recreate the worksheet below (the title is in cell A30:

| Total Hours For Each Doctor | |
|---|---|
| Doctor | Hours |
| JC | |
| EC | |
| PB | |
| CW | |
| LK | |
| MG | |

☞ In cell B32, insert the CountIf function to determine the number of hours John Carter (JC) is scheduled to work during the week. Confused? Follow the steps below:
☞ Click in cell B32.
☞ Click Insert, Function. From the Category list, select All.
☞ From the collection of functions, select CountIf.
☞ In the dialog box, specify the range of cells. That is, in which cells should Excel look to find the data? (B3:H26).
☞ Then specify the criteria (what should Excel look for?). In this case type JC.
☞ Click the OK button. Notice the cell now tells you how many cells in the range contain JC, which tells you how many hours he is scheduled to work.
☞ Repeat these steps for each of the doctors.
☞ Your answers should be: JC (34) EC (19), PB (25), CW (31), LK (29), and MG (30).
☞ Save the worksheet (you will use this worksheet later).
☞ Print one copy of the worksheet.
☞ Close the worksheet. Close Excel.

The primary purpose of a worksheet is to incorporate formulas to convert data into information. However, to enhance a worksheet's appearance and to focus the reader's attention to its most salient parts, you should format the worksheet. In this project, you will learn how to format a worksheet. First, start Excel, close the task pane, and create the worksheet below.

☞ In cell B2 type JAN and the other months as shown.
☞ In cell A3, type INCOME and the other labels in column A as shown. Notice that some of the labels are so long that they "spill over" into column B. The contents of a cell will spill over if the adjacent cell is empty.
☞ Enter the values as shown.

|  | JAN | FEB | MAR | APR |
|---|---|---|---|---|
| INCOME | 1800 | 1800 | 1800 | 1800 |
| EXPENSES |  |  |  |  |
| HOME | 896 | 925 | 965 | 754 |
| AUTO | 256 | 239 | 368 | 372 |
| FOOD | 125 | 145 | 169 | 187 |
| TOTAL EXPENSES |  |  |  |  |
| NET INCOME |  |  |  |  |

☞ In cell B8 enter a formula that sums the three values above it to compute total expenses. Even though B8 appears to have the "spilled over" label from cell A8, ignore it and enter the formula. After you enter the formula, notice that the label in A8 is truncated (cut off). When a cell's contents are longer than the width of the column in which it resides, the contents will be truncated if the adjacent cell contains data.
☞ In C8, D8, and E8, enter a formula to sum the three values above each cell to compute total expenses for each month.
☞ In cells B9, C9, D9, and E9, enter a formula that subtracts total expenses from income to compute net income.
☞ If you entered the data and formulas correctly, the Net Income values will be as follows (if your values differ from these, figure out what you did wrong and fix it. After all, by now you know that when your stuff differs from my stuff, you are wrong and I am right):

| NET INCOME | 523 | 491 | 298 | 487 |
|---|---|---|---|---|

☞ Save the worksheet (name it EP3-Home Budget).

## CHANGE COLUMN WIDTHS

As mentioned above, if the data you enter is longer than the cell in which it resides, one of two things will happen. If there is nothing in the cell to the right, the longer-than-cell data will "spill over" into the cell to the right. If the cell to the right contains data, the longer-than-cell data will be cut short (truncated). All the data is still in the cell. You just can't see it. In such cases (and when you want to shrink the size of cells), you will want to resize the width of columns.

To practice automatically adjusting the width of a column to accommodate the widest entry in the column, do the following:
☞ Point to the border between the column A and the column B headers until the mouse pointer looks like a bi-directional arrow.

☞ Double-click. The width of column A adjusts so that you can see all the data in each cell in the column.
☞ Repeat these steps to adjust columns B, C, D, and E.

To practice manually adjusting widths, do the following:
☞ Point to the border between the column headers until the mouse pointer looks like a bi-directional arrow (in this case, point to the border between column B and column C).
☞ Drag the border to the right to widen the column or to the left to make if narrower. When it becomes the desired size, release the mouse button. As you drag, notice that the width of the column is shown. Drag the border to the right until the column is 6.14 characters wide. Release the mouse button.
☞ Repeat these steps for columns C, D, and E.

To practice adjusting multiple column widths, do the following:
☞ Select the columns (in this case, select columns B to E by dragging over their column headers).
☞ Click Format, Column, Width (by the way, you could also right click and find this command on the shortcut menu).
☞ Specify the desired width (specify 8). Click OK.

## CHANGE ROW HEIGHTS

You just learned how to adjust the column widths. Sometimes, you will want to adjust the height of rows. To do so, you can either use the menu bar command (if you have many rows to adjust) or you can drag the border (if you have a few to adjust). For now, there's no need to practice this. If you know how to change the width of a column, then you know how to change the height of a row.

## ALIGN DATA

Excel assumes that any data that begins with an alphabetic character (A, B, C, etc.) is a label and any data that begins with a numeral (1,2,3, etc.) is a value. By default, labels are left aligned in each cell and values are right aligned. You may want to change the way Excel aligns labels and values within each cell (or, even across multiple cells). Below, you will center labels within cells and then you will center a title across multiple cells. The method differs for each.

To practice changing alignment within a cell, do the following:
☞ Select the data (select the labels for the months).
☞ Click an alignment button on the toolbar (in this case, click the Center alignment button).

To practice centering data across cells, do the following:
☞ Type the data in the left-most cell in the range over which it is to be centered (type HOME BUDGET in cell A1).
☞ Select the cell containing the title and the cells to the right which define the range across which you want to center the title (in this case, drag over cells A1 to E1).
☞ Click the Merge and Center toolbar button (it has a lowercase "a" with an arrow on each side (←a→).
☞ The five cells are now merged into one cell and the title is centered within the newly-merged cell.
☞ Save the modified worksheet.

## CHANGE FONTS

The font type (shape of characters), the font size (dimension of characters), and the font color can be changed.

To practice changing the font, do the following:
- ☞ Select the cells containing the data to be changed (in this case, select the title "HOME BUDGET").
- ☞ Click Format, Cells, Font.
- ☞ Choose the desired font type (Arial) and size (18). Notice the variety of other font-related choices available.
- ☞ Click OK. Notice that the font of the title is Arial 18.
- ☞ Repeat the above steps to change the font of the labels in column A and in row 2 to Arial 12. If any label in column A is now truncated (cut short), widen the column so that you can see all of the labels in the column.

## APPLY ENHANCEMENTS

Enhancements include bold, italics, and underline. These are often applied to emphasize key points in a worksheet. You can apply one, any two, or all three of these enhancements.

To practice applying enhancements, do the following:
- ☞ Select the text to be enhanced (select the title).
- ☞ Click the Bold and the Underline toolbar buttons.
- ☞ Click anywhere outside of the selected text to deselect it.
- ☞ Select the labels in column A and in row 2.
- ☞ Click the Italic toolbar button.
- ☞ Click anywhere outside of the selected text to deselect it.

## SET THE MARGINS

To change the margins in an Excel Worksheet, click File, Page Setup, Margins and specify the desired margins. While there is no need to change the margins in your worksheet now, please take a look at how that would be done.

## INDENT LABELS

In word processing, to indent text, you press the Tab key. In a worksheet, pressing the Tab key makes the next cell the active cell. So, to indent text, use the Increase Indent toolbar button.

To practice indenting labels in a worksheet, do the following:
- ☞ Click the cell where the label resides (in this case, click the cell containing the label "Home").
- ☞ Click the Increase Indent toolbar button (it looks like a few lines of text with a small arrow pointing to the right). Notice that the word "Home" is now indented.
- ☞ Repeat these steps to indent the "Auto" and "Food" labels.

## CHANGE THE PAGE ORIENTATION

By default, Excel worksheets are printed vertically (called portrait orientation). If your worksheet is wider than it is high, it may be better to print it horizontally (landscape orientation).

To practice changing the page orientation, do the following:
- ☞ Click File, Page Setup. Click the Page tab.
- ☞ In the Orientation area, click Landscape. Click OK.
- ☞ To see the worksheet, click File, Print Preview.
- ☞ Click the Close button on the Print Preview feature bar.
- ☞ Since your worksheet is not wider than it is high, repeat the above steps to change the orientation back to portrait.
- ☞ To see the worksheet, click File, Print Preview.
- ☞ Click the Close button on the Print Preview feature bar.

## SELECT NUMBER FORMATTING

Worksheet values can be formatted in numerous ways (e.g., as money in various currencies or as scientific notation).

To practice applying number formatting, do the following:

- ☞ Select the data (drag over cells B3 to E9).
- ☞ Click Format, Cells, Number.
- ☞ Select a category (in this case, select Currency).
- ☞ If necessary, select U.S. Dollars ($) and 2 decimal places.
- ☞ Click OK. Notice that some cells contain a series of pound signs (#####), indicating that the cells are too narrow to display the values. This happened because you just made the values wider than they were by adding a dollar sign and two decimal places.
- ☞ Widen the columns so that ###### is removed from each cell and your values are fully displayed in the cells.

## APPLY BORDERS & SHADING

To enhance the appearance of a worksheet or to emphasize parts of a worksheet, you can apply borders and/or shading.

To practice applying a border, do the following:
- ☞ Select the worksheet (drag over cells A1 to E9).
- ☞ Click Format, Cells, Border.
- ☞ Select the desired border, style, and color (select any). Note: you must select the line style and color (on right side) before you select the border (on the left side).
- ☞ Click OK. Click elsewhere to deselect the worksheet.

To practice applying shading, do the following:
- ☞ Since we want to apply different shadings to various parts of the worksheet, click in A1 (since we previously merged A1 to E1 into one cell, the cell from A1 to E1 is selected).
- ☞ Click Format, Cells, Patterns.
- ☞ Select the desired shading (select any color you like).
- ☞ Click OK. Click elsewhere to deselect the cells.
- ☞ Select cells A2 to E9 (drag over the cells).
- ☞ Click Format, Cells, Patterns.
- ☞ Select the desired shading (select any color you like).
- ☞ Click OK. Click elsewhere to deselect the cells.

## USE AUTOFORMAT

You can rapidly improve the appearance of your worksheet by applying a preset collection of formats to it, whereby all of your previously-applied formats (borders, shading, etc.) will be removed and a coordinated set of formats will be applied.

To practice using the AutoFormat feature, do the following:
- ☞ Select the entire worksheet (drag over cells A1 to E9).
- ☞ Click Format, AutoFormat. Samples appear.
- ☞ Take a few minutes to look at the wide range of formats available here (scroll down to see more of them).
- ☞ Click the format you like, then click OK. The AutoFormat feature removes your formats and applies its own formats.
- ☞ Click anywhere outside of the selected text to deselect it.
- ☞ If you don't like the way your table looks, either apply another AutoFormat style or click the Undo button until you return to the way your table looked before you used AutoFormat.
- ☞ Type your name in cell A20.
- ☞ Save the worksheet. Print the worksheet. Close Excel.

## CLEAR FORMATS

By the way, a cell can contain either a label, a value, or a formula. In addition to one of these, a cell can contain formats (fonts, borders, shading, etc.). To remove a label, value, or a formula, select the cell and press the Delete key. To remove the formats found in a cell, select the cell and click Edit, Clear, Formats. If you want to remove everything in a cell (the label, value, or formula AND all the formats), then click Edit, Clear, All.

## EXERCISE 1: CROSSWORD

Use the clues below to complete the crossword puzzle.

### ACROSS

1. To copy data, I select it and then I click Edit, ___.
4. To remove formats, I would click Edit, ___, Formats.
6. In Exercise 7 on page E-14, Dopie's worksheet has a line around it. This line is called a ___.
8. Documents printed ___ will be 11" wide and 8 ½" high.
12. The ___ of a document relates to how the text is printed on the paper (e.g., 8½" or 11" width).
14. If the data you enter is longer than the cell in which it resides, and there is nothing in the cell to the right, the longer-than-cell data will "___ over" into the next cell.
16. To manually resize the width of a column or height of a row, ___ the border of the column or row header.
18. If the data you enter is longer than the cell in which it resides, and if the cell to the right contains data, the longer-than-cell data will be ___ (cut short).

### DOWN

2. Documents printed ___ will be 8½" wide and 11" high.
3. When I drag the border of a column header to resize the column, the mouse pointer looks like a two-pointed __.
5. A ___ identifies the data in a row or column.
7. To center data across cells, select the cells. Then click the Merge and ___ toolbar button.
9. To change margins or orientation, click File, Page ___.
10. ___ signs in a cell indicate that the cells are too narrow to display the values.
11. To indent text within a cell, press the ___ Indent toolbar button.
13. A ___ is a number to be mathematically manipulated.
15. Another way of saying "start" Excel, is to say "___" Excel.
17. Another name for memory.

## EXERCISE 2: TRUE-FALSE

For each of the following eight statements, place a T or an F on the line to indicate if the statement is True or False.

1. ___To remove formats, click File, Remove, Formats.
2. ___"Truncated" is a fancy word for "cut short" or "cut off".
3. ___The Center toolbar button centers data within a cell.
4. ___A single cell can contain both data and formats.
5. ___I can not change the widths of columns.
6. ___By default, a label will be left aligned in a cell.
7. ___If #### signs appear in a cell, the column is too wide.
8. ___I can put a border around a single cell.

## EXERCISE 3: IDENTIFY TERMS

Below are eight definitions. Below the definitions are eight lines. In each line, write the word that matches the definition.

1. The orientation of a worksheet printed 11" wide.
2. The A, B, C. etc. along the top of a worksheet.
3. The way data lines up within the cell.
4. The toolbar button used to indent data within a cell.
5. A word or phrase that identifies what is in a row or column.
6. A number that will be mathematically manipulated.
7. The 1, 2, 3, etc. along the left edge of a worksheet.
8. The orientation of a worksheet printed 8 ½" wide.

1. _____  5. _____
2. _____  6. _____
3. _____  7. _____
4. _____  8. _____

## EXERCISE 4: TRUE-FALSE

For each of the following seven statements, place a T or an F on the line to indicate if the statement is True or False.

1. ___I can put shading in a single cell.
2. ___Data in cell A6 may be truncated if data exists in B6.
3. ___By default, a label will be right aligned in a cell.
4. ___To use AutoFormat, click Format, AutoFormat.
5. ___Right aligned data will appear at the right end of a cell.
6. ___To remove formats, click Edit, Clear, Formats.
7. ___The dimension of the characters is the font type.

## EXERCISE 5: TRUE-FALSE

For each of the following seven statements, place a T or an F on the line to indicate if the statement is True or False.

1. ___Data in B8 may spill over into C8, if data exists in C8.
2. ___I can not change the height of rows.
3. ___By default, a value will be right aligned in a cell.
4. ___To use AutoFormat, click View, AutoFormat.
5. ___To remove formats, click File, Clear, Formats.
6. ___To set the margins, click File, Page Setup.
7. ___The shape of characters is the font type.

## EXERCISE 6: MATCHING

Below are two sheets of paper. Which one's orientation is portrait and which is landscape?

1. _____  2. _____

## EXERCISE 7: CREATE AND FORMAT A WORKSHEET

☞ Start Excel, close the task pane, and recreate the worksheet below. The following steps will provide needed details.
☞ Column A is 17 characters wide.
☞ Columns B through E are each 9.43 characters wide.
☞ The title is in cell A1 and it is bold 14-point Arial.
☞ The title in row 1 is centered across columns A to E.
☞ The subtitle in row 2 is 12-point Arial.
☞ The subtitle in row 2 is centered across columns A to E.
☞ All other labels and values are 10-point Arial.
☞ The months are bold, underlined, and centered in cells.
☞ In cells B6 to E6, multiply drinks sold and unit price.
☞ In cells B9 to E9, subtract expenses from gross income.
☞ In cell B11, add the net income for the four months.
☞ In cell B12, compute average monthly net income.
☞ Money values are in U.S. currency with 2 decimal places.
☞ Medium gray shading is applied to rows 1 and 2.
☞ Light gray shading is applied to all other rows.
☞ A thick single line borders the worksheet.
☞ A thick single line is under row 2.
☞ A thin single line is under the values in rows 5 and 8.
☞ A double line is under the values in row 9.

### DOPIE TAYLOR'S LEMONADE STAND

| Income Statement | | | | |
|---|---|---|---|---|
| | **JUN** | **JUL** | **AUG** | **SEP** |
| Drinks Sold | 136 | 256 | 196 | 76 |
| Unit Price | 1.31 | 1.26 | 1.34 | 1.34 |
| Gross Income | | | | |
| | | | | |
| Expenses | 17.14 | 26.88 | 28.81 | 11.17 |
| Net Income | | | | |
| | | | | |
| Total Income | | | | |
| Average Income | | | | |
| | | | | |

This Income Statement was created by Ernest T. Bass

☞ If you entered the data and formulas correctly, Total Income will be $781.20; Average Income will be $195.30. If your values differ from these, you made a mistake. Find your mistake and fix it before proceeding.
☞ Save the worksheet (name it EP3-Dopie).
☞ In cell A14, replace Ernest's name with your name.
☞ In cell A14, indent the text.
☞ Insert a new column at column A and a new row at row 1. If a Format Painter button appears, ignore it.
☞ Check for spelling errors (click in cell A1, then click Tools, Spelling to start the spell checker from the top of the sheet).
☞ Use Print Preview to view your worksheet.
☞ Change the Page Orientation to Landscape.
☞ Use Print Preview to view your landscaped worksheet.
☞ Save the worksheet (you will use this worksheet later).
☞ Print your worksheet. Close the workbook. Close Excel.

## EXERCISE 8: FORMAT A WORKSHEET

In Exercise 6 (page E-10), you created a Weekly Payroll Summary for the Wonder Furniture Company and saved it to your disk under the filename of "EP2-Wonder". Start Excel, close the task pane, and open the "EP2-Wonder" file. Save it as "EP3-Wonder". If you don't have it, redo that exercise. Then, follow the instructions below to format the worksheet.
☞ Resize columns A to E to be 15 characters wide.
☞ Center the title across columns A to E.
☞ Change the font of the title to Arial 14.
☞ Apply a dark, bold border around the worksheet.
☞ Apply Medium gray shading to the title row.
☞ Apply light gray shading to the remaining rows.
☞ Center the employee's names in the cells.
☞ Italicize and underline the title of the worksheet.
☞ Make the Net Pay figures in Bold.
☞ Save the worksheet (you will use this worksheet later).
☞ Print your worksheet. Close the workbook. Close Excel.

## EXERCISE 9: FORMAT A WORKSHEET

In Exercise 5 (page E-9), you inserted some formulas into an Arrest Report for the 15th Precinct and saved it under the filename of "EP2-NYPD". Open that file and save it as "EP3-NYPD". If you don't have it, redo that exercise. Then, follow the instructions below to format the worksheet.
☞ Center the title across columns A to F.
☞ Change the font of the title to Arial 12.
☞ Apply a thin border around the worksheet and around each cell in the worksheet.
☞ Apply Medium gray shading to the title row.
☞ Apply light gray shading to the remaining rows.
☞ Center the column headings in the cells.
☞ Apply bold enhancement to the title of the worksheet.
☞ Save your modified worksheet.
☞ Print your worksheet. Close the workbook. Close Excel.

## EXERCISE 10: FORMAT A WORKSHEET

In Exercise 7 (page E-10), you inserted some formulas into a summary for Conner Construction Company. You saved it to your diskette under the filename of "EP2-Conner". Open that file and save it as "EP3-Conner". If you don't have it, redo that exercise. Then, return to this exercise.
☞ Center the title across columns A to F.
☞ Apply a double-lined border around the worksheet, but not around each cell.
☞ Apply light gray shading to the title row.
☞ Center the column labels in the cells.
☞ Underline the title of the worksheet.
☞ Save the worksheet (you will use this worksheet later).
☞ Print your worksheet. Close the workbook. Close Excel.

## EXERCISE 11: FORMAT A WORKSHEET

In Exercise 8 (page E-10), you modified a Work Schedule for the ER at County General. You saved it to your diskette under the filename of "EP2-ER". Open that file and save it as "EP3-ER". If you don't have it, redo that exercise. Then, do the following:
☞ Format the worksheet using whatever borders, shading, enhancements, fonts, etc., you want.
☞ When the worksheet is the way you want it, save it (you will use this worksheet later).
☞ Print your worksheet.
☞ Close the workbook.
☞ Close Excel.

The smallest particle of information about a person or event is a field (e.g., first name, last name, city, state, zip ). A collection of related fields is a record (e.g., Dozer, Pannell, Las Vegas, Nevada, 89130). A collection of related records is a database. A database program permits you to store, organize, and retrieve data. The power behind a database program is its ability to retrieve data in customized ways. Customized lists can be retrieved based upon any field in the database. For instance, colleges use database programs which contain information about each student. When the college wants to send a schedule of classes for a remote campus to currently registered students who live near the remote campus, a mailing list can be created by extracting all the records for students who have zip codes that indicate they live near the remote campus.

### CREATE A DATABASE
☞ Start Excel and close the task pane.
☞ Widen columns A, B, and C to be 20 characters wide.
☞ Begin in A1 and type the data below.

| FIRSTNAME | LASTNAME | CITY | ST | ZIP |
|---|---|---|---|---|
| Chandler | Bing | New York | NY | 10152 |
| Bart | Simpson | Springfield | MA | 11144 |

☞ Continue entering data (the data found below). As you type data, Excel looks in the column for similar previously-entered data and may guess what you want to type in the current cell. For instance, when you start to type "Seattle", notice that Excel guesses the city to be Springfield. In this case, Excel is wrong. So, just continue to type the city as Seattle.

| Niles | Crane | Seattle | WA | 98132 |
|---|---|---|---|---|
| Hank | Hill | Arlan | TX | 79914 |

☞ Continue entering data (the data found below) in row 6. As you start to type "Simpson", Excel again guesses the name. In this case, Excel is right. So, accept the suggestion by pressing the Tab key and continue to enter the data as shown below:

| Lisa | Simpson | Springfield | MA | 11144 |
|---|---|---|---|---|
| Al | Bundy | Chicago | IL | 60612 |
| Walter | O'Reilly | Ottumewa | IA | 52501 |
| Marge | Simpson | Springfield | MA | 11144 |
| Dozer | Pannell | Las Vegas | NV | 89146 |
| Bobby | Hill | Arlan | TX | 79914 |
| Kelly | Bundy | Chicago | IL | 60612 |
| Frasier | Crane | Seattle | WA | 98117 |
| Bud | Bundy | Chicago | IL | 60612 |
| Cosmo | Kramer | New York | NY | 10103 |
| Homer | Simpson | Springfield | MA | 11144 |
| Peggy | Bundy | Chicago | IL | 60612 |
| George | Costanza | New York | NY | 10112 |

☞ Save the database to your diskette (name it EP4-Friends).

### EDIT A RECORD
To practice editing a record, do the following:
☞ Double-click the cell containing the data to be edited (double-click the cell containing Walter O'Reilly's city).
☞ Remove the "e" from "Ottumewa".
☞ Click outside of the cell to deselect it.

### FIND & REPLACE DATA
If you have a single record that needs to be edited, the above steps will work just fine. However, sometimes a single correction needs to be made in multiple locations. For instance, if an item of data was incorrectly entered in many places, you could use the Find and Replace feature to locate each erroneous entry and replace it with the correct entry.

To practice using Find and Replace, do the following:
☞ Click Edit, Replace.
☞ In the Find What box, enter the data to be found (in this case, you need to replace each instance of "Arlan" with "Arlen". So, type Arlan in the Find What box).
☞ In the Replace With box, enter the replacement data, which in this case would be Arlen.
☞ Click Find Next. The first instance of "Arlan" is found (you may need to move the dialog box to see the entry).
☞ To replace the data this time only, click Replace.
☞ The next instance of the incorrect entry is found.
☞ To replace all instances of the data, click Replace All.

### SORT RECORDS
You can sort the records using any field (first name, last name, city, state, or zip code) in the database. Because it is easy to sort your records in ways that you do not intend, it is always a good idea to save the workbook before you attempt to sort the database. This way, if you end up with a jumbled database, you can always close the workbook without saving it, and you can open the workbook in the condition it was in before you attempted to sort it. So, before continuing, save the workbook (simply click the Save toolbar button).

To practice sorting records, do the following:
☞ Select any cell in the database.
☞ Click Data, Sort. The Sort dialog box appears.
☞ Since your database has a header row identifying the various fields, select the Header row radio button at the bottom of the dialog box, if it is not already selected.
☞ In the Sort by drop-down list, click the field that you want the database sorted by (in this case, click City).
☞ Click a radio button, ascending (A -Z) or descending (Z-A). In this case, click Ascending, if it is not already selected.
☞ Click OK. Notice your database is now sorted in alphabetical order by city.
☞ Repeat the above steps to sort the database by State.
☞ Repeat the above steps to sort the database by Zip.
☞ Sort the database by Lastname.
☞ If the database sorted properly, go ahead and save it.

### DELETE A RECORD
To practice deleting a record, do the following:
☞ Select the row that contains the unwanted record (in this case, select the row with the record for Dozer Pannell).
☞ Click Edit, Delete.

## INSERT A NEW RECORD

It is often desirable to add a record to a database. Since your database is now in alphabetical order by last name, you might want to add a record to the database so that the newly-added record will be in alphabetical order as well.

To practice inserting a new record, do the following:
☞ Insert a row where you want the new record to reside (in this case, insert a new row where your name would go). Remember, to insert a row, click the row header and then click Insert, Rows. Notice that when you insert a row, the records that were in that row and in every row below that row move down one row to make room for the new row.
☞ In the newly-inserted row, insert a record of yourself.

## USE AUTOFILTER

In many databases, you may have hundreds, if not thousands of records. With such databases, there will be times when you will want to rapidly identify records that meet a certain criterion. To do so, you could use the AutoFilter feature.

To practice filtering records, do the following:
☞ Select any cell in the database.
☞ Click Data, Filter, AutoFilter. Notice that a drop-down arrow appears next to each field name in the first row.
☞ Click the AutoFilter arrow for the city field. Notice that the drop-down list contains each city found in the column along with some additional items (All, Top 10, and Custom).
☞ Click Springfield. Notice that records appear in which the city field is "Springfield". All other records are filtered out. Notice that the AutoFilter arrow changed color to indicate that the database has been filtered via this field.
☞ Click the AutoFilter arrow for the city field.
☞ Click All. Notice that all the records now reappear and the AutoFilter arrow reverts back to its original color indicating that the database is no longer filtered via this field.

Sometimes, you will want to create a list based on more than one piece of data. Say, that you want a list of the records for folks who live in either New York or Chicago. If you followed the steps above, you could obtain a list for New York or a list for Chicago. But, you could not create a single list. To create a custom list of this type, use the custom filtering feature.

To practice using custom filtering, do the following:
☞ Click the AutoFilter arrow for the City field.
☞ Click Custom from the drop-down list. The Custom AutoFilter dialog box appears with four text boxes.
☞ Click the list arrow in the top-left text box of the dialog box.
☞ Click Equals from the drop-down list.
☞ Click the list arrow in the top-right text box.
☞ Click New York from the drop-down list.
☞ Click the Or radio button.
☞ Click the list arrow in the bottom-left text box.
☞ Click Equals from the drop-down list.
☞ Click the list arrow in the bottom-right text box.
☞ Click Chicago from the drop-down list.
☞ Click OK. Note that records with a city field of either New York or Chicago appear. Other records are filtered out.
☞ Click the AutoFilter arrow for the City field.
☞ Click All. Notice that all the records now reappear.

To practice turning AutoFilter off, do the following:
☞ Click Data, Filter, AutoFilter. (AutoFilter arrows disappear).

## NAME A WORKSHEET

When you start Excel, a workbook with three worksheets opens, each of which is identified by a tab at the bottom of the screen. The current worksheet (the one with your database) is called Sheet1. When you use more than one worksheet in a workbook, you can organize the sheets by giving each tab a name that identifies what is in the worksheet. By doing so, you won't have to guess what's in each sheet.

To practice naming a worksheet, do the following:
☞ Double-click the Sheet1 tab. Its name will be highlighted.
☞ Type TV Friends. Press the Enter key.
☞ Repeat these steps to name Sheet2 Real Friends and name Sheet 3 Enemies.

## MOVE A WORKSHEET TAB

Sometimes, you will want to place the sheet tabs in a different order. For instance, you might have sheets for each month of the year, but they may not be in correct order. You would want to move the tabs so the months are in chronological order.

To practice moving worksheet tabs, do the following:
☞ Drag and drop the tab to a new location. In this case, since enemies are more important than friends (they can have a greater impact on your life than friends), move the "enemies" tab to be the first one in the list of tabs.

## INSERT A WORKSHEET

Sometimes, you will need more than three sheets in a workbook. For instance, if you need a sheet for each day of the week or for each month of the year.

To practice inserting a new sheet, do the following:
☞ Click Insert, Worksheet. A new sheet tab appears.
☞ Rename the new sheet tab, Relatives.
☞ Move the Relatives sheet tab so it appears as the third tab in the list of tabs (it should be between the TV Friends and the Real Friends tabs).

## DELETE A WORKSHEET

From time to time, it is common to want to delete a worksheet.

To practice deleting a worksheet, do the following:
☞ Click the sheet tab of the sheet to be deleted. In this case, you believe that you have no enemies. You are mistaken about that, but let's say that you believe everyone is your friend. Click the Enemies sheet tab.
☞ Click Edit, Delete Sheet. Notice the sheet tab disappears. Now, you only have three sheets.
☞ Save the workbook.
☞ Print the database.
☞ Close the workbook.
☞ Close Excel.

## USE A TEMPLATE

By the way, you don't need to construct each worksheet from scratch. Excel provides templates (patterns) of commonly-used worksheets (e.g., invoices, purchase orders, loan amortization schedules). To view them, click File, New. The New Workbook task pane appears. From the task pane, click Templates On My Computer (or General Templates). From this collection you can rapidly create a variety of worksheets. Take a moment and look at some of the templates available. Someday, you may need to use these. When done, close Excel.

## EXERCISE 1: CROSSWORD
Use the clues below to complete the crossword puzzle.

### ACROSS
1. Jerry, George, Elaine, and Cosmo are in ___ order.
5. Cosmo, Elaine, George, and Jerry are in ___ order.
6. To rapidly identify records meeting certain conditions, I use the ___ feature.
8. To delete a worksheet, click ___, Delete Sheet.
11. In an Excel database, each ___ contains a field.
12. To modify a record in a database.
14. To rename a worksheet tab, first you would ___ click the tab. Then you would type in the new name.
15. When you start Excel, you get a workbook which consists of ___ worksheets (how many?).
16. To move a worksheet within a workbook, drag its ___.
17. To rearrange the records in a database so that they appear in some type of logical order (e.g., alphabetical).

### DOWN
1. A collection of related records.
2. Is Dozer a cat?
3. A collection of related fields.
4. The smallest particle of information about a person or event (e.g., first name, last name, city, state, zip code).
7. In an Excel database each ___ contains a record.
9. Excel provides patterns for many common worksheets. Each pattern is a ___. To view one, click File, New.
10. To move data, I would select the data and then click Edit ___.
13. To add a sheet to a workbook, click ___, Worksheet.
14. To rearrange the order of records, click ___, Sort.

## EXERCISE 2: TRUE-FALSE
For each of the following eight statements, place a T or an F on the line to indicate if the statement is True or False.

1. ___To delete a worksheet, click Edit, Delete Sheet.
2. ___To delete a record, I can delete the row where it resides.
3. ___In an Excel database, each column is a record.
4. ___A field is the smallest bit of information about a person.
5. ___A person's first name is an example of a record.
6. ___AutoFilter will extract records that meet certain conditions.
7. ___By default, a workbook contains four worksheets.
8. ___Excel is a soda produced by the Coca-Cola Company.

## EXERCISE 3: IDENTIFY TERMS
Below are six definitions. Below the definitions are six lines. In each line, write the word that matches the definition.

1. A collection of related records.
2. The smallest bit of information about a person or event.
3. Sorting order that puts items in alphabetical order.
4. Sorting order that puts items in reverse alphabetical order.
5. A collection of related fields.
6. To extract database records that meet specific conditions.

1. _____    4. _____
2. _____    5. _____
3. _____    6. _____

## EXERCISE 4: TRUE-FALSE
For each of the following eight statements, place a T or an F on the line to indicate if the statement is True or False.

1. ___To delete a column, I can delete the row where it resides.
2. ___To add a worksheet, click Insert, Worksheet.
3. ___In an Excel database, each column is a field.
4. ___Sorting in ascending order would alphabetize the records.
5. ___In an Excel database, the top row identifies field names.
6. ___AutoClip will extract records that meet certain conditions.
7. ___To delete a worksheet, click Delete, Worksheet.
8. ___A phone number is an example of a field.

## EXERCISE 5: TRUE-FALSE
For each of the following eight statements, place a T or an F on the line to indicate if the statement is True or False.

1. ___I can rename a worksheet tab.
2. ___In an Excel database, each row is a field.
3. ___To find worksheet templates, click File, New.
4. ___To add a worksheet, click Add, Worksheet.
5. ___I can sort my database.
6. ___I can move a worksheet tab by dragging the tab.
7. ___To delete a field, I can delete the row where it resides.
8. ___A zip code is an example of a record.

## EXERCISE 6: MATCHING
A database, a field, and a record differ as to how much information each provides. Match each of the three terms below with a description of the amount of information it provides.

| A. Database | B. Field | C. Record |
| --- | --- | --- |

1. ___Least amount of information.
2. ___Not the least, but not the most amount of information.
3. ___Most amount of information.

## EXERCISE 7: CREATE, SORT, & FILTER A DATABASE

Dozer has decided that he wants a girlfriend. I've tried to tell him that he will end up with a lot of grief and a broken heart, but he won't listen to me. He has devised a plan to identify the perfect girlfriend. So far, he has created a database consisting of records for each candidate in the neighborhood. Please start Excel, close the task pane, make columns A to D 15 characters wide, and recreate Dozer's database (shown below). Note: your columns will be of different widths than those shown below.

| BREED | ORIGIN | IQ | HEIGHT (") |
|---|---|---|---|
| Beagle | England | High | 14 |
| Briard | France | Medium | 25 |
| Boxer | Germany | Medium | 23 |
| Bulldog | England | Low | 14 |
| Chihuahua | Mexico | High | 8 |
| Greyhound | Egypt | Low | 27 |
| Lhasa Apso | Tibet | High | 10 |
| Papillon | France | High | 10 |
| Pekingese | China | Medium | 9 |
| Afghan | Afghanistan | Low | 26 |
| Airedale | England | Low | 23 |
| Poodle | France | Medium | 15 |
| Brittany | France | Medium | 19 |
| Schnauzer | Germany | High | 19 |
| Dachshund | Europe | High | 9 |
| Dalmatian | Europe | High | 21 |
| Samoyed | Siberia | High | 21 |
| Braque Francais | France | High | 22 |
| Char-Pei | China | Medium | 19 |
| Chow Chow | China | Medium | 18 |

☞ Save your database (call it EP4-Dozer's Girlfriend).

☞ The boxer is moving to Iowa. Since Dozer isn't interested in a long-distance romance, please delete the boxer's record by deleting the row in which her record resides.

☞ Sort the database by Breed in ascending order.

☞ A 25", high-IQ, collie from Scotland has moved into the house vacated by the boxer. Insert a new record for her. To do so, insert a new row in the proper place (insert the new row so that the collie's record will appear in alphabetical order with the other dogs' records).

☞ Dozer has heard that French dogs are romantic. He also wants a girlfriend with a high IQ. Use AutoFilter to extract the records for dogs of French origin possessing high IQs.

☞ Since Dozer is intimidated by tall dogs (any dog over twelve inches tall), which dog should Dozer ask for a date? _____.

☞ Remove the filter.

☞ Save your database. Close the workbook. Close Excel.

## EXERCISE 8: WORK WITH MULTIPLE SHEETS

Sometimes, it is helpful to have more than one worksheet in a workbook and to have formulas that refer to the cells in the other worksheets. In this exercise, you will create an income statement for the first three months of the year. Then, you will create a statement summarizing the individual statements.

☞ Start Excel. Close the task pane.

☞ Notice that you get three worksheets.

☞ Name the sheets "Jan," "Feb," and Mar."

☞ Insert a new worksheet. Name it "Summary".

☞ Save your workbook (call it EP4-Q1 Budget).

☞ Move the "Summary" tab so it appears after the Mar sheet.

☞ In the Jan sheet, recreate the sheet below placing the title (Dozer, Inc.) so it is centered from A1 to B1 and the subtitle (Income Statement) so it is centered from A2 to B2.

| Dozer, Inc. | |
|---|---|
| Income Statement | |
| Revenue | |
| Expenses | |
| Net Income | |

☞ In B5, insert a formula to subtract Expenses from Revenue. At this moment, the values for Revenue and Expenses for this month are unknown, so the result of your formula will be zero. Later, we will know the Revenues and Expenses and when we insert those values, the formula will compute the correct Net Income.

☞ Copy the Jan sheet (the one you just created) and paste it into the Feb, Mar, and Summary sheets. Be sure to paste it so that it appears in cells A1 to B5.

☞ In each of the four sheets, widen Column A to be 14 wide.

☞ In the Summary sheet, click cell B3. Here you want a formula that sums the Revenue values in each of the prior 3 worksheets. To create this formula type = and go to the Jan sheet and click in the Revenue cell (B3). Type + and go to the Feb sheet and click in the Revenue cell (B3). Type + and go to the Mar sheet and click in the Revenue cell (B3). Then, press the Enter key. You are taken back to the Summary sheet where the result of the formula will appear. Since the Revenue values in the other worksheets have not yet been entered, the result is zero. Later, after the values for Revenue are inserted in each worksheet, the formulas you just inserted will compute the summary of those values.

☞ In the Summary worksheet, copy the formula you just created for B3 (Revenue) to cell B4 (Expenses). Again, since the first three worksheets have not had any values entered into them, the result for each formula is zero.

☞ Imagine that January has passed and you now know what the revenues and expenses were. Go to the Jan sheet and insert these values: Revenue (1425) and Expenses (851).

☞ Imagine that February has passed and you now know what the revenues and expenses were. Go to the Feb sheet and insert these values: Revenue (1865) and Expenses (1196).

☞ Imagine that March has passed and you now know what the revenues and expenses were. Go to the Mar sheet and insert these values: Revenue (2659) and Expenses (1392).

☞ Go to the Summary sheet. Your totals on the Summary sheet should be: Revenue (5949), Expenses (3439), and Net Income (2510). If you did not get these results, you did something wrong. Find the error and fix it.

☞ Save your worksheet. Close the workbook. Close Excel.

While the primary purpose of a worksheet is to convert data into information, the resulting information can be confusing to readers who get lost in its complexity. In order to simplify the interpretation of the information, you may want to transform it into a chart. By doing so, people can easily see the trends in the data and can compare various outcomes. In this project you will convert your worksheet to charts. First, start Excel, close the Task Pane, and create the worksheet below. Be sure that the title is centered across columns A-F in row 1.

| DOZER & ASSOCIATES SECURITY SERVICES PAYROLL | | | | | |
|---|---|---|---|---|---|
| | SAM | ACE | JAKE | JIM | MIKE |
| MAY | 125 | 125 | 60 | 30 | 40 |
| JUNE | 146 | 152 | 65 | 40 | 45 |
| JULY | 165 | 169 | 75 | 50 | 55 |
| TOTAL | | | | | |

☞ In the Total row, enter a formula to sum each worker's pay.
☞ Type your name in cell A45.
☞ Save the workbook (name it EP5-Dozer Security).

## CREATE A CHART
To practice creating a chart, do the following:
☞ Select the cells containing the data to be charted including the column and row labels if you want them to appear in the chart (in this case, drag over cells A2 to F5). Since you want to create a chart comparing monthly payroll for each person, do not drag over the totals in Row 6.
☞ Click Insert, Chart. The first of four Chart Wizard dialog boxes appears.
☞ Click the Standard Types tab. This tab provides a list of chart types on the left. For each chart type selected, a list of chart sub-types is displayed on the right.
☞ From the Chart Type list, click a chart type. Notice the sub-types displayed. Click other chart types and see what is available.
☞ Since you want a column chart, click Column.
☞ From the Chart Sub-type list, select the type desired (click the one at the top, left corner). Below the samples, you are told that this is a Clustered Column chart and what kind of data it best represents. Click the Next button.
☞ The second Chart Wizard box (Source Data) appears.
☞ Click the Data Range tab. Look at the sample of your chart. Below the sample are two radio buttons. Click the one that is not currently selected. Look at the sample of your chart. Notice that the data labels that were on the X axis switched places with the data labels in the legend. Click the other radio button to switch back to the way it was. Decide how you want your chart to display the data by selecting the proper radio button (in this case, leave the Rows radio button selected). Click the Next button.
☞ The third Chart Wizard dialog box (Options) appears. It has several tabs. You can explore them to discover what options are available. For now, click the Titles tab.
☞ In the Chart Title text box, type Dozer Security Payroll - Dozer Pannell (replace Dozer's name with your name).
☞ In the X-axis text box, enter Associates.
☞ In the Y-axis text box, enter Monthly Pay. Click Next.
☞ The fourth Chart Wizard dialog box (Location) appears.

Here you are asked if you want the chart placed in its own worksheet or on the current worksheet.
☞ Click the As Object In radio button (this will place the chart on the current sheet with the data from which it is derived).
☞ Click the Finish button.
☞ The chart appears. Click outside the chart to deselect it.
☞ Save your modified worksheet.

## DELETE A CHART
In the process of editing and formatting a chart, you may find that it becomes so ugly that you simply want to start all over with it. In such cases you will want to delete an existing chart.

To practice deleting a chart, do the following:
☞ Select the chart (point in the chart until the "Chart Area" tooltip appears). If the Chart toolbar appears, close it.
☞ Click. Sizing handles appear around the chart.
☞ Press the Delete key. The chart is gone.
☞ Click the Undo button to have the chart return.

## MOVE A CHART OR ITS OBJECTS
You may want to move a chart or an individual object within a chart. For instance, you may want to move the title box, the legend box, or plot area.

To practice moving a chart, do the following:
☞ Point in the chart until the "Chart Area" box appears.
☞ Drag and drop the chart elsewhere (in this case, move the chart so that its top, left corner resides in cell A10).
☞ Click outside of the chart to deselect it.

To practice moving chart objects, do the following:
☞ Point to the object (in this case, point to the chart title).
☞ Drag and drop it to its new location (in this case, move it to the left side of the chart).
☞ Click elsewhere to deselect the object.
☞ Repeat the above steps to move the legend to the bottom, right corner of the chart.
☞ Save your modified worksheet.

## RESIZE A CHART OR ITS OBJECTS
After you have created a chart, you may want to resize it. Or, you might want to resize individual objects (e.g., the plot area or the legend). You resize a chart or its objects the same way you resize a window or a graphic image.

To practice resizing a chart or its objects, do the following:
☞ Select the chart (point in the chart until the "Chart Area" tooltip appears).
☞ Click. Sizing handles appear around the chart.
☞ Drag and drop any handle to resize the chart (resize the chart so that it resides in the range A10:H25).
☞ Click elsewhere to deselect the chart.

To practice resizing an object in a chart, do the following:
☞ Select the object (point in the legend box until the "Legend" tooltip appears).
☞ Click. Sizing handles appear around the legend box.
☞ Drag and drop any handle to resize the legend box.
☞ Click elsewhere to deselect the object.
☞ Repeat the above steps to resize the Plot Area.

## FORMAT A CHART

You can customize the way the chart looks in numerous ways.

To practice formatting the title of a chart, do the following:
- ☞ Double click on the title. A dialog box appears.
- ☞ Click the Font tab and format the title as Arial 12-pt, Red).
- ☞ Click OK. Click elsewhere to deselect the object.

.

To practice changing the text in a title, do the following:
- ☞ Select the title. Sizing handles appear around the title box.
- ☞ Click in front of "Payroll" to place the insertion point there.
- ☞ Type Services and press the space bar to insert a space.

To practice changing a chart's bar colors, do the following:
- ☞ Double click a bar (in this case, double click one of the bars representing May). A dialog box appears.
- ☞ Select an area fill (select yellow).
- ☞ Click OK. Click elsewhere to deselect the object. Notice that the bars representing May are now yellow. Repeat these steps to make the June bars blue and the July bars green. Notice that your chart is nice and colorful. This is great if you have a color printer. However, some folks don't. Therefore, when some folks print a chart, their printer converts colors to shades of gray. Colors, which are easily differentiated on a monitor, may print in indistinguishable shades of gray. To overcome this, you can change the colors of the elements in your chart so that when they are converted to various shades of gray, the differences will be easily recognized. Or, you could use patterns instead of colors.

To practice using patterns, do the following:
- ☞ Double click a bar (double click one of the May bars).
- ☞ Select an area fill (select black at top left corner of samples).
- ☞ Click the Fill Effects button. Click the Pattern tab.
- ☞ Click any pattern you like. Click OK. Click OK.
- ☞ Click elsewhere to deselect the object. Note that all the bars that represent May have the pattern. Repeat the above steps to select different patterns for the June and July bars.

To practice formatting numbers, do the following:
- ☞ Double click a number (double click any number on the Y axis). A dialog box appears.
- ☞ Click the Number tab.
- ☞ Select a format (in this case, click Currency).
- ☞ Select U.S. Dollars ($) with no decimal places. Click OK.
- ☞ Save your modified worksheet.

## USE THE PRINT PREVIEW FEATURE

To see how the document will look before you print it, you can use the Print Preview feature. This is especially valuable when dealing with worksheets, because many worksheets will run off the page to the right or include charts that may not appear where you want them. By using Print Preview, you will save paper and toner by reducing the number of printouts.

To practice previewing the worksheet, do the following:
- ☞ Be sure the chart is not selected (if needed, click outside of the chart to have the sizing handles disappear).
- ☞ Click File, Print Preview. You will see a preview of the worksheet and the chart the way it will print out. Notice that the title looks stupid on the left side of the chart. You may want to move the title, but you can't change anything while in the Print Preview screen. So, you'll need to close this

screen and return to the normal view.
- ☞ Click Close on the Print Preview bar (don't click the Close button on Excel's title bar).
- ☞ Move the title so it is centered in the chart.

To practice previewing the chart only, do the following:
- ☞ Select the chart (click in it so the sizing handles appear).
- ☞ Click File, Print Preview. You will see a preview of the chart the way it will print out without the worksheet.
- ☞ Click Close on the Print Preview bar.
- ☞ Save your modified worksheet.

## PRINT A CHART

Your main concern in printing a worksheet is that the entire chart be printed at the proper location.

To print just the chart, do the following:
- ☞ If it is not already selected, click in the chart to select it.
- ☞ Click the Print toolbar button (looks like a printer).

To print the chart and the worksheet data, do the following:
- ☞ Be sure the chart is not selected.
- ☞ Click the Print toolbar button (looks like a printer).

## CREATE A PIE CHART

Some data is best represented with a pie chart, which gets its name from the fact that it looks like a pie, each piece of which represents specific data. Thus, pie charts are excellent for representing how the parts compare with each other and with the whole. Below, you will create a pie chart which represents the total salaries for each employee.

To practice making a pie chart, do the following:
- ☞ Select the cells containing the data to be charted (in this case, select cells B2 to F2 and the hold down the Ctrl key while you select the cells in B6 to F6).
- ☞ Click Insert, Chart. The first of four Chart Wizard dialog boxes appears. Click the Standard Types tab. From the Chart Type list, click Pie.
- ☞ From the Chart Sub-type list, select the specific type desired (click the one at the top, left corner). Click Next.
- ☞ In the second dialog box, make sure the Rows radio button is selected. Then click Next.
- ☞ In the third dialog box, type Total Payroll - Dozer Pannell as a title (replace Dozer's name with your name). Click Next.
- ☞ In the Fourth dialog box, make sure the As Object In radio button is selected. Then click Finish.
- ☞ Move and resize the Chart so it resides in A27 to H40.
- ☞ Double click on the pie. A dialog box appears.
- ☞ Click the Data Labels tab.
- ☞ Click the Value check box. Click OK.
- ☞ Click elsewhere to deselect the object. Notice that the actual value appears next to each slice.
- ☞ Double click on any value. A dialog box appears.
- ☞ Click the Number tab. Select a format (Currency).
- ☞ Select U.S. dollars ($) with no decimal places.
- ☞ Click the Font tab. Select Arial 8. Click OK.
- ☞ Click elsewhere to deselect the object. Notice that the dollars signs appear next to each slice.
- ☞ Save the workbook.
- ☞ Print one copy of this pie chart so that the only thing that appears on the printout is this chart.
- ☞ Close the workbook.
- ☞ Close Excel.

## EXERCISE 1: CROSSWORD
Use the clues below to complete the crossword puzzle.

### ACROSS
2. A work ___ is a collection of columns and rows forming millions of cells.
4. To get a context-sensitive shortcut menu, I would ___.
5. A vertical collection of cells.
8. All formulas start with an ___ sign.
9. Is Dozer is the smartest cyberdog on the planet?
12. The ___ is the part of a chart that contains the columns, lines, or pie that represents the data in a chart.
14. The intersection of a column and a row.
15. To ___ a chart or an element in a chart, I would click it.
16. Dozer Pannell is a Super Cyber ___.

### DOWN
1. The horizontal plane of a plot area is the X-___.
3. The name of the program we use to create worksheets.
5. A pictorial representation of my data that takes the form of columns, lines, or pie slices.
6. I can ask the Office Assistant a question by clicking ___.
7. To ___ a selected chart or element of a chart, I would simply click outside of it. The boxes mentioned in 11 Down will then disappear.
10. To save toner and paper, I often want to view my chart and worksheet before I print it out. To do so, I use the Print ___ feature, which shows me the page on-screen.
11. If I click in a chart or in any element of a chart, little boxes called sizing ___ appear on the borders and corners. I can then drag one of these to resize the chart. If I click outside of the chart, these boxes disappear.
13. The box in a chart that identifies the various columns, lines, or pie slices in the chart.

## EXERCISE 2: TRUE-FALSE
For each of the following seven statements, place a T or an F on the line to indicate if the statement is True or False.

1. ___The bars or lines of a chart appear in the legend.
2. ___Pie, line, column, and bar are types of charts.
3. ___The vertical plane of a plot area is the X-Axis.
4. ___To deselect a chart, click outside of the chart.
5. ___To delete a chart, select it and then press the Delete key.
6. ___I can resize the legend within a chart.
7. ___Once created, I can not move the title of a chart.

## EXERCISE 3: TRUE-FALSE
For each of the following seven statements, place a T or an F on the line to indicate if the statement is True or False.

1. ___The first step to creating a chart is to select the data.
2. ___The bars or lines of a chart appear in the plot area.
3. ___The horizontal plane of a plot area is the Y-Axis.
4. ___To select a chart, double click in the chart.
5. ___Print Preview lets me see the worksheet before I print it.
6. ___A chart is a pictorial representation of my data.
7. ___The boxes around a selected chart are moving handles.

## EXERCISE 4: CREATE A PIE CHART
In Exercise 11 (page E-14), you formatted a schedule of work hours for each doctor. You saved it to your diskette under the filename "EP3-ER". Open that file and save it as "EP5-ER". If you don't have it, redo that exercise. Then do the following:
☞ Create a 3-D pie chart that depicts the total number of hours each doctor is scheduled to work during the week.
☞ The title for the pie chart should be ER Hours.
☞ Move and resize the chart so that it covers the range of cells defined as A39:E47.
☞ Use Print Preview to see what the worksheet and chart will look like when printed. Will it all print on one page? If not, return to your worksheet and resize the columns, rows, and/or the chart until it will all print on one page.
☞ Save your modified worksheet with its new chart.
☞ Print your worksheet. Close the workbook. Close Excel.

## EXERCISE 5: CREATE A COLUMN & A PIE CHART
In Exercise 8 (page E-14), you formatted a Weekly Payroll worksheet for the Wonder Furniture Company. You saved it to your diskette under the filename "EP3-Wonder". Open that file and save it as "EP5-Wonder". If you don't have it, redo that exercise. Then do the following:
☞ Create a column chart that depicts the number of hours each employee worked during each day of the week.
☞ The title for the chart should be Wonder Furniture Payroll. and the label for the Y Axis should be "Hours Worked".
☞ Move and resize the column chart so that it covers the range of cells defined as A24:E36.
☞ Create a pie chart showing each worker's weekly net pay.
☞ The title for the pie chart should be Weekly Net Pay.
☞ Move the pie chart so it appears below the column chart.
☞ Resize the pie chart so it is as wide as the column chart.
☞ Use Print Preview to see what the worksheet and charts will look like when printed. Will it all print on one page? If not, return to your worksheet and resize the columns, rows, and/or the charts until it will all print on one page.
☞ Save your modified worksheet with its new charts.
☞ Print your worksheet. Close the workbook. Close Excel.

## EXERCISE 6: CREATE A LINE & A PIE CHART

In Exercise 7 (page E-14), you created an income statement for Dopie Taylor and saved it to your diskette as "EP3-Dopie". Open that file and save it as "EP5-Dopie". If you don't have it, redo that exercise. Then do the following:

☞ Create a line chart (any kind of line chart you want) that depicts Gross Income for each of the four months that the lemonade stand was in business.
☞ The title for the chart should be Dopie's Gross Income.
☞ Move and resize the line chart so that it appears below the data from which it is derived and is the same width as the data from which it is derived.
☞ Delete the legend in the chart.
☞ Create a 3-D Exploded Pie chart that depicts Dopie's Net Income for each of the four months.
☞ The title for the pie chart should be Dopie's Net Income.
☞ Move the pie chart so that it appears below the line chart.
☞ Resize the pie chart so it's the same width as the line chart.
☞ Use Print Preview to see what the worksheet and charts will look like when printed. Will it all print on one page? If not, return to your worksheet and resize the columns, rows, and/or the charts until it will all print on one page. Note: when you originally created this file, you were told to change the orientation to Landscape. Therefore, the document is still in landscape orientation. So, you might need to change the page orientation to portrait to make the worksheet and the two charts fit on one page.
☞ Save your modified worksheet with its new charts.
☞ Print your worksheet.
☞ Close the workbook. Close Excel.

## EXERCISE 7: CREATE A LINE & A DOUGHNUT CHART

In Exercise 10 (page E-14), you formatted a worksheet for Conner Construction Company and saved it to your disk as "EP3-Conner". Open that file and save it as "EP5-Conner". If you don't have it, redo that exercise. Then, do the following:

☞ Create a line chart depicting total expenses for each month.
☞ The title for the line chart should be Total Expenses.
☞ Move the line chart to appear below the data from which it is derived and resize it to be as wide as the data from which it is derived.
☞ Delete the legend.
☞ Create a doughnut chart depicting the average expense for each type of material.
☞ The title for the doughnut chart is Average Expenses.
☞ Move the doughnut chart so it appears below the line chart.
☞ Resize the chart so that it is as wide as the line chart.
☞ Use Print Preview to see what the worksheet and charts will look like when printed. Will it all print on one page? If not, return to your worksheet and resize the columns, rows, and/or the charts until it will all print on one page.
☞ Save your modified worksheet with its new charts.
☞ Print your worksheet.
☞ Close the workbook. Close Excel.

## EXERCISE 8: IDENTIFY ELEMENTS OF A CHART

Identify the following elements of a typical column chart.

1. _____The box identifying what each column represents .
2. _____Words that identify the chart (the name of the chart).
3. _____The box containing the actual columns.
4. _____The vertical line on the left side of the plot area.
5. _____The horizontal line at the bottom of the plot area.

## EXERCISE 9: CREATE A WORKSHEET & TWO CHARTS

Recreate the worksheet below which represents the sales activity of the salesmen for the Igit Wigit Sales Company. The data (representing millions of dollars in sales) is presented for each salesman for each of three years.

| THE IGIT WIGIT SALES COMPANY | | | |
|---|---|---|---|
| TOTAL SALES PER SALESMAN | | | |
| (In Millions of U.S. Dollars) | | | |
| | 1997 | 1998 | 1999 |
| Conner | 25 | 36 | 23 |
| Loman | 15 | 21 | 12 |
| Roma | 8 | 6 | 3 |
| Seinfeld | 11 | 27 | 19 |

☞ Compute the total sales for each salesman (if you enter the data and formulas correctly, your results will be as follows: Conner ($84), Loman ($48), Roma ($17), Seinfeld ($57).
☞ Each salesman gets a 6% commission. Compute each man's commission (if you enter the data and formulas correctly, your results will be as follows: Conner ($5.04), Loman ($2.88), Roma ($1.02), and Seinfeld ($3.42).
☞ Change the commission to 8%. Each person's amount of commission will automatically be recalculated. Your results should now be as follows: Conner ($6.72), Loman ($3.84), Roma ($1.36), and Seinfeld ($4.56).
☞ Apply enhancements, currency formats, borders, and/or shading, etc., to give the sheet a professional appearance.
☞ Type your name somewhere on the worksheet.
☞ If needed, widen columns to eliminate any truncation.
☞ Save the worksheet (call it EP5-Igit Wigit Sales Company).
☞ Create a clustered column chart that depicts the four salesmen's sales for each of the three years.
   ☞ Put the names of the salesmen on the X-axis
   ☞ Put the years in the legend.
   ☞ The title of the chart should be "Yearly Sales"
   ☞ The X-axis title should be "Salesmen"
   ☞ The Y-axis title should be "In Millions"
   ☞ Format the Y-axis values to be in U.S. dollars with no decimal places.
   ☞ Resize the chart so that it is the same width as the data in your worksheet.
☞ Create a 3-D pie chart that depicts total sales for each salesman.
   ☞ Put the names of the salesmen in the legend.
   ☞ The title of the chart should be "Total Sales"
   ☞ Resize the chart so that it is the same size as the column chart.
☞ Move the charts so that they appear below the data.
☞ Use Print Preview to see if the data and the two charts will all print on one sheet of paper. If they do not, resize the charts so that all of the stuff will fit on one page.
☞ Save your modified worksheet.
☞ Print your worksheet.
☞ Close the workbook.
☞ Close Excel.

## EXCEL COMPREHENSIVE
# E X E R C I S E S

## EXERCISE 1: TRUE-FALSE
For each of the following seven statements, place a T or an F on the line to indicate if the statement is True or False.

1. ___In an Excel database, each column is a record.
2. ___To select a column, I would click its column header.
3. ___To remove formats, click Edit, Clear, Formats.
4. ___If #### signs appear in a cell, the column is too wide.
5. ___"Truncated" is a fancy word for "cut short" or "cut off".
6. ___I can enter labels, values, or formulas in a cell.
7. ___Data in cell A6 may be truncated if data exists in B6.

## EXERCISE 2: IDENTIFY TERMS
Below are eight definitions. Below the definitions are eight lines. In each line, write the word that matches the definition.

1. The place where the address of the active cell is displayed.
2. Sorting order that puts items in reverse alphabetical order.
3. A vertical collection of cells.
4. A collection of related records.
5. A collection of worksheets that I will save as a single file.
6. The smallest bit of information about a person.
7. A matrix of columns and rows.
8. Each of these has an alphabetic name (A, B, C . . .).

1. _____   5. _____
2. _____   6. _____
3. _____   7. _____
4. _____   8. _____

## EXERCISE 3: TRUE-FALSE
For each of the following seven statements, place a T or an F on the line to indicate if the statement is True or False.

1. ___To select an entire worksheet, click the Select All button.
2. ___A record is the smallest bit of information about a person.
3. ___To view formulas instead of the results, press Ctrl + V.
4. ___To select a range of cells, I drag over the cells.
5. ___The Name box displays the contents of the current cell.
6. ___Unless I create more, a workbook will have 4 worksheets.
7. ___To move to the next cell, press the Tab key.

## EXERCISE 4: IDENTIFY TERMS
Below are eight definitions. Below the definitions are eight lines. In each line, write the word that matches the definition.

1. A synonym for "active" cell.
2. A cell reference that changes when it is copied.
3. The toolbar button with an "Σ" on it.
4. The 1, 2, 3, etc. along the left edge of a worksheet.
5. The A, B, C. etc. along the top of a worksheet.
6. The way data lines up within the cell.
7. The toolbar button used to indent data within a cell.
8. A word identifying the data in a row or column.

1. _____   5. _____
2. _____   6. _____
3. _____   7. _____
4. _____   8. _____

## EXERCISE 5: IDENTIFY TERMS
Below are six definitions. Below the definitions are six lines. In each line, write the word that matches the definition.

1. The intersection of a row and a column.
2. A collection of related fields.
3. A worksheet printed 11" wide has a this type of orientation.
4. A horizontal collection of cells.
5. Sorting order that puts items in alphabetical order.
6. Each of these has a numeric name (1, 2, 3 . . .).

1. _____   4. _____
2. _____   5. _____
3. _____   6. _____

## EXERCISE 6: TRUE-FALSE
For each of the following seven statements, place a T or an F on the line to indicate if the statement is True or False.

1. ___An active cell is the same thing as the current cell.
2. ___A worksheet is a collection of workbooks.
3. ___The address at the intersection of 3 and C is C3.
4. ___AutoSum is used to sum a column or row of values.
5. ___Each row has an alphabetic name (A, B, C, etc).
6. ___The Formula Bar Enter button has a "✔" on it.
7. ___Each column has an numeric name (1, 2, 3, etc).

## EXERCISE 7: TRUE-FALSE
For each of the following six statements, place a T or an F on the line to indicate if the statement is True or False.

1. ___All formulas start with a "=" sign.
2. ___The Center toolbar button centers data within a cell.
3. ___A horizontal collection of cells is a row.
4. ___I cannot add entries into the AutoCorrect feature.
5. ___The Formula Bar displays the location of the active cell.
6. ___Relative cell references don't change when copied.

## EXERCISE 8: IDENTIFY TERMS
Below are six definitions. Below the definitions are six lines. In each line, write the word that matches the definition.

1. A number that will be mathematically manipulated.
2. The symbol used to create an absolute cell reference.
3. Each row of an Excel database contains one of these.
4. A cell reference that does not change when it is copied.
5. The orientation of a worksheet printed 8 ½" wide.
6. All formulas begin with this sign.

1. _____   4. _____
2. _____   5. _____
3. _____   6. _____

## EXERCISE 9: KNUCKLEHEAD PAINTERS INCOME
Several months ago, my three cousins Zack, Zeke, and Zeb started a house painting business. Since they love the Three Stooges, they called their company Knucklehead Painters. A First Quarter Income Summary for Knucklehead Painters is provided (next page). Recreate the Income Summary and then represent the pertinent data with the requested charts. The steps that follow will guide you through the process and will give you details about various elements of the worksheet and the charts.

## PART A: CREATE AND FORMAT A WORKSHEET
- ☞ Enter your full name in cell A1.
- ☞ Change the width of column B to 20.
- ☞ Enter the title in B3 (title is in uppercase--capital letters).
- ☞ Center the title across columns B to E.
- ☞ Underline the title and format it to be in Arial 14-point type.
- ☞ Enter the subtitle (First Quarter . . . ) in B4
- ☞ Center the subtitle across columns B to E.
- ☞ Format the subtitle to be in Arial 12.
- ☞ Apply medium gray shading to the title and subtitle cells and light gray shading to all the other cells.
- ☞ Enter the column labels (JAN, FEB, MAR) in row 5.
- ☞ Center the column labels in each cell.
- ☞ Bold the title, subtitle, and the column labels.
- ☞ Format the column labels to be in Arial 12-point type.
- ☞ Enter the row labels in Column B.
- ☞ Indent the itemized expenses (Paint, Plaster, and Tools) once and indent "Total Expenses" twice.
- ☞ Save your work (call it EC-Knucklehead Painters).

### KNUCKLEHEAD PAINTERS
#### First Quarter Income Summary

|  | JAN | FEB | MAR |
|---|---|---|---|
| Revenue | 4259 | 3652 | 2569 |
| Expenses | | | |
| Paint | 1942 | 1697 | 1175 |
| Plaster | 125 | 425 | 256 |
| Tools | 85 | 46 | 57 |
| Total Expenses | | | |
| Net Income | | | |

## PART B: INSERT FORMULAS
- ☞ In the Total Expenses row, insert a formula that sums the three itemized expenses.
- ☞ In the Net Income row, insert a formula that subtracts total expenses from revenue to calculate the net income.
- ☞ When you complete the formulas, net income should be JAN (2107), FEB (1484), and MAR (1081). If your answers differ from mine, that means that I am right and you are wrong. So, go back and find your mistake. It may be that you incorrectly entered data in one or more cells. Or, perhaps you incorrectly constructed your formulas. Look at each cell to see where the problem lies.
- ☞ Display all values in U.S. currency with 2 decimal places.
- ☞ Make sure all the data is visible (nothing is truncated).
- ☞ Apply a border around the worksheet.

## PART C: CREATE CHARTS
- ☞ Create a clustered column chart depicting the itemized expenses (paint, plaster, and tools) for each month. Include a chart title that reads "Itemized Expenses".
- ☞ Resize the chart so it is the same width as your worksheet.
- ☞ Create a pie chart that represents net income for each month. Include a chart title that reads "Net Income".
- ☞ Resize the chart so it is the same width as your worksheet.
- ☞ Correct any spelling errors. Save your modified worksheet.

## PART D: PRINT YOUR DOCUMENT
Use Print Preview to see what your worksheet and charts will look like when printed. If they will print on one sheet of paper using portrait orientation, print it. If the worksheet and the two charts do not fit on one page, resize the worksheet columns, resize the charts, etc. until everything will print on one sheet. When all is good, print one copy. Close the workbook.

## EXERCISE 10: USING MULTIPLE WORKSHEETS
In Exercise 9, you created a worksheet using the first quarter data. Below is the summarized data for all quarters of the year.

> Quarter 1: Revenues (10480) and Expenses (5808).
> Quarter 2: Revenues (9854) and Expenses (5698).
> Quarter 3: Revenues (11524) and Expenses (6524).
> Quarter 4: Revenues (8654) and Expenses (4587).

Open a new workbook and create a separate worksheet for each of the quarters. Insert a formula that subtracts Expenses from Revenue to determine the Net Income for each quarter. When done, you will have four worksheets in one workbook. Each worksheet will simply list the Revenue, Expenses, and Net Income for that quarter. The 1st worksheet will look like this:

| Revenue | 10480 |
|---|---|
| Expenses | 5808 |
| Net Income | 4672 |

- ☞ After creating the first 4 worksheets, insert a new worksheet.
- ☞ Rename each worksheet tab (call them Q1, Q2, Q3, Q4, and Annual). Make sure the tabs are in the proper order.
- ☞ In the Annual worksheet, create a worksheet summarizing the data in the preceding four quarterly sheets.
- ☞ If your formulas and data are correct, net income in the Annual worksheet will be $17,895.
- ☞ In cell A20 of the Annual worksheet, enter your name.
- ☞ Save the workbook (call it EC-Annual).
- ☞ Print one copy of the Annual worksheet.

## EXERCISE 11: KNUCKLEHEAD PAINTERS DATABASE
The database below represents the gallons of paint in the back of the company truck. Recreate the database below.

| PAINT | TYPE | COLOR | GALLONS |
|---|---|---|---|
| Latex | Interior | White | 4 |
| Oil based | Exterior | Green | 11 |
| Oil based | Interior | Tan | 8 |
| Latex | Exterior | Brown | 6 |
| Oil based | Exterior | Yellow | 14 |
| Latex | Interior | Peach | 3 |
| Latex | Exterior | White | 7 |

- ☞ Click Tools, Spelling to check for spelling errors.
- ☞ Save your database (call it EC-Database).
- ☞ Sort the records (ascending) by type, by paint, and by color.
- ☞ Filter the database to find out how many gallons of yellow oil based exterior paint are in the truck.
- ☞ Close the workbook. Close Excel.

## PAGE E-5: EXERCISE 1

| Across | Down |
|---|---|
| 2. Tabs | 1. Workbook |
| 4. Formula | 3. Select All |
| 6. Enter | 5. Active |
| 7. Box | 9. Tab |
| 8. Worksheet | 10. Cancel |
| 11. Label | 11. Left |
| 12. Value | 14. Right |
| 13. Frame | 15. Column |
| 15. Cell | 16. Move |
| 19. AutoCorrect | 17. Row |
| | 18. Copy |

## PAGE E-5: EXERCISE 2
1. F: A vertical collection of cells is a column. A row consists of a horizontal collection of cells.
2. F: I can delete a column or a row.
3. T
4. T
5. T
6. T
7. F: The address at the intersection of row 3 and column C is C3.

## PAGE E-5: EXERCISE 3
1. T
2. T
3. F: The Formula Bar displays the contents of the active (current) cell. The location of the active (current) cell can be found in the Name Box.
4. F: Entries can be added to or deleted from the AutoCorrect feature.
5. T
6. T
7. F: Unless I create more, a workbook will have three, not two worksheets.

## PAGE E-5: EXERCISE 4
1. Column
2. Workbook
3. Row
4. Worksheet
5. Column Header
6. Name Box
7. Row Header
8. Cell

## PAGE E-5: EXERCISE 5
1. F: A worksheet is not a collection of workbooks. Instead, a workbook is a collection of worksheets.
2. F: I can add a column or a row.
3. T
4. T
5. T
6. T
7. F: Excel does have a spell checker.

## PAGE E-5: EXERCISE 6
1. T
2. F: A horizontal collection of cells is a row. A column is a vertical collection of cells.
3. F: Each column has an alphabetic name (A, B, C, etc). Each row has a numeric name (1. 2, 3, etc.).
4. T

5. F: The Name box is where the location of the active (current) cell is displayed. It's not where I type my name or anything else.
6. T

## PAGE E-9: EXERCISE 1

| Across | Down |
|---|---|
| 3. Formula | 1. Name |
| 5. Save | 2. Memory |
| 6. One | 3. Function |
| 8. AutoSum | 4. Header |
| 11. Equal | 7. Escape |
| 13. Absolute | 9. Marquee |
| 15. Relative | 10. Column |
| 17. Enter | 12. Dollar |
| 18. Book | 14. Sheet |
| | 16. Tab |

## PAGE E-9: EXERCISE 2
1. T
2. F: To view formulas instead of the results, press Ctrl + ~.
3. F: The Formula Bar Enter button has a green check mark on it, not an "E".
4. F: Relative cell references will change when copied. Absolute cell references will not change when copied
5. T
6. T
7. T
8. F: A file consists of one workbook. A workbook may contain numerous worksheets, but when you save the sheets, they are all saved as one workbook and they become one file.

## PAGE E-9: EXERCISE 3
1. D
2. A
3. B
4. C

## PAGE E-9: EXERCISE 4
1. AutoSum
2. Absolute
3. Relative
4. Equal (=)
5. Name Box
6. Dollar Sign ($)

## PAGE E-13: EXERCISE 1

| Across | Down |
|---|---|
| 1. Copy | 2. Portrait |
| 4. Clear | 3. Arrow |
| 6. Border | 5. Label |
| 8. Landscape | 7. Center |
| 12. Orientation | 9. Setup |
| 14. Spill | 10. Pound |
| 16. Drag | 11. Increase |
| 18. Truncated | 13. Value |
| | 15. Load |
| | 17. RAM |

## PAGE E-13: EXERCISE 2
1. F: To remove formats, I would click Edit, Clear, Formats.
2. T
3. T
4. T
5. F: I can change the widths of columns.
6. T
7. F: If #### signs appear in a cell, the column is too narrow to display its contents, not too wide.
8. T

## PAGE E-13: EXERCISE 3
1. Landscape
2. Column Headers
3. Alignment
4. Increase Indent
5. Label
6. Value
7. Row Headers
8. Portrait

## PAGE E-13: EXERCISE 4
1. T
2. T
3. F: By default, a label will be left aligned in a cell. Values are, by default, right aligned.
4. T
5. T
6. T
7. F: The dimension of the characters is the font size. The font type indicates the shape of the characters.

## PAGE E-13: EXERCISE 5
1. F: Data in B8 will not "spill over" into C8, if data exists in C8. Instead the data in B8 will be cut off (truncated) to allow the data in C8 to be seen. If no data is in C8, the data in B8 will "spill over".
2. F: I can change the height of rows.
3. T
4. F: To use AutoFormat, I would click Format, AutoFormat.
5. F: To remove formats, I would click Edit, Clear, Formats.
6. T
7. T

## PAGE E-13: EXERCISE 6
1. Landscape
2. Portrait

## PAGE E-17: EXERCISE 1

| Across | Down |
|---|---|
| 1. Descending | 1. Database |
| 5. Ascending | 2. No |
| 6. AutoFilter | 3. Record |
| 8. Edit | 4. Field |
| 11. Column | 7. Row |
| 12. Edit | 9. Template |
| 14. Double | 10. Cut |
| 15. Three | 13. Insert |
| 16. Tab | 14. Data |
| 17. Sort | |

## PAGE E-17: EXERCISE 2
1. T
2. T
3. F: In an Excel database, each column is a field. Each row is a record.
4. T
5. F: A person's first name is an example of a field, not a record. Remember, a field is the smallest particle of information about a person, place, thing, or event. A record is a collection of related fields.
6. T
7. F: By default, a workbook contains three worksheets, not four. I can create a fourth one, or many of them, but by default, I get three.
8. F: Excel is a sophisticated spreadsheet program produced by the fine folks at Microsoft. The folks at Coca-Cola make lots of great stuff, but they don't make the Excel spreadsheet program (not yet, anyway).

## PAGE E-17: EXERCISE 3
1. Database
2. Field
3. Ascending
4. Descending
5. Record
6. Filter

## PAGE E-17: EXERCISE 4
1. F: This statement makes no sense. A column is a vertical collection of cells and a row is a horizontal collection of cells. They are two different things and, therefore, you can't delete one by deleting the other one. Duh!
2. T
3. T
4. T
5. T
6. F: AutoFilter will extract records that meet certain conditions. I don't have a clue what AutoClip is--or even if it exists.
7. F: To delete a worksheet, click Edit, Delete Sheet.
8. T

## PAGE E-17: EXERCISE 5
1. T
2. F: In an Excel database, each row is a record. Each column is a field.
3. T
4. F: To add a worksheet, click Insert, Worksheet.
5. T
6. T
7. F: To delete a field, I can delete the column where it resides, not the row. Remember, fields reside in columns: records reside in rows.
8. F: A zip code is an example of a field, not a record. Remember, a field is the smallest particle of information about a person, place, thing, or event. A record is a collection of related fields.

## PAGE E-17: EXERCISE 6
1. B
2. C
3. A

## PAGE E-21: EXERCISE 1
**Across**
2. Sheet
4. Right Click
5. Column
8. Equal
9. Yes
12. Plot Area
14. Cell
15. Select
16. Dog

**Down**
1. Axis
3. Excel
5. Chart
6. Help
7. Deselect
10. Preview
11. Handles
13. Legend

## PAGE E-21: EXERCISE 2
1. F: The bars or lines of a chart appear in the plot area. The legend identifies what the various lines or bars represent.
2. T
3. F: The vertical plane of a plot area is the Y-Axis. The horizontal plane of a plot area is the X-Axis.
4. T
5. T
6. T
7. F: Once created, I can move the title of a chart.

## PAGE E-21: EXERCISE 3
1. T
2. T
3. F: The horizontal plane of a plot area is the X-Axis. The vertical plane of a plot area is the Y-Axis.
4. F: To select a chart, click in the chart. If I double-click in the chart, a dialog box will appear.
5. T
6. T
7. F: The boxes around a selected chart are sizing handles, not moving handles.

## PAGE E-22: EXERCISE 8
1. Legend
2. Title
3. Plot Area
4. Y-Axis
5. X-Axis

## PAGE E-23: EXERCISE 1
1. F: In an Excel database, each column is a field; each row is a record.
2. T
3. T
4. F: If #### signs appear in a cell, the column is too narrow to display its contents, not too wide.
5. T
6. T
7. T

## PAGE E-23: EXERCISE 2
1. Name Box
2. Descending
3. Column
4. Database
5. Workbook
6. Field
7. Worksheet
8. Column Header

## PAGE E-23: EXERCISE 3
1. T
2. F: A field is the smallest bit of information about a person, place, thing, or event. A record is a collection of related fields.
3. F: To view the formulas in the cells instead of the results, press Ctrl + ~.
4. T
5. F: The Name box displays the location of the current (active) cell; the Formula Bar displays the contents of the current (active) cell.
6. F: Unless I create more, a workbook will have three worksheets, not four.
7. T

## PAGE E-23: EXERCISE 4
1. Current
2. Relative Reference
3. AutoSum
4. Row Headers
5. Column Headers
6. Alignment
7. Increase Indent
8. Label

## PAGE E-23: EXERCISE 5
1. Cell
2. Record
3. Landscape
4. Row
5. Ascending
6. Row Headers

## PAGE E-23: EXERCISE 6
1. T
2. F: A worksheet is not a collection of workbooks. Instead, a workbook is a collection of worksheets.
3. T
4. T
5. F: Each row has a numeric name (1, 2, 3, etc). Each column has an alphabetic name (A, B, C, etc).
6. T
7. F: Each column has an alphabetic name (A, B, C, etc). Each row has a numeric name (1, 2, 3, etc).

## PAGE E-23: EXERCISE 7
1. T
2. T
3. T
4. F: Entries can be added to or deleted from the AutoCorrect feature.
5. F: The Formula Bar displays the contents of the active (current) cell. The Name box displays the location of the active (current) cell.
6. F: Relative cell references change when copied. Absolute cell references do not change when copied.

## PAGE E-23: EXERCISE 8
1. Value
2. Dollar Sign ($)
3. Record
4. Absolute Reference
5. Portrait
6. Equal (=)

**A drive**: A secondary storage device that writes to and reads from a floppy disk. Also called a floppy drive.

**absolute references**: A cell reference in a formula that does not change when the formula is copied elsewhere. The opposite of a relative reference. A relative reference is converted into an absolute reference by placing a dollar sign in front of the row and/or the column reference.

**active cell**: The cell into which typed data will be entered (i.e., the selected cell). Also called the current cell.

**address**: The location of a cell denoted by the column and row heading (e.g., the intersection of column E and row 6, creates a cell with an address of E6).

**alignment**: The way the data lines up within a cell or across multiple cells.

**AutoCorrect**: A feature that corrects commonly-misspelled words and capitalizes the first word in each sentence automatically.

**AutoComplete**: A feature that automatically completes partially entered data. For instance, if you enter "Seattle" in a worksheet, and later in that same column you type an "S", AutoComplete will guess that you intend to enter Seattle again and will do so for you. If you did not intend to enter "Seattle" continue to type and the guess will disappear. If you did intend to enter "Seattle", simply press the Tab key to accept the guess.

**AutoFill**: A feature that permits the rapid entry of sequential data. For instance, if you type Monday in cell A1 and drag the fill handle to cell G1, the remaining days of the week will be entered in those cells.

**AutoFilter**: A feature used to extract records that meet prescribed conditions.

**AutoFormat**: A feature that applies a preset collection of formats to a worksheet.

**AutoSum**: A feature that will rapidly sum the values in a column or row.

**backspace key**: The key that deletes data to the left of the insertion point.

**cell**: The intersection of a row and a column wherein labels, values, formulas, and/or formats reside.

**chart**: A pictorial representation of data, generally in the form of columns, lines, or a pie.

**Chart Wizard**: A series of dialog boxes that ask me to provide the specific details during the creation of a chart.

**click**: The act of rapidly pressing the left mouse button one time, generally done to select an on-screen object.

**close**: The process of removing a file or a program from memory.

**column**: A vertical collection of cells.

**copy**: To place text elsewhere while maintaining the original text where it was.

**current cell**: The cell into which typed data will be entered (i.e., the selected cell). Also called the active cell.

**delete**: To remove (erase).

**delete key**: The key that deletes data to the right of the insertion point.

**Dozer**: The smartest cyberdog on the planet.

**double-click**: The act of rapidly pressing the left mouse button two times.

**drag**: To move the mouse.

**drag and drop**: The act of pointing to an object on the screen, holding down the left mouse button, moving the mouse, and then releasing the mouse button, thereby moving the object. In essence you have dragged and then dropped the object.

**edit**: To modify a document.

**enhancements**: Bold, italics, and underline.

**Excel**: Software created by Microsoft that permits complex and rapid manipulation of values.

**field**: The smallest particle of information about a person or an event (e.g., first name, or last name, or zip code).

**fill handle**: The little black box at the bottom right corner of a selected cell that, when dragged, fills adjacent cells with data utilizing the AutoFill feature.

**filtering**: Extracting records from a database that meet certain conditions. Also, having unwanted mail diverted to the Trash folder instead of being sent to the Inbox.

**font color**: The color of the characters.

**font size**: The dimension of the characters.

**font type**: The shape of the characters.

**format painter**: A feature that will copy the formats residing in text and will apply those same formats to other text.

**formula**: The instructions that tell Excel how to manipulate the values in other cells.

**formula bar**: The location (below the toolbar) where the contents of the current (active) cell are displayed.

**functions**: A collection of formulas provided by Excel.

**insertion point**: The on-screen blinking vertical line identifying where entered text will appear. Some folks refer to this as a cursor.

**landscape orientation**: A document printed on paper that is 11 inches wide and 8-1/2 inches high.

**launch**: To put a program or data into memory. Also called start, load, or open.

**load**: To place a program or data into memory. Also called start, launch, or open.

**margins**: The space between the text and the edges of the paper.

**marquee**: Aa blinking dotted border which looks like a theater marquee.

**maximize button**: The button (on the title bar) that, when clicked, will make the window fill the entire screen.

**memory**: The temporary location where the data and programs currently being used by a processor reside. Also called RAM (an acronym for Random Access Memory).

**menu bar**: The bar (under the title bar) which consists of a series of command categories. To access specific commands in a category, click the item on the menu bar.

**minimize button**: The button that, when clicked, will make the window become the size of a taskbar button.

**move**: To place text elsewhere while removing the original text from where it was.

**move handle**: A vertical bar on a toolbar that, when dragged, will allow the user to move the toolbar.

**name box**: The box that displays the address of the current (active) cell.

**office assistant**: A Microsoft help feature that displays a character in the form of a paper clip that asks you to pose a question for him to answer.

**open**: To place a program or data into memory. Also called start, load, or launch.

**page breaks**: The location in a worksheet where the printer will cease to print one page and will load another sheet of paper before continuing to print. Page breaks are automatically inserted whenever your document contains more data than can be printed on one page.

**page orientation**: The way the print appears on the page. If 11" wide, the page has a landscape orientation; if 8-12" wide, the page has a portrait orientation.

**paste options button**: A button that appears below text that has been copied and then pasted into a document. If you click the Paste Options button you will be able to select how you want to paste the text.

**portrait orientation**: A document printed on paper that is 8-1/2 inches wide and 11 inches high.

**print preview**: A feature that permits you to see how each page of your document will look before you print the document.

**record**: In a database, a collection of fields about a particular person or event.

**redo button**: The toolbar button that, when clicked, will undo the last undo done. It has a crooked arrow pointing to the right.

**references**: The cell addresses in a formula.

**right-click**: The act of rapidly pressing the right mouse button one time.

**row**: A horizontal line of cells in a worksheet.

**save**: The act of placing a copy of the document that is currently in memory into secondary storage.

**select**: To identify an object, text, or image to which you wish to do something.

**select all button**: The button at the top left corner of the worksheet frame that, when clicked, will select all the cells in the worksheet.

**shortcut menu**: A context-sensitive menu that appears when I right click. Also called a Quick Menu.

**sort**: To rearrange records in a database in some logical order.

**spreadsheet**: A collection of rows and columns forming cells into which data is entered for the primary purpose of mathematically manipulating the values. Also called a worksheet.

**tab key**: The key used to indent a line in word processing or to move from cell to cell in a table or in a worksheet.

**task pane**: A pane that sometimes appears at the right side of the screen which provides for rapid selection of features.

**taskbar**: The horizontal grey bar, typically at the bottom of the desktop, upon which the Start button resides.

**template**: A document file with customized format, content, and features, usually accessed by clicking File, New in the program.

**toolbar**: A collection of picture buttons that, when clicked, execute a command. These buttons typically appear below the menu bar.

**undo button**: The toolbar button that, when clicked, will reverse the last action taken. It has a crooked arrow pointing to the left.

**view**: A menu bar item that lets me choose the way stuff looks on the screen. For instance, in My Computer, the way the icons appear (thumbnails, tiles, icons, list, or details).

**workbook**: A collection of worksheets that, when saved, becomes one file.

**worksheet**: A collection of rows and columns forming cells into which data is entered for the primary purpose of mathematically manipulating the values. Also called a spreadsheet.

# DOZER'S QUINTESSENTIAL GUIDE TO MICROSOFT® POWERPOINT®

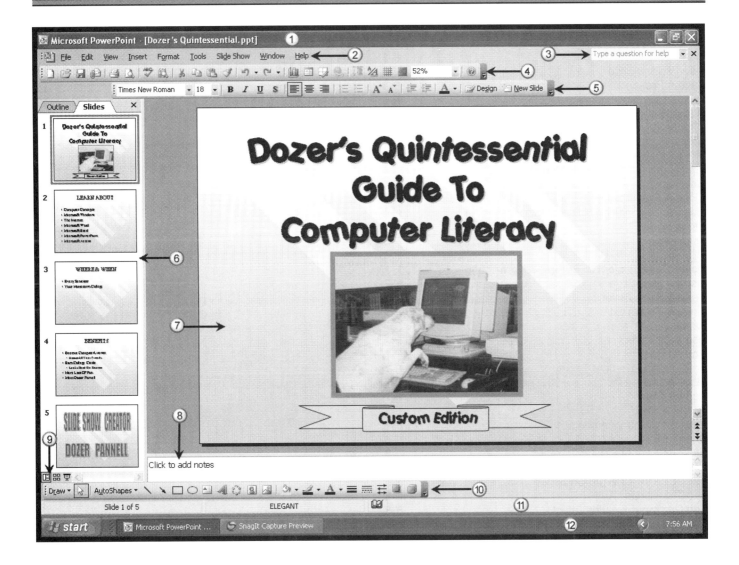

1. Title bar (identifies the program and the document being used)
2. Menu bar (collection of menu items, each of which contains commands)
3. Help (a great place to find answers to all your questions)
4. Standard toolbar (collection of picture buttons, each of which accesses a command)
5. Formatting toolbar (collection of picture buttons, each of which accesses a command)
6. Slide/Outline pane (displays either thumbnails or outlines of your slides)
7. Slide pane (displays the selected slide)
8. Notes pane (displays speaker notes)
9. View toolbar (changes the way your slides appear on the screen)
10. Drawing toolbar (buttons for drawing objects in your slides)
11. Status bar (displays information, such as the number of slides and type of template used)
12. Taskbar (contains the Start button, open windows buttons, etc.)

## Dozer's Quintessential Guide To Microsoft PowerPoint
# TABLE OF CONTENTS

In addition to allowing us to present our ideas in a variety of dynamic ways via a computerized slide show, PowerPoint permits us to create a hard copy of our slide show in paper or overhead transparency form. The opportunities to inspire and educate an audience via PowerPoint are endless.

## START (LOAD, OPEN, LAUNCH) POWERPOINT
To use PowerPoint, it must be placed into memory (RAM).

To start PowerPoint, do the following:
☞ Click the Start taskbar button. Point to All Programs.
☞ On the sub-menu, click Microsoft PowerPoint (If you don't see it, open additional menus until you find it).

## SURVEY THE POWERPOINT SCREEN
The PowerPoint screen contains elements that are common to many Windows-based programs, including:
☞ Title bar (top of screen) identifies the program and presentation being used. In addition, the Close, Minimize, Maximize, and Restore buttons reside on the title bar.
☞ Menu bar (below title bar) contains command categories (when one is clicked, a list of commands appears. To see all the commands, click the double-down arrow on the list).
☞ Toolbars (below menu bar) consist of picture buttons. If clicked, a command is executed. Each toolbar has a Move handle (vertical bar) at its left edge. If you point the mouse to a Move handle, the pointer will become a four-pointed arrow. If the Standard and Formatting toolbars appear in one line, drag the Move handle of the Formatting toolbar down so that the Formatting toolbar occupies its own line. Otherwise, you won't be able to see all the toolbar buttons.
☞ PowerPoint window (space where your slides reside).

## USE THE TASK PANE
From time to time, the task pane will appear on the right side of the screen. Its contents change, depending on what you are doing. Since you just started PowerPoint, the task pane wants to know what you want to do (if the task pane is not visible, click View, Task Pane to have it appear). Since you want to create a new presentation, just close the task pane (click the X at the top right corner of the task pane). The task pane disappears, but it will appear later as you attempt other tasks.

## CHOOSE A LAYOUT
When you create a new slide show, PowerPoint provides a Title layout for Slide 1 and a Title And Text layout for subsequent slides. If you don't want these layouts for your slides, you can choose others. For now, we'll use the layouts PowerPoint chooses. Later, we'll choose our own layouts.

## INSERT TEXT
Text is placed in text boxes (also called placeholders).

To practice inserting text in a text box, do the following:
☞ Click in the Title text box (placeholder). That is, click in the box that says "Click To Add Title".
☞ Type your Text (In this case, type Dozer's Quintessential Guide To Computer Literacy).
☞ Click in the Subtitle placeholder.
☞ Type your text (in this case, type Custom Edition).

## INSERT A NEW SLIDE
To practice inserting new slides, do the following:
☞ Click Insert, New Slide (or click the New Slide button which is on the Formatting toolbar). A Title And Text slide appears.
☞ Click in the Title placeholder and type LEARN ABOUT.
☞ Click in the Text placeholder and type the following list:

Computer Concepts
Microsoft Windows
The Internet
Microsoft Word
Microsoft Excel
Microsoft PowerPoint

☞ Click Insert, New Slide (or click the New Slide button). A new Title And Text slide appears.
☞ Click in the Title placeholder and type BENEFITS.
☞ Click in the Text placeholder and type the following list:

Become Computer Literate
Amaze All Your Friends
Earn College Credits
Looks Good On Resume
Have Lots Of Fun
Meet Dozer Pannell

☞ Click Insert, New Slide (or click the New Slide button). A Title And Text slide appears. But, this time, you don't want a bulleted list. You want a Title Only slide. So, to change the layout, point the mouse to various layouts in the task pane. Notice that as you point to each, its name appears. When you find the Title Only slide (not the Title Slide, but the Title Only slide), click it. Notice that the Title And Text slide has been replaced with a Title Only slide.
☞ In the placeholder, type Slide Show Creator: X (replace X with your name).

## SAVE A PRESENTATION (SLIDE SHOW)
While creating a presentation, it resides in memory. To be able to retrieve it later, you will want to save your slide show.

To practice saving a slide show, do the following:
☞ Insert a diskette into the floppy drive.
☞ Click File, Save (the Save As dialog box opens).
☞ From the Save In list box, select the 3 ½ Floppy (A:) drive.
☞ In the File Name box, enter the name PP1-Dozer's Guide.
☞ Click the Save button.

## CHANGE VIEWS
There exists more than one way to view the contents of the PowerPoint window. The views are changed by clicking the buttons on the View toolbar (the itsy bitsy toolbar located near the bottom left corner of the window. By the way, "itsy bitsy" is a highly-technical term meaning very small). The views are:

| View | Contents |
|---|---|
| Normal | Displays Slide, Outline/slide, & Notes panes |
| Slide Sorter | Displays multiple thumbnail slides |
| Slide Show | Runs the slide show |

To practice changing the view, do the following:
- ☞ Click the Slide Sorter View button on the View toolbar. Notice that thumbnails of all four slides appear.
- ☞ Click the Normal View button on the View toolbar. Three panes appear: A slide pane, an outline/slide pane, and a notes pane. Notice the outline/slide pane (left pane) has two tabs and a Close button. The Outline tab displays an outline of the text in each slide; the Slide tab displays a thumbnail of each slide. Click each tab to see the different views. If you can't see the thumbnails, drag the right edge of the outline/slide pane to the right to enlarge the pane. If you click the close button in the outline/slide pane, the entire pane will go bye-bye. To have it reappear, click the Normal View button on the View toolbar.
- ☞ The Slide Show button will be described in the next section.

## RUN A PRESENTATION (SLIDE SHOW)
To practice running a presentation, do the following:
- ☞ In the Outline/slide pane (left side of screen) click Slide 1 (this will tell PowerPoint to start the slide show with Slide 1).
- ☞ Click the Slide Show button on the View toolbar (the first slide appears).
- ☞ When you want the next slide to appear, click the mouse. Continue to click until you get to the end of the slide show.
- ☞ When told that you have reached the end of the slide show, click anywhere on the screen. Note that if you ever want to end a slide show before you view all the slides, right click on the slide and click End Show or press the Esc key.

## CHOOSE A DESIGN TEMPLATE
You can apply a design template (background scheme) for your slides. Dozens of design templates are provided.

To practice choosing a design template, do the following:
- ☞ Click Format, Slide Design (or click the Design button which is on the Formatting toolbar).
- ☞ In the Slide Design task pane, use the scroll bar to view the variety of designs available for use.
- ☞ Point the mouse to any one and you will be told its name.
- ☞ Find the Capsules template and click it (if your machine does not have the Capsules template, pick another one).
- ☞ Run your slide show again. It should be much prettier.

## CREATE A PLACEHOLDER (TEXT BOX)
When creating a slide show, some slides have placeholders in which you enter your desired text. The number and location of placeholders is determined by the layout chosen. For instance, the Title And Text slide layout has two placeholders, one on top of the other; the Title and 2-Column Text slide layout has a placeholder at the top and two below it so that your slide can have two columns of text. When you want to have additional text boxes on a slide, you can create some.

To practice creating a text box, do the following:
- ☞ In Normal View, select Slide 1. Click Insert, Text Box.
- ☞ Move the mouse pointer onto the slide (notice that the mouse pointer looks like an upside-down cross).
- ☞ Drag to create a text box (in this case create a one-inch long text box under "Custom Edition").
- ☞ In the text box, type Written by Steve Pannell). Don't be concerned If your text wraps into two lines. We'll fix that later. For now, just type the line of text and then click outside of the box to deselect it.
- ☞ Save your modified slide show.

## MOVE AND RESIZE A PLACEHOLDER
As previously mentioned, placeholder locations are determined by the layout chosen. On the other hand, when you create your own placeholders (text boxes), they appear where you create them. Sometimes, you'll want to move or resize a placeholder.

To practice moving and resizing a placeholder, do the following:
- ☞ In Slide 1, click on "Written by Steve Pannell" to select its text box.
- ☞ Point to a sizing handle. The mouse pointer turns into a two-pointed arrow. Drag the handle so that the text box is just long enough so that the text does not wrap within the box, but not longer than is needed to display its contents.
- ☞ Put the mouse pointer on one of the borders until the mouse pointer looks like a four-pointed arrow.
- ☞ Drag the text box to the desired location (in this case, drag it to the bottom right corner of the slide).
- ☞ Save your modified slide show.
- ☞ Starting from Slide 1, run your slide show.

## PRINT A PRESENTATION (SLIDE SHOW)
You can print your slide show in a variety of ways. For instance, you can print each slide on a separate sheet of paper, or you can print up to nine slides on a single sheet.

To practice printing handouts of your slides, do the following:
- ☞ Click File, Print. The Print dialog box appears.
- ☞ If you wanted to print each slide on a separate sheet of paper, you would indicate which slides to print in the Print Range area. For now, let's not print slides this way.
- ☞ To print up to nine slides on a single handout, select Handouts in the Print What list box.
- ☞ In the Color/Grayscale box, select Color. Do this even if you don't have a color printer. Otherwise, some slides will not print the background graphics. By choosing "color" a non-color printer will print the background in shades of gray.
- ☞ Since this slide show only has four slides, in the Slides Per Page list box, select 4. Click OK and get your printout.

## GET HELP
The Office Assistant will ask for your questions. If you see the paper clip dude on the screen, click him. If you don't see him, click Help, Show The Office Assistant to have him appear.

## CLOSE A PRESENTATION (SLIDE SHOW)
When you're done working on a presentation, you'll want to close it. Remember, there's more than one close button. The one on the title bar closes the program; the one on the menu bar closes the presentation. Close the presentation, but leave PowerPoint open. If asked if you want to save changes you've made, click Yes. You will use this slide show later.

## OPEN A PRESENTATION (SLIDE SHOW)
To edit, format, or run an existing presentation, you will need to open it (i.e., place a copy of it in memory). To do so, click File, Open. Then select the drive and folder from the Look In box that contains your "PP1-Dozer's Guide" file. Select the file and click the Open button.

## CLOSE POWERPOINT
To close PowerPoint (remove it from memory), click the Close button (the X at the top right corner of the window). If asked if you want to save your file, click Yes.

# EXERCISES

## EXERCISE 1: CROSSWORD

Use the clues below to complete the crossword puzzle. (Note: the Answer Key can be found beginning on page F-17).

### ACROSS

1. At the top right corner of the window, there is a button with an X on it. This is the ___ button.
3. To run a slide show, I click the Slide Show button on the ___ toolbar.
5. PowerPoint is designed to create presentations. The presentation is often referred to as a ___.
9. To see how my slide show looks or to use it while giving a presentation, I will need to ___ it.
10. To have a permanent copy of a presentation, I will ___ it to a diskette or to the hard drive.
11. When running a slide show, I can stop the show at any point by right clicking to access a shortcut menu from which I would click ___ Show.
12. When in Normal view, the pane on the left side of the screen has two tabs: an ___ tab and a Slide tab.
14. I can find answers about PowerPoint by using the Office ___, which normally appears in the form of a paper clip.
15. When you create a slide show, text is entered into a box called a ___.
19. The slide show program we are using is called ___.
20. To close my presentation, but keep PowerPoint open, would I click the Close button on the title bar?
22. When you are creating a slide show and you want to add another slide, you would click Insert, ___ Slide.
23. The view that displays a slide pane, an outline/slide pane, and a notes pane is the ___ View.
24. If you copy text from one place to another, the text will be in ___ places.
27. I can create ___, which are printouts of slides that can be given to an audience.
29. At the left end of many toolbars, there is a thin vertical bar called a ___, which by dragging it, will allow me to move the entire toolbar.

### DOWN

2. If I click on the screen while running a slide show, the next ___ is displayed.
4. PowerPoint is a presentations program created by the fine folks at ___.
5. When in Normal view, the pane on the left side of the screen has two tabs: a ___ tab and an Outline tab.
6. To create, modify, or run a slide show, I first must put it into memory. To do so, I would ___ it.
7. Another name for a slide show.
8. The ___ View displays multiple thumbnail slides.
13. A ___ box is found in some dialog boxes. By clicking the arrow next to this box, I can access a collection of items, any of which can be selected.
16. To move a placeholder, put the mouse pointer on its border until the mouse pointer turns into a four-pointed ___. Then drag the placeholder to its new location.
17. I can enhance the appearance of my slides by applying a background to my slides called a ___ template.
18. While you are creating a presentation, it resides in ___. If power is lost, you may lose all of your work.
20. Is Dozer a Cyber Cat?
21. Another word for memory.

23. PowerPoint provides an extensive help feature that will answer most any question you may have about the program. Is this help feature called the Office Agent?
24. Another name for 15 Across is a ___ box.
25. If you drag a sizing handle, you can ___ a placeholder.
26. The words File, Edit, View, and Insert are found on the menu ___.
28. Is PowerPoint made by the Coca-Cola Company?

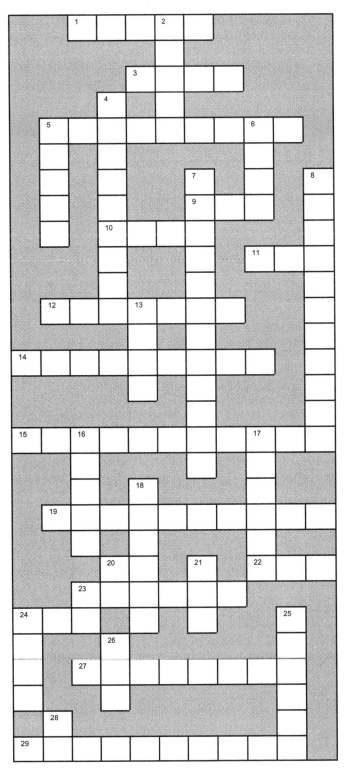

## EXERCISE 2: IDENTIFY TERMS

Below are eight definitions. Below the definitions are eight lines. In each line, write the word that matches the definition.

1. The menu bar item I click to learn how to use PowerPoint.
2. The company that makes the PowerPoint program.
3. The blinking, vertical bar marking where text will be entered.
4. The "X" button at the top right corner of a window.
5. The collection of background patterns used in PowerPoint.
6. The box on a slide in which text is placed.
7. The toolbar with Normal, Slide Sorter, & Slide Show buttons.
8. The act of viewing a slide show.

1. _____   5. _____
2. _____   6. _____
3. _____   7. _____
4. _____   8. _____

## EXERCISE 3: MATCHING

For each statement, identify the view being described by placing the letter of the view in the line preceding each statement.

| A. Normal |
| B. Slide Show |
| C. Slide Sorter |

1. ___Displays multiple thumbnail slides.
2. ___Runs the slide show.
3. ___Displays a Slide, Outline/slide, and Notes Pane.

## EXERCISE 4: TRUE-FALSE

For each of the following seven statements, place a T or an F on the line to indicate if the statement is True or False.

1. ___To "load" a program is to "start" a program.
2. ___The title bar is at the top of the PowerPoint window.
3. ___The menu bar has picture buttons on it.
4. ___The Office Assistant normally looks like a paper clip.
5. ___Closing a presentation removes it from memory.
6. ___Once I create a slide show, I can't modify it.
7. ___The Print toolbar button prints one copy of my slide show.

## EXERCISE 5: CREATE A SLIDE SHOW

Create a slide show about secondary storage devices. The actual information for each slide is provided below.

**SLIDE ONE**: Use the Title Slide layout.
☞  Click in the Title placeholder.
☞  Type Secondary Storage.
☞  Click in the Subtitle placeholder.
☞  Type Permanent Place To Store Programs And Data.

**SLIDE TWO**: Use the Title And Text layout.
☞  Click in the Title placeholder.
☞  Type Secondary Storage Devices.
☞  Click in the Text placeholder and type the following:

```
Diskettes
Hard Drives
CD-ROMs
Zip Disks
Magnetic Tapes
```

☞  Before you continue, please take a moment to save your slide show (name it PP1-Storage).

**SLIDE THREE**: Use the Title And Text layout.
☞  Click in the Title placeholder.
☞  Type Diskettes.
☞  Click in the Text placeholder and type the following:

```
1.44 MB Capacity
Hard Plastic Cover
Shutter Mechanism
Used In "A" Drive
Can Be Written Upon Many Times
Random Access To Data
```

**SLIDE FOUR**: Use the Title And Text layout.
☞  Click in the Title placeholder.
☞  Type Hard Drives.
☞  Click in the Text placeholder and type the following:

```
10-60+ GB Capacity
Also Called "C" Drive
Can Be Written Upon Many Times
Random Access To Data
```

**SLIDE FIVE**: Use the Title And Text layout.
☞  Click in the Title placeholder.
☞  Type CD-ROMs.
☞  Click in the Text placeholder and type the following:

```
680 MB Capacity
Can't Be Written Upon By User
Random Access To Data
```

**SLIDE SIX**: Use the Title And Text layout.
☞  Click in the Title placeholder.
☞  Type Zip Disks.
☞  Click in the Text placeholder and type the following:

```
100 or 250 MB Capacity
Can Be Written Upon Many Times
Random Access To Data
```

**SLIDE SEVEN**: Use the Title And Text layout.
☞  Click in the Title placeholder.
☞  Type Magnetic Tapes.
☞  Click in the Text placeholder and type the following:

```
20+ GB Capacity
Used Mostly For Backups
Can Be Written Upon Many Times
Sequential Access To Data
```

**SLIDE EIGHT**: Use the Title Only layout.
☞  Click in the Title placeholder.
☞  Type Slide Show Creator: X (replace X with your name).
☞  Starting with Slide 1, run your slide show.
☞  To enhance its appearance, apply a design template (choose any template you like).
☞  Run your slide show again. Does the application of a design template improve the appearance of your slide show? Try several different design templates until you find the one you like best.
☞  Save your modified slide show (you will use it later).
☞  Since you have eight slides, print a handout, nine slides to a page.
☞  Close the slide show.
☞  Close PowerPoint.

In this project, you will use the "PP1-Dozer's Guide" slide show you created on page F-3. If you haven't created that slide show yet, or if you've lost it, please return to page F-3 and recreate that show. Then, you will be ready to start this project.

Once you have created a slide show, you may decide that you need to edit it (correct mistakes or update data) or format it (change its appearance). This project will demonstrate some basic editing and formatting options.

## INSERT A NEW SLIDE
Sometimes, after creating a slide show, you'll want to insert an additional slide.

To practice inserting a new slide, do the following:
☞ Start PowerPoint, open "PP1-Dozer's Guide", and save it as "PP2-Dozer's Guide ".
☞ Click the Normal View button on the View toolbar.
☞ In the Outline/slide pane, click on Slide 3.
☞ Click Insert, New Slide (or, click the New Slide button).
☞ Notice that a new slide appears below Slide 3 and that the original Slide 4 has been renumbered to be Slide 5. Also notice the new slide has a Title And Text layout. Since this is what we want, there is no need to change it.
☞ In the Title placeholder, type WHEN & WHERE?
☞ In the Text placeholder, type the following:

```
Every Semester
Your Hometown College
```

## UNDO & REDO ACTIONS
When you make a mistake, you can reverse the action by clicking the Undo toolbar button (it has a crooked arrow pointing to the left) which will undo the last action taken. If you then click the Undo button again, the second-to-last action will be undone. If you undid something you did not want to undo, you can restore the action by the clicking the Redo toolbar button (it has a crooked arrow pointing to the right).

## MOVE AND COPY TEXT
To move text, select the text and click Edit, Cut. Then click where you want it and click Edit, Paste. Follow these steps to copy text, except, click Copy instead of Cut from the Edit menu.

## REPLACE TEXT
You can have PowerPoint search through your entire slide show to find specific text and replace it with other text. To use this feature, click Edit, Replace to access a dialog box where you can specify what text to find and the replacement text.

## USE AUTOCORRECT
AutoCorrect will automatically correct many errors. To add or delete items from AutoCorrect, click Tools, AutoCorrect Options.

## CORRECT SPELLING
To check the spelling, click Tools, Spelling. PowerPoint will find each misspelled word and provide suggestions for correction.

## PROMOTE AND DEMOTE TEXT
All text is not equal in importance. For instance, a subtitle is generally of lesser prominence than a title and some items in a bulleted list are generally subordinate to other items in the list. To communicate the importance of some text over other text, you may need to promote the important text and/or demote the less important text.

To practice demoting text, do the following:
☞ In the Outline/slide pane, click on Slide 3
☞ In the Slide pane, click in "Amaze All Your Friends".
☞ Click the Increase Indent toolbar button (it looks like a few lines of text with a right-pointing arrow). Notice that the item is indented, which indicates it has been demoted.
☞ Repeat the above two steps to demote "Looks Good On Resume" and "Meet Dozer Pannell".
☞ Note: Promoting text is done the same way as demoting text, except you click the Decrease Indent toolbar button (it looks like a few lines of text with a left-pointing arrow).

## MOVE A SLIDE
If you find that a slide would work better in a different location in the presentation, you can move the slide.

To practice moving a slide, do the following:
☞ Click the Slide Sorter View button on the View toolbar.
☞ Click the slide that needs to be moved (in this case, click Slide 4). Notice a border appears around the slide.
☞ Click Edit, Cut (the slide is sent to the clipboard).
☞ Click where you want the slide to be pasted (in this case, click between Slide 2 and Slide 3). Notice that the insertion point appears between the two slides.
☞ Click Edit, Paste (the slide is inserted).

## COPY A SLIDE
The steps to copy a slide are identical to the steps to move a slide with one exception. To move a slide, you send it to the clipboard by clicking Edit, Cut. To copy a slide, you send it to the clipboard by clicking Edit, Copy. Since all other steps are the same, there's no need to practice copying slides now.

## DELETE A SLIDE
If you find that you no longer need a slide, you can delete it.

To practice deleting a slide, do the following:
☞ In Slide Sorter View, click Slide 4 (the Benefits slide).
☞ Press the Delete key. Notice that Slide 4 is removed and that the remaining slide is renumbered.
☞ Click the Undo button. The previously deleted slide returns and the slides are renumbered.
☞ Save your slide show.

## APPLY TEXT ENHANCEMENTS
Enhancements include bold, italics, underline, and text shadow. These are applied to text to emphasize key points. You can apply one, any two, any three, or all four of these enhancements to text.

To practice applying enhancements, do the following:
☞ In Normal View, select Slide 1.
☞ In the Slide pane, click on "Written by Steve Pannell".
☞ Select the text in that placeholder.
☞ Click the Italics (I) and Underline (U) toolbar buttons.
☞ Click outside the box. The text has these enhancements.

## CHANGE FONTS

The font type (shape of the characters) and the font size (dimension of the characters) can be changed.

To practice changing fonts, do the following:
☞ Select the "Written by Steve Pannell" text in Slide 1.
☞ Click Format, Font. Select the font (Arial), the size (24) and a text color you like. Click OK. If the text is too long to appear in one line, resize the text box so the text appears in only one line.
☞ Select the "Benefits" title in Slide 4. Click Format, Font. Select Arial 54 and any text color you like. Click OK.

## USE THE FORMAT PAINTER

If you have a format that needs to be applied to other places in your presentation (e.g., chapter titles, headings), you can select each instance of the text and individually apply the formats. In long slide shows, this would be time consuming. The Format Painter will copy formats with greater speed and accuracy.

To practice using the Format Painter, do the following:
☞ Select the text that has the desired formats (select the title "Benefits" in Slide 4). Notice that the title has several formats applied to it (font type, size, and color).
☞ Double-click the Format Painter toolbar button (looks like a paint brush).
☞ Select the text to have formats applied (in slides 1-3, select each title).
☞ Click the Format Painter button to turn this feature off.
☞ Starting with Slide 1, run your slide show. Notice that all of the titles now have the same formats as the Slide 4 title.

## ALIGN TEXT

Text can be aligned so that the straight edge is on the left side of the placeholder (align left), or on the right side of the placeholder (align right), or centered within the placeholder (center). The toolbar has one button for each alignment style and each of these buttons has an image which shows how the alignment will look.

To practice aligning text, do the following:
☞ In the Outline/slide pane, click Slide 2.
☞ Click the title in Slide 2 to select the placeholder.
☞ Click the desired alignment button on the toolbar (in this case, click any alignment button). The title is realigned.
☞ Change the alignment on Slide 3 and Slide 4.

## USE THE PEN TO WRITE ON SLIDES

While running a presentation, you can focus the audience's attention onto specific parts of a slide by writing on the slide. PowerPoint provides a multi-colored pen for this purpose.

To practice writing on a slide, do the following:
☞ Beginning with Slide 1, run your slide show.
☞ Right click on Slide 1 (a shortcut menu appears).
☞ Click Pointer Options, Pen Color (or Ink Color), and the desired color.
☞ In the slide, hold down the left mouse button and move the mouse to draw on the slide.
☞ Since the pointer is now a pen, you can't click to have the next slide appear. Instead, press the Enter key to view each slide, writing on each slide. When the slide show ends, if you are asked "Do you want to keep your ink annotations?", click Discard to turn the pen off.

## ADD TRANSITIONS

PowerPoint provides a collection of transitions, each of which determines how one slide disappears and the next appears.

To practice applying transitions, do the following:
☞ In Normal view, select Slide 1.
☞ From the menu bar, click Slide Show, Slide Transition (the Slide Transition task pane appears).
☞ Click a type of transition. Notice that a transition preview is provided. To see the preview again, click the Play button. Keep selecting transitions until you find one you like.
☞ From the Speed list box, select the speed of the transition. To see the transition again, click the Play button.
☞ From the Sound list box, select a desired sound. To see the transition again, click the Play button.
☞ In the Advance Slide area, choose how you want the slides to advance. That is, do you want a slide to remain displayed until you click the mouse or do you want the slide to advance to the next slide after a specified lapse of time. In this case you want each slide to remain on the screen until you click the mouse. So, make sure a check mark appears in the On Mouse Click check box and that the Automatically After check box is empty.
☞ To apply the transition to all slides, click Apply To All Slides.
☞ Run your slide show.
☞ If you don't like the transitions or sound, change it and rerun the slide show until you find a combination you like.
☞ Save your modified slide show.

## ADD CUSTOM ANIMATION EFFECTS

While Transitions determine how the slides appear, animations determine how specific text or images on a single slide appears. There are countless ways and reasons to animate text. For instance, if you have a slide with bullets on it, you may want to display the bullets one at a time. By doing so, your audience will not get ahead of you as you give your presentation.

To practice adding custom animation effects, do the following:
☞ In Normal view, select Slide 2.
☞ From the menu bar, click Slide Show, Custom Animation. Notice that the Custom Animation task pane appears.
☞ Select the part of the slide you want to animate (in this case, select the bulleted list).
☞ In the Custom Animation task pane, click the Add Effect button. A list effect types will appear
☞ Point to Entrance on the list. A list of specific effects appears. Select an effect. A preview appears. To see the preview again, click the Play button.
☞ Use the various boxes in the Custom Animation task pane to select the Start (make it On Click), Direction (whatever you like), and speed (whatever you like) of the animation. Take a few moments to experiment with various choices.
☞ To see the animation, click the Play button. Keep selecting and playing animations until you find one you like.
☞ Repeat these steps to add an animation effect to the bulleted lists found in slides 3-4.
☞ Beginning with Slide 1, run your slide show. Each time you click on a slide, another bullet appears using the animation effect you choose. If you like your slide show, save it. If you don't like it, fix what you don't like and then save it. You will use this slide show later.
☞ Since you have 5 slides, print a handout, 6 slides to a page.
☞ Close the slide show.
☞ Close PowerPoint.

## EXERCISE 1: CROSSWORD
Use the clues below to complete the crossword puzzle.

### ACROSS

3. To move a slide, I would select the slide and then I would click Edit ___ to send it to the clipboard. Then, I'd paste it elsewhere.
4. To rapidly and accurately substitute a specific word in your slide show with another word, use the ___ feature.
7. The Decrease Indent toolbar button will ___ a bullet item.
9. When I start PowerPoint, I am putting the program into ___.
12. The ___ feature automatically corrects common errors and capitalizes the first word in each sentence.
13. The way the characters line up vertically in relation to the left or right edge of a placeholder.
14. When you do something that you did not want to do, you can reverse the action by clicking the ___ button.
16. To make the left edge of the characters line up vertically straight within the placeholder, I would ___ align the text.
17. In the ___ area of the Slide Transition task pane, I can choose an audio effect (e.g., chime, applause) for when one slide disappears and the next appears.
19. In PowerPoint Project 1, we learned that one of the layouts available permits you to display a bulleted list in two ___ which means that there will be more than one vertical arrangement of bullets on the slide.
22. Is Dozer the smartest cyberdog on the planet?
25. The Increase Indent toolbar button will ___ a bullet item.
27. Dozer's favorite treat is a dog ___.
28. You can find answers by using the ___ Assistant, which normally appears as a paper clip cartoon character.
30. To ___ a slide show, I click the Slide Show button on the View toolbar.
31. The "B" on the toolbar button stands for ___.
32. The words File, Edit, View, and Help are on the ___ bar.

### DOWN

1. When you want a permanent copy of your slide show, you will want to ___ it to a diskette or to the hard drive.
2. A ___ wavy line identifies a possible spelling error.
3. If I select a slide and click Edit, Copy, the slide goes to the ___board.
5. When I select Normal View, I see a Slide ___, an Outline/slide ___ and a Notes ___.
6. The ___ is a toolbar button (looks like a paint brush) that lets you rapidly apply formats to parts of a presentation.
8. To make the right edge of the characters line up vertically straight within the placeholder, I would ___ align the text.
10. PowerPoint provides a collection of slide ___, which determine how each slide will disappear and how the next will appear.
11. To move, copy, or delete text or a slide, I would first ___ the text or the slide.
15. If you click Undo and decide that you want to undo the undo, you can click the ___ toolbar button.
18. When you ___ text or a slide, the original (source) text or slide will remain where it was and a duplicate of it will be placed in a new location (the destination).
20. When you ___ text or a slide, the original (source) text or slide will be removed from where it was and is placed in its new location (the destination).
21. The shape of the characters is the font ___.
23. Sometimes, we call a presentation a slide ___.
24. Does the "U" on the toolbar button stand for "Undo"?
25. I can enhance the appearance of my slides by applying a background to my slides called a ___ template.
26. While you are creating a presentation, it resides in ___. If the power goes out, you will lose what is in there.
29. To end a slide show, I can right click on a slide to access a shortcut menu from which I can click ___ Show.
30. Another word for 26 Down.
31. The bold, italics, and underline buttons can be found on the tool___.

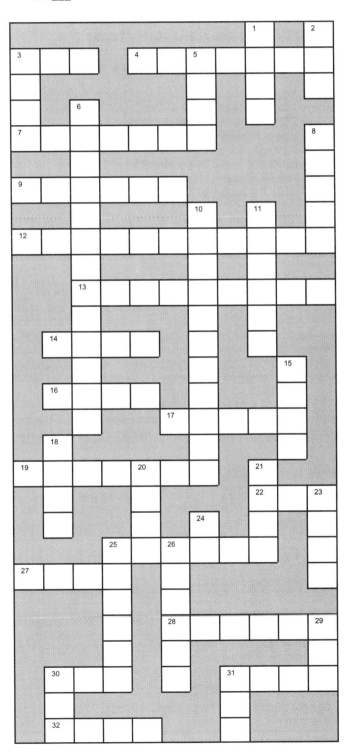

## EXERCISE 2: TRUE-FALSE

For each of the following eight statements, place a T or an F on the line to indicate if the statement is True or False.

1. ___After I copy a slide, it will appear in two places.
2. ___The Undo button has a crooked arrow pointing to the left.
3. ___Red wavy lines identify possible spelling errors.
4. ___Font size refers to the dimensions of the characters.
5. ___The Redo button has a crooked arrow pointing to the left.
6. ___The blinking, vertical bar is the mouse pointer.
7. ___To replace text, click Edit, Replace.
8. ___After I move a slide, it will appear in two places.

## EXERCISE 3: IDENTIFY TERMS

Below are eight definitions. Below the definitions are eight lines. In each line, write the word that matches the definition.

1. The toolbar button with the picture of a paint brush on it.
2. The shape of the characters.
3. The Office Assistant typically looks like this.
4. The type of possible error denoted by red wavy underlines.
5. A moved slide will appear in how many places?
6. The way text lines up in a placeholder.
7. The feature that automatically corrects many common errors.
8. The bar at the bottom of the screen (the Start button is on it).

1. _____     5. _____
2. _____     6. _____
3. _____     7. _____
4. _____     8. _____

## EXERCISE 4: EDIT AND FORMAT A SLIDE SHOW

In Exercise 5 (page F-6), you created a slide show and saved it using the name "PP1-Storage." Start PowerPoint and close the task pane. Open "PP1-Storage" and save it as "PP2-Storage". If you haven't created that slide show yet, or if you did create it and lost it, please return to page F-6 and recreate that show. Then return to this exercise.

### PART A: INSERT NEW SLIDES

Your Storage slide show does not have a slide for CD-RWs or a slide for USB drives. So, insert two slides so they appear after Slide 7.

### NEW SLIDE EIGHT:
☞ Use the Title And Text layout.
☞ Click in the Title placeholder.
☞ Type CD-RWs.
☞ Click in the Text placeholder and type the following:

> 680 MB Capacity
> Can Be Written Upon Many Times
> Random Access To Data

### NEW SLIDE NINE:
☞ Use the Title And Text layout.
☞ Click in the Title placeholder.
☞ Type USB Drives.
☞ Click in the Text placeholder and type the following:

> Typically 16 to 256 MB Capacity
> Can Be Written Upon Many Times
> Random Access To Data

### PART B: EDIT A SLIDE
☞ Since you now have two new slides, Slide 2 needs to be edited. To do so, insert two new bullets (CD-RWs & USB Drives) to appear below "Magnetic Tapes" on Slide 2.
☞ Also, in Slide 1, change "Place" so that it reads "Places". Save your modified slide show.

### PART C: CREATE A TEXT BOX
☞ Create a text box at the bottom of Slide 10 and type your email address in the box.
☞ Resize and move the box so it appears at the bottom center of the slide.
☞ Save your modified slide show.

### PART D: DEMOTE TEXT
☞ On the Diskettes slide (Slide 3), demote "Hard Plastic Cover" and "Shutter Mechanism".

### PART E: MOVE A SLIDE
☞ In Part A, you inserted two new slides. Move the CD-RWs slide so that it appears between the CD-ROMs slide and the Zip Disks slide.
☞ Then, move the USB Drives slide so that it appears in front of the Zip Disks slide.
☞ Go to the Secondary Storage Devices slide (Slide 2) and move the "CD-RWs" and the "USB Drives" bullets so they appear between the CD-ROMs and the Zip Disks bullets.

### PART F: DELETE A SLIDE
☞ You have decided that you do not want the Magnetic Tape slide. So, delete that slide from the slide show.
☞ Go to your Secondary Storage Devices slide (Slide 2) and delete the Magnetic Tape bullet in that slide.

### PART G: FORMAT SLIDES
☞ Change each slide title to appear underlined and italicized.
☞ Change the color of the titles (pick any color you like). Remember, the easy way to do this is to change one title and then to use the Format Painter to apply those changes to the other titles.

### PART H: USE THE PEN
☞ Run the slide show. As you view slides 3-8, use the pen to circle the capacity of each type of secondary storage (remember, to turn on the pen, start the show, right click, click Pointer Options, Pens Color (or Ink Color), and pick the desired color for the pen). Notice that with the pen selected, you can't advance to the next slide by clicking on the slide. Instead, press the Enter key or the spacebar to advance to the next slide.

### PART I: ADD SLIDE TRANSITIONS
☞ Add a slide transition to your slide show. Apply the same transition to all your slides.
☞ Starting with Slide 1, run the show.

### PART J: ADD CUSTOM ANIMATION EFFECTS
☞ Apply a custom animation effect to the bulleted lists found in Slides 2-8.
☞ Run your slide show. If you don't like something, fix it. When you are proud of your work, save it. You will use this slide show later.

### PART K: PRINT HANDOUTS
☞ Print a handout with nine slides to the page.
☞ Close the slide show. Close PowerPoint.

In this project, you will use the "PP2-Dozer's Guide" slide show you created on page F-7. If you haven't created that slide show yet, or if you've lost it, please return to page F-7 and recreate that show. Then, you will be ready to start this project.

A presentation's appearance can be enhanced by incorporating symbols, clipart, bullets, tables, AutoShapes, and action buttons along with the text. This project will show you how.

## INSERT A SYMBOL
PowerPoint comes with an extensive collection of non-keyboard characters (symbols) that, once inserted in a slide, can be treated much like keyboard characters. That is, they can be moved, copied, resized, edited, and deleted.

To practice inserting a symbol, do the following:
- ☞ Start PowerPoint and open "PP2-Dozer's Guide" and save it as "PP3-Dozer's Guide ".
- ☞ Put the insertion point where you want the symbol inserted (put it in front of the "LEARN ABOUT" title of Slide 2).
- ☞ Click Insert, Symbol. Click the Font list arrow. Click a font. The dialog box displays the symbols in the font you selected. Look at the collection of symbols. Look for a symbol of a book. If the selected font does not have that symbol, click other fonts until you find a book. Note: all of the symbols needed in this project can be found in either the webdings or wingdings font lists. When you find a book, click it.
- ☞ Click Insert, Close. The book appears in the slide.
- ☞ Put the insertion point at the end of the title of Slide 2. Repeat the above steps to insert another symbol of a book (note you can find the "book" symbol in the Recently Used Symbols collection at the bottom of the Symbol dialog box). When done, you should have a symbol of a book in front of and at the end of the "LEARN ABOUT" title.
- ☞ Go to Slide 3 and insert a symbol of a clock in front of and at the end of the "WHERE & WHEN" title.
- ☞ Go to Slide 4 and insert a symbol of a smiley face in front of and at the end of the "BENEFITS" title.

## INSERT IMAGES FROM THE MICROSOFT GALLERY
The Microsoft Gallery is a collection of clipart images that you can insert into your slide shows. Once inserted, images can be moved, copied, resized, edited, or deleted.

To practice inserting clip art, do the following:
- ☞ In Normal view, select Slide 2.
- ☞ Click Insert, Picture, Clip Art.
- ☞ In the Insert Clip Art task pane's Search Text box, enter a word that describes the clipart you want. In this case, since Slide 2 is all about learning, type in a word having to do with learning (e.g., "books").
- ☞ Press the Enter key. Be patient. It may take a minute or so for the thumbnail images to appear. If needed, use the task pane's scroll bar to view all the images. If you don't find an image you like, do another search, using other words (e.g., "school" or "education" or "teacher") until you find an image you like. Then, click the image to insert it to the slide (again, be patient, after clicking the image, it may take a while for the image to actually be inserted into the slide).
- ☞ The image is placed in a graphics box with sizing handles.
- ☞ Click outside of the box (the sizing handles disappear).

To practice resizing an image, do the following:
- ☞ Click on the image to select it. Point to any sizing handle until the mouse pointer looks like two-pointed arrow. Drag the handle until the box is the desired size.
- ☞ Click outside of the graphics box to deselect it.

To practice moving an image, do the following:
- ☞ Put the mouse pointer inside of the box so the pointer looks like a four-pointed arrow.
- ☞ Drag and drop the box to the right side of the bulleted list.
- ☞ Click outside of the graphics box to deselect it.
- ☞ Repeat the above steps to insert, resize, and move a clipart image (any image you like) onto Slide 4.

To practice editing an image, do the following:
- ☞ Click on the image to select it. The Picture toolbar appears (if it doesn't appear, click View, Toolbars, Picture). You can edit the image in many ways (e.g., crop it, change colors in it, rotate it, put a border around it, etc). Experiment with the various buttons on the Picture toolbar to edit the image.
- ☞ Click outside of the graphics box to deselect it.

To practice deleting an image, do the following:
- ☞ Click on the image to select it. Press the Delete key.
- ☞ Click the Undo button to have the image reappear.
- ☞ Click outside of the graphics box to deselect it.
- ☞ Save your modified slide show.

## INSERT IMAGES FROM YOUR DISKETTE
In addition to inserting images from the Microsoft Gallery, you can insert images from your disk, a CD, or the C drive. Once inserted, an object can be moved, copied, resized, edited, and deleted. First, you need to save some images to your disk.

To save images to your diskette, do the following:
- ☞ Start Internet Explorer and go to **www.dozer.pannell.com** (or www.pannell.biz).
- ☞ Click the My Quintessential Guide To Computer Literacy link.
- ☞ Right click on the picture of Dozer using a computer.
- ☞ On the shortcut menu, click Save Picture As.
- ☞ Indicate where to save it (save it on your floppy disk).
- ☞ Notice that the filename "cyberdozer" is supplied. Use it.
- ☞ Click the Save button. The picture is saved to your disk.
- ☞ While on this web page, scroll down to see the walking paw prints. Right click on them and save the animation to your diskette. Use "pawswalk" as its name. You'll need it later.
- ☞ Use the Internet to find and then save an image of one of your college campus buildings (name it college).

To practice inserting an image from a disk, do the following:
- ☞ In Normal view, select Slide 1.
- ☞ Click Insert, Picture, From File.
- ☞ In the Look in box, select the 3 ½ Floppy (A:) drive.
- ☞ Select the "cyberdozer" file and click the Insert button.
- ☞ Resize the image as desired.
- ☞ Move the image (move it wherever you think it looks best).
- ☞ Go to slide 3, insert, resize, and move the "college" picture so that it appears under the bulleted list.
- ☞ At the top of Slide 1, insert the Pawswalk file. Resize its graphics box to span across the slide. The image won't be animated yet, but it will be later when you run the slide show.

## USE WORDART

With WordArt, the image is not of clipart or a photo, but is text. In this part of the project, you will be replacing the ugly text in Slide 5 with spectacular WordArt text (well, maybe "spectacular" is overstating the degree of improvement, but it'll be better).

To practice using WordArt, do the following:
- ☞ In Slide 5, select the placeholder (Slide Show Creator . . .)
- ☞ Delete the placeholder (click one of its borders and press the Delete key twice).
- ☞ Click Insert, Picture, WordArt.
- ☞ Click a style (choose any style you like). Click OK. The Edit WordArt Text dialog box appears.
- ☞ Type Slide Show Creator. Click OK.
- ☞ Point to any character in the image. When the mouse pointer looks like a four-pointed arrow, drag the image to move it wherever you think it looks best.
- ☞ Click outside of the image to deselect it.
- ☞ Repeat the above steps to create another WordArt graphic that consists of your name.
- ☞ Resize and move the two WordArt images so that your name appears below "Slide Show Creator".

To practice changing the color of WordArt, do the following:
- ☞ To select the WordArt, click on one of the characters (in this case, click on any character in "Slide Show Creator"). The WordArt toolbar should appear (if it does not, click View, Toolbars, WordArt to have it appear).
- ☞ From the WordArt toolbar, click the Format WordArt button (it looks like a paint bucket).
- ☞ In the dialog box, click the Colors and Lines tab.
- ☞ In the Fill area, click the Color list box to access a collection of colors for the text. If you want to access more colors, click the More Colors button. When you find what you want, click it.
- ☞ In the Line area, click the Color list box to access a collection of colors for the borders of the text. In this case, click No Line. Then click OK.
- ☞ If you don't like the color or effect of your WordArt, repeat the above steps to change it. Note: depending on the style of WordArt you choose, you may not be able to change its color. If this happens, you can change the style and then change its color. Or, you could learn to like the color of the existing style.
- ☞ Repeat the above steps to apply the same color or fill to the "your name" WordArt in the slide.
- ☞ Save your modified slide show.

## CHANGE BULLETS

As you know, one way to organize data is to use bullets to separate and highlight each item on a list. When you created slides 2-4, PowerPoint choose the type of bullets to use. You can change those bullets.

To practice choosing bullets, do the following:
- ☞ In Slide 2, select the bulleted list placeholder in the slide.
- ☞ Drag over the items in the bulleted list.
- ☞ Click Format, Bullets and Numbering.
- ☞ In the dialog box, click either the Numbered or Bulleted tab (in this case, click the Bulleted tab).
- ☞ From the small selection of bullets, you could choose one you like. But, there are thousands of others to choose from. To access them, click the Customize button. Note that these are the same characters you found when you inserted

symbols earlier in this project. You could use one of them, but, let's find some other bullets. So, click Cancel.
- ☞ Click the Picture button. A large collection of picture bullets appears. Scroll down to find the one you like best.
- ☞ Click the desired image. Click OK.
- ☞ Your bullets have been changed.
- ☞ Now, replace the ugly bullets in slides 3-4 with the pretty ones you selected in the prior steps.

## DRAW OBJECTS

To practice drawing objects, do the following:
- ☞ Select Slide 5.
- ☞ On the Drawing toolbar (if it's not located near the bottom of the screen, click View, Toolbars, Drawing), click the desired drawing tool (in this case, click the rectangle). Move the mouse pointer onto the slide. Drag a border around your name. Release the mouse button.
- ☞ If the object obscures your name, click Draw, Order, Send To Back. If the text is still hidden, click the Fill Color arrow button (next to the paint bucket) and select a color you like from the menu or select No Fill if you don't want any color.
- ☞ To resize the object, point to any border until the mouse pointer looks like a four-pointed arrow and click. Sizing handles appear. Drag a handle to resize the object.
- ☞ Repeat the above steps to draw an oval around the "Slide Show Creator" line. Resize and move the object, if needed.

## INSERT AUTOSHAPES

If your artistic ability is somewhat limited, you may want to insert AutoShapes into your slides instead of drawing objects.

To practice inserting AutoShapes, do the following:
- ☞ Select Slide 1.
- ☞ From the Drawing toolbar, click AutoShapes, Stars and Banners, Down Ribbon.
- ☞ Drag the mouse to create a ribbon. Release the mouse.
- ☞ Resize and move the ribbon so that "Custom Edition" appears in it. If the ribbon obscures the text, click Draw, Order, Send To Back. If the text is still hidden, then click the Fill Color arrow button and select a color you like from the menu or select No Fill if you don't want any color.

## INSERT ACTION BUTTONS

You can insert buttons onto your slides that, when clicked, will do a variety of things (e.g., go to another slide in the show, or go to a web page, or simply provide an audio effect).

To practice inserting action buttons, do the following:
- ☞ Select slide 5 (the last slide).
- ☞ Click Slide Show, Action Buttons.
- ☞ Choose the desired button (select the Home action button).
- ☞ Drag the mouse pointer on the slide to create the button. When you release the mouse button, the Action Settings dialog box appears.
- ☞ In the Hyperlink To box, select First Slide. Click OK.
- ☞ Resize the button and move it to the bottom of the slide.
- ☞ Repeat the above steps to insert a Sound action button on Slide 1. Use any sound you like.
- ☞ Run your slide show. On Slide 1, click the Sound Action button; on Slide 5, click the Home Action button to jump to the first slide. After running the show, if you like it, save it. If you don't like it, fix it and then save it.
- ☞ Since you have 5 slides, print a handout, 6 slides to a page.
- ☞ Close the presentation. Close PowerPoint.

## EXERCISE 1: CROSSWORD

Use the clues below to complete the crossword puzzle.

### ACROSS

1. PowerPoint is a presentations program produced by the fine folks at ___.
5. Is Dozer a cat?
7. To change the color of WordArt, I would click the ___ WordArt button from the WordArt toolbar.
10. PowerPoint provides a variety of background patterns for my slides (e.g., blends, capsules, crayons, echo). Each pattern is a Design ___.
13. The ___ determines the quantity and location of the placeholders in each slide. Common examples include: Title Only, Title And Text, Title Only, and Organization Chart.
14. If you select some text (or an image) and then you press the ___ key, the selected text (or image) will disappear.
15. To ___ an image, point to one of the small boxes mentioned in 22 Across and drag the box until the image is the desired size.
18. To end a slide show, I can ___ click on a slide to access a shortcut menu from which I can click End Show.
19. The "B" on the toolbar button stands for ___.
22. When a graphic image is selected, little squares called sizing ___ will appear on the corners and borders. These allow me to resize the image.
23. A graphic image that is not of clipart or a photo, but is text.

### DOWN

2. If you click the Undo toolbar button and decide that you want to undo the undo, you can click the ___ toolbar button.
3. The collection of characters mentioned in 16 Down are so extensive that they reside in groups such as Wingdings, Webdings, and MS Outlook. Each group is called a ___.
4. If I click the ___ toolbar button, the printer will print a hard copy of each of my slides in my presentation.
6. If I have an image saved and I want to insert that image into a slide, I would click Insert, Picture, ___.
8. To take a slide that is in one location and put it elsewhere so that it then appears in only one place.
9. The collection of images mentioned in 11 Down reside in the Microsoft Clip ___.
11. PowerPoint comes with a collection of images that I can insert into my presentations. To access this collection of images, I would click Insert, Picture, Clip___.
12. Is PowerPoint a word processing program?
14. The smartest cyberdog on the planet is ___ Pannell.
16. Non-keyboard characters, such as ♫, ✄, and ☞ are ___.
17. When I am done using a program, I will want to take it out of memory. To do so, I would click the ___ button, which has an "X" on it. Since more than one of these exist, I would be sure to click the one on the title bar.
20. To insert an image into a presentation, I do not "open the file". Instead, I click ___, Picture.
21. To insert a banner, I would click the ___Shape button on the Drawing toolbar. Then I would click Stars and Banners, and finally I would click the banner I like best.
22. I can create ___outs, which are printouts of slides that can be given to an audience.

## EXERCISE 2 TRUE-FALSE

For each of the following eight statements, place a T or an F on the line to indicate if the statement is True or False.

1. ___ ♫, ✈, and ✄ are examples of smileys.
2. ___ To select a graphic image, I right click in it.
3. ___ To insert an image into PowerPoint, click File, Open.
4. ___ I can resize WordArt.
5. ___ WordArt is an image in the form of text.
6. ___ The Microsoft Gallery contains clipart.
7. ___ To deselect an image, click inside of the image.
8. ___ I can move WordArt.

## EXERCISE 3: CREATE A PHOTO SLIDE SHOW

Take a moment to think about an entertainer that you like. It could be an actor, singer, or comedian. Or, it could be a cartoon character or a famous dog, cat, or rat. Once you have identified the character, start PowerPoint and start Internet Explorer. Use Google to find five pictures of the character. Then create a slide show that has six slides: The first slide will use WordArt for the title of the slide show. The next five slides will each display one of the pictures, resized to cover the entire slide. When done, run your show to see if you like it. If you don't like it, fix it. Save your show to your diskette.

## EXERCISE 4: ENHANCE A SLIDE SHOW VIA GRAPHICS

This exercise will give you the opportunity to enhance a slide show by incorporating graphics. To do this exercise, you will need to use a previously-created slide show. In Exercise 4 on page F-10, you edited a slide show and saved it as "PP2-Storage." Start PowerPoint and open "PP2-Storage" and save it as "PP3 Storage". If you haven't created that slide show yet, or if you created it and lost it, please return to page F-10 and recreate that show. Then return to this exercise.

### PART A: FIND & SAVE IMAGES FROM THE INTERNET

Use Internet Explorer to find each image listed in the table below. As you find each image, save it to your diskette. Use the slide number for each image's name. For example, when you find an image of a diskette, enter its name as <u>Slide 3 Image</u>.

| SLIDE | IMAGE |
|---|---|
| Slide 3 | Diskette |
| Slide 4 | Hard Drive |
| Slide 5 | CD-ROM |
| Slide 6 | CD-RW |
| Slide 7 | USB Drive |
| Slide 8 | Zip Disk |

### PART B: INSERT IMAGES FROM A DISKETTE

☞ Insert each of the images in the appropriate slide.
☞ Resize and move each image as you please.
☞ Starting with Slide 1, run your slide show. If any image needs to be moved or resized, do so.
☞ When you like the way the slide show looks, save your modified slide show.

### PART C: CHANGE BULLETS

☞ In slides 2-8, change the bullets to be picture bullets. Pick any picture bullet you like.
☞ Save your modified slide show.

### PART D: USE WORDART

☞ In Slide 1, change the title (Secondary Storage) to be WordArt (any style of WordArt you like).
☞ Resize and move the WordArt, as needed.
☞ Change the color of the WordArt so it coordinates with your design template.
☞ Using the same WordArt style and color, change the title in the last slide so that it is two different WordArt images. One for the "Slide Show Creator" line and another for the "your name" line.
☞ Resize and move the WordArt as needed.

### PART E: INSERT A TABLE

Some data is best organized by placing it in a table (a matrix of rows and columns). The intersection of each row and column forms a cell, a location where data is placed. Once the table is created, you can enter text, add or delete rows or columns, adjust column widths, merge cells, apply enhancements, change fonts, align text, apply borders and shading, etc.

☞ Create a new slide to appear between Slides 8 and 9 (use the Title And Table slide layout). This layout includes a table which you will use to summarize the capacities of each storage device.
☞ Click in the Title placeholder and type <u>Storage Capacities</u>.
☞ Double click where it says "Double Click To Add Table".
☞ Specify the number of rows and columns. In this case, you want a table like the one below. So, you will need to create a table with two columns and eight rows.
☞ Once you make these choices, click OK.

### PART F: FORMAT A TABLE AND ENTER DATA

☞ Merge the cells in Row 1 (select the cells in row 1, right click, and then click Merge Cells from the shortcut menu).
☞ Enter the data as shown in the table below.
☞ Center the text in rows 1-2. If needed, resize the columns to ensure that the text does not wrap within a cell.
☞ Change the font color of the text in rows 1-2 to match the colors found in your slides.

| SECONDARY STORAGE DEVICES | |
|---|---|
| TYPE | CAPACITY |
| Diskette | 1.44 MB |
| Hard Drive | 10-30+ GB |
| CD-ROM | 680 MB |
| CD-RW | 680 MB |
| USB Drive | 16-256+ KB |
| Zip Disk | 100 or 250 MB |

### PART G: INSERT A SYMBOL

☞ On Slide 10 (the last slide), insert a symbol of a mailbox in front of and at the end of your email address. The mailbox symbol can be found in the Wingdings font list.
☞ Change the font size of your email address and of the symbol to be 36 points.
☞ If needed, resize and move the text box wherein your email address resides.
☞ Change the color of the two mailboxes and your email address to match the color of your slides.

### PART H: DRAW OBJECTS & INSERT AUTOSHAPES

☞ In slide 10 (the last slide), draw an oval around your name.
☞ In the last slide, insert a Double Wave Banner AutoShape so that your email address appears in it.

### PART I: INSERT ACTION BUTTONS

☞ At the bottom of the last slide, insert a Home action button that, when clicked, will take you to a web site (in this case, have it linked to your first slide).
☞ Starting with Slide 1, run the slide show. When you get to the last slide, click the action button to be sure it works.
☞ Save your modified slide show.

### PART J: PRINT HANDOUTS

☞ Print a handout, six slides to a page. Since you have ten slides, your printout will be two pages.
☞ Close PowerPoint.

## POWERPOINT COMPREHENSIVE
# E X E R C I S E S

### EXERCISE 1: IDENTIFY TERMS
Below are eight definitions. Below the definitions are eight lines. In each line, write the word that matches the definition.

1. The blinking, vertical bar marking where text will be entered.
2. The "X" button at the top right corner of a window.
3. A moved slide will appear in how many places?
4. The Office Assistant typically looks like this.
5. The feature that automatically corrects many common errors.
6. The shape of the characters.
7. The menu bar item I click to access the Office Assistant.
8. The company that makes the PowerPoint program.

1. _____     5. _____
2. _____     6. _____
3. _____     7. _____
4. _____     8. _____

### EXERCISE 2: TRUE-FALSE
For each of the following eight statements, place a T or an F on the line to indicate if the statement is True or False.

1. ___The Office Assistant normally looks like a paper clip.
2. ___Closing a presentation removes it from memory.
3. ___To open a slide show, I click Open, Slide Show.
4. ___To "load" a program is to "start" a program.
5. ___The menu bar has picture buttons on it.
6. ___Font size refers to the shape of the characters.
7. ___Once I create a slide show, I can't modify.
8. ___To "start" a program is to "launch" a program.

### EXERCISE 3: TRUE-FALSE
For each of the following eight statements, place a T or an F on the line to indicate if the statement is True or False.

1. ___To move or copy a slide, I would first select the slide.
2. ___Red wavy lines identify possible grammar errors.
3. ___After I copy a slide, it will appear in one place.
4. ___To deselect an image, click outside of the image.
5. ___The menu bar is above the title bar.
6. ___AutoCorrect corrects common errors automatically.
7. ___The Undo button has a crooked arrow pointing up.
8. ___The blinking, vertical bar is the insertion point.

### EXERCISE 4: TRUE-FALSE
For each of the following eight statements, place a T or an F on the line to indicate if the statement is True or False.

1. ___After I move a slide, it will appear in one place.
2. ___The Microsoft Gallery contains clipart.
3. ___Font type refers to the size of the characters.
4. ___After I copy a slide, it will appear in two places.
5. ___To select a graphic image, I right click in it.
6. ___The blinking, vertical bar is the mouse pointer.
7. ___I can resize WordArt.
8. ___The title bar is at the bottom of the PowerPoint window.

### EXERCISE 5: MATCHING
Below is a list of three ways to view slides. Below the list is another list of statements, each of which describes one of the various views. For each descriptive statement, identify the view being described by placing the letter of the view in the line preceding each statement.

> A. Normal
> B. Slide Show
> C. Slide Sorter

1. ___Runs the slide show.
2. ___Displays multiple thumbnail slides.
3. ___Displays a Slide, Outline/slide, and Notes Pane.

### EXERCISE 6: TRUE-FALSE
For each of the following eight statements, place a T or an F on the line to indicate if the statement is True or False.

1. ___ I can move WordArt.
2. ___A toolbar has picture buttons on it.
3. ___The Close button on the title bar has a "C" on it.
4. ___To insert an image into PowerPoint, click File, Open.
5. ___Text is inserted at the location of the mouse pointer.
6. ___The Office Assistant typically looks like a thumb tack.
7. ___The Print toolbar button prints one copy of my slide show.
8. ___To replace text, click Edit, Replace.

### EXERCISE 7: TRUE-FALSE
For each of the following eight statements, place a T or an F on the line to indicate if the statement is True or False.

1. ___The blinking, vertical bar is the move handle.
2. ___♫, ✈, and ✄ are examples of symbols.
3. ___After I move a slide, it will appear in two places.
4. ___The Undo button has a crooked arrow pointing down.
5. ___WordArt is an image in the form of text.
6. ___Red wavy lines identify possible spelling errors.
7. ___When I open a slide show, I put a copy of it in memory.
8. ___The Redo button has a crooked arrow pointing to the left.

### EXERCISE 8: IDENTIFY TERMS
Below are eight definitions. Below the definitions are eight lines. In each line, write the word that matches the definition.

1. The way text lines up in a placeholder.
2. Background patterns used in PowerPoint slides.
3. The box on a slide into which text is placed.
4. The toolbar button with the picture of a paint brush on it.
5. The bar at the bottom of the screen (the Start button is on it).
6. The type of possible error denoted by red wavy underlines.
7. The toolbar with Normal, Outline/slide, & Slide Sorter buttons.
8. The act of viewing a slide show.

1. _____     5. _____
2. _____     6. _____
3. _____     7. _____
4. _____     8. _____

## EXERCISE 9: CREATE A HARDWARE SLIDE SHOW

Please create a slide show about hardware input devices.

### PART A: CHOOSE LAYOUTS AND CREATE SLIDES

Start PowerPoint and create the following slides.

**SLIDE ONE**: Use the Title Slide layout.
☞ Type <u>HARDWARE</u> in the Title placeholder.
☞ Type <u>Components That Create A Computer System</u> in the Subtitle placeholder.

**SLIDE TWO**: Use the Title And Text layout.
☞ Type <u>TYPES OF HARDWARE</u> in the Title placeholder.
☞ Type <u>Input</u>, <u>Processing</u>, <u>Storage</u>, and <u>Output</u> in the Text placeholder. Type these words, one per line, so that you have a bulleted list.

**SLIDE THREE**: Use the Title And Text layout.
☞ Type <u>COMMON INPUT DEVICES</u> in the Title placeholder.
☞ Type <u>Mouse</u>, <u>Keyboard</u>, <u>Microphone</u>, and <u>Scanner</u> in the Text placeholder. Type these words, one per line, so that you have a bulleted list.
☞ Save your slide show. Name it <u>PC-Hardware</u>

**SLIDE FOUR**: Use the Title Slide layout.
☞ Type <u>MOUSE</u> in the Title placeholder.
☞ Type <u>Enters Commands And Moves/Resizes Objects</u> in the Subtitle placeholder.

**SLIDE FIVE**: Use the Title Slide layout.
☞ Type <u>KEYBOARD</u> in the Title placeholder.
☞ Type <u>Inputs Data & Commands</u> in the Subtitle placeholder.

**SLIDE SIX**: Use the Title Slide layout.
☞ Type <u>MICROPHONE</u> in the Title placeholder.
☞ Type <u>Enters Data Via Voice</u> in the Subtitle placeholder.

**SLIDE SEVEN**: Use the Title Slide layout.
☞ Type <u>SCANNER</u> in the Title placeholder.
☞ Type <u>Produces A Digitized Copy Of Text Or Image</u> in the Subtitle placeholder.

**SLIDE EIGHT**: Use the Title Only layout
☞ In the Title placeholder, type <u>Slide Show Creator: X</u> (replace X with your name)
☞ Save your slide show.

### PART B: CHANGE BULLETS

☞ In slides 2 and 3, change the bullets (choose any type you like).

### PART C: CREATE A TEXT BOX

☞ Create a text box at the bottom of the last slide and type your email address in the box.
☞ Resize and move the box so it appears at the bottom center of the slide.

### PART D: CHOOSE A DESIGN TEMPLATE

☞ Choose a design template for your slide show and have the template applied to all your slides.
☞ Run your slide.

### PART E: INSERT NEW SLIDES

☞ Insert the following two slides after the Keyboard slide.

**NEW SLIDE SIX**: Use the Title Slide layout.
☞ Type <u>DIGITAL CAMERA</u> in the Title placeholder.
☞ Type <u>Takes A Digitized Picture For Use By A Computer</u> in the Subtitle placeholder.

**NEW SLIDE SEVEN**: Use the Title Slide layout.
☞ Type <u>BAR CODE READER</u> in the Title placeholder.
☞ Type <u>Reads UPCs (Universal Product Codes)</u> in the Subtitle placeholder.

### PART F: MOVE SLIDES

☞ Move the Microphone slide to appear after the Scanner slide in the slide show.
☞ Save your modified slide show.

### PART G: EDIT SLIDES

☞ In Part E, you inserted a Digital Camera and a Bar Code Reader slide. So, edit Slide 3 to include a Digital Camera and a Bar Code Reader bullet.
☞ In Part F, you moved the Microphone slide. So, in slide 3, move the Microphone bullet so it appears after the Scanner bullet.

### PART H: DELETE SLIDES

☞ Delete the Bar Code Reader slide.
☞ Delete the Bar Code Reader bullet from Slide 3.

### PART I: FORMAT SLIDE ELEMENTS

☞ Format the titles for slides 1-8 to appear in Bold, Underlined, Arial 40, left aligned, and any color of your choice.

### PART J: INSERT GRAPHICS

☞ Find an Internet image of a mouse, keyboard, digital camera, scanner, and microphone. Save each image to your disk.
☞ Insert the appropriate image in slides 4-8. Resize and move each image as needed. When you like the way the images look, save your modified slide show.

### PART K: INSERT WORDART

☞ In Slide 1, change the "Hardware" title to be some type of WordArt. Resize and move the WordArt, as needed.

### PART L: DRAW OBJECTS & INSERT AUTOSHAPES

☞ In Slide 1, insert an Up Ribbon Banner Autoshape so that the "Hardware" WordArt title appears in it.
☞ In Slide 9, draw a rectangle around your email address.
☞ Save your modified slide show.

### PART M: INSERT AN ACTION BUTTON

☞ In Slide 9 (the last slide), insert an Action button that, when clicked, will make Slide 1 appear.
☞ Save your modified slide show.

### PART N: ADD TRANSITIONS & ANIMATE TEXT

☞ Apply a slide transition to all your slides (use any type you like).
☞ In slides 2 & 3, animate the bulleted lists using any type custom animation you like.
☞ Run you show. If you like you slide show, save it. If there is anything about it you don't like, fix it and then save it.

### PART O: PRINT HANDOUTS

☞ Since your slide show has nine slides, print a handout, nine slides to a page.
☞ Close the slide show. Close PowerPoint.

## PAGE F-5: EXERCISE 1

| Across | Down |
|--------|------|
| 1. Close | 2. Slide |
| 3. View | 4. Microsoft |
| 5. Slide Show | 5. Slide |
| 9. Run | 6. Open |
| 10. Save | 7. Presentation |
| 11. End | 8. Slide Sorter |
| 12. Outline | 13. List |
| 14. Assistant | 16. Arrow |
| 15. Placeholder | 17. Design |
| 19. PowerPoint | 18. Memory |
| 20. No | 20. No |
| 22. New | 21. RAM |
| 23. Normal | 23. No |
| 24. Two | 24. Text |
| 27. Handouts | 25. Resize |
| 29. Move Handle | 26. Bar |
| | 28. No |

## PAGE F-6: EXERCISE 2
1. Help
2. Microsoft
3. Insertion Point
4. Close Button
5. Design Templates
6. Placeholder (text box)
7. View
8. Run

## PAGE F-6: EXERCISE 3
1. C
2. B
3. A

## PAGE F-6: EXERCISE 4
1. T
2. T
3. F: The menu bar has words on it. The toolbar has picture buttons on it.
4. T
5. T
6. F: Once I create a slide show, I can modify it as often as I wish.
7. T

## PAGE F-9: EXERCISE 1

| Across | Down |
|--------|------|
| 3. Cut | 1. Save |
| 4. Replace | 2. Red |
| 7. Promote | 3. Clip |
| 9. Memory | 5. Pane |
| 12. AutoCorrect | 6. Format Painter |
| 13. Alignment | 8. Right |
| 14. Undo | 10. Transitions |
| 16. Left | 11. Select |
| 17. Sound | 15. Redo |
| 19. Columns | 18. Copy |
| 22. Yes | 20. Move |
| 25. Demote | 21. Type |
| 27. Bone | 23. Show |
| 28. Office | 24. No |
| 30. Run | 25. Design |
| 31. Bold | 26. Memory |
| 32. Menu | 29. End |
| | 30. RAM |
| | 31. Bar |

## PAGE F-10: EXERCISE 2
1. T
2. T
3. T
4. T
5. F: The Redo button has a crooked arrow pointing to the right. The Undo button has a crooked arrow pointing to the left.
6. F: The blinking, vertical bar is the insertion point, not the mouse pointer.
7. T
8. F: After I move a slide, it will appear in only one place. If I were to copy a slide, it would appear in more than one place.

## PAGE F-10: EXERCISE 3
1. Format Painter
2. Font Type
3. Paper Clip
4. Spelling
5. One
6. Alignment
7. AutoCorrect
8. Taskbar

## PAGE F-13: EXERCISE 1

| Across | Down |
|--------|------|
| 1. Microsoft | 2. Redo |
| 5. No | 3. Font |
| 7. Format | 4. Print |
| 10. Template | 6. From File |
| 13. Layout | 8. Move |
| 14. Delete | 9. Gallery |
| 15. Resize | 11. Art |
| 18. Right | 12. No |
| 19. Bold | 14. Dozer |
| 22. Handles | 16. Symbols |
| 23. WordArt | 17. Close |
| | 20. Insert |
| | 21. Auto |
| | 22. Hand |

## PAGE F-13: EXERCISE 2
1. F: ♫, ✈, and ✂ are examples of symbols. Examples of smileys would be d:) or 8-(.
2. F: To select a graphic image, I click in it. If I were to right click the image, I would get what I always get when I right click--a shortcut menu.
3. F: To insert an image into PowerPoint, I click Insert, Picture. Then I click From File if the picture is saved to a disk. Or, I click Clip Art if it is in the Clipart Gallery.
4. T
5. T
6. T
7. F: To deselect an image, click outside of the image. If I click in the image, I would be selecting the image.
8. T

## PAGE F-15: EXERCISE 1
1. Insertion Point
2. Close button
3. One
4. Paper Clip
5. AutoCorrect
6. Font Type
7. Help
8. Microsoft

## PAGE F-15: EXERCISE 2
1. T
2. T
3. F: To open a slide show, I click File, Open.
4. T
5. F: The menu bar has words on it. The toolbar has picture buttons on it.
6. F: Font size refers to the dimension of the characters. The shape of the characters is called the font type.
7. F: Once I create a slide show, I can modify it as often as I want to.
8. T

## PAGE F-15: EXERCISE 3
1. T
2. F: Red wavy lines identify possible spelling errors. Possible grammar errors are identified with green wavy lines.
3. F: After I copy a slide, it will appear in more than one place. It will be where it was (source) and it will be where I paste it (destination).
4. T
5. F: The menu bar is below the title bar.
6. T
7. F: The Undo button has a crooked arrow pointing to the left, not up.
8. T

## PAGE F-15: EXERCISE 4
1. T
2. T
3. F: The font type refers to the shape of the characters. The font size identifies the dimension of the characters.
4. T
5. F: To select a graphic image, I click in it. If I were to right click on the image, I would get what I always get when I right click--a shortcut menu.
6. F: The blinking, vertical bar is the insertion point, not the mouse pointer.
7. T
8. F: The title bar is at the top of the PowerPoint window, not at the bottom of the window.

## PAGE F-15: EXERCISE 5
1. B
2. C
3. A

## PAGE F-15: EXERCISE 6
1. T
2. T
3. F: The Close button has an "X" on it, not a "C".
4. F: To insert an image into PowerPoint, I click Insert, Picture. Then I click From File if the picture is saved to a disk. Or, I click Clip Art if it is in the Clipart Gallery.
5. F: Text is inserted where the insertion point is located, not where the mouse pointer is located.
6. F: You can change the way it looks, but the Office Assistant typically looks like a paper clip, not a thumb tack.
7. T
8. T

## PAGE F-15: EXERCISE 7

1. F: The blinking, vertical bar is the insertion point, not the move handle.
2. T
3. F: After I move a slide, it will appear in only one place. If I were to copy it, it would appear in more than one place, but moving it takes it from where it was and puts it where you want it to be.
4. F: The Undo button has a crooked arrow that points to the left, not down.
5. T
6. T
7. T
8. F: The Redo button has a crooked arrow that points to the right. The Undo button has a crooked arrow pointing to the left.

## PAGE F-15: EXERCISE 8

1. Alignment
2. Design Templates
3. Placeholder (Text Box)
4. Format Painter
5. Taskbar
6. Spelling
7. View
8. Run

☞ Dozer's Quintessential Guide To Microsoft PowerPoint ☜

**A drive**: A secondary storage device that writes to and reads from a floppy disk. Also called a floppy drive.

**action button**: A button on a slide that, when clicked during the running of the slide show, will initiate some pre-determined action, such as loading another slide, accessing a web site, or producing an audio effect.

**alignment**: The way the text lines up within a slide or placeholder.

**AutoCorrect**: A feature that corrects commonly-misspelled words and capitalizes the first word in each sentence automatically.

**AutoShapes**: A collection of geometric shapes, such as arrows, banners, boxes, lines, callouts, etc., that can be placed in a document or on a slide.

**backspace key**: The key that deletes data to the left of the insertion point.

**bullet**: A symbol (e.g., a dot, check mark, or star) used to separate and highlight items in a list.

**click**: The act of rapidly pressing the left mouse button one time, generally done to select an on-screen object.

**clipart**: Artwork that can be viewed on screen, inserted into a document, or sent via email.

**close**: The process of removing a file or a program from memory.

**column**: A vertical collection of cells in a table.

**copy**: To place text elsewhere while maintaining the original text where it was.

**custom animation effects**: The variety of ways titles or bulleted lists can appear on the slide .

**delete**: To remove (erase).

**delete key**: The key that deletes data to the right of the insertion point.

**demote**: To decrease the importance of an item. In an outline or bulleted list, an item is demoted by indenting it. In PowerPoint an Increase Indent toolbar button is used to accomplish this.

**design template**: A collection of these exists from which you can choose. Each provides a background pattern for the slides.

**Dozer**: The smartest cyberdog on the planet.

**double-click**: The act of rapidly pressing the left mouse button two times.

**drag**: To move the mouse.

**drag and drop**: The act of pointing to an object on the screen, holding down the left mouse button, moving the mouse, and then releasing the mouse button, thereby moving the object. In essence you have dragged and then dropped the object.

**drawing toolbar**: A toolbar containing buttons which allow you to insert a variety of objects such as arrows, banners, boxes, lines, callouts, etc. Once inserted, these objects can be moved and resized in the document

**edit**: To modify a document.

**enhancements**: Bold, italics, underline, and text shadow.

**font color**: The color of the characters.

**font size**: The dimension of the characters.

**font type**: The shape of the characters.

**format painter**: A feature that will copy the formats residing in text and will apply those same formats to other text.

**handouts**: A printed document containing an individual slide or multiple slides printed on each sheet of paper, used for distribution to an audience so folks will have something to write on during the presentation and something to take with them for later review.

**insertion point**: The on-screen blinking vertical line identifying where entered text will appear. Some folks refer to this as a cursor.

**launch**: To place a program or data into memory. Also called start, load, or open.

**layout**: The quantity and location of the text boxes (placeholders) in each slide. The slide show creator can choose from a variety of layouts, including title, bullets, columns, clipart, etc.

**load**: To place a program or data into memory. Also called start, launch, or open.

**maximize button**: The button (on the title bar) that, when clicked, will make the window fill the entire screen.

**memory**: The temporary location where data and programs currently being used by a processor reside. Also called RAM (an acronym for Random Access Memory).

**menu bar**: The bar (under the title bar) which consists of a series of command categories. To access specific commands in a category, click the item on the menu bar.

**Microsoft Gallery**: A collection of clipart.

**minimize button**: The button that, when clicked, will make the window become the size of a taskbar button.

**move**: To place text elsewhere while removing the original text from where it was.

**move handle**: A vertical bar on a toolbar that, when dragged, will allow the user to move the toolbar.

**normal**: The view that displays three panes: Slide pane (the slide), Notes pane (place to insert notes), and a Outline/slide pane (place where you can choose to view an outline of your text or thumbnails of your slides.

**office assistant**: A Microsoft help feature that displays a character in the form of a paper clip that asks you to pose a question for him to answer.

**open**: To place a program or data into memory. Also called start, load, or launch.

**outline/slide pane**: The pane found when under Normal view wherein two tabs exist: Outline tab, which, when selected, will provide an outline of the text in each slide and a Slide tab which will display a thumbnail each slide.

**paste options button**: A button that appears below text that has been copied and then pasted into a slide. If you click the Paste Options button you will be able to select how you want to paste the text.

**pen**: A feature that allows you to write on slides while running the slide show.

**placeholder**: The boxes into which text is entered onto a slide. Also called a text box.

**PowerPoint**: A program developed by Microsoft that permits us to create dynamic slide shows so as to enhance any audience presentation. presentation: A category of software that permits us to create dynamic slides shows.

**presentation**: A category of software that permits us to create dynamic slides shows.

**Print Preview**: A feature that permits you to see how each page of your document will look before you print the document.

**promote**: To increase importance of an item. In an outline or bulleted list, an item is promoted by having it appear closer to the left margin than other less important items. In PowerPoint a Decrease Indent toolbar button is used to accomplish this.

**redo button**: The toolbar button that, when clicked, will undo the last undo done. It has a crooked arrow pointing to the right.

**right-click**: The act of rapidly pressing the right mouse button one time.

**row**: A horizontal line of cells in a table.

**run**: The process of viewing a slide show. Or, what Dozer does when anyone opens the refrigerator.

**save**: The act of placing a copy of the document that is currently in memory into secondary storage.

**select**: To identify an object, text, or image to which you wish to do something.

**shortcut menu**: A context-sensitive menu that appears when I right click. Also called a Quick Menu.

**slide show view**: The view in which the slide show is running.

**slide sorter view**: The view in which numerous thumbnail slides are displayed on the screen.

**symbols**: Non-keyboard characters that can be placed in documents (e.g., ♫, ✉, and ✿).

**table**: A collection of columns and rows forming cells into which data is entered.

**task pane**: A pane that sometimes appears at the right side of the screen which provides for rapid selection of features.

**taskbar**: The horizontal grey bar, typically at the bottom of the desktop, upon which the Start button resides.

**template**: A document file with customized format, content, and features, usually accessed by clicking File, New in the program.

**text shadow button**: In PowerPoint, in addition to the B, I, and U enhancement buttons, there is an "S" enhancement button which applies a shadow to the text.

**toolbar**: A collection of picture buttons that, when clicked, execute a command. These buttons typically appear below the menu bar.

**transitions**: The way one slide disappears and the next slide appears. This can include both video and audio elements.

**undo button**: The toolbar button that, when clicked, will reverse the last action taken. It has a crooked arrow pointing to the left.

**view**: A menu bar item that lets me choose the way stuff looks on the screen. For instance, in My Computer, the way the icons appear (thumbnails, tiles, icons, list, or details).

**WordArt**: A graphic image in the form of text.

# DOZER'S QUINTESSENTIAL GUIDE TO MICROSOFT® ACCESS

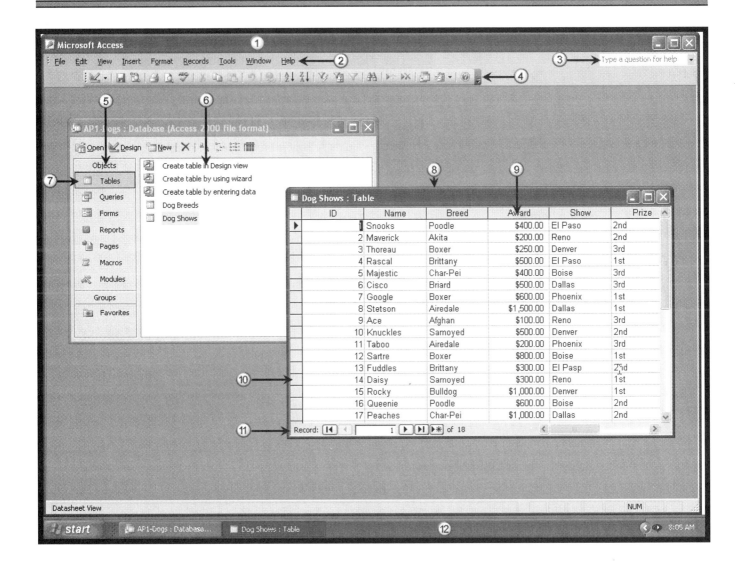

1. Title bar (identifies the program being used)
2. Menu bar (collection of menu items, each of which contains commands)
3. Help (a great place to find answers to all your questions)
4. Toolbar (collection of picture buttons, each of which accesses a command)
5. Objects bar (displays a list of objects)
6. Objects list (a list of objects and ways to create more of them)
7. Selected object (generates a specific Objects list)
8. Datasheet view (displays table contents in rows and columns)
9. Column Selector button (click to select the column)
10. Row Selector button (click to select the row)
11. Records buttons (finds and displays other records)
12. Taskbar (contains the Start button, open windows buttons, etc.)

Access is a program that stores, organizes, and retrieves data. For instance, colleges use database programs which contain information about each student. When a college wants to send a schedule of classes for a remote campus, a mailing list can be created by extracting all the records for students who have zip codes that indicate they live near the remote campus.

A database stores data in a hierarchy (various levels). The smallest particle of information about a person, place, thing, or event is a field (e.g., first name, last name, city, state, or zip). A collection of related fields is a record (e.g., Dozer, Pannell, Las Vegas, Nevada, 89130). A collection of related records is a table. A collection of related tables is a database.

## START (LOAD, OPEN, LAUNCH) ACCESS
To use Access, it must be placed into memory (RAM).

To start Access, do the following:
☞ Click the Start taskbar button and point to All Programs.
☞ On the sub-menu, click Microsoft Access (If you don't see it, open additional menus until you find it).

## SURVEY THE ACCESS SCREEN
The Access screen contains elements, including:
☞ Title bar (top of screen) identifies the program and database being used. In addition, the Close, Minimize, Maximize, and Restore buttons reside on the title bar.
☞ Menu bar (below the title bar) contains command categories. When one is clicked, a list of commands appears. To see all the commands, click the double-down arrow on the list.
☞ Database toolbar (below the menu bar) consists of picture buttons. If clicked, a command is executed.
☞ Task Pane appears on the right side of the screen. Its contents change, depending on what you are doing. Since you just started Access, the task pane wants to know what you want to do (if the task pane is not visible, click View, Toolbars, Task Pane to have it appear).

## CREATE A DATABASE TABLE
The first step in creating a database is to think about what types of information you need to store, organize, and retrieve. Then, you distill that information into fields and assemble the related fields into separate tables. Let's create a database of dog breeds with five fields: Breed, Origin, Weight, Height, and IQ.

To practice creating a table, do the following:
☞ From the Task Pane, click Blank Database (If Blank Database is not an option in the Task Pane, click Create A New File. Then, you will be able to click Blank Database).
☞ Insert a diskette and select the 3½ Floppy (A:) drive from the Save In list box of the File New Database dialog box.
☞ In the File Name box, enter the name AP1-Dogs.
☞ Click the Create button. You will then have a database window on top of the Access window. The Database window has two parts. On the left side of the window, the Objects bar provides a list of objects. Objects include tables, queries, forms, reports, etc. that you will use. When an object is selected, the Objects list appears on the right side of the window. It provides a list of specific ways to work with the selected object.
☞ From the Objects bar, click Tables (if not already selected).
☞ Notice that the Objects list provides a list of ways to create

a table. Since we'll use the Design view to create our table, double-click Create Table in Design View. The Table window appears. It has three columns to permit us to specify a name, a type, and a description for each field. And, it has many rows, each of which can contain a field.
☞ Maximize the window. In the cell below Field Name, type the first field name (in this case, type Breed).
☞ Press the Tab key to move to the Data Type cell. By default, "Text" is the data type selected. If you wanted another data type, you would select it from the list box. Since "Text" is the one we want, leave it as is.
☞ Press the Tab key to move to the Description cell. This cell provides an optional place to fully describe the field. Since the field name (breed) clearly identifies the field, we'll leave the Description cell blank.
☞ Press the Tab key to move to Row 2 and enter a field name of Origin.
☞ Press the Tab key and specify the data type to be Text.
☞ Press Tab and, in the Description cell, describe what is meant by "origin" (in this case type Country of Origin).
☞ In Row 3 enter a field name of Weight.
☞ Even though a weight is a number, we will never use it in any mathematical formulas. So specify the data type to be Text.
☞ In the Description cell, type Adult Weight in Pounds.
☞ In Row 4 enter a field name of Height.
☞ Since we will never use it in any mathematical formulas, specify the data type to be Text.
☞ In the Description cell, type Adult Height in Inches.
☞ In Row 5 enter a field name of IQ.
☞ Specify the data type to be Text.
☞ As IQ is self-explanatory, leave the Description cell blank.

## DESIGNATE A PRIMARY KEY
Every record in a table should have a field that differentiates it from any other record in the table so that no two records will have the same value for that field. That unique field should be designated as the primary key for that table. For instance, in the table you just created, it is possible that two or more dogs will have the same origin, IQ, weight, or height. On the other hand, only one record will exist for each breed. So, only the Breed field could be designated as a primary key.

To practice designating a primary key, do the following:
☞ Right click the row selector (the button on the left end of each row) for the row containing the desired field (in this case, the Breed field).
☞ Click Primary Key from the shortcut menu.
☞ Notice the row selector now has a picture of a key on it.

## SAVE A TABLE
Even though you saved your database when you started to create it, any table you create within your database will need to be saved as well. Think of a database as a "container" which holds all your objects, like this table.

To practice saving a table, do the following:
☞ Click File, Save. In the Save As box, name it Dog Breeds.
☞ Click OK.

## INSERT A FIELD
If you want a new field to be at the end of the table, just enter the field name, data type, and description in the row below the

last field. If you want to insert a new field between two other existing fields, insert a new row where desired.

To practice inserting a field, do the following:
☞ Right click the row selector for the row where you want a new row. In this case, insert a new row where the third is.
☞ Click Insert Rows from the shortcut menu.
☞ In the new row, enter a field name of Color, specify the data type as text, and leave the Description cell empty.

### DELETE A FIELD
If you no longer need one of the fields in the table, delete it.

To practice deleting a field, do the following:
☞ Right click the row selector for the row containing the field to be deleted (in this case, the Weight field row).
☞ Click Delete Rows from the shortcut menu.
☞ Repeat the above two steps to delete the Color field.
☞ Your table now has four fields (breed, origin, height, and IQ).

### MOVE A FIELD
After you've created fields, you may want to rearrange the order.

To practice moving a field, do the following:
☞ Click the row selector for the row to be moved (in this case, click the row selector for the Height field).
☞ Drag the row selector to the row where the IQ row is and release the mouse button. The Height field now appears below the IQ field in the table.
☞ Save your modified table (click File, Save).

### ENTER RECORDS INTO A TABLE
While we created the table in Design View, we will enter records using Datasheet View. As you enter each record, Access will automatically save your work.

To practice entering records in a table, do the following:
☞ Click View, Datasheet View. The table opens in Datasheet View with each field name at the top of each column. Click in the cell below the Breed field name and type the breed of the first record (in this case, type Beagle).
☞ Press Tab to move to the next field. Type England.
☞ Press Tab to move to the next field. Type High.
☞ Press Tab to move to the next field. Type 14.
☞ Press Tab to move to the second row in the Breed column and repeat the above steps to enter the following records:

| Breed | Origin | IQ | Height |
|---|---|---|---|
| Briard | France | Medium | 25 |
| Boxer | Germany | Medium | 23 |
| Bulldog | England | Low | 14 |
| Chihuahua | Mexico | High | 8 |
| Greyhound | Egypt | Low | 27 |
| Lhasa Apso | Tibet | High | 10 |
| Papillon | France | High | 10 |
| Pekingese | China | Medium | 9 |
| Afghan | Afghanistan | Low | 26 |

| Chow Chow | China | Medium | 18 |
|---|---|---|---|
| Akita | Japan | High | 26 |
| Airedale | England | Low | 23 |
| Brittany | France | Medium | 19 |
| Schnauzer | Germany | High | 19 |
| Dachshund | Germany | High | 9 |
| Samoyed | Siberia | High | 21 |

☞ Since Access saved each record as you entered it, there is no need to save the table. It's already saved.

### CLOSE AND OPEN A TABLE
When done working on a database, you'll want to close it.

To practice closing and opening a table, do the following:
☞ There's more than one Close button. The one on the title bar closes the program; the one on the menu bar closes the current object, which in this case is a table. So, to close the table, but leave Access open, click the Close button that appears at the right end of the menu bar.
☞ When the Database window appears, notice that your newly-created Dog Breeds table is on the Objects list.
☞ Imagine that you have discovered that you need to add two more records to your table. To do so, double-click the Breeds table icon to open the table. Notice that your records are now in alphabetical order by the primary key (breed).
☞ At the bottom of the table, add these two records:

| Char-Pei | China | Medium | 19 |
|---|---|---|---|
| Poodle | France | Medium | 15 |

☞ Close the table. You don't need to save your newly-modified table. Access did it for you. To confirm this fact, double-click the Dog Breeds table on the Objects list and locate the two records you just entered. Note: those records will be in alphabetical order with the other records in the table.

### GET HELP
The Office Assistant (the paper clip dude) can help with Access. If he's not on the screen, click Help, Show The Office Assistant. To have him disappear, right click him and then click Hide.

### COMPACT A DATABASE
As you proceed to the next few projects, you will be creating forms, reports, and queries, each of which need to be saved. Even if you delete some of these objects, the space they occupied is not efficiently freed up on your diskette. So, to keep your database from becoming too big to fit on your diskette, you will need to compact it. You can set up your database to compact automatically each time you close it.

To set up automatic compacting, do the following:
☞ Click Tools, Options. Click the General tab.
☞ Select Compact on Close. Click OK.

### CLOSE ACCESS
To close Access (remove it from memory), click the Close button (the X at the top right corner of its window).

NOTE: The files you created in this project will be needed later.

## EXERCISE 1: CROSSWORD

Use the clues below to complete the crossword puzzle (Note: the Answer Key can be found beginning on page G-21).

### ACROSS

3. The smallest particle of information about a person, place, thing, or event.
7. Access is a program created by the fine folks at ___.
8. Another word for load or launch.
10. From time to time, the task ___ will appear on the right side of the screen. Its contents change, depending on what you are doing. For instance, when you start Access, it wants to know what you want to do first.
11. The ___ bar appears below the title bar and it contains command categories (e.g., File, Edit, View, Insert).
12. A primary ___ is a field that will contain a unique data value for each record in the table.
14. The ___ View is used to create tables.
16. The ___ View is used to enter data into a table.

### DOWN

1. A collection of related fields is a ___.
2. When you start Access, you are actually placing the program into memory. Another word for memory is ___.
4. A collection of related tables is a ___.
5. I can click Help, Show The ___ Assistant, to find a paper clip character who will provide guidance.
6. A ___ key is a field that will contain a value different from any other record.
8. When I ___ a database (or a table within a database), I am placing a copy of what is in memory onto a more permanent place (e.g., my diskette).
9. A collection of related records is a ___.
13. Is the database program we are using called Access?
15. Street, City, State, Zip are each most likely a field ___.

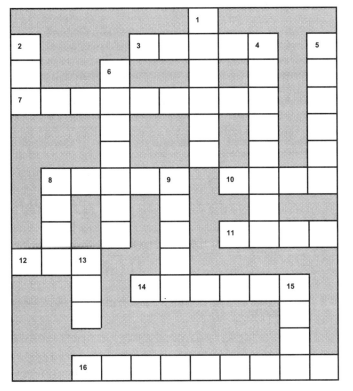

## EXERCISE 2: MATCHING

For each statement, identify the term being described by placing the letter of the term in the line preceding each statement.

> A. Database
> B. Field
> C. Record
> D. Table

1. ___ A collection of related tables.
2. ___ A collection of related fields.
3. ___ A collection of related records.
4. ___ The smallest particle of information.

## EXERCISE 3: TRUE-FALSE

For each of the following eight statements, place a T or an F on the line to indicate if the statement is True or False.

1. ___ A field is a collection of related tables.
2. ___ The title bar is at the top of the Access window.
3. ___ The menu bar has picture buttons on it.
4. ___ The Office Assistant normally looks like a paper clip.
5. ___ A table is a collection of related fields.
6. ___ The Database Toolbar has picture buttons on it.
7. ___ A collection of related records is a field.
8. ___ To "load" a program is to "start" a program.

## EXERCISE 4: MATCHING

For each statement, identify the view being described by placing the letter of the view in the line preceding each statement.

> A. Datasheet view
> B. Design view

1. ___ The view used to create a table.
2. ___ The view used to enter data into a table.

## EXERCISE 5: FIND A WORD

Each of the following nine statements describes a word. The actual word referred to can be found in the matrix below. Some are backwards, some are diagonal, and some are horizontal. Circle each word.

1. A collection of related fields.
2. A collection of related records.
3. A collection of related tables.
4. The smallest particle of information.
5. The database program we are learning about in this book.
6. The view used to create tables.
7. The "X" button at the top right corner of a window.
8. A ___ key identifies a field containing a unique value.
9. Another word for memory.

| P | C | L | T | T | E | O | L | G | D | R |
|---|---|---|---|---|---|---|---|---|---|---|
| R | D | A | T | A | B | A | S | E | T | A |
| I | C | T | R | E | B | M | B | P | C | M |
| M | L | H | F | I | E | L | D | C | K | B |
| A | O | O | D | R | O | C | E | R | J | V |
| R | S | M | S | P | B | S | A | E | N | O |
| Y | E | U | D | E | S | I | G | N | I | W |

## EXERCISE 6: CREATE A DATABASE TABLE

Dozer's Digital Devices, Inc. (DDD) buys, refurbishes, and resells used computers and monitors. The owner, Dozer, wants to take better control of his business. He's asked you to help. Will you? If so, please create a database for him.

☞ Start Access. On a diskette, create a new database (call it AP1-Inventory).

☞ In Design View, create a table. The first field name is "Model", the data type is "Text", and the description is "Manufacturer's Model Number".

☞ The second field is "Date", the data type is "Text", and the description is "Date Unit Was Manufactured".

☞ The third field name is "Cost", the data type is "Currency" (select Currency from the Data Type drop down list). The description is "Dozer's Cost To Acquire".

☞ The fourth field name is "SKU", the data type is "Text", and the description is "Stock Keeping Unit". By the way, a sku is a number assigned to items to help control inventory.

☞ Between the first and second fields, insert a new field called "Warehouse", with a "Text" data type, and a "Warehouse Where Unit Is Stored" description.

☞ Dozer has decided that he doesn't need to keep information about the date of manufacture. So, delete the Date field.

☞ Move the fields so that they are in the following order: SKU, Cost, Model, and Warehouse.

☞ Since Dozer assigns a different inventory number (SKU) to each individual monitor, no two records will have the same data value for the SKU field. Therefore, designate the SKU field as the Primary key.

☞ Save your table (name it Monitor SKUs).

## EXERCISE 7: SET UP AUTOMATIC COMPACTING

The database you are now working on will be used in the following three exercises and in the next three projects where you will be creating forms, reports, and queries, each of which need to be saved. Even if you delete some of these objects, the space they occupied is not efficiently freed up on your diskette. So, to keep your database from becoming too big to fit on your diskette, you will need to compact it. Please set up this database to compact automatically each time you close it. If you forgot how to do this, see page G-4.

## EXERCISE 8: ENTER RECORDS INTO A TABLE

The records for the Monitor SKUs table need to be entered. Using the Datasheet View, please enter the records below. While you do so, you may notice that the floppy drive light keeps coming on. That's because Access will save your work as you enter it. In the prior exercise, you had to save your table when you were done with it. That's because in the prior exercise, you were creating the table. Now, you are entering records into that table. A table must be saved when you are done creating it; records being entered into a previously-saved table are saved as you enter them. Use Datasheet View to enter these records.

| SKU | Cost | Model | Warehouse |
|-----|------|-------|-----------|
| 268 | 26.56 | Z44 | West Coast |
| 295 | 27.64 | Z88 | East Coast |
| 214 | 35.69 | Z66 | West Coast |
| 278 | 38.25 | FX95 | East Coast |

☞ Close the table, but leave Access open.

☞ Open the table and insert the following record into it.

| SKU | Cost | Model | Warehouse |
|-----|------|-------|-----------|
| 236 | 19.59 | CX75 | West Coast |

☞ Close the table, but leave Access open.

## EXERCISE 9: CREATE A DATABASE TABLE

In Exercise 6, you created a database (AP-1 Inventory) with a table (Monitor SKUs) to store data about the specific monitors Dozer has in inventory. From time to time, Dozer will need to know the exact specifications of his various models of monitors. For instance, if a buyer wants to know about the dot-pitch and the resolution of a particular monitor, Dozer wants to be able to provide that information swiftly. So, he needs a table to store the specifications for each model of monitor.

☞ In the AP-1 Inventory database, use Design View to create a table.

☞ The first field is "Brand", the data type is "Text", and the description is "Brand Name of Monitor".

☞ The second field is "Dot-Pitch", the data type is "Text". Leave the Description cell blank.

☞ The third field is "Size", the data type is "Text". Leave the Description cell blank.

☞ The fourth field is "Model", the data type is "Text", and the description is "Manufacturer's Model Number".

☞ The fifth field is "Refresh Rate", the data type is "Text". Leave the Description cell blank.

☞ Between the third and fourth fields, insert a new field called "Resolution", with a "Text" data type, and a "Maximum Resolution" description.

☞ Dozer has decided he doesn't want a Refresh Rate field. So, delete that field from the table.

☞ Move the fields so that they are in the following order: Brand, Model, Resolution, Size, and Dot-Pitch.

☞ Since each model will have only one record in this table, no two records will have the same data value for the Model field. Therefore, designate the Model field as the primary key.

☞ Save your table. Since this table will store data about each model's specifications (name it Monitor Specs).

## EXERCISE 10: ENTER RECORDS INTO A TABLE

Dozer normally buys and sells only Zony and Zell monitors. The records for the Monitor Specs table need to be entered. Using the Datasheet View, please enter the following five records.

| Brand | Model | Resolution | Size | Dot-Pitch |
|-------|-------|------------|------|-----------|
| Zell | CX75 | 1280 x 1024 | 15 | .28 |
| Zell | FX95 | 1600 x 1200 | 19 | .26 |
| Zony | Z44 | 1280 x 1024 | 19 | .26 |
| Zony | Z66 | 1600 x 1200 | 19 | .26 |
| Zell | QX66 | 1024 x 768 | 17 | .25 |

☞ Close the table, but leave Access open.

☞ Open the Monitor Specs table. Insert the following record.

| Brand | Model | Resolution | Size | Dot-Pitch |
|-------|-------|------------|------|-----------|
| Zony | Z88 | 1600 x 1200 | 19 | .26 |

☞ Close the table and close Access.

**NOTE**: The files you created in this project will be needed later.

In this project you will use the AP-1 Dogs database you created on page G-3. If you don't have that database, go to page G-3 and create it. You will then be ready to start this project.

## OPEN A DATABASE
To work with an existing database, you will need to open it.

To practice opening an existing database, do the following:
☞ Start Access and click File, Open. From the Look In box, select the drive that contains your database.
☞ Select the AP-1 Dogs file and click Open.

## CREATE ANOTHER TABLE IN A DATABASE
Your AP1-Dogs database has one table (Dog Breeds). In this project, you will create another table and will learn how to create and use forms to enter records into a table.

To practice creating another table, do the following:
☞ From the Objects bar, click Tables.
☞ Double-click Create Table in Design View.
☞ The Table window appears. In the cell below Field Name, type your first field name (in this case, type Name).
☞ Specify the data type to be Text.
☞ Press the Tab key and type Dog's Name in the Description cell to clarify that the name will be the dog's, not the owner's.
☞ In Row 2 enter a field name of Breed.
☞ Specify Text as data type. Leave the Description cell blank.
☞ In Row 3 enter a field name of Award.
☞ Specify Currency as data type (select Currency from the Data Type drop down list). Leave the Description cell blank.
☞ In Row 4, enter a field name of Show.
☞ Specify the data type to be Text.
☞ Press Tab. In the Description cell, type Location of Show to clarify that the field identifies the dog show location.
☞ In Row 5 enter a field name of Prize.
☞ Specify Text as data type. Leave the Description cell blank.
☞ You may recall that a primary key is used to identify a field that will have a unique data value from any other field in that table. In our "Dog Breeds" table, there was one record for each breed. So, we designated the "Breed" field as the primary key. In this table, no field will contain a unique data value. In this table, even the Breed field may have duplicate data values (e.g., a specific breed might win more than one dog show). So no fields in this table qualify to be a primary key. In the next step, when you save the table without designating a primary key, you'll be asked to do so.
☞ To save the table, click File, Save.
☞ Enter a name (Dog Shows), and click OK.
☞ You will be told that no primary key has been defined and you will be asked if you want to create a primary key. Click Yes. Your table will be saved and you will be returned to the Datasheet View. Notice that the first row is now the primary key. Access will assign a unique number to each record.
☞ Close the table, but leave Access open.

## CREATE A FORM
You now have a database with two tables. You may recall that after you created the "Dog Breeds" table (in Project 1), you switched to the Datasheet view and entered records by typing each record in a row. Another way to enter records is to create a form into which you could enter each record. By doing so, the record-entry process becomes less tedious, faster, and more accurate. We will use a wizard (a series of dialog boxes that will guide us through the process) to create our form.

To practice creating a form, do the following:
☞ From the Objects bar, click Forms.
☞ From the Objects list, double-click Create Form By Using Wizard. Notice that the Form Wizard dialog box appears.
☞ From the Tables/Queries list box, select the table for which you want to create a form (in this case, select Dog Shows).
☞ From the Available Fields list, double-click each field you want in the form (you want them all). Each time you double click a desired field, it will appear in the Selected Fields box. By the way, you could also click the >> button to have all the fields move to the Selected Fields box at once.
☞ When all the fields are in the Selected Fields box, click Next.
☞ Select the Columnar layout for your table and click Next.
☞ Choose a style for your form and see what it looks like. Select another one. When you find one you like, click Next.
☞ You are now asked to provide a title (name) for your form (name it Dog Shows).
☞ Make sure the Open the Form To View Or Enter Information option is chosen and then click the Finish button. The Dog Shows form appears.

## ENTER RECORDS INTO A TABLE VIA A FORM
Now that you have created a form for the Dog Shows table, you can enter records into the form. Each form contains a box for inputting each field in a specific record. Let's enter records into the Dog Shows table via the form.

To practice entering records via a form, do the following:
☞ Maximize the form window, if not already maximized.
☞ In the Name field box, type the dog's name (Snooks).
☞ Press Tab to move to the Breed field box and type Poodle.
☞ Press Tab to move to the Award field box and type (400).
☞ Press Tab to move to the Show field box and type Phoenix).
☞ Press Tab to move to the Prize box and type the prize (2$^{nd}$).
☞ Press Tab. Since there are no more field boxes in the form, a form for a new record appears.
☞ In the new form, press Tab to move to the Name field box.
☞ Enter following records:

| Name | Breed | Award | Show | Prize |
|---|---|---|---|---|
| Maverick | Akita | 200 | Reno | 2nd |
| Thoreau | Boxer | 250 | Denver | 3rd |
| Rascal | Brittany | 500 | El Paso | 1st |
| Majestic | Char-Pei | 400 | Boise | 3rd |
| Cisco | Briard | 500 | Dallas | 3rd |
| Google | Boxer | 600 | Phoenix | 1st |

☞ Look at the Record buttons (bottom left corner of the window). You should have seven records in your table.
☞ Click View, Datasheet View to see your data in that view. Remember, you could have entered your data using the Datasheet view as you did on your Dog Breeds table. But, using a form to enter the data is just another way to do it.
☞ To return to the Form View, click View, Form View.

## CREATE A LIST BOX

When you were entering data in the form, you may have noticed that typing all that stuff gets somewhat boring. If many of your records have identical data values for some fields, you can speed up the data-entry process (and increase accuracy) by adding list boxes to your form. For instance, in the current table, you had to enter either 1st, 2nd, or 3rd place for each record. You also had to enter cities, many of which will be repeated in future records. If you create list boxes containing the possible choices, you could then simply select the choice from the list. By the way, you could also create combo boxes, which are similar to list boxes with one exception. With a list box, you can only pick what's on the list; with a combo box, you can pick from the list or go ahead and type in a data value that is not on the list. Both list boxes and combo boxes are made virtually the same way, so we'll only create list boxes for our form.

To practice creating a list box, do the following:

☞ Click View, Design View. The form will appear in Design view along with the Toolbox toolbar (if the Toolbox does not appear, click View, Toolbox).

☞ To see more of the form (the grid with the dots), drag the bottom border of the grid to make the form taller.

☞ On the Toolbox, make sure the Control Wizards button is selected (looks like a magic wand with some stars).

☞ Click the List Box button on the Toolbox (to find it, point to each button to have a Tooltip identify the button).

☞ Move the mouse to the grid. Notice that the mouse pointer changes shape, indicating you've chosen to create a list box.

☞ Drag the mouse on the grid below the field boxes and release the mouse button. The List Box Wizard appears.

☞ Select the method you'll use to enter the values on the list (in this case, select I Will Type In The Values That I Want).

☞ Click the Next button. The next page of the wizard appears.

☞ In the first cell, type the first data value. In this case, type Boise, press Tab to go to the next cell and type Dallas, and continue until you've entered Denver, El Paso, Phoenix, and Reno. When done, click the Next button.

☞ Select Store That Value In This Field. From the drop down list, select the field associated with the list (in this case, select the Show field).

☞ Click the Next button. The next page of the wizard appears.

☞ Type the label for the list (type Show) and click Finish.

☞ The actual values you put in the box do not appear in Design View. They will appear when you go back to Form View.

☞ To create a second list box, click the List Box button on the Toolbox.

☞ Drag the mouse on the grid below the field boxes and release the mouse button. The List Box Wizard appears.

☞ Select I Will Type In The Values That I Want. Click Next.

☞ In the first cell, type the first data value (in this case, type 1st).

☞ Press Tab to go to the next cell and type 2nd.

☞ Press Tab to go to the next cell and type 3rd.

☞ When done, click the Next button. The next page appears.

☞ Select Store That Value In This Field. From the drop down list, select the field associated with this list (in this case, select the Prize field).

☞ Click the Next button. The next page of the wizard appears.

☞ Type the label for the list (type Prize) and click Finish.

☞ The actual values you put in the list do not appear in Design View. They will appear when you go back to Form View.

## MODIFY A FORM

To change the appearance of a form, here are a few tips.

To practice modifying a form, do the following:

☞ In Design View, a form is a collection of controls. Each field name is a control and each data field box is a control.

☞ To change the size of a control, click the control and then drag one of its sizing handles. Go ahead and resize each of the two list boxes so you can see all the options on each list. Since you cannot actually see the items in each list, after you make each list box bigger, you will need to click View, Form View to see if you made it big enough. Then, to return to the Design View, click View, Design View.

☞ Since you've created list boxes for the Show and Prize fields, delete the original Show and Prize field controls. To do so, click each one and press the Delete key.

☞ Move the Show list box under the Award controls and the Prize list box under the Show list box. To do so, click in a control and move the mouse until the mouse pointer looks like a hand. Then drag and drop the list to its new location.

☞ Right click in a data field box, point to Fill/Back Color, and click a color. With the box selected, double-click the Format Painter toolbar button (looks like a paint brush) and then click each of the other field boxes to apply the same color. When done, click the Format Painter button to turn it off.

☞ Click View, Form View to see what your newly-modified form looks like. If you don't like anything about it, click View, Design View and modify it some more.

☞ Now, let's enter a few records with our newly-improved form.

☞ In Form View, click Insert, New Record. Enter these records. Use the list boxes to enter the data values for the Show and Prize fields. And, when one record is complete, press Tab to have the next record appear.

| Name | Breed | Award | Show | Prize |
|------|-------|-------|------|-------|
| Stetson | Airedale | 1500 | Dallas | 1st |
| Ace | Afghan | 100 | Reno | 3rd |
| Knuckles | Samoyed | 500 | Denver | 2nd |
| Taboo | Airedale | 200 | Phoenix | 3rd |
| Sartre | Boxer | 800 | Boise | 1st |
| Fuddles | Brittany | 300 | El Paso | 2nd |
| Daisy | Samoyed | 300 | Reno | 1st |
| Rocky | Bulldog | 1000 | Denver | 1st |
| Queenie | Poodle | 600 | Boise | 2nd |
| Peaches | Char-Pei | 1000 | Dallas | 2nd |
| Bandit | Papillon | 150 | El Paso | 3rd |

☞ Look near the bottom left corner of the window to see how many records are in your table. If there aren't 18, your table is not correct. To fix it, click View, Datasheet View and compare your records with those found on this page and on page G-7. Add any missing records and delete any duplicate records so that you have 18 records.

☞ Close the form. If asked if you want to save it, click Yes. Note, you won't be saving the records you entered (they were saved automatically when you entered them). You will be saving the structure (design) of the form for later use.

☞ Close Access.

NOTE: The files you created in this project will be needed later.

## EXERCISE 1: CROSSWORD

Use the clues below to complete the crossword puzzle (Note: the Answer Key can be found beginning on page G-21).

### ACROSS

2. If I have a field called "Zip Code" and I enter "89130" as the zip code in a specific record, the "89130" is the ___ value for that field.
4. To create a form, sometimes it's easier to use a ___, which is a series of dialog boxes that will guide me through a process.
8. Dozer's favorite database program (the one we are using) is called Microsoft ___.
10. "Tables", "Forms", and "Queries" are ___ within a database.
13. To work with an existing database, you first need to ___ it so that it will be in memory (RAM).
14. After I select an object from the Objects bar, the Objects ___ appears which provides various ways for me to work with the specific object I selected.
16. The database program we are learning about was created by the fine folks at ___.

### DOWN

1. The smallest particle of information in a database.
3. A collection of related records.
5. The ___ View is used to enter data into a table.
6. The ___ View is used to create tables.
7. A collection of related tables.
9. When you look at your form in Design View, you can see that each field has two parts; the field name and a data value box into which you enter the data for that field. Each of these two parts can be resized and/or moved and each is called a ___.
11. If I try to save a table without defining a field as the primary key, will Access remind me to do so?
12. You can create a ___ into which you could enter the data for each record.
15. Is a collection of related records called a field?

## EXERCISE 2: TRUE-FALSE

For each of the following eight statements, place a T or an F on the line to indicate if the statement is True or False.

1. ___ A form is used to enter data into a table.
2. ___ To work with a database, you'll need to open it.
3. ___ The words "Tables" and "Forms" are on the Objects bar.
4. ___ A database could contain more than one table.
5. ___ The paper clip dude is called a wizard.
6. ___ "Create Table in Design View" is on an Objects list.
7. ___ When using a form, pressing Tab moves to the next field.
8. ___ I can create a table in Datasheet View.

## EXERCISE 3: IDENTIFY TERMS

Below are eight definitions. Below the definitions are eight lines. In each line, write the word that matches the definition.

1. The view used to create a form.
2. The view used to enter records into a table.
3. A list of items on a form from which I can select data values.
4. In Design View, each field consists of two of these.
5. A series of dialog boxes that guides you through a process.
6. This is used to identify a field with a unique data value.
7. The view used to create a table.
8. A collection of related fields.

1. _____    5. _____
2. _____    6. _____
3. _____    7. _____
4. _____    8. _____

## EXERCISE 4: TRUE-FALSE

For each of the following eight statements, place a T or an F on the line to indicate if the statement is True or False.

1. ___ A table is used to enter data into a form.
2. ___ Each field on a form has two controls.
3. ___ The words "Tables" and "Forms" are on the Objects list.
4. ___ A database can contain only one table.
5. ___ Once my form is created, I can modify its appearance.
6. ___ "Create Table in Design View" is on the Objects bar.
7. ___ A form is a collection of controls.
8. ___ I can create a table in Design View.

## EXERCISE 5: EXPLAIN CONCEPTS

Dozer is confused. He doesn't understand why anyone would need to create a form. Explain to him what a form is used for and why it is helpful to use them.

_____
_____
_____
_____
_____
_____
_____
_____
_____
_____
_____
_____
_____
_____
_____
_____

## EXERCISE 6: CREATE A FORM

In Exercises 6-10 on page G-6, you created a database for Dozer's Digital Devices, Inc. (AP-1 Inventory). In that database, you created two tables, one to store data about his inventory of monitors (Monitor SKUs) and another to store data about the specifications of each model of monitor (Monitor Specs). To do the next few exercises, you'll use that database. If you haven't created it, or if you've lost it, go back to page G-6 and do exercises 6-10. You will then be prepared to do the following exercises. In this particular exercise, you will create a form.

☞ Start Access and open the AP-1 Inventory database.
☞ Use a wizard to create a form for the Monitor SKUs table using all the fields from that table (name the form Monitor SKUs.
☞ Create a list box for the model field. The list should include: CX75, DX55, FX95, LX45, MX30, QX66, SX88, Z22, Z44, Z66, and Z88 (name the list box Model).
☞ Create a list box for the warehouse field. The box should include two items: East Coast and West Coast (name the list box Warehouse).
☞ Go to Form View. Are the list boxes you just created big enough to display all the items on each? If not, go to Design view and resize them so they are big enough, but not too big.
☞ Since you've created two list boxes, delete the original model and the warehouse controls.
☞ Move the Model list box so it appears below the Cost control and move the Warehouse list box so it appears below the Model list box.
☞ Apply a Fill/Back Color to each data value control.
☞ Close the form. If asked if you want to save the design of your form, click Yes.

## EXERCISE 7: ENTER RECORDS USING A FORM

Your Monitor SKUs table already has some records in it. You might recall that you entered some when you did Exercise 8 on page G-6. At that time, you used the Datasheet View to enter some records. In Exercise 6 above, you created a form. The purpose of a form is to provide another way to enter records into a table. So, let's use your newly-created form to enter some additional records into your table. Open the "Monitor SKUs" form, click Insert, New Record, and enter the following records. Use the list boxes to speed up the process and to increase accuracy.

| SKU | Cost | Model | Warehouse |
|-----|------|-------|-----------|
| 224 | 18.57 | DX55 | East Coast |
| 249 | 24.89 | Z22 | West Coast |
| 251 | 19.46 | DX55 | West Coast |
| 285 | 26.76 | SX88 | East Coast |
| 262 | 20.54 | LX45 | East Coast |
| 273 | 26.32 | MX30 | West Coast |
| 281 | 26.98 | Z88 | East Coast |
| 233 | 26.45 | QX66 | East Coast |
| 219 | 18.95 | CX75 | West Coast |
| 205 | 34.69 | Z66 | East Coast |

☞ Close the form, but leave Access open.

☞ Open the Monitor SKUs form and enter these records.

| 222 | 37.59 | FX95 | West Coast |
|-----|-------|------|-----------|
| 298 | 37.96 | Z66 | East Coast |
| 235 | 25.57 | Z44 | West Coast |
| 284 | 25.85 | QX66 | West Coast |

☞ Close the form, but leave Access open.

## EXERCISE 8: CREATE A FORM

In Exercise 6, you created a form for the Monitor SKUs table and then in Exercise 7, you used that form to enter records into that table. Dozer also needs a form for the Monitor Specs table.

☞ Use a wizard to create a form for the Monitor Specs table using all its fields (name the form Monitor Specs).
☞ Create a list box for the brand field. The list will include Zell and Zony (name the list box Brand).
☞ Create a list box for the model field. The list should include: CX75, DX55, FX95, LX45, MX30, QX66, SX88, Z22, Z44, Z66, and Z88 (name the list box Model).
☞ Create a list box for the resolution field. The list box should include the following three items: 1024 X 768, 1280 x 1024, and 1600 x 1200 (name the list box Resolution).
☞ Create a list box for the size field. The list has the following three items: 15, 17, and 19 (name the list box Size).
☞ Create a list box for the dot-pitch field. The list has the following three items: .25, .26, and .28 (name the list box Dot-Pitch).
☞ Go to Form View. Are the list boxes you just created big enough to display all the items on each? If not, go to Design view and resize them so they are big enough, but not too big.
☞ Since you've created five list boxes, delete the original brand, model, resolution, size, and dot-pitch controls.
☞ Move the list boxes so they appear in the following order: Brand, Model, Resolution, Size, and Dot-Pitch.
☞ Apply a Fill/Back Color to each data value control.
☞ Close the form. If asked if you want to save the design of your form, click Yes.

## EXERCISE 9: ENTER RECORDS USING A FORM

In Exercise 10 on page G-6, you used the Datasheet View to enter records into your Monitor Specs table. In Exercise 8 above, you created a form. The purpose of a form is to provide another way to enter records into a table. So, let's use your newly-created form to enter some additional records into your table. Open the "Monitor Specs" form and enter the following records. Use the list boxes to speed up the process and to increase accuracy.

| Brand | Model | Resolution | Size | Dot-Pitch |
|-------|-------|-----------|------|-----------|
| Zony | Z22 | 1280 x 1024 | 17 | .28 |
| Zell | DX55 | 1024 x 768 | 15 | .28 |
| Zell | SX88 | 1600 x 1200 | 17 | .25 |
| Zell | LX45 | 1280 x 1024 | 15 | .25 |
| Zell | MX30 | 1280 x 1024 | 17 | .28 |

☞ Close the form and then close Access.

NOTE: The files you created in this project will be needed later.

Microsoft Access is a database program that stores, organizes, and retrieves data. The power behind a database program is its ability to retrieve data in customized ways. Information can be retrieved based upon any field in the database. In this project you will run some queries (ask some questions) to retrieve information from your database.

## OPEN A DATABASE
Start Access and open the AP1-Dogs database you created on page G-3 and later modified on page G-7. If you don't have that database, please return to those pages and recreate it. Then, you will be ready to start this project.

## CREATE A QUERY USING A SINGLE TABLE
In Project 1, you created the Dog Breeds table and used the Database view to enter records into the table. In Project 2, you created the Dog Shows table, created a form to assist in the entry of the records, and then you actually used that form to enter records. Both tables are saved as a single database called "AP1-Dogs". Now that your database is complete, you can use it to learn lots of neat stuff by querying it (asking it a question). For instance, you might want to know: What breeds won 1ˢᵗ place prizes at the various dog shows? Or, what prizes were won by dogs with high IQs? Or, what was the total amount of all awards for all the shows? When you query a database, Access will provide a record set (a list of records that answer your question). And, if you save your query as an object in your database, you can retrieve it later. A query can be created in Design View or via a wizard. Later, we'll learn how to create a query in Design View, but first let's use a wizard.

To practice querying a database, do the following:
- From the Objects bar, click Queries.
- Double-click Create Query By Using Wizard (the Simple Query Wizard dialog box will appear).
- From the Tables/Queries list box, select the table that contains the data to be queried. Since you want to know which prizes were won by which breeds, select the table that contains that data (the Dog Shows table).
- The Available Fields box provides a list of all the fields in the Dog Shows table. Double click each field needed to answer your question. Each time you double click a desired field, it will move to the Selected Fields box (in this case, double click the breed field and then the prize field).
- Click the Next button to go to the next page of the wizard.
- In the What Title Do You Want For Your Query text box, type a name for your query (call it Breeds Prizes).
- Click the Finish button. A window displays the results of your query. If needed, maximize the window. Notice that the results are not in any particular order. We'll fix that next.

## SORT A QUERY
It's easier to find information when it's organized in some logical way. You can sort (reorganize) the information provided by your query either in ascending order (ABC or 123) or in descending order (ZYX or 321). And, you can do so with any field.

To practice sorting a query, do the following:
- Click anywhere in the column for the field by which you want the records sorted (in this case, the Breed column).
- Click Records, Sort, Sort Ascending. Notice that the records are now sorted alphabetically by breed, which makes it

easier to comprehend the information.
- To sort the records by Prize, click in the Prize column and click Records, Sort, Sort Ascending. After sorting the records, you can easily see which breeds won 1ˢᵗ, 2ⁿᵈ, and 3ʳᵈ place prizes.
- Close the Query window, but leave Access open. If asked if you want to save the changes to the query, click Yes.

## CREATE A RELATIONSHIP BETWEEN TABLES
In addition to querying a single table, your query can extract information from more than one table. However, before you can do so, you must create a connection (relationship) between the tables. In your database, you have two tables. The Dog Breeds table stores the origin, IQ, and height of each dog breed. The Dog Shows table stores the name, breed, award, show, and prize won by specific dogs. If you wanted to know something that requires the data from both tables, you will need to create a query that tells Access to extract the needed data from those two tables. For instance, if you wanted to know the IQ of dogs who won 1ˢᵗ place prizes, you would need to extract data from both of your tables. But, first, you must create a link between them. That link is called a relationship. By the way, the ability to connect two or more tables in a database provides awesome benefits. For instance, since I can extract data from more than one table, I can construct my tables to avoid something called data redundancy, which occurs when the same data is kept in more places than is necessary. Let's establish (define) the relationship between our two tables.

To practice creating a relationship, do the following:
- In the Database window, click Tools, Relationships. The Show Table dialog box will appear (if it does not appear, click Relationships, Show Table to have it appear). The Show Table dialog box will provide a list of the tables in your database. In your case, there are two tables; Dog Breeds and Dog Shows.
- Click Dog Breeds and then click the Add button.
- Click Dog Shows and then click the Add button.
- Click the Close button in the dialog box to close it. Notice that each of your tables (Dog Breeds and Dog Shows) appears in its own box within the Relationships window and that each box displays a list of the fields found in each table. If needed, resize the windows so that you can see all the fields in each. Also notice that the primary key for each table is displayed in bold.
- You now need to choose which fields to link between the two tables. There are some rules to follow. For instance, while they don't need to have the same name, the fields must contain the same type of information and be of the same data type. Most often, a primary field from one table is linked to a field in another table.
- Since the primary field in the Dog Breeds table is "Breed", let's link that field to a field in the Dog Shows table that has the same type of information and data type (i.e., Breed). To do so, point the mouse to the Breed field in the Dog Breeds table and drag and drop it to the Breed field in the Dog Shows table. When you release the mouse button, the Edit Relationships dialog box will appear.
- In the Edit Relationships dialog box, notice that the two tables are identified along with the fields used to link them. Also, there are three check boxes. The first one asks if you want to enforce referential integrity. Sounds a bit ominous,

doesn't it? Here's what it's asking. You just linked a primary key field to a foreign key field (the foreign key field is the Breed field in the Dog Shows table). So, if you enforce referential integrity, you are telling Access to make sure that in the future, any data entered into the foreign key field must match data in the primary key field of the other table. If you ever try to violate referential integrity by typing in data that has no exact match in the primary key field, Access will give you an error message. The other two check boxes, if selected, will tell Access to either automatically update the foreign key field data when you change its corresponding data in the primary key field or will tell Access to delete the data in the foreign key field if the corresponding data is changed in the primary key field. Hey, let's not choose any of the three. But, knowing how inquisitive you are, I thought I'd go ahead and explain what those boxes are for. Otherwise, you'd stay up all night trying to figure it all out.

☞ In the Edit Relationships dialog box, click Create. Notice that there is now a line connecting the two fields indicating that the tables are now related (linked) via those two fields.

☞ Close the Relationship window. When asked if you want to save the changes in its layout, click Yes.

## CREATE A QUERY USING MORE THAN ONE TABLE
Earlier in this Project, you ran a query on a single table. Now that you've created a relationship between the two tables, you can extract information that resides in both of them.

To practice querying more than one table, do the following:
☞ From the Objects bar, click Queries.
☞ Double-click Create Query By Using Wizard (the Simple Query Wizard dialog box will appear).
☞ From the Tables/Queries list box, select a table containing data to be queried. Since you want to know which awards and prizes were won by which breeds and the IQ of each breed, you will need to capture the breed, award, prize, and IQ fields. Since the required data exists in both tables, you will need to capture fields from their respective tables.
☞ Select the Dog Breeds table from the Tables/Queries list.
☞ The Available Fields box provides a list of all the fields in the Dog Breeds table. Double click each field needed to answer your question (in this case, double click the Breed field and then the IQ field).
☞ From the Tables/Queries list, select the Dog Shows table.
☞ The Available Fields box provides a list of all the fields in the Dog Shows table. Since you already have the Breed and IQ fields from the other table, you now only need the Award and the Prize fields from this table. So, go ahead and double click Award and Prize to have each added to the Selected Fields list.
☞ The Selected field box should now contain four fields (breed, IQ, award, and prize). Click the Next button to go to the next page of the wizard.
☞ When asked if you would like a detail or a summary query, select Detail and then click the Next button.
☞ In the What Title Do You Want For Your Query text box, type a name (call it Breed IQ Award Prize).
☞ Click Finish. A window displays the results of your query. If needed, maximize the window.
☞ Sort the records in descending order by Award.
☞ Close the window, but leave Access open. If asked to save the design of the query, click Yes.

## CREATE A QUERY USING THE DESIGN VIEW
So far, we've created two queries using a wizard, which made the process rather simple. However, in more complex queries, the limitations inherent in a wizard might prevent us from creating our query. In such cases, we might need to create a query using the Design View. Below, we'll create a query to find out which breeds won 1st prizes that came with awards of $500 or more. By doing so, all breeds winning 2nd and 3rd place prizes will be eliminated, as well as any 1st place prize winners who were awarded less than $500.

To practice creating a query in Design View, do the following:
☞ From the Objects bar, click Queries.
☞ Double-click Create Query in Design View. The Show Table dialog box appears.
☞ Click the Dog Breeds table.
☞ Click the Add button.
☞ Click the Dog Shows table.
☞ Click the Add button and close the Show Table dialog box.
☞ The Select Query window appears with windows for the Dog Breeds and Dog Shows tables appearing above a grid. Your goal is to get the desired fields to appear in the grid. The easiest way to accomplish this feat is to simply double click each desired field. So, since your query is to find the IQ, award, and prize for each breed, from the Dog Breeds table, double-click Breed and then double-click IQ.
☞ Notice that those fields are now in the grid.
☞ From the Dog Shows window, double-click Award and Prize. Now, the grid contains the fields needed for your query. If you made a mistake, you can clear the grid by clicking Edit, Clear Grid. Then you can start over.
☞ Notice that each field's Show Box has a check mark, indicating that the field will appear in the query results. If you were to run the query, you'd get a list of all the breeds along with each breed's IQ, award, and prize. But, what if you didn't want all that information. What if you only wanted the records where a dog received a 1st place prize and the award was for at least $500? To have that happen, you'll need to set additional criteria.
☞ Click in the cell at the intersection of the Criteria row and the Prize column. Enter your criteria (condition). In this case enter =1st to indicate that you don't want any 2nd or 3rd place prize winners.
☞ Click in the cell at the intersection of the Criteria row and the Award column. Enter your criteria (condition). In this case enter >=500 to indicate that you want only records where the award was for an amount greater than (>) or equal to (=) $500.
☞ Run the query (click the Run toolbar button, which looks like a big red exclamation point). Notice that the results include only 1st place winners who received $500 or more in award. In your database, there was another 1st place winner, but that dog was awarded $300. So, that record does not appear in the query results.
☞ Sort the records in ascending order by breed.
☞ Close the window. When asked if you want to save your changes to the design of the query, click Yes.
☞ In the Save As window, enter a query name (name it 1st Prize >=500). Click OK.
☞ Close Access.

NOTE: The files you created in this project will be needed later.

## EXERCISE 1: CROSSWORD

Use the clues below to complete the crossword puzzle (Note: the Answer Key can be found beginning on page G-21).

### ACROSS

1. When you want to extract information from a database, you can create and then run a ___.
4. The smallest particle of information about a person, place, thing, or event in a database is a ___.
5. To Open an Access database, you will first want to click the ___ button to find the program (this button is at the left end of the taskbar).
7. A ___ key is a field within a table that will contain a data value different from any other record in that table.
10. Is a wizard and a query the same thing?
11. Words like Tables, Queries, and Forms can be found on the Objects ___.
12. Learning about computers is lots of ___.
14. To create a form or a query, sometimes its easier to use a ___, which is a series of dialog boxes that guide us through a process.
16. Data ___ occurs when the same data is kept in more places than is necessary in a database. To overcome this problem, a database often consists of more than one table.
18. You can create simplistic queries with a wizard, but if your query is somewhat complex, you will need to create the query in Design ___, where you can provide more details about the query.
19. The top part of the Select Query window displays a window for each table you've selected. From the windows, you double-click any fields you want to be in your query. When you double-click a field, it is placed in the bottom part of the Select Query window. The bottom part consists of a series of row and columns and it is called the ___.
20. The words "rat, cat, bat" are in descending order; the words "bat, cat, rat" are in ___ order.

### DOWN

1. When you perform a "query", you are simply asking Assess to find the answer to a ___.
2. Can I query more than one table at one time?
3. When I am done creating a relationship between two or more tables, I will want to ___ it so that I can use it at a later time.
6. A collection of related records.
7. When I initially start Access, the Task ___ appears at the right side of the screen. From it, I can choose to create a new database or open an existing one.
8. I can run a query on one table without one of these being created, but if the information I need is in two or more tables, I will need to create a ___ between the tables before creating my query.
9. If you enforce ___ integrity, you are telling Access to make sure that in the future, any data entered into the foreign key field must match data in the primary key field of the other table.
13. Is Dozer a cat?
15. When creating a query in Design View, in addition to providing the desired fields, you sometimes will want to set ___ (conditions) to permit Access to find precisely the information you want.
17. Dozer is the smartest cyber___ on the planet.

## EXERCISE 2: TRUE-FALSE

For each of the following six statements, place a T or an F on the line to indicate if the statement is True or False.

1. ___A query is a question you ask.
2. ___The names Jim, Kim, Tim, are in descending order.
3. ___A wizard is a series of dialog boxes.
4. ___I can query a 1-table, but not a 2-table database.
5. ___A primary key identifies a field with a unique value.
6. ___The numbers 6, 5, 4, 3, 2, 1 are in descending order.

## EXERCISE 3: IDENTIFY TERMS

Below are eight definitions. Below the definitions are eight lines. In each line, write the word that matches the definition.

1. A question you ask.
2. A series of dialog boxes that makes query creation easier.
3. The series of rows and columns in the Select Query window.
4. The smallest particle of information in a database.
5. To put information in some logical order.
6. A collection of related fields.
7. Where words like Tables, Queries, and Forms can be seen.
8. A collection of related records.

1. _____   5. _____
2. _____   6. _____
3. _____   7. _____
4. _____   8. _____

## EXERCISE 4: CREATE A QUERY VIA A WIZARD

This exercise and the ones that follow require that you use a database that you originally created on page G-6 and then modified on page G-10. If you didn't do Exercises 6-9 on page G-10, or if you've lost that database, go back and do those exercises before proceeding. Then you will be prepared for the fun stuff on this page.

☞ Start Access and open the AP-1 Inventory database.
☞ Use a wizard to create a query that answers the question "In which warehouse is each SKU located?" Hint: since the SKU and the warehouse fields are in the Monitor SKUs table, that's the table you will need to query.
☞ Save the query (name it <u>SKU Warehouse</u>).
☞ If needed, maximize the window.
☞ Sort the query results in ascending order by warehouse. There should be 19 records in the query results and the first record should be for SKU 262.
☞ Close the Query window, but leave Access open. Since you sorted the query, you will be asked if you want to save the changes to the query design. Click Yes.

## EXERCISE 5: CREATE A QUERY VIA A WIZARD

☞ Use a wizard to create a query that answers the question "What is the size and the resolution of each model of monitor?" Hint: since the model, size, and the resolution fields are in the Monitor Specs table, that's the table you will need to query.
☞ Save the query (name it <u>Monitor Size Resolution</u>).
☞ Sort the query results in ascending order by resolution. There should be 11 records in the query results and the first record should be model DX55, size 15", and resolution 1024 x 768 resolution.
☞ Close the Query window, but leave Access open. When asked if you want to save the changes to the query design, click Yes.

## EXERCISE 6: CREATE A TABLE RELATIONSHIP

In each of the prior two exercises, you created a query that extracted data from only one table. You may recall that to query a database where the required data resides in more than one table, a relationship between the tables must be created. This exercise will have you create such a relationship.

☞ The AP-1 Inventory database has two tables. Create a link between the two using the model fields in each table.
☞ When done, close the Relationship window. When asked if you want to save the changes in the layout, click Yes.

## EXERCISE 7: CREATE A QUERY OF TWO TABLES

In the prior exercise, you created a relationship between the two tables. Now that you've done that, it's possible to query your database and extract information that resides in more than one table.

☞ Use a wizard to create a query that answers the question "What is the brand, model number, and cost of each SKU?" Hint: Use the Monitor SKUs table to get the SKU and the cost data and use the Monitor Specs table to get the brand and model number data.
☞ Save the query (name it <u>SKU Cost Brand Model</u>).
☞ Sort the query results in descending order by cost. There should be 19 records in the query results and the first record should be SKU 278, cost $38.25, brand Zell, and model FX95.
☞ Close the Query window, but leave Access open. When asked if you want to save the changes to the query design, click Yes.

## EXERCISE 8: CREATE A QUERY IN DESIGN VIEW

In Exercises 3-6, you created several queries using a wizard, which is an excellent way to swiftly query a database if your question is rather simplistic. However, when the question is more complex, a wizard will be an inadequate tool for query creation. In such cases, it's often best to create a query in Design View where you can provide more intricate details.

☞ Use the Design View to create a query that asks the question "What is the cost of each 19" monitor in the West Coast warehouse?" Hint: Use the Monitor SKUs table to get the Cost and the Warehouse data and use the Monitor Specs table to get the Size data.
☞ In the criteria row of the warehouse column, be sure to specify that you only want records involving the West Coast warehouse.
☞ In the criteria row of the size column, be sure to specify that you only want records involving 19 inch monitors.
☞ Run the query.
☞ Sort the query results in ascending order by cost. There should be four records in the query results with costs of $25.57, $26.56, $35.69, and $37.59.
☞ Close the query window, but leave Access open. When asked if you want to save the changes to the query design, click Yes. Name it <u>West Coast 19 Cost</u>.

## EXERCISE 9: CREATE A QUERY IN DESIGN VIEW

☞ Use the Design View to create a query that asks the question "What is the total value of all monitors in the East Coast warehouse?" Hint: since both the cost and the warehouse data is in the Monitor SKUs table, that's the only table you will need to query.
☞ Since we've not previously created a query where the total amount of a field was calculated, I'll provide some help. First, go ahead and click Queries from the Objects bar and then double-click Create Query in Design View.
☞ As always from the Show Table window, you will need to select the tables needed and in the Select Query window you will need to double-click each field (Cost and Warehouse) needed from the table that appears above the grid. So far, the steps are the same as before.
☞ Now, to get the query to total the data values in a field, click the Total toolbar button (∑). You may recall that in Excel, this button was called the AutoSum button. In Access, it's called the Total button.
☞ After you click the Total button, notice that a new row is added to the grid. The new row is the "Total" row.
☞ Click in the Total row of the grid in the Cost column to get the list box arrow to appear. Then click the list box arrow and select Sum from the list.
☞ In the criteria row of the warehouse column, be sure to specify that you only want records involving the East Coast warehouse.
☞ Run the query. There should be one record in the query results and it should indicate that the total cost of all monitors in the East Coast warehouse is $257.84 .
☞ Close the query window, but leave Access open. When asked if you want to save the changes to the query design, click Yes and name it <u>East Coast Total Cost</u>.
☞ Close Access.

**NOTE**: The files you created in this project will be needed later.

A report is just like a query in that it extracts information found in the database based upon your criteria. However, the advantage to creating a report is that you can add formats (fonts, graphics, etc.) to enhance its appearance. In short, you would run a query if you wanted to see the results on the monitor; you would create a report if you wanted to print out the results in an attractive document. In this project you will use the AP-1 Dogs database you created on page G-3 and later modified in Projects 2 and 3. If you don't have that database, go back and create it. You will then be ready to start this project.

### CREATE REPORTS USING AUTOREPORT

There is more than one way to create a report. The AutoReport feature is helpful to quickly create a report if you want all the data in a single table to be included in the report.

To practice creating a report with AutoReport, do the following:
- ☞ Start Access and open the AP-1 Dogs database.
- ☞ From the Objects bar, click Reports.
- ☞ From the toolbar, click the New button.
- ☞ in the New Report dialog box, click the type of AutoReport you want. AutoReport: Columnar arranges records vertically and on the report. AutoReport: Tabular arranges records horizontally. For our report, click AutoReport: Tabular.
- ☞ From the list box near the bottom of the dialog box, select the table where the desired data resides (in this case, select the Dog Shows table).
- ☞ Click OK. Your report will appear in Print Preview.
- ☞ Click View, Design View. At the top of the report, click the Dog Shows title. In the box, after the word "Shows", type your name in parenthesis. For example, if Dozer were doing this, his title would read "Dog Shows (Dozer Pannell)".
- ☞ Close the report, but leave Access open. When asked if you want to save the changes to the report design, click Yes.
- ☞ In the Save As window, enter a report name (name it Dog Shows). Click OK.

### CREATE A REPORT FROM ONE TABLE USING A WIZARD

The AutoReport feature is great when you want to quickly create a report. However, if you want more control over the content and the appearance of your report, you might want to use a wizard to create it.

- ☞ From the Objects bar, click Reports.
- ☞ From the Objects list, double-click Create Report By Using Wizard (the Report Wizard dialog box will appear).
- ☞ From the Tables/Queries list box, select the table that contains the data needed for your report. Dozer wants a report that will list each breed, its height, and its IQ. Since all of that data can be found in the Dog Breeds table, select the Dog Breeds table from the Tables/Queries list box.
- ☞ The Available Fields box provides a list of all the fields in the Dog Breeds table. Double-click each field needed to answer your question (in this case, double click the Breed field, the Height field, and the IQ field).
- ☞ Click the Next button to go to the next page of the wizard.
- ☞ When asked if you want to add grouping levels, click Next.
- ☞ To specify the order of the records on your report, use each list box to choose the order and use the button next to each list box to specify either ascending (ABC) or descending (ZYX). To change from Ascending to Descending, just click the button next to each list box. In this case, you want the

records sorted by Breed in ascending order.
- ☞ Click the Next button to go to the next page of the wizard.
- ☞ Specify the layout (Tabular) and the orientation (Portrait) for your report. Tabular arranges the records horizontally on the report, columnar arranges the records vertically, and justified arranges the records horizontally with field names for each report. Portrait prints the report 8 ½" wide and 11" high and landscape prints the report 11" wide and 8 ½" high.
- ☞ Click the Next button to go to the next page of the wizard.
- ☞ Specify a style for your report (select Corporate).
- ☞ Click the Next button to go to the next page of the wizard.
- ☞ In the What Title Do You Want For Your Report text box, type a name for your report (call it Breed Height IQ).
- ☞ Click the Finish button. The report will be saved to your AP-1 Dogs database and it will appear in Print Preview.
- ☞ Click View, Design View. At the top of the report, click the "Breed Height IQ" title. If you can't see the entire title in the box, drag a sizing handle to make the box wider. Then, in the box, after "IQ", type your name in parenthesis.
- ☞ Close the report, but leave Access open. When asked if you want to save the changes to the report design, click Yes.
- ☞ From the Objects list, double-click the Breed Height IQ report to open it.
- ☞ Print the report. Then close it, but leave Access open.

### CREATE A REPORT FROM TWO TABLES USING A WIZARD

So far, you've created a report using the AutoReport feature and then another report using the wizard. In both cases, the report extracted information from only one table. Now, let's create a report where the desired information is in two tables.

- ☞ From the Objects bar, click Reports.
- ☞ Double-click Create Report By Using Wizard (the Report Wizard dialog box will appear).
- ☞ From the Tables/Queries list box, select the table containing the data needed for your report. Dozer wants a report that will list each dog who entered any dog show, its breed, its height, its IQ, and the award won. Since some of that data is in the Dog Shows table and some of it is in the Dog Breeds table, the report will need to use both tables. So, first select the Dog Breeds table from the Tables/Queries list box.
- ☞ From the Available Fields box, double-click each field needed to answer your question (in this case, double click the Breed field, the Height field, and the IQ field).
- ☞ From the Tables/Queries list box, click the Dog Shows table.
- ☞ The Available Fields box provides a list of all the fields in the Dog Breeds table. Double-click the Show field, the Name field, and the Award field to have those fields move to the Selected Fields box. Note: the Selected Fields box should have six fields: breed, height, IQ, show, name, and award.
- ☞ Click the Next button to go to the next page of the wizard.
- ☞ You are now asked to specify how you want to view your data. You only get this page of the wizard when you create a report that uses more than one table. It wants to know by which table do you want the report organized. In this case, select By Dog Breeds.
- ☞ Click the Next button to go to the next page of the wizard.
- ☞ When asked if you want to add grouping levels, click Next.
- ☞ To specify the order you wish to have the records appear on your report, use each list box to choose the order and use the button next to each list box to specify either ascending (ABC) or descending (ZYX). In this case, you want the

records sorted by Name in ascending order.
☞ Click the Next button to go to the next page of the wizard.
☞ Specify the layout and orientation. Note that earlier, when you created a report that used only one table, the layout choices were Columnar, Tabular, or Justified. When your report uses data from more than one table, you get different layout choices. In this case, select Stepped as the layout and select Portrait for the orientation.
☞ Click the Next button to go to the next page of the wizard.
☞ Specify a style for your report (select Corporate).
☞ Click the Next button to go to the next page of the wizard.
☞ In the What Title Do You Want For Your Report text box, type a name for your report (call it Dog Awards).
☞ Click the Finish button.
☞ The report will be saved to your AP-1 Dogs database and it will appear in Print Preview.
☞ Click View, Design View. At the top of the report, click the "Dog Awards" title. In the box, after "Awards", type your name in parenthesis.
☞ Close the report, but leave Access open. When asked if you want to save the changes to the report design, click Yes.
☞ From the Objects list, double-click the Dog Awards report.
☞ Print the report. Then close it, but leave Access open.

## CREATE A REPORT FROM A QUERY

So far, you've created three reports. One using AutoReport and two using a wizard. In each case, the report extracted its contents from one or two tables. You can also create a report of a query. Remember, in Project 3, you created queries (asked questions). The results of each query appeared on the screen. A report is just like a query except you create a report when you want to print out your results. Let's create a report using one of the queries you created in Project 3.

☞ From the Objects bar, click Reports.
☞ Double-click Create Report By Using Wizard (the Report Wizard dialog box will appear).
☞ From the Tables/Queries list box, select the query for which you wish to create a report (select the Breeds Prizes)
☞ The Available Fields box provides a list of both of the fields in the Breeds Prizes query: breed and prize, both of which need to be moved to the Selected Fields box.
☞ Click the Next button to go to the next page of the wizard.
☞ When asked if you want to add grouping levels, click Next.
☞ Specify the order you wish to have the records appear on your report (in this case, sort by Prize in descending order).
☞ Click the Next button to go to the next page of the wizard.
☞ Specify the layout (Tabular) and the orientation (Portrait).
☞ Click the Next button to go to the next page of the wizard.
☞ Specify a style for your report (select Corporate).
☞ Click the Next button to go to the next page of the wizard.
☞ In the What Title Do You Want For Your Report text box, type a name for your report (call it Breeds Prizes).
☞ Click the Finish button.
☞ The report will be saved to your AP-1 Dogs database and it will appear in Print Preview.
☞ Click View, Design View. At the top of the report, click the "Breeds Prizes" title. In the box, after "Prizes", type your name in parenthesis.
☞ Close the report, but leave Access open. When asked if you want to save the changes to the report design, click Yes.
☞ From the Objects list, double-click the Breeds Prizes report.
☞ Print the report. Then close it, but leave Access open.

## MODIFY A REPORT

Once created, you may want to modify a report.

To practice modifying a report, do the following:
☞ Open the Breeds Prizes report.
☞ Click View, Design view, if necessary.
☞ In Design view, your report will consist of field names along with the value for each field. Each field name is called a control and each data field box is a control.
☞ Click a control to select it (click any control). Once clicked, it will have a sizing handle on each corner and on each border. You can drag a handle to resize the control. Just for the fun of it, resize a few controls.
☞ To move a control, click in a control and move the mouse until the mouse pointer looks like a hand. Then drag and drop the list to its new location. Just for the fun of it, drag and drop a few controls to move them around on the report.
☞ Right click in a data field box, point to Fill/Back Color, and click a color. With the box selected, double-click the Format Painter toolbar button (looks like a paint brush) and then click the other field boxes to apply the same color. When done, click the Format Painter button to turn it off.
☞ Click View, Print Preview to see what the newly-modified report looks like. If you don't like anything about it, click View, Design View and modify it some more.
☞ Save your modified report (click File, Save).

## INSERT IMAGES IN A REPORT

You can enhance the appearance of a report by inserting an image or two. It might be a company logo, or simply an image that is related to the information found on the report.

To practice inserting an image, do the following:
☞ First, let's go get an image. Start Internet Explorer and find a picture of a dog on the Internet.
☞ Right-click on the picture and click Save Picture As from the shortcut menu. Save the image to your disk (call it Dog).
☞ Close Internet Explorer.
☞ Open the Breeds Prizes report and click View, Design View.
☞ Since you want to place the image in the header of the report, expand the size of the Report Header section (drag its bottom border down a bit).
☞ On the Toolbox, click the Image button.
☞ Drag the mouse in the Report Header area to create a box into which the image will appear. When you release the mouse button, the Insert Picture dialog box will appear.
☞ In the Look In box find the "Dog" image you saved.
☞ Click the image and click OK.
☞ If the image is bigger than the box, right-click in the box and click Properties from the shortcut menu. The Properties dialog box appears. In it, click the Format tab, then click in the Size Mode box to have the list box arrow appear. From the list box, click Zoom. Close the dialog box.
☞ Now, if needed, move and resize the image.
☞ Click View, Print Preview to see what the newly-modified report looks like. If you don't like anything about it, click View, Design View and modify it some more.
☞ Close the report, but leave Access open. When asked if you want to save the changes to the report design, click Yes.
☞ From the Objects list, double-click the Breeds Prizes report.
☞ Print the report.
☞ Close Access.

## EXERCISE 1: CROSSWORD

Use the clues below to complete the crossword puzzle (Note: the Answer Key can be found beginning on page G-21).

### ACROSS

1. To have your report printed 11" wide and 8½" high, you would choose the ___ orientation.
4. If you want to insert an image in a report or change the size or location of the controls, you would switch to ___ View.
5. How many orientation choices are there?
6. When you want to extract information from a database, you can run a query. You could then view the information on the computer monitor. However, if you want to print out the information, you would want to create a ___.
9. Are the names Corky, Dozer, and Skooter in descending order?
12. Is Access produced by AOL?
13. The ___ feature will quickly create a report when you want all the data in a single table to be included in the report.
15. The ___ of a report refers to the way the report is printed on the paper (portrait or landscape).
16. A collection of related records.
19. When creating a report with a wizard, you get to select the ___ of the report (e.g., Corporate, Compact, Formal).
20. In addition to creating a report from a table, can I also create a report from a query?
21. If you want to insert an image into a report, you will need to use the Design View and insert the image onto the ___, the part of the window with all the little dots on it.
24. A ___ is a series of dialog boxes that guide us through a process.
25. When you want to extract information from a database, you can create and then run a ___.

### DOWN

1. After I select an object from the Objects bar, the Objects ___ appears which provides various ways for me to work with the specific object I selected.
2. When I am done creating a report, it will appear on the screen in ___ Preview.
3. The ___ Painter toolbar button has a picture of a paint brush on it.
7. Tables, queries, forms, and reports are called ___.
8. When you look at your report in Design View, you can see that each field has two parts; the field name and a data value box into which you enter the data for that field. Each of these two parts can be resized and/or moved and each is called a ___.
10. The ___ of a table refers to how the records will be displayed (e.g., tabular, columnar, justified).
11. To have your report printed 8½" wide and 11" high, you would choose the ___ orientation.
14. You can create a report using the AutoReport feature if your report will extract data from only ___ table.
17. The numbers 56, 68, 89, and 92 are in ___ order.
18. The smallest particle of information about a person, place, thing, or event.
22. A collection of related fields.
23. Words like Tables, Queries, and Forms can be found on the Objects ___.

## EXERCISE 2 TRUE-FALSE

For each of the following six statements, place a T or an F on the line to indicate if the statement is True or False.

1. ___ Portrait and Seascape are two types of orientation.
2. ___ Reports, queries, forms, and tables are objects.
3. ___ A report can be created from a table or from a query.
4. ___ A wizard is a series of dialog boxes.
5. ___ A query is a question you ask.
6. ___ AutoReport will only create a report from one table.

## EXERCISE 3: IDENTIFY TERMS

Below are six definitions. Below the definitions are six lines. In each line, write the word that matches the definition.

1. A collection of related fields.
2. A series of dialog boxes that makes query creation easier.
3. A question you ask.
4. The smallest particle of information in a database.
5. The orientation of a report printed 11" wide and 8½" high.
6. The orientation of a report printed 8½" wide and 11" high.

1. _____    4. _____
2. _____    5. _____
3. _____    6. _____

## EXERCISE 4: CREATE A REPORT USING AUTOREPORT

This exercise and the ones that follow require that you use the AP1-Inventory database originally created on page G-6 and then modified on pages G-10 and G-14. If you don't have that database, go back and do those exercises before proceeding.

☞ Start Access and open the AP1-Inventory database.
☞ Use the AutoReport: Tabular feature to create a report of the contents of the Monitor Specs table.
☞ At the end of the report title, type your name in parenthesis.
☞ Save the report (name it <u>Monitor Specs</u>).
☞ Print the report. Close the report, but leave Access open.

## EXERCISE 5: CREATE A REPORT OF A QUERY

☞ Use a wizard to create a report of the SKU Cost Brand Model query. Use all the fields in the query.
☞ When asked how you want to view the data, select By Monitor SKUs.
☞ When asked about grouping levels, just click Next.
☞ When asked how to sort the records in the report, sort them in ascending order by cost.
☞ When asked about the layout and orientation, choose a tabular layout and a portrait orientation.
☞ When asked to choose a style, select Compact.
☞ When asked to name your report, name it <u>SKU Cost</u>.
☞ At the end of the report title, type your name in parenthesis.
☞ Print the report.
☞ Close the report; leave Access open. When asked if you want to save the changes to the report design, click Yes.

## EXERCISE 6: CREATE A REPORT USING A WIZARD

☞ Use a wizard to create a report that will list each SKU along with its model number, location and brand.
☞ When asked how you want to view the data, select By Monitor SKUs.
☞ When asked about grouping levels, just click Next.
☞ Sort the records by model number in ascending order.
☞ Select a tabular layout and a portrait orientation.
☞ When asked to choose a style, select Compact.
☞ When asked to name your report, name it <u>SKU Location</u>.
☞ At the end of the report title, type your name in parenthesis.
☞ Print the report.
☞ Close the report; leave Access open. When asked if you want to save the changes to the report design, click Yes.

## EXERCISE 7: MODIFY A REPORT & INSERT AN IMAGE

☞ In Exercise 6, you created a SKU Location report. Open it.
☞ Resize the title box so that it is as wide as the report.
☞ Center the title within the title box.
☞ Use the Fill/Back Color option to fill the title box with a color.
☞ Start Internet Explorer and search the Internet to find a picture of a computer monitor.
☞ Save the picture to your diskette.
☞ If the picture is bigger than the box, fix it.
☞ Insert the image under the title of the report.
☞ If needed, move the image so it is centered in the report.
☞ Use Print Preview to see what your report will look like. If you don't like anything about it, go back and fix it.
☞ When you like the appearance of the report, save it.
☞ Print one copy of the report.
☞ Close the report, but leave Access open.
☞ You should have two printouts of your SKU location report (one from Exercise 6 and one from this exercise). Compare the two reports. The information is the same on each report, but the enhances made in this exercise should have improved the appearance of the report.

## EXERCISE 8: CREATE A REPORT USING AUTOREPORT

☞ Use the AutoReport: Tabular feature to create a report of the contents of the Montors SKU table.
☞ At the end of the report title, type your name in parenthesis.
☞ Save the report (name it <u>Monitor SKUs</u>).
☞ Print the report. Close the report, but leave Access open.

## EXERCISE 9: CREATE A REPORT OF A QUERY

☞ Use a wizard to create a report of the West Coast 19 Cost query. Use all the fields in the query.
☞ When asked how you want to view the data, select By Monitor SKUs.
☞ When asked about grouping levels, just click Next.
☞ When asked how to sort the records in the report, sort them in descending order by cost.
☞ When asked about the layout and orientation, choose a columnar layout and a landscape orientation.
☞ When asked to choose a style, select Compact.
☞ When asked to name your report, name it <u>West Coast 19.</u> If asked to Enter A Parameter Value, leave the text box empty and just click OK.
☞ At the end of the report title, type your name in parenthesis.
☞ Print the report.
☞ Close the report; leave Access open. When asked if you want to save the changes to the report design, click Yes.

## EXERCISE 10: CREATE A REPORT USING A WIZARD

☞ Use a wizard to create a report that will list each model, its resolution, size, dot-pitch, and cost.
☞ When asked how you want to view the data, select By Monitor SKUs.
☞ When asked about grouping levels, just click Next.
☞ Sort the records by model number in ascending order.
☞ Select a tabular layout and a portrait orientation.
☞ When asked to choose a style, select Compact.
☞ When asked to name your report, name it <u>Model Info</u>.
☞ At the end of the report title, type your name in parenthesis.
☞ Print the report.
☞ Close the report; leave Access open. When asked if you want to save the changes to the report design, click Yes.

## EXERCISE 11: MODIFY A REPORT & INSERT AN IMAGE

☞ In Exercise 10, you created a Model Info report. Open it.
☞ Resize the title box so it is as wide as the report.
☞ Center the title within the title box.
☞ Use the Fill/Back Color option to fill the title box and the other field boxes with a color.
☞ In Exercise 7, you found an image of a computer monitor on the Internet and saved it to your diskette. Insert that image under the title of the report.
☞ If the picture is bigger than the box, fix it.
☞ If needed, move the image so it is centered in the report.
☞ Use Print Preview to see what your report will look like. If you don't like anything about it, go back and fix it.
☞ When you like the appearance of the report, save it.
☞ Print one copy of the report.
☞ Close the report, but leave Access open.
☞ You should have two printouts of your Model Info report (one from Exercise 10 and one from this exercise). Compare the two reports. The information is the same on each report, but the enhances made in this exercise should have improved the appearance of the report.
☞ Close Access.

## EXERCISE 1: CROSSWORD

Use the clues below to complete the crossword puzzle (Note: the Answer Key can be found beginning on page G-21).

### ACROSS

1. The record-entry process becomes less tedious, faster, and more accurate if you create a ___, which contains boxes into which you input the data value for each field.
5. When you are creating a table in Design view, the first column asks you to provide a field ___.
8. When you ___ a database, you are placing a copy of it onto a permanent storage device, such as a diskette, or a hard drive. By doing so, you will be able to retrieve it later.
9. A ___ key is a field that will contain a value different from any other record in the table.
11. A collection of related records.
12. A collection of related fields.
14. The task ___ appears on the right side of the screen. Its contents change, depending on what you are doing.
15. A ___ is a series of dialog boxes that will guide you through a process (e.g., creating a form or performing a query).
16. Is Dozer a cat?
17. A ___ is a question you ask.
20. To find the answer to a question about Access, click the ___ menu bar button.
21. To arrange records in some logical order.
22. To have a report printed 8½" wide and 11" high, you would choose the ___ orientation.

### DOWN

2. When you have a question about how to do something in Microsoft Access, you can click Help, Show The ___ Assistant, to access a friendly paper clip character who will provide guidance.
3. The ___ bar appears below the title bar and it contains command categories, such as File, Edit, View, etc.
4. If you click a control in a report while in Design view, each corner and each border of the control will have a little box on it called a ___ handle. If you were to drag one of those boxes, you can resize the control.
6. The fine folks at ___ produce the Access program.
7. A primary ___ is a field with a unique value.
8. When you place the Access program or a specific database into memory, you are loading it. Another word for load is ___.
10. The ___ View is used to create tables or forms.
12. I can run a query on one table without one of these being created, but if the information I need is in two or more tables, I will need to create a ___ between the tables before creating my query.
13. Microsoft Access is a ___ program that stores, organizes, and retrieves data.
18. When you want to extract information from a database, you can run a query. You could then view the information on the computer monitor. However, if you want to print out the information, you would want to create a ___.
19. A query, a report, or a form is sometimes called an ___.

## EXERCISE 2: CREATE A DATABASE

Dozer's Digital Devices, Inc. (DDD) is a company that buys, refurbishes, and resells used computers and monitors. You did such a splendid job creating a database for Dozer's inventory of monitors that he wants you to create a computer inventory database for his company.

### PART A: CREATE A TABLE

☞ Start Access and create a new database (call it DDD CPUs).
☞ In Design View, create a table with the following fields.
☞ The first field is "Memory", the data type is "Text", and the description is "Amount of RAM".
☞ The second field is "Brand", the data type is "Text", and the description is "Brand Name of Computer".
☞ The third field is "Modem", the data type is "Text", and the description is "Modem Speed".
☞ The fourth field is "Model", the data type is "Text", and the Description is "Manufacturer's Model Number".
☞ The fifth field is "Hard Drive", the data type is "Text", and the description is "Hard Drive Capacity".

☞ Between the second and the third field, insert a new field called "Speed", with a "Text" data type, and a "Processor Speed in MHZ" description.
☞ Since many people no longer use modems, Dozer thinks that knowing about the modem is not important. So, delete that field from the table.
☞ Move the fields so that they are in the following order: Brand, Model, Speed, Memory, and Hard Drive.
☞ Designate the Model field as the Primary key.
☞ Save the table (name it CPU Specs).

### PART B: SET UP AUTOMATIC COMPACTING
Set this database to compact automatically when you close it.

### PART C: ENTER RECORDS INTO A TABLE
Using the Datasheet View, enter the following records into the CPU Specs table.

| Brand | Model | Speed | Memory | Hard Drive |
|-------|-------|-------|--------|------------|
| Zony | Z99R | 667 | 256 | 8 |
| Zell | CP48 | 400 | 128 | 6 |
| Zony | Z77R | 333 | 64 | 4 |
| Zell | CP78 | 550 | 128 | 10 |
| Zell | CP58 | 466 | 64 | 4 |
| Zony | Z33R | 266 | 64 | 2 |

☞ Close the table, but leave Access open.

### PART D: CREATE ANOTHER TABLE
☞ In Design View, create a table. The first field name is "Model", the data type is "Text", and the description is "Manufacturer's Model Number".
☞ The second field name is "Cost", the data type is "Currency" (select Currency from the Data Type drop down list). The description is "Dozer's Cost To Acquire".
☞ The third name is "SKU", the data type is "Text", and the description is "Stock Keeping Unit". By the way, a sku is a number assigned to items to help control inventory.
☞ Between the first and second fields, insert a new field called "Warehouse", with a "Text" data type, and a "Warehouse Where Unit Is Stored" description.
☞ Move the fields so that they are in the following order: SKU, Cost, Model, and Warehouse.
☞ Designate the SKU field as the Primary key.
☞ Save your table (name it CPU SKUs).
☞ Close the table, but leave Access open.

### PART E: CREATE FORMS
Since there are many records in the CPU SKUs table, create a form to help in the data-entry process.
☞ Create a form for the CPU SKUs table using all its fields.
☞ Choose a Columnar layout and an International style.
☞ Name the form CPU SKUs.
☞ Create a list box for the model field which includes the following items: CP48, CP58, CP78, Z33R, Z77R, and Z99R.
☞ Create a list box for the warehouse field which includes the following items: East Coast and West Coast.
☞ Resize each list box so it is big enough to display all its contents, but not too big.
☞ Delete the original model and warehouse controls and move the new list boxes where the original controls were located.
☞ Apply a Fill/Back Color to each data value control.

☞ Close the form, but leave Access open. When asked if you want to save the changes to the form design, click Yes.

### PART F: ENTER RECORDS USING FORMS
Using the form you created in Part D, enter the following records into the CPU SKUs table.

| SKU | Cost | Model | Warehouse |
|-----|------|-------|-----------|
| 325 | 41.15 | Z77R | East Coast |
| 385 | 46.95 | CP48 | West Coast |
| 345 | 51.05 | CP58 | West Coast |
| 369 | 42.52 | Z77R | West Coast |
| 342 | 97.58 | Z99R | West Coast |
| 312 | 62.52 | CP78 | East Coast |
| 384 | 41.05 | Z77R | East Coast |
| 394 | 48.89 | CP58 | West Coast |
| 367 | 35.67 | Z33R | West Coast |
| 393 | 47.77 | CP48 | West Coast |
| 387 | 39.84 | Z77R | East Coast |
| 371 | 36.95 | Z33R | East Coast |
| 311 | 49.95 | CP58 | East Coast |

☞ Close the table, but leave Access open.

### PART G: CREATE A RELATIONSHIP BETWEEN TABLES
Create a relationship between the two tables. Use the model fields in each table to create the link.

### PART H: CREATE QUERIES
Create queries to answer each of the following questions:
☞ What is the brand, model, speed, memory, hard drive capacity and warehouse location of each SKU? Save the query (name it SKU Summary).
☞ What is the total cost of all computers in the East Coast warehouse? Save the query (name it East Coast Cost).
☞ Which SKUs found in the West Coast warehouse have processor speeds of at least 400MHz? Save the query (name it SKU West 400 MHZ).

### PART I: CREATE A REPORT
☞ Create a report of the "SKU Summary" query using all the fields in the query.
☞ When asked how you want to view the data, select By CPU SKUs.
☞ When asked about grouping levels, just click Next.
☞ When asked how to sort the records in the report, sort them in ascending order by speed.
☞ When asked about the layout and orientation, choose a tabular layout and a portrait orientation.
☞ Choose any style and layout you like.
☞ Name the report SKU Summary.
☞ At the end of the report title, type your name in parenthesis.
☞ From the Internet, find a picture of a computer system. Save the image to your diskette. Then, insert the image at the top of your report.
☞ Print your report. Close the report. Close Access.

## PAGE 5: EXERCISE 1

| Across | Down |
|--------|------|
| 3. Field | 1. Record |
| 7. Microsoft | 2. RAM |
| 8. Start | 4. Database |
| 10. Pane | 5. Office |
| 11. Menu | 6. Primary |
| 12. Key | 8. Save |
| 14. Design | 9. Table |
| 16. Datasheet | 13. Yes |
| | 15. Name |

## PAGE G-5: EXERCISE 2

1. A
2. C
3. D
4. B

## PAGE G-5: EXERCISE 3

1. F: A field is the smallest particle of information about a person, place, thing, or event (e.g., first name, last name, city, state, or zip ). A collection of related fields is a record, a collection of related records is a table, and a collection of related tables is a database.
2. T
3. F: A menu bar has words (e.g., File, Edit, View, Insert) on it and is typically found under the title bar in a window. On the other hand, a toolbar has picture buttons on it and is typically found under the menu bar in a window.
4. T
5. F: A table is a collection of related records. Each record is a collection of related fields.
6. T
7. F: A field is the smallest bit of information about a person, place, thing, or event (e.g., first name, last name, city, state, or zip ). A collection of related records is a database.
8. T

## PAGE G-5: EXERCISE 4

1. B
2. A

## PAGE G-5: EXERCISE 5

1. Record
2. Table
3. Database
4. Field
5. Access
6. Design
7. Close
8. Primary
9. RAM

## PAGE G-9: EXERCISE 1

| Across | Down |
|--------|------|
| 2. Data | 1. Field |
| 4. Wizard | 3. Table |
| 8. Access | 5. Datasheet |
| 10. Objects | 6. Design |
| 13. Open | 7. Database |
| 14. List | 9. Control |
| 16. Microsoft | 11. Yes |
| | 12. Form |
| | 15. No |

## PAGE G-9: EXERCISE 2

1. T
2. T
3. T
4. T
5. F: The paper clip dude is the Office Assistant. He will answer your questions about Access. A wizard is a series of dialog boxes that are useful in creating forms, reports, or queries.
6. T
7. T: However, when you get to the last field of a record, pressing the Tab key will take you to the first field of the next record.
8. T

## PAGE G-9: EXERCISE 3

1. Design View
2. Datasheet View
3. List box
4. Controls
5. Wizard
6. Primary Key
7. Design View
8. Record

## PAGE G-9: EXERCISE 4

1. F: A table is a collection of records. The actual records can be entered into the table using either the Datasheet View or a form.
2. T
3. F: The words "Tables" and "Forms" are on the Objects bar, not the Objects list. When I select one of the objects on the Objects bar, the Objects list displays a list of ways to work with the specific object I selected.
4. F: A database can have many tables. In fact, most databases do contain more than one table.
5. T
6. F: The words "Create Table in Design View" can be found on an Objects list, not on the Objects bar. They would appear on the Objects list after you select "Table" from the Objects bar.
7. T
8. T

## PAGE G-9: EXERCISE 5

You can enter records into a table with the Datasheet View. Or, if you create a form, you can use the form to do so. Nobody "needs" to create a form. However, doing so can speed up the data entry process and most likely increase the accuracy of the entries as well.

## PAGE G-13: EXERCISE 1

| Across | Down |
|--------|------|
| 1. Query | 1. Question |
| 4. Field | 2. Yes |
| 5. Start | 3. Save |
| 7. Primary | 6. Table |
| 10. No | 7. Pane |
| 11. Bar | 8. Relationship |
| 12. Fun | 9. Referential |
| 14. Wizard | 13. No |
| 16. Redundancy | 15. Criteria |
| 18. View | 17. Dog |
| 19. Grid | |
| 20. Ascending | |

## PAGE G-13: EXERCISE 2

1. T
2. F: The names Jim, Kim, and Tim are not in descending order. They are in ascending order. If sorted in descending order, the list would be Tim, Kim, Jim. Ascending order places the items in either alphabetical (ABC) or numerical (123) order. Descending order places the items in reverse alphabetical order (ZYX) or in numerical order from highest to lowest (321).
3. T
4. F: I can query a database regardless of how many tables it has. If I use more than one table in my query, a relationship between the tables needs to be created, but once created, I can query as many of the tables as desired.
5. T
6. T

## PAGE G-13: EXERCISE 3

1. Query
2. Wizard
3. Grid
4. Field
5. Sort
6. Record
7. Objects Bar
8. Table

## PAGE G-17: EXERCISE 1

| Across | Down |
|--------|------|
| 1. Landscape | 1. List |
| 4. Design | 2. Print |
| 5. Two | 3. Format |
| 6. Report | 7. Objects |
| 9. No | 8. Control |
| 13. AutoReport | 10. Layout |
| 15. Orientation | 11. Portrait |
| 16. Table | 14. One |
| 19. Style | 17. Ascending |
| 20. Yes | 18. Field |
| 21. Grid | 22. Record |
| 24. Wizard | 23. Bar |
| 25. Query | |

## PAGE G-17: EXERCISE 2

1. F: Portrait and Landscape are two types of orientation. A seascape is a painting of the ocean, which has nothing to do with Access.
2. T
3. T
4. T
5. T
6. T

## PAGE G-17: EXERCISE 3

1. Record
2. Wizard
3. Query
4. Field
5. Landscape
6. Portrait

**PAGE G-19: EXERCISE 1**

| Across | Down |
|---|---|
| 1. Form | 2. Office |
| 5. Name | 3. Menu |
| 8. Save | 4. Sizing |
| 9. Primary | 6. Microsoft |
| 11. Table | 7. Key |
| 12. Record | 8. Start |
| 14. Pane | 10. Design |
| 15. Wizard | 12. Relationship |
| 16. No | 13. Database |
| 17. Query | 18. Report |
| 20. Help | 19. Object |
| 21. Sort | |
| 22. Portrait | |

☞ Dozer's Quintessential Guide To Microsoft Access ☜

**A drive**: A secondary storage device that writes to and reads from a floppy disk. Also called a floppy drive.

**Access**: A program developed by Microsoft that permits us to create and manipulate data bases.

**ascending**: The order of items that exists when they are in alphabetical (A, B, C) or numerical order (1, 2, 3).

**AutoReport**: A feature that quickly creates reports that extract information from only one table.

**click**: The act of rapidly pressing the left mouse button one time, generally done to select an on-screen object.

**close**: The process of removing a file or a program from memory.

**column**: A vertical collection of cells.

**combo box**: A box in a form from which you can select items or you can go ahead and type in your own items when you are entering data into a table. Using a combo box, speeds up the data entry process and increases the accuracy of the entries.

**control**: Each element in a report (e.g., each field name and each value for each field).

**data redundancy**: The condition that exists when data is stored in more places than necessary within your database.

**data type**: When creating a table in Datasheet view you will specify the type of data that will be entered into each field (e.g., Text, Currency).

**database**: A collection of related tables, each of which contains data.

**datasheet view**: The view where data is entered into a table.

**delete**: To remove (erase).

**delete key**: The key that deletes data to the right of the insertion point.

**descending**: The order of items that exists when they are in reverse alphabetical (Z, Y, X) or numerical order (3, 2, 1).

**description cell**: The place where you can enter a description of each field when creating a table in Datasheet view.

**Design View**: The view where tables are created.

**Dozer**: The smartest cyberdog on the planet.

**double-click**: The act of rapidly pressing the left mouse button two times.

**drag**: To move the mouse.

**drag and drop**: The act of pointing to an object on the screen, holding down the left mouse button, moving the mouse, and then releasing the mouse button, thereby moving the object. In essence you have dragged and then dropped the object.

**field**: The smallest particle of information about a person, place, thing, or event (e.g., first name, last name, city, state, or zip code)

**field value**: The data assigned to each field in a record. Also called simply a value.

**floppy drive**: A secondary storage device that writes to and saves from a floppy disk. Also called the A Drive.

**form**: An object used to enter data into a table. It will have each field name listed along with a text box into which the field value will be entered.

**Form View**: The view where data is entered into a table via a form.

**format painter**: A feature that will copy the formats residing in text and will apply those same formats to other text.

**grid**: In Design View, the controls can be found here. And, the can be moved from one place on the grid to another place.

**insertion point**: The on-screen blinking vertical line identifying where entered text will appear. Some folks refer to this as a cursor.

**landscape**: The orientation of the report on the printed page wherein the report is printed 11" wide and 8 ½:" high.

**launch**: To place a program or data into memory. Also called start, load, or open.

**layout**: The way the various records will be displayed in a report (e.g., tabular, columnar, justified)

**list box**: A box in a form from which you can select items when you are entering data into a table. Using a list box, speeds up the data entry process and increases the accuracy of the entries.

**load**: To place a program or data into memory. Also called start, launch, or open.

**maximize button**: The button (on the title bar) that, when clicked, will make the window fill the entire screen.

**memory**: The temporary location where data and programs currently being used by a processor reside. Also called RAM (an acronym for Random Access Memory).

**menu bar**: The bar (under the title bar) which consists of a series of command categories. To access specific commands in a category, click the item on the menu bar.

**minimize button**: The button that, when clicked, will make the window become the size of a taskbar button.

**move**: To place text elsewhere while removing the original text from where it was.

**move handle**: A vertical bar on a toolbar that, when dragged, will allow the user to move the toolbar.

**object**: The parts of a database (e.g., tables, queries, forms, reports).

**Objects bar**: The bar on the left side of the Database window that lists objects.

**Objects list**: The list that appears on the right side of the Database window when an object has been selected from the Objects bar. It provides a list of ways to work with the currently selected object.

**office assistant**: A Microsoft help feature that displays a character in the form of a paper clip that asks you to pose a question for him to answer.

**open**: To place a program or data into memory. Also called start, load, or launch.

**orientation**: The way a report is printed on the a page (see portrait and landscape).

**portrait**: The orientation of the report on the printed page wherein the report is printed 8 ½:" wide and 11" high.

**primary key**: A field in a table that has a unique value (i..e., no other record in the table will have the same value).

**print preview**: A feature that permits you to see how each page of your document will look before you print the document.

**query**: The process of asking a question, the answer of which can be found in the database.

**record**: A collection of related fields.

**Record buttons**: A series of buttons near the bottom left corner of the screen which indicate how many records are in the table and which record is currently being viewed. In addition, the buttons permit you to move from one record to another within the table.

**referential integrity**: The condition whereby any data which is entered into a foreign key field must match data in the primary key field of a related table.

**relational database**: A database in which the tables are related to each other, thereby permitting queries to be run which extract data from more than one table within the database.

**relationship**: A link between tables which permits queries to be run that require the extraction of data which resides in more than one table within the database.

**report**: A document containing the information derived from a database.

**restore button**: The button (on the title bar) that, when clicked, will make the window the size it was when it was last manually resized.

**right-click**: The act of rapidly pressing the right mouse button one time.

**row**: A horizontal line of cells in a table.

**row selector**: The button on the left end of each row In Datasheet View.

**run**: The act of having Access perform the query to extract information from the database.

**Run toolbar button**: The toolbar button that looks like a big red exclamation point which is used to run a query.

**save**: The act of placing a copy of the document that is currently in memory into secondary storage.

**select**: To identify an object, text, or image to which you wish to do something.

**shortcut menu**: A context-sensitive menu that appears when I right click. Also called a Quick Menu.

**sizing handle**: The little boxes that appear on each border and corner of a selected image or control. By dragging one of these handles, the image or control can be resized.

**sort**: To rearrange in some logical order.

**style**: The general format of a report or form. Common styles are Corporate, International, or Compact.

**table** A collection of related records.

**task pane**: A pane that sometimes appears at the right side of the screen which provides for rapid selection of features.

**taskbar**: The horizontal grey bar, typically at the bottom of the desktop, upon which the Start button resides.

**title bar**: The horizontal bar at the top of the window that identifies the program and the database being used.

**toolbar**: A collection of picture buttons that, when clicked, execute a command. These buttons typically appear below the menu bar.

**undo button**: The toolbar button that, when clicked, will reverse the last action taken. It has a crooked arrow pointing to the left.

**value**: The specific data assigned to each field in a record.

**wizard**: a series of dialog boxes that will guide us through the process.

# Dozer's Quintessential Guide to Computer Literacy

## COMPREHENSIVE INDEX

# A Personal Message From Dozer

My old man, Steve, told me that I could put anything I wanted on the last page of this book. After all, the book is named after me. So, after taking a good long nap, I decided to put "The Pet's Bill of Rights" here. Please take good care of your pets; they take good care of you.   --Your Pal, Dozer

# THE PET'S BILL OF RIGHTS

1. We have the right to be full members of your family.
We thrive on social interaction, praise, and love.

2. We have the right to stimulation.
We need new games, new toys, new experiences, and new smells to be happy.

3. We have the right to regular exercise.
Without it, we could become hyper, sluggish...or fat.

4. We have the right to have fun.
We enjoy acting like clowns now and then; don't expect us to be predictable all the time.

5. We have the right to quality health care.
Please stay good friends with our vet!

6. We have the right to a good diet.
Like some people, we don't know what's best for us. We depend on you.

7. We have the right not to be rejected because of your expectations that we be
great show dogs or show cats, watchdogs, hunters, or baby-sitters.

8. We have the right to receive proper training.  Otherwise, our good relationship could
be marred by confusion and strife - and we could become dangerous to ourselves and others.

9. We have the right to guidance and correction based on
understanding and compassion, rather than abuse.

10. We have the right to live with dignity...
and to die with dignity when the time comes.

☞ Comprehensive Index ☜